# BALANCING CONSTITUTIONAL RIGHTS

The language of balancing is pervasive in constitutional rights jurisprudence around the world. In this book, Jacco Bomhoff offers a comparative and historical account of the origins and meanings of this talismanic form of language, and of the legal discourse to which it is central. Contemporary discussion has tended to see the increasing use of balancing as the manifestation of a globalization of constitutional law. This book is the first to argue that 'balancing' has always meant radically different things in different settings. Bomhoff makes use of detailed case studies of early postwar US and German constitutional jurisprudence to show that the same unique language expresses both biting scepticism and profound faith in law and adjudication, and both deep pessimism and high aspirations for constitutional rights. An understanding of these radically different meanings is essential for any evaluation of the work of constitutional courts today.

JACCO BOMHOFF is Associate Professor of Law at the London School of Economics and Political Science.

## CAMBRIDGE STUDIES IN CONSTITUTIONAL LAW

The aim of this series is to produce leading monographs in constitutional law. All areas of constitutional law and public law fall within the ambit of the series, including human rights and civil liberties law, administrative law, as well as constitutional theory and the history of constitutional law. A wide variety of scholarly approaches is encouraged, with the governing criterion being simply that the work is of interest to an international audience. Thus, works concerned with only one jurisdiction will be included in the series as appropriate, while, at the same time, the series will include works which are explicitly comparative or theoretical – or both. The series editors likewise welcome proposals that work at the intersection of constitutional and international law, or that seek to bridge the gaps between civil law systems, the US, and the common law jurisdictions of the Commonwealth.

*Series Editors*

David Dyzenhaus, *Professor of Law and Philosophy,*
*University of Toronto, Canada*
Adam Tomkins, *John Millar Professor of Public Law,*
*University of Glasgow, UK*

*Editorial Advisory Board*

T.R.S. Allan, Cambridge, UK
Damian Chalmers, LSE, UK
Sujit Choudhry, Toronto, Canada
Monica Claes, Maastricht, Netherlands
David Cole, Georgetown, USA
K.D. Ewing, King's College London, UK
David Feldman, Cambridge, UK
Cora Hoexter, Witwatersrand, South Africa
Christoph Moellers, Goettingen, Germany
Adrienne Stone, Melbourne, Australia
Adrian Vermeule, Harvard, USA

# BALANCING
# CONSTITUTIONAL RIGHTS

## The Origins and Meanings of Postwar
## Legal Discourse

JACCO BOMHOFF

CAMBRIDGE
UNIVERSITY PRESS

# CAMBRIDGE
## UNIVERSITY PRESS

University Printing House, Cambridge CB2 8BS, United Kingdom

Cambridge University Press is part of the University of Cambridge.

It furthers the University's mission by disseminating knowledge in the pursuit of education, learning and research at the highest international levels of excellence.

www.cambridge.org
Information on this title: www.cambridge.org/9781107622487

© Jacco Bomhoff 2013

This publication is in copyright. Subject to statutory exception and to the provisions of relevant collective licensing agreements, no reproduction of any part may take place without the written permission of Cambridge University Press.

First published 2013
First paperback edition 2015

*A catalogue record for this publication is available from the British Library*

*Library of Congress Cataloguing in Publication data*
Bomhoff, J. (Jacco)
Balancing constitutional rights : the origins and meanings of postwar legal discourse / Jacco Bomhoff.
pages   cm. – (Cambridge studies in constitutional law)
Includes bibliographical references and index.
ISBN 978-1-107-04441-8 (hardback)
1. Proportionality in law.   2. Constitutional law.
3. Civil rights.   4. Jurisprudence–Philosophy.   I. Title.
K247.B65 2013
342.08′5–dc23
2013023418

ISBN 978-1-107-04441-8 Hardback
ISBN 978-1-107-62248-7 Paperback

Cambridge University Press has no responsibility for the persistence or accuracy of URLs for external or third-party internet websites referred to in this publication, and does not guarantee that any content on such websites is, or will remain, accurate or appropriate.

Die Rechtsprechung zu den Grundrechten und deren Dogmatik sind in den letzten Jahren so sehr von der Theorie der Abwägung dominiert worden, dass weder deren vielfach unausgesprochen gebliebenen Voraussetzungen noch dogmatische Alternativen überhaupt Konturen gewinnen konnten.

*Karl-Heinz Ladeur, Kritik der Abwägung in der Grundrechtsdogmatik, 2004*

Over the past few decades, with little justification or scrutiny, balancing has come of age. […] Without a pause, our minds begin analysis of [constitutional law] questions by thinking in terms of the competing interests. Before we have time to wonder whether we ought to balance, we are already asserting the relative weights of the interests. Constitutional law has entered the age of balancing.

T. Alexander Aleinikoff, Constitutional Law in the Age of Balancing, 1987

[European] Continental legal theory is uncannily 'other' for an American, perhaps because just about everything in our legal culture is present in theirs, often translated word for word, but nothing seems to have the same meaning.

Duncan Kennedy, *A Critique of Adjudication (fin de siècle)*, 1997

# CONTENTS

# ACKNOWLEDGEMENTS

I am particularly grateful to Janneke Gerards for her unwavering support during all the different phases of work on this project. For critical readings and stimulating conversations along the way, I thank Maurice Adams, Eduard Bomhoff, Antoine Buyse, Neil Duxbury, Jan Komárek, Peter Kugel, Susan Marks, Kai Möller, Jo Murkens, Andrew Lang, Mitchel Lasser, Anne Meuwese, Ralf Michaels, Marthias Reimann, Anne-Isabelle Richard, Helen Reece, Annelise Riles, Felix Ronkes Agerbeek, Yaniv Roznai, Mathias Siems, Emmanuel Voyiakis, Catherine Valcke, Grégoire Webber, Michael Wilkinson, Lorenzo Zucca and Peer Zumbansen. Jan Kleinheisterkamp provided invaluable encouragement and advice. The generosity of these colleagues and friends is not to be confused with any responsibility for what follows. Special thanks are due to Frederick Schauer, Martijn Polak and Janneke Gerards for commenting on the doctoral manuscript on which this book is based. Emma and Matthias have been quiet – and not so quiet – sources of inspiration and playful distraction. Andrea's patience and support would merit mention on every page. This book is dedicated to her, *s láskou*.

~

# Introduction

## A.  The local meanings of balancing

This book is about the origins and meanings of one of the central features of postwar Western legal thought and practice: the discourse of balancing in constitutional rights jurisprudence. This discourse is pervasive in legal systems around the globe. Paradoxically though, its very ubiquity makes it in some ways more difficult to grasp. One important reason for this is the widespread assumption that identical, or nearly identical, terminology will mean more or less the same thing wherever it appears. That – normally unstated – assumption is only reinforced by the ways in which the imagery of weights and proportions corresponds to popular and scholarly notions of what constitutional rights justice should look like.

The central argument of this book is that references to balancing, of rights, values or interests, in case law and legal literature, have a far wider and richer range of meanings than conventional accounts allow for. On a most basic level, this argument builds on a change in perspective from balancing as something we think judges do, to something we know judges say they do – a shift in emphasis, that is, from balancing as doctrine, technique or principle to balancing as discourse. The project for the next few chapters is to uncover what this balancing discourse means to local actors in different legal systems.

These local meanings of balancing, as I show in a case study of German and US constitutional rights jurisprudence, can and do differ dramatically. Uncovering these different meanings matters. This is, after all, the legal language that, more than any other currently in use, constitutional rights jurisprudence turns to for justification, legitimization and critique. This book aims to contribute to an understanding of how so much has come to be invested, in so many different and contradictory ways, in this one particular, talismanic form of legal language.

1

## B.   A puzzle: reconciling turns to balancing and legalism

The discipline of comparative law offers a hard-won but simple lesson for any study of legal discourse: it would be little short of astonishing if similar language, even the same words translated as literally as possible, *did* have the same meaning in different legal systems and cultures. In comparative project after project, as soon as rudimentary elements of context, history and mentality are taken into account, cracks quickly begin to appear in even the sternest façades of uniformity.

And yet, curiously, when it comes to one of the central preoccupations of late twentieth- and early-twenty-first-century constitutional jurisprudence, these lessons are often, apparently, forgotten. Instead, the rise of the language of balancing and proportionality is commonly invoked as the foundation for extraordinarily far-reaching comparative claims.[1] Such claims tend to amalgamate a familiar torrent of references to weighing in case law and legal literature into some form of 'globalization of constitutional law', understood to be a worldwide, or almost worldwide, movement of convergence on a 'global model' of rights adjudication, possibly underpinned by an emergent, shared 'ultimate rule of law'.[2]

Some of this may in fact capture contemporary trends. It is not unreasonable to assume that judiciaries operating in interconnected societies and often facing similar issues might turn to somewhat similar legal methods, doctrines or philosophies. But certainly insofar as they relate to balancing, these claims of convergence also face some formidable obstacles. One way of bringing these into focus is by asking how this inferred global turn towards a shared model relates to classic accounts of differences between styles of legal reasoning among different legal systems and cultures. Of particular interest, from that perspective, are studies from within a rich tradition that has sought to cast such differences in terms of a formal versus substantive dichotomy.

Classic comparative accounts of law and legal reasoning in the US and Europe have often invoked sets of sliding scales that run between some

---

[1] The relationship between balancing and proportionality is a contested issue in many legal systems. But whether, in analytical terms, 'balancing' is seen as part of proportionality, or whether proportionality is seen as a 'balancing' test (the two most common perspectives), the two categories are clearly part of the same broad family of discourse. See further Chapter 1, Section B.2.

[2] See, e.g., Beatty (2004); Law (2005); Möller (2012); Schlink (2012). These convergence accounts tend to take an ambivalent position on the position of the US. See, e.g., Weinrib (2006); Tushnet (2009); Möller (2012), pp. 17ff.

conception of legal formality on one extreme, and one or more of formality's opposites on the other, in order to frame salient differences. In this way, the syllogistic mode of reasoning found in the official, published decisions of the French *Cour de cassation* and the efforts by the German nineteenth-century Pandectists and their successors to build a coherent and gapless legal system have long served to ground the argument that law and legal reasoning in Continental Europe are traditionally overwhelmingly 'formal', or 'legalist'.[3] Legal reasoning in the US, by contrast, is commonly thought to be more 'pragmatic', 'policy-oriented', 'open-ended', or, in the most general terms, more 'substantive'. The orthodox argument in this field is that while American and Continental-European jurisprudence were both strongly formal in orientation at the end of the nineteenth century, American legal reasoning has since been subjected to a devastating Realist critique that has unmasked legal formality as 'merely a kind of veneer'.[4] Legal thinking in Europe, notably in Germany, was at one time early in the twentieth century in thrall of a very similar line of critique. But attacks on legal formality, or belief in law's autonomy, simply have never had the same long-term impact on mainstream European jurisprudence as they had in the US.[5]

It is when this historical narrative is extended to take postwar developments into account that a close connection to the topic of balancing appears. The rise of constitutional rights adjudication during this period, this story typically continues, has come to undermine these long-established differences. This is because leading courts in Europe and elsewhere outside the US have adopted a style of reasoning in rights cases that appears to be surprisingly and radically open-ended and pragmatic – in short: *informal*, or less legalist. 'A common cliché has it that legal systems from the common law tradition produce case law, while so-called continental legal systems strive for codification and a more systematic jurisprudence', Georg Nolte notes, for example, in a comparative study of European and US constitutional rights law. Nolte continues: 'The question, however, is whether *the opposite* is not true for today's constitutional adjudication', adding that '[i]n its freedom of expression case law, for example, the US Supreme Court strives to develop "tests" that are on a similar level of abstraction as legislation [while] The European Court of Human Rights and the German *Bundesverfassungsgericht* on the other

---

[3] For discussion and nuance see Lasser (2004).
[4] See, e.g., Riles (2000), p. 5.
[5] On legal formality, see further Chapter 1, Section D.

hand, typically insist on a balancing of "all the relevant factors of the case"'.[6] Nolte sees these European examples as following an approach to constitutional adjudication that is, overall, 'less rigorous' than that found in the US.[7]

As this quotation illustrates, the stories of the rise of balancing and of the supposed de-formalization of postwar legal reasoning in the constitutional rights context, are intimately related. The turn towards balancing and proportionality reasoning by European courts and other non-US courts is read as a turn away from legal formality – a turn away from reliance on legal rules, from 'rigour' in legal thinking, and from belief in the possibility of juridical autonomy more generally. Conversely, it is the US Supreme Court's preference for 'rules' and its encasement of balancing in the form of 'tests' that make its constitutional rights reasoning more formal.

This account of the role of balancing in constitutional rights adjudication, it seems, can support only one conclusion. And that is that judicial balancing and legal formality are radical opposites. This, certainly, is the dominant American view in this area.[8] The idea of constitutional law 'in an age of balancing', as one famous depiction has it, is very much the idea of law in an age of lost faith in legal formality. Adjudication, on this view, can be no more – and is no more – than a pragmatic, ad hoc, instrumentalist approach to deciding cases. The courts' balancing rhetoric is the principal expression of this realization. And so, it is not surprising to see US lawyers describe value- and interest-balancing, 'all things considered judgments', and proportionality reasoning as manifestations of *'the form that reason will take when there is no longer a faith in formalism'*.[9] 'As long as belief in a formal science of law is strong', Yale Law School's Paul Kahn writes, 'the reasoned judgments of a court look different from the "all things considered" judgments of the political branches. When

---

[6] Nolte (2005), pp. 17–18 (emphasis added). See also, e.g., Grey (2003), p. 474: '[A]ccording to conventional wisdom, the general style of legal thought in [the US] has long been more pragmatic, or less formalistic, than in other systems. Over the last half-century, other legal systems have taken up judicial review, and now seem themselves to be moving away from traditionally more formal approaches to law'.

[7] *Ibid.*, p. 18. For a classic German statement, see Forsthoff (1959), pp. 145ff. See also Schlink (2012), p. 302 (under influence of proportionality and balancing '[c]onstitutional cultures with a doctrinal tradition will progressively be transformed in the direction of a culture of case law').

[8] See, e.g., Schor (2009), p. 1488 ('Courts around the globe have turned away from formalism and towards proportionality analysis or balancing tests.')

[9] Kahn (2003), pp. 2698–99 (emphasis added).

reasonableness replaces science, however, the work of a court looks like little more than prudence.'[10]

This conception, of course, fits snugly with the broader American story in which balancing and the rise of scepticism – the more familiar designation of a loss of faith – in law are intimately related. But when developments in other countries than the US are taken into account, problems emerge. The loss of faith narrative quite clearly *does not work*. To begin with, the available evidence suggests rather strongly that legal systems outside the US have not, over the past decades, experienced anything like an American-style surge in scepticism about law and judicial institutions. So, for example, where US lawyers continue to fret over the familiar counter-majoritarian dilemma, German writers and judges worry, conversely, that '[t]he German faith in constitutional jurisdiction must not be allowed to turn into a lack of faith in democracy'.[11] But the evidence against a sceptical turn outside the US is much broader and encompasses many more systems. The embrace of supra-national courts such as the European Court of Human Rights or the International Criminal Court, for example, but also the fundamentally constructive nature of most doctrinal writing in many legal systems are telling signs of a pervasive 'faith in and hope for law'.[12] These are, if anything, manifestations of a 'turn to legalism' rather than any turn towards scepticism and pragmatism.[13]

Further tangles to this basic puzzle are now quick to surface. Is it really plausible that legal cultures with a long tradition of high formalism and of attachment to legal doctrine and legal rigour, like those in Continental

---

[10] *Ibid.*

[11] Häberle (1980), p. 79. Cited by the then president of the *Bundesverfassungsgericht*, Jutta Limbach, in Limbach (2000), p. 9. See also Casper (2002).

[12] Kennedy (1985), p. 480 (describing the seminal work of Rudolf Wiethölter). See also Zimmermann (1996), p. 583 (contrasting American scepticism with European – Continental and English – faith in law as an autonomous discipline). For recent case studies voicing similar observations, see Saiman (2008) and Kuo (2009).

[13] Pildes (2003), pp. 147ff. Pildes continues: 'It is quite intriguing – and enormously significant [...] – that the attachment to legalism and judicial institutions outside the United States is reaching this peak in the same period in which within the United States there has been general and increasing scepticism about judicial institutions' (*Ibid.*). Legalism, in all of its common meanings – rule-following, logical deduction, conceptualism and most comprehensively, belief in some form and degree of autonomy for the juridical – is essentially connected to the idea of legal formality. Cf. Shklar (1964), pp. 33ff; Wieacker (1990), pp. 23ff. Here, legalism and formalism are both used to refer to an attitude of faith in and commitment to the possibility of the (semi)-autonomy of the juridical field. If there is any difference between the terms, it is that formalism refers more specifically to the one-sided concern to *uphold* this autonomy, whereas legalism designates a commitment to managing the *co-existence* of formal and substantive elements in law.

Europe, would suddenly have abandoned these long-held views? If so: did lawyers in these systems retain their belief in legal formality in other areas of law, but abandon it completely in the field of constitutional rights adjudication, where balancing now dominates? Or has legal formality been entirely disenchanted, and have German judges and legal scholars, to use the most striking example, really 'replaced legal science' and centuries of conceptual refinement with mere reasonableness and prudential reasoning? If so, it might be asked, why does private law adjudication and scholarship in European countries, like Germany, still look so very different from American legal theory and practice? Why, come to think of it, does German and European *constitutional* law scholarship still look so very different from its US counterpart?

And on the American side of this story, too, matters do not quite fit. Granted, the specific idea of balancing as anti-formality, or non-law, could still hold in this setting. But if there really has been a comprehensive loss of faith in the formal attributes of law and legal reasoning, why would American courts and commentators still bother to encase balancing-based reasoning within the confines of strict rules and multi-part tests? Surely these elaborate legal constructs, designed specifically to dam in what are seen as the most pernicious aspects of open judicial weighing, must signal some remaining commitment to legal formality and doctrinal craftsmanship?

## C.  Rethinking balancing, rethinking legalism

The main argument of this book consists of a three-part answer to this puzzle of how turns to balancing and to legalism might be reconciled. First: balancing does not mean the same thing everywhere. Second: analysing these different meanings reveals that the opposition between balancing and legal formality does not hold in all contexts. These different meanings, in turn, do not allow for a simple conclusion that European and other non-US adjudication styles have become pragmatic, policy-oriented or informal in the sense these terms are commonly understood. And third: rethinking the meaning of balancing brings with it a need to rethink the nature of legalism itself.[14] Not only 'balancing', but also the

---

[14] There is a possibility that balancing in, say, South Africa, India or Israel could emanate from – and be embedded within – rather more indigenous legalisms, best understood as purposeful rejections of (parts of) the Western tradition. That possibility cannot be discounted on the basis of the narrower comparative project undertaken here, with its focus on US and Continental-European constitutional jurisprudence. But even if

central organizing terms of 'formal' and 'substantive', and the very character of legalism as an attitude to law, carry different meanings in these different settings.

This argument is developed by way of a case study on German and US jurisprudence. It was in these two systems that, at virtually exactly the same time in the late 1950s, high courts first began to discuss constitutional rights issues in balancing terms. Chapters 3 and 4 discuss both these judicial references and the surrounding scholarly and judicial discourse in some detail. In both these settings, these first judicial references followed earlier virtually simultaneous invocations of balancing in scholarly legal debates of the early twentieth century, in the context of the *Interessenjurisprudenz* in Germany and Sociological Jurisprudence in the US. These earlier invocations are studied in Chapter 2. Adopting this narrow lens of two parallel sets of self-identified balancing debates should make it possible to uncover the meanings of the discourse of balancing at its inception.

Throughout this book, but most particularly in Chapter 5, these different meanings will be translated into the conceptual vocabulary of the formal versus substantive opposition.[15] The discourse of balancing, I argue, is the principal contemporary site for where the formal and the substantive in law meet. And certainly as between German and US jurisprudence *everything* about these encounters is different. Where a rule-based, constraining formality is predominant in the US, legal formality in German jurisprudence is conceptual and exhortative, even perfectionist. The substantive in law, which equals policy and pragmatism in the US, finds expression in an extraordinarily powerful and complex set of ideas known as 'material constitutionalism' in Germany. And where the formal and the substantive co-exist in a constant state of conflict and unstable compromise in US law, German jurisprudence continually strives for synthesis.

In no small part, the astounding capacity of the discourse of balancing to mean all things to all people rests precisely on the many different ways it gives shape to the discursive management of the formal versus substantive opposition in law. Balancing can stand for both intuitive reasoning that is formalized to an unusual degree, and for formal legal reasoning

---

for these other settings a more radical rethinking of legalism may be required, it still seems difficult to sever completely the connection between legalism as a general faith in the juridical, and legal formalism as faith in the possibility of juridical *autonomy* more specifically.

[15] See further Chapter 1, Section D.

that is unusually open. Balancing can be both an admission of the limitations of formal legal analysis, and an attempt to stretch formal legal reasoning as far as it might go. Balancing can be principle and policy, conceptual synthesis and pragmatic compromise. Balancing, I argue in the final chapter of this book, can form the centrepiece of a mode of reasoning that 'substantivizes' its formality, and of a discourse that is in an important sense 'formally substantive'.[16] And when what is emblematic for legal reasoning in different settings is not so much the fact that it combines both more formal and more substantive elements, *but how it does so*,[17] studying the discourse of balancing opens up a uniquely privileged vantage point from which to analyse and compare what legal reasoning, in these different places, to a large extent, is all about.

For that last – large – question, the discourse of balancing proves revealing in a final, perhaps unexpected, way. If formalism and legalism are, at heart, expressions of beliefs relating to qualities ascribed to legal institutions – those qualities that make up the 'internal dynamics of juridical functioning',[18] – then *the character of those beliefs* may well vary in ways that could be distinctive for the communities of legal actors who hold them. And in this regard too, the discourse of balancing occupies a unique position. This is because this particular language can be the expression of both a deep-seated scepticism towards the legal, and of a faith in law of such fervour and ambition that non-believers may find difficult to take seriously. I argue in Chapters 4 and 5 that the discourse of balancing in US constitutional rights jurisprudence reveals a faith in law that is halting, tentative and always constrained by powerful sceptical tendencies. The tropes that typically surround the vocabulary of balancing show this very clearly: 'bright lines' wobble on 'slippery slopes', 'absolutes' are 'relativized' and formalism itself is 'pragmatical' and in need of 'empirical support'. The relative strengths of these contradictory impulses are continuously subject to reassessment, as 'spectres' from earlier misguided eras continue to haunt, 'revisionism' is revisited and American jurisprudence as a whole is described as existing in a permanent state of 'schizophrenia'.[19] It is revealing to compare these figures of speech with the tropes surrounding the vocabulary of balancing in Germany. There,

---

[16] Recourse to inelegant terminology seems inevitable in this area. See Summers & Atiyah (1987), p. 30 (coining what they call the 'ugly word' of 'substantivistic' reasoning); Kalman (1986), p. 36 (using 'autonomousness' as synonym for formalism).

[17] See Lasser (2004), p. 155.

[18] Bourdieu (1987). See also Unger (1986), pp. 1ff.

[19] For references, see Chapter 5, and especially Section E therein.

a list of dominant terms would have to include words such as *dialektisch* (dialectical), *prinzipiell* (principled), *durchtheoretisiert* (fully theorized), *Einheitsbildung* (fostering of unity), *'logisch-teleologisch'* (logical-teleological), *Optimierung* (optimization) and *Synthese* (synthesis).

In one sense, all of what follows in this book builds on a simple contrast. If there is even some marginal consensus on the kinds of differences identified in simple lists like these, then we must begin to rethink the apparent commonality of the discourse we seem to share. If so much else about the language of American and German or European lawyers is *so* different, surely when the same or similar words do appear, they will come with different meanings, even radically different meanings?

This, then, is what I hope to show: that the discourse of balancing, for all its global pervasiveness, does not mean the same thing everywhere. Balancing, instead, has come to rule our legal imagination because, Humpty Dumpty-like, it means exactly that which everyone, everywhere, expects, wants and fears it to mean. Those expectations, as illustrated in the two – really only mildly caricatured – lists above, are consistently more ambitious, more hopeful for the power of legal ideas in German and Continental-European jurisprudence than in the US. This ambition is not a good in and of itself. That much is demonstrated by the Orwellian flights of conceptual fancy engaged in by some legal scholars under fascism. But it is this same ambition that has now also served, for more than half a century, to uphold a liberal constitutional order with a reach that is unprecedented. A reach, in addition, that would be unthinkable in the US. I argue in this book that the different meanings of the discourse of balancing – as the cornerstone of a 'perfect constitutional order' and as a 'dangerous doctrine' – are central to these radically different understandings.

The irresistible propensity in balancing to conform to expectations – those of its advocates, but also of its critics – is the source of its strengths, but also of its weaknesses. The dominance of the discourse means that these strengths and weaknesses reverberate widely. And so, while this book may disappoint in not offering suggestions on how to (or how not to) balance, it does stem from the conviction that uncovering the contingency of our received interpretations must itself be a worthwhile project.

# 1

## Questioning a global age of balancing

The aim of this book is to uncover different local meanings for the language of balancing. This chapter begins that project by first challenging the diametrically opposite claim: the suggestion that constitutional jurisprudence finds itself in a global age of balancing. In Section A, I discuss what this opposing claim means and what its foundations and implications are. The remainder of the chapter sets out the contours of the challenge. Section B shows how comparative studies of balancing and proportionality commonly fail to distinguish between balancing as discourse and as process, and discusses how this conflation sustains an overly uniform understanding of what balancing is. An alternative approach is presented in Section C. Balancing, I argue, should be approached, not as a fixed analytical structure, but as a form of legal argument. The meaning of this argument can be studied in terms of the contribution legal actors in any given system think it is able to make to the legitimization of the exercise of public authority under law. In Section D, I relate this legitimization imperative to an underlying dilemma shared by Western legal orders: that of maintaining law's essential semi-autonomy, or, in other words: of the discursive management of the formal versus substantive opposition. As a universal dilemma with local manifestations, the formal versus substantive opposition is a useful point of reference for comparative studies of legal discourse. It is also, of course, instrumental to solving the puzzle set out in the Introduction, of how turns to balancing might be reconciled with turns to legalism – a puzzle to which Chapter 5 will return. Section E, finally, introduces the case studies of balancing discourse in German and US jurisprudence that occupy Chapters 2, 3 and 4.

## A.   A hegemonic discourse

### 1.   Doctrine, theory, portrait

The language of weights and weighing makes up much of the way we talk now in modern Western law. *How much* exactly, though, is not all that easy to say.

First, there are the judicial balancing references. Courts in many parts of the Western world often use very similar sounding balancing-related language in their decisions in constitutional or fundamental rights cases. In the second half of the twentieth century, the US Supreme Court, the Supreme Court of Canada, the German *Bundesverfassungsgericht* (Federal Constitutional Court), the Court of Justice of the European Union and the European Court of Human Rights, to list a number of prominent examples in Europe and North America,[1] have all come to regularly invoke the need to balance rights, interests or values when dealing with fundamental rights cases.[2]

This same language figures heavily in constitutional legal scholarship within these systems. Primarily in response to judicial references of the kinds cited above, legal scholars have over the past sixty years developed a wealth of doctrinal commentary and critical evaluation, mostly consisting of intricate lessons for courts on when and how (not) to balance. This kind of scholarship grew so quickly that by 1965 already one American constitutional lawyer exclaimed: '[s]o much has been written on the subject that the writers […] have no doubt told us more about balancing than we wanted to know'.[3]

Balancing's hold on legal thinking, however, extends far beyond doctrinal commentary. Legal scholars have come to invoke the theme of

---

[1] Examples from Germany and the US are discussed in Chapters 3 and 4. For Canada, see, e.g., SCC *R.* v. *Oakes*, [1986] S.C.R. 103, par. 70 (balancing individual and societal interests as part of a proportionality test) and La Forest (1992). For Europe, see, e.g., ECtHR *Sunday Times* v. *The United Kingdom*, 2 EHRR 245, par. 6 (1979); ECtHR *Soering* v. *The United Kingdom*, 11 EHRR 439, par. 89 (1989) (a 'search for a fair balance' between general and individual interests is 'inherent in the whole of the Convention'); CJEU Case C-169/91 *Council of the City of Stoke on Trent and Norwich City Council* v. *B & Q plc* [1992] ECR I-6635, par. 15 (balancing as part of a principle of proportionality); CJEU Case C-112/00 *Schmidberger Internationale Transporte und Planzüge* v. *Austria*, 2003 ECR I-5659, par. 82 (need for a 'fair balance' between EU freedoms and human rights). See further van Gerven (1999), pp. 42ff (proportionality in EU law as 'a complex balancing test').

[2] For a comprehensive recent overview see Barak (2012). See also Law (2005).

[3] Karst (1965), p. 22.

balancing as a common focal point, a trope, for more abstract theoretical discussions of law and adjudication generally. A range of influential post-war writers, from the late Ronald Dworkin in the US to Jürgen Habermas in Germany, have all turned to the phenomenon of explicit judicial balanc-ing in order to frame broad arguments on the nature of rights and adju-dication. Dworkin's famous conception of rights as 'trumps', for example, was developed initially as part of a response to the first invocations of balancing at the US Supreme Court during the 1950s.[4] In work of this kind, the theme of balancing becomes a favourite prism through which local actors observe and evaluate their own constitutional law practices and understandings.

There is more, though. Following-on from these references in case law and scholarship, recent decades have witnessed a subtle transfor-mation in perspective. Balancing is now often seen no longer as merely a phenomenon within constitutional adjudication, or as a lens through which to study constitutional law or even as possibly the most impor-tant lens through which to do so, but as an emblematic characteristic of constitutional law as such. In many Western jurisdictions, it has become increasingly common to invoke the language of balancing as an essen-tial element of the locally held 'self-image' of constitutional legal thought and practice.[5] Balancing, in these images, is part of what defines a par-ticular constitutional legal system, culture or epoch for its inhabitants. American constitutional law, for example, was said in the late 1980s to find itself in an age of balancing.[6] The arrival of balancing tests, accord-ing to another American observer, heralded 'the beginning of modern-ism in American legal thought'.[7] And in German legal writing, balancing is seen as a new '*Rechtsparadigma*' ('a paradigm of law')[8] or a new '*Staatsgrundkonzeption*' ('a conception of the foundations of the State' – predictably: a 'balancing State').[9]

---

[4] Dworkin (1977), pp. 198ff (describing 'the balancing metaphor' as 'the heart of the error' in the US Supreme Court's model of rights). Dworkin began his legal career as a clerk for Judge Learned Hand, a notable – critical – participant in the debates on balancing canvassed in Chapter 4. See also Ely (1980), pp. 105ff. For Habermas, judicial balancing mocks the 'strict priority' that ought to be accorded to fundamental rights and leads to arbitrariness in adjudication. See Habermas (1996), pp. 256–59.
[5] See Lasser (1995), p. 1344.
[6] Aleinikoff (1987).    [7] Horwitz (1992), p. 131.
[8] Ladeur (1983). For the position in the US, see Kennedy (1997), p. 324 ('balancing became a paradigm for constitutional decision in one area after another' after 1945).
[9] See Leisner (1997), pp. 20, 174. See also Schlink (1976); Kommers (2006), p. 13.

All these references to the language of balancing, its invocations in case law and doctrine, but also as part of the imagery that legal actors use to make sense of their own constitutional law beliefs and practices, make up the discourse of balancing in contemporary constitutional jurisprudence.

## 2.   Convergence and contrast

The reach of the language of balancing extends beyond domestic and regional legal systems and into the discipline of comparative constitutional law, where it has emerged as an important conceptual organizational tool. In this context, the language generally figures in one of two principal ways: to voice ideas of universality or convergence, and as a marker of salient contrasts.

Studies of the first kind, in their most ambitious guises, invoke notions of descriptive or normative universality for balancing. Balancing, on these views, is either or both a universally valid description of what 'actually happens' in constitutional adjudication, and/or a universally desirable ideal for what should happen. One early study along these lines, for example, claimed that '[j]ustices everywhere, who have the responsibility of deciding constitutional controversies, know that their task involves the identification and balancing of competing societal interests', before going on to list examples of the recognition of the 'inevitability' of balancing in case law and literature from an extensive collection of systems.[10] More recently, the Canadian scholar David Beatty has posited that the principle of proportionality – which for him encompasses a notion of balancing – is 'an integral, indispensable part of every constitution'.[11] Using reasoning and doctrines that are, strikingly, 'virtually identical', balancing courts in different systems in Beatty's view are doing no more than explicitly recognizing this universal principle.[12]

Other studies, still within this broad similarity-focused framework, describe the spread of references to balancing not in terms of universal normative appeal, but from a more dynamic, political science oriented perspective, as part of a contemporary 'globalization of legal thought',[13] or a trend of 'judicial globalization'.[14] In this vein, Alec Stone Sweet and

---

[10]   Antieau (1985), p. 125. See also Antieau (1977).
[11]   Beatty (2004), pp. 162ff.
[12]   Beatty (1995), pp. 15ff.
[13]   Kennedy (2006).
[14]   Grey (2003), p. 484. See also Law (2005).

Jud Mathews observe: 'Over the past fifty years proportionality balancing [...] has become a dominant technique of rights adjudication in the
world'.[15] Another example of this approach is Thomas Grey's argument
that the broad formulation of post-1945 constitutional rights guarantees
and the influence and prestige of the European Court of Human Rights
and the Court of Justice of the European Union, have helped spread a
'policy-oriented pragmatic style of adjudication' throughout Europe
and beyond.[16] The core of this new judicial pragmatism, in Grey's view,
consists of 'purposive reasoning, balancing and proportionality'.[17] And
Duncan Kennedy, finally, has argued that 'balancing of conflicting considerations' is one of two defining characteristics of a 'globalization of
legal thought' which, from origins in US law, has gone on to conquer the
postwar legal world.[18]

Comparative scholarship of a second variety, on the other hand, takes
up the language of balancing rather to frame contrasts between legal systems. Studies in this vein build on the assumption that differences in the
ways legal communities do, or do not, use balancing-based language matter, and that analysing these differences is a suitable way to go about framing salient points of comparison between legal systems and cultures.

The main thrust of these studies has been to contrast US constitutional jurisprudence with experiences in Canada, Europe and elsewhere.
Kent Greenawalt, for example, has compared US and Canadian freedom
of expression adjudication by asking whether courts use a 'balancing'
approach in which they 'openly weigh factors', or a 'conceptual' approach,
relying on 'categorical analysis'.[19] Greenawalt concludes that in this
area '[t]he Canadian Supreme Court is developing a distinctive balancing approach [...] and avoids relying as much upon categorical analysis
as do US courts'.[20] Frederick Schauer has similarly contrasted different
approaches to freedom of expression adjudication through a balancing
lens. He writes: 'there is a view, widespread in Canada, in Europe and in
South Africa [and elsewhere], that American free-speech adjudication is
obsessed with categorization and definition. Under this view, American

---

[15] Stone Sweet & Mathews (2008), p. 72. See also Stone Sweet (2004).
[16] Grey (2003), pp. 484–85.    [17] *Ibid.*, p. 486.
[18] Kennedy (2006), pp. 21–22. The other characteristic is 'neo-formalism'; the two endure
   in a state of 'unsynthesized coexistence': See Stone Sweet (2003), p. 674. For a critique of
   this view insofar as it purports to describe German and European jurisprudence, see
   Chapter 5, Section D.
[19] Greenawalt (1992), pp. 5–10.
[20] *Ibid.*, p. 32. See also Beschle (2001), pp. 187–88; Harding (2003), p. 430.

free speech adjudication disingenuously [...] masks the difficult weighing process that the Canadian, European and South African structure both facilitates and makes more transparent'.[21]

### 3.    A global community of discourse?

These two approaches, while obviously coming to very different substantive conclusions, proceed on the basis of the same methodological assumption. In both, it is tacitly taken for granted that the language of balancing has the same meaning wherever it surfaces. If it did not, comparative observations based on the incidence of this language, as well as any conclusions framed using this language, would obviously become unstable. In this sense, both the similarity- and the contrasts-focused approaches locate themselves within a global age of balancing: an age in which even those wanting to emphasize differences between legal systems find themselves having to rely on this unifying language to make their point.

Comparative lawyers would do well, however, to heed Mirjan Damaška's warning, that any semblance of such a 'community of discourse' – of an apparently shared conceptual language – could lack substance, and could in fact be 'mainly a rhetorical achievement'.[22] That risk seems particularly acute when such a community would have to exist on the kind of grand, global scale that comparative studies of balancing commonly claim for it. Awareness of this danger opens up a host of fascinating questions. Can we assume so easily that all these courts and lawyers referring to balancing and weighing do in fact mean the same thing, and that they are understood in the same way by their audiences? Is balancing as a shared focal point for debates on the nature of rights, law and adjudication really as shared and common as it appears to be, once the boundaries of individual legal systems are crossed? What kinds of distortions are likely when legal actors accustomed to understanding their own systems through a balancing prism look outwards, at the practices and understandings of others?

These questions have so far largely escaped sustained academic attention.[23] They all raise the fundamental question of how the discipline of

---

[21] Schauer (2005), pp. 50–51.    [22] Damaška (1986), pp. 67–68.

[23] Recent studies do emphasize the idea that balancing and proportionality will often 'coexist with attention to historically specific aspects of national constitutions' or that 'the way in which balancing is done will differ depending on a society's history and expectations'. See Beschle (2001), p. 189 (emphasis added); Jackson (2004), p. 810 (emphasis

comparative law should engage with the pervasiveness of the language of balancing in contemporary constitutional adjudication practice, critique and theory.

## B.    Balancing as process and as discourse

Imagine if you will the familiar setting of a round-table faculty seminar on some question of constitutional rights jurisprudence. Having been quiet for a while, one participant now begins to nod with growing impatience. 'This all sounds very interesting', she says, 'but you do *of course* realize that all of what we have been discussing turns on nothing more than a simple balancing exercise.' She then describes how, in the given problem area, courts either routinely openly balance or weigh; that they balance without saying they do so; or that they should be balancing certain factors in a particular way. Just as inevitable as this first intervention is the response it provokes. '*That*', another participant says of what has just been presented, 'is *not really* balancing'. Reactions now are likely to be mixed. Some of those in attendance will probably think that it is important to settle this preliminary matter first, and to be clear about what this alleged balancing *is*. Others, though, are likely to feel a sense of loss over a debate that moments earlier had been about *real* issues – a right to housing, perhaps, or individual liberties in the face of counter-terrorism actions – and that has now turned into a discussion of, what, really? Semantics? Or something of greater salience after all?

### 1.    A lens and an object

Familiar debates like these illustrate the predicament the discipline of comparative constitutional law finds itself in today. They are the most intimate, localized manifestations of the general discursive and conceptual environment within which all comparative lawyers must move. But that environment, of course, also constitutes the very terrain of which they are trying to make sense, and this often on a global scale. Here is one account of how the discipline has fared in its attempts to do just that.

Judicial and academic discussions of balancing are commonly triggered by simple language: by the incidence of words such as 'balancing', 'weighing', or in some cases 'proportionality', and their derivations, in

added). See also Grimm (2007); Cohen-Eliya & Porat (2009), p. 372. They do not, however, discuss the idea that balancing *itself* might mean different things in different settings.

case law and commentary. In standard discussions, what initially makes a judicial opinion a balancing opinion, or what characterizes a court as a balancing court, is simply the occurrence of a peculiar form of legal language. Balancing, in these approaches is, at least initially, simply something judges say they do.[24]

Despite this initial reliance on language however, the ultimate concern of these studies is overwhelmingly with balancing as an analytical construct – as something that judges and lawyers are thought to actually do.[25] This preoccupation with the analytics of balancing, or with balancing as process, has a long tradition. It characterized the first balancing debates within the German school of the *Interessenjurisprudenz* and America's proto-Realist Sociological Jurisprudence, during the early decades of the twentieth century. These authors saw balancing as a 'process' of adjustment and calibration between opposing social interests,[26] and as a 'method' of lawfinding.[27] This early choice of emphasis on process is not surprising. After all, the understanding of law in terms of conflicting interests to be weighed and mediated that prompted these writers' interest in balancing in the first place, was itself just one manifestation of a broader intellectual trend that advocated looking at legal institutions in terms of their functions – a trend culminating in Felix Cohen's provocative functionalist credo 'a thing *is* what it does'.[28] It is important to note, then, that from the outset, in the work of these early twentieth-century writers, judicial balancing as lens and balancing as object shared the same intellectual foundations.

This relationship between balancing and a functional view of legal institutions is on particularly stark display in the area of comparative legal studies. In that field, functionalism has long been the focal point for virtually all discussions of method.[29] Using the idea of shared 'problems' as their starting point, scholars working in the functionalist tradition aim

---

[24] Or, of course, something that academic commentators say judges do.

[25] For reliance on this distinction in the study of legal argumentation see, e.g., Wasserstrom (1961); Bell (1986); MacCormick & Summers (1991).

[26] Pound (1943), p. 4.

[27] See, e.g., Heck (1932a), pp. 120ff; Heck (1932b), pp. 108ff.

[28] Cohen (1935), p. 52. See, e.g., Pound (1921), p. 450 (referring to both the recognition of 'the problem of harmonizing or compromising conflicting or overlapping interests' and to 'a functional point of view' as part of the intellectual legacy of Oliver Wendell Holmes). Neither Roscoe Pound nor Philipp Heck would have accepted Cohen's statement in its starkest form.

[29] Michaels (2006a), p. 340. See also Frankenberg (1985); Kennedy (1997); Grosswald Curran (1998).

to compare the 'solutions' found in different legal systems.[30] References to balancing, on this view, are simply manifestations of such solutions to a common problem. Comparative law as a whole even, in the words of one early commentator, amounted to nothing more than a 'necessary supplement and continuation of the jurisprudence of interests'.[31]

This early preoccupation with what balancing does, and with how it does it, remains pervasive. In contemporary studies, balancing is a 'method of constitutional interpretation',[32] balancing and proportionality are 'doctrines' relying on certain similar 'thought processes',[33] 'proportionality balancing' is an 'analytical procedure' and a 'technique of rights adjudication'.[34] And although they are virtually always prompted by language, it is with the implications of this 'technique' or this 'process' for decisions in concrete cases, for the institutional position of the judiciary, etc., that studies of balancing and proportionality are ultimately concerned.

## 2.  Conflating process and discourse: three problems of comparative method

In a methodological move that tends to remain unarticulated, investigations of balancing and proportionality commonly conflate these two dimensions of discourse and process. Balancing references are taken as reliable indicators of the presence of a particular underlying analytical process. Once they have served this role, scholarly attention quickly shifts to this purportedly underlying process itself and to *its* implications, for constitutional practice and theory. Balancing's discursive dimension, as a result, disappears from view. A central claim underlying the case studies in this book is that this conflation of process and discourse and the attendant neglect of balancing's discursive dimension are problematic when used in comparative legal scholarship.

To begin with, such comparative studies face problems when trying to *identify* what counts as balancing in a foreign system. If that is a difficult

---

[30] Cf. Yntema (1956), p. 903; Frankenberg (1985), p. 438; Zweigert & Kötz (1998), p. 34.

[31] Rheinstein (1931), p. 2899; cited and translated in Michaels (2006a), p. 349. Philipp Heck, the leading German representative of the *Interessenjurisprudenz*, noted how his conception of 'interests' reduced differences between legal systems and allowed for easier comparison. See Heck (1932a), p. 133. See also Kahn-Freund (1966), p. 51; Frankenberg (1985), p. 434; Kennedy (1997), p. 589.

[32] Aleinikoff (1987), p. 944.

[33] Cohen-Eliya & Porat (2009), p. 385.

[34] Stone Sweet & Mathews (2008), p. 72.

enough question in any local setting, as illustrated by the earlier vignette of the faculty debate, these issues are more complex still in any study that crosses borders. For one, foreign judges and lawyers could be using terms that are locally – that is, in their jurisdiction – seen as closely related or even equivalent to 'real' balancing. But this alternative terminology may be entirely unfamiliar to the outside observer. Examples could include 'means/ends rationality', a 'least restrictive means test', or 'strict scrutiny' in the US context, and *Optimierung* ('optimization') or *praktische Konkordanz* ('practical concordance') in German law.[35] Also, of course, with the question of balancing's nature contested at home, there is no reason to assume this will be a settled matter abroad. Just how little can be taken for granted becomes clear when the German *Bundesverfassungsgericht* is described as having arrived at decisions cast in balancing language 'without any *real* balancing',[36] or when a US Supreme Court Justice is labelled as 'a balancer who seldom uses the word'.[37] My point here is simply that the comparative lawyer does not know beforehand whether the language of balancing in the foreign setting is always used in the same basic sense, or whether it refers to a range of different conceptualizations of decision making. Nor does she know whether alternative terms are used as real substitutes for the language of balancing, or whether they have fundamentally different meanings.

The most pressing example in this area has to be the issue of 'proportionality', a term already encountered in some of the quotations cited earlier. Proportionality is often discussed alongside balancing, both by courts and in academic literature, and is generally seen as similar to, or more precisely as encompassing, balancing as an analytical process.[38] But there are also clear indications of difference, both within and among systems. Both Canadian and German jurisprudence, for example, show evidence of sustained efforts to distinguish proportionality from what is locally seen by some as a 'free-wheeling balancing process'.[39] And while the concept of proportionality dominates constitutional practice and theory in Germany, Canada and many other systems, where it counts as

---

[35] On these terms see further Chapters 3, 4 and 5.
[36] Schlink (1976), pp. 20–21 ('*ohne eigentliche Abwägung*') (emphasis added in translation).
[37] Karst (1965), p. 24. The reference was to Justice Brennan.
[38] See, e.g., Alexy (2002), p. 67. But see Grey (2003), p. 505.
[39] See, e.g., Weinrib (1986), p. 479 and pp. 500ff (the Canadian Supreme Court's 'singular' reference to balancing in *Oakes* is 'at odds' with the gist of its own approach to proportionality).

one of the overarching general principles of constitutional adjudication, it only surfaces in very specific contexts in US constitutional law, where no such general concept is thought to exist.[40] Given these differences, it is not easy to determine *a priori* to what extent 'proportionality' decisions should be compared with 'balancing' case law.[41]

Two further difficulties of comparative method relate to the *interpretation* of balancing, once identified. First, there is the risk that in trying to construe a stable analytical process of balancing underlying foreign legal materials, comparative scholars may in fact be projecting their own experiences and understandings. That is, they may be too quick to assume that the analytical process underlying foreign references to balancing will be the essentially similar to the analytical process signalled by balancing references in their own legal system. This is the familiar problem of the risk of homeward bias in comparative studies. Common depictions of balancing as a solution to a supposedly ubiquitous counter-majoritarian dilemma, for example, or as an answer to an allegedly inevitable problem of the relativity of rights, should be treated with caution on this ground.

Finally, there is the problem of what could be called the one-dimensionality of meaning. This label refers to the idea that balancing's underlying analytical structure – assuming that such a structure could be identified by the comparative lawyer – is likely to constitute only one aspect of the meaning of the language of balancing in a particular setting. References to balancing instead may stand for much more than simply a process of decision making cast in a particular analytical form. Directing all efforts of inquiry at this analytical structure risks closing off many important questions that could be much more revealing of a foreign legal system.[42]

Through their conflation of process and discourse, then, the dominant approaches to the study of balancing in comparative constitutional law have largely left unexamined a broad range of significant questions concerning one of the most striking trends in global contemporary

---

[40]  See, e.g., Grimm (2007), p. 384. US constitutional doctrine often invokes factors like the purpose of governmental action and the impact of governmental action on individuals, either in combination or separately. But this reasoning is not developed as a comprehensive 'proportionality test' and not labelled as such. See, e.g., Fallon (1997b), p. 111.

[41]  See, e.g., Beatty (1993), p. 544 (American constitutional doctrines as 'simply the balancing and proportionality principles by other names'). The relationship between balancing and proportionality is a live issue in many systems. See, e.g., van Gerven (1999), pp. 49ff; Engle (2012).

[42]  For an early recognition of this problem, see Lepaulle (1922), p. 845 (the view of law as a 'mere balancing of interests' involves the indefensible postulate that 'the legal system is an impartial, impassive receptacle in which more or less automatic reactions take place').

constitutional law. Furthermore, the risk that comparative scholars, in construing balancing as process, may unwittingly project their domestic experiences onto foreign systems means there is a real danger that answers obtained to the questions that these approaches *do* ask might be flawed.

## C.    Local meaning, legitimacy, relativity

This book proposes a new direction for the comparative study of balancing. Rather than seeing terms like 'balancing' and 'weighing', or 'proportionality', merely as the reflection of a fixed, stable underlying analytical process, it is possible to engage directly with this language and with the discourse to which it is central. The question to be asked, then, is what this discourse means to its local participants.

The elaboration of this alternative approach starts with a basic proposition. References to balancing or proportionality, in judicial opinions or academic legal writing, figure in a context of legal argumentation. Judges and writers referring to balancing do so in order to argue for or against a particular legal outcome, a specific doctrinal position or a more general understanding of the role of law and courts in society. In effect, from an external perspective, the most neutral answer to the question of what balancing *is*, is simply a form of legal argument.[43] As in ordinary language, this meaning will be governed by the rules of a locally prevalent 'grammar' of legal discourse.[44] But although this grammar will naturally differ from system to system, it will always remain, at least in some basic respects, a distinctively legal – 'typically juridical' – grammar.[45] The methodological framework used in this book is based on the idea that comparative legal studies can make strategic use of what we know about these 'typically juridical' characteristics of Western law. Three dimensions of this shared juridical logic are of particular relevance. The first two – the legitimization imperative and the relativity of the meaning of legal arguments – are discussed in this section. The third, concerning the formal versus substantive opposition, is presented in the next.

---

[43] It is irrelevant, from this perspective, whether local participants *themselves* see balancing in this way. If local legal actors see balancing as an unambiguous analytical structure with a fixed function, then *that* may be the local meaning of balancing as argument. The point, however, is that this has to be a question rather than a starting assumption.

[44] See, e.g., Balkin (1991), p. 1845. See further Bomhoff (2012a).

[45] See Bourdieu (1987), pp. 816ff (labelling this 'the internal logic of juridical functioning').

A first principal characteristic of juridical logic stems from the basic demand that courts in liberal democracies should, in principle, offer publicly stated reasons for their decisions whenever they exercise public authority in order to settle social, political or moral controversies. Publicly stated reasoning, in short, is a necessary condition for the legitimacy of the exercise of judicial power.[46] By implication, to the extent that any element of judicial discourse is an argument, it will always be possible to read its meaning in terms of the contribution it is locally understood to make to either the legitimization or the critique of the exercise of public authority under law.[47]

My claim here is not that judges will always have grand questions of legitimacy foremost in mind, or even that they will always be fully conscious of the broader implications of their arguments in any specific case. What I do argue, though, is that whenever a court invokes a particular type of legal argument, they are necessarily also insisting, albeit normally tacitly, that it is *appropriate* for them to be relying on that type of argument in this situation. They must be taken, in other words, to assert that they are operating within the local range of *acceptable* arguments.[48] The strength and variety of the reasons locally seen as supporting the use of any specific argument to justify the exercise of public authority under law – the reasons underlying this argument's acceptability, that is – can be labelled as its 'legitimizing force'.[49]

This assumption of course applies most directly to the work of courts. But it is relevant also for legal discourse among other kinds of participants

---

[46] See, e.g., Hart (1959), p. 99; Hart (1961), p. 205; Müller (1966), p. 209 (referring to '*rechtsstaatlichea Begründungszwang*' – the duty to give reasons, as imposed by the rule of law); MacCormick (1978), pp. 12ff. Intriguingly, the rise of this demand for adequate justification was contemporaneous with the balancing debates of the 1950s and 1960s canvassed in Chapters 3 and 4. In this sense, the same caveat as to the connections between 'lens' and 'object', raised earlier with regard to balancing and functionalism, is pertinent here too.

[47] This approach originates in the study of political discourse. See Pocock (1981); Pocock (2009), p. 3, p. 16. For its application in legal studies, see, e.g., Kahn (2001), p. 145 ('the character of knowledge claims within the legal order is a function of [the] need for legitimacy'). See further Bomhoff (2012a).

[48] Cf. Bobbitt (1982), pp. 6–8; Bell (1986), pp. 45–56.

[49] Legitimacy is used here as a *sociological* concept of acceptance with a particular *legal* constituency. For the purposes of this study, that constituency is confined to what Marc Galanter has called 'the higher reaches' of the law 'where the learned tradition is propounded'. This means especially judges at higher courts, the legal scholarly community and leading advocates. Legitimacy, as used here, is also an *abstract* concept, assessed on *local* standards by a local audience. See further Galanter (1974), p. 147; Summers (1978), p. 716; Bell (1986), p. 46; Bobbitt (1989), p. 1239; Fallon (2005).

in the legal order. This is because they too will be subject to the conventions and constraints that come with having to operate within the range of locally acceptable arguments. This ensures that 'legitimizing force' will always be one dimension, though not necessarily the only dimension, of any argument's local meaning.[50]

A second characteristic of juridical logic flows from the widely shared understanding in Western systems that legal actors will always have some degree of choice with regard to the specific arguments they invoke in defending and challenging exercises of public authority under law.[51] This is not to say that this possibility of choice will always and everywhere be perceived in similar terms. In some settings, otherwise familiar forms of argument may effectively be off-limits, while others may be dominant to the point of hegemony. What is advocated is merely an understanding that legal arguments are conventions upheld by participants and that, therefore, the argumentative landscape of any given system could look different if these participants made different choices.[52] This possibility of choice means that any argument's contribution to the projects of legitimization and critique will always be a relative contribution, which can only be understood by way of comparison within a particular system.[53] This basic relativity of meaning pervades all uses of legal arguments, not only by judges but also by other participants in legal discourse.

The advantage of this alternative perspective is that the nature of balancing's legitimizing contribution – the ways in which balancing is taken to be relevant, its success or failure as a legal argument, even its very analytical structure – can be left open as questions for the foreign system to answer. In this approach it is possible that the language of balancing may not always and everywhere signal the same underlying analytical process. Or that, even if similar processes are involved, they will come

---

[50] For the sociological critique that use of the concept of 'legitimation' rests on the unrealistic assumption 'that every element of a legal system contributes to the maintenance of the whole', see Hyde (1983), p. 422. Here, I merely claim that local participants will – or at least could – interpret any element of legal discourse as *either* serving to uphold *or* as critiquing the legitimacy of the exercise of public power, or in any event that such a reading will give a reasonably accurate understanding of this discourse to an outside observer. Cf. Bomhoff (2012a), pp. 79ff.

[51] Cf. Bomhoff (2012a), pp. 83ff.

[52] Bobbitt (1982), pp. 6ff. On this view of argument as audience-dependent, see, e.g., Perelman (1963).

[53] On the relational character of meaning and other basic (post)-structuralist insights in the study of discourse see, e.g., Pocock (1981); Toews (1987), pp. 881ff; Fisher (1997), p. 1068; Clark (2004), pp. 138ff. See also Kennedy (1979); Heller (1984); Kennedy (1987); Koskenniemi (2005).

with fundamentally different implications. Rather than having to identify a specific, uniform structure and function for balancing as doctrine
beforehand, this alternative approach asks why *this* particular court and
its audience see a need to balance – whether it is because they feel that
this is what the protection of a particular fundamental right or perhaps
the task of judges in a democracy is fundamentally about, for example,
or because judges cannot agree on anything more than that some sort of
accommodation between individual and societal interests is important.[54]
It then analyses the answers in the context of locally prevalent ideals of
legitimacy.

## D.   Balancing, the formal and the substantive

### 1.   *Law's* proprium

There is overwhelming evidence for the proposition that actors in all
Western legal systems are faced with some variant of a basic dilemma
of managing these systems' relative autonomy.[55] This relative autonomy
of the juridical sphere constitutes not only a valid descriptive account of
Western law, but also crucially, a normative ideal intimately connected to
the idea of legitimacy.

In the Western tradition, law, in order to qualify as law, has to be somewhat autonomous, somewhat closed-off from other sources of value,
such as morality, religion, ideology, social relations or economics. In the
vocabulary made famous by Max Weber, this means that law, by definition, as a normative ideal, and by experience, is and has to be somewhat
*formal.*[56] But at the same time, law, in order to be acceptable as law and

---

[54]  See, e.g., Justice Brennan of the US Supreme Court in *New Jersey* v. *T.L.O.* 469 US 325,
369–71 [1985] (balancing as no more than 'a convenient umbrella under which a majority
that cannot agree on a genuine rationale can conceal its differences').

[55]  See, e.g., Friedman (1966), pp. 148, 161, 170 ('legalism', as a type of reasoning based on
formal logic 'within a closed system of legal rules and concepts [...], is a feature which
can and does appear whenever certain conditions prevail in a legal system – the duty to
decide; the duty to give reasons; a closed canon of principles or rules; legal functionar-
ies whose roles do not legitimately allow for the making of law'); Berman (1983), pp. 7–8
(a first 'principal characteristic' of the Western legal tradition is a 'relatively sharp distinction [...] between *legal* institutions [...] and *other* types of institutions') (emphasis in
original); Wieacker (1990), pp. 23ff.

[56]  See Weber (1925), pp. 63ff. Weber's scheme is famously opaque, in no small part because
it attempts to distinguish not only 'formal' from substantive, but also 'rational' from
'irrational'. On the 'exclusionary' character of Weber's formality see, e.g., Trubek (1985),
pp. 930ff. For an account of legal formality as 'closedness' see Schauer (1988), pp. 536ff.

to have any hope of functioning at least somewhat effectively in modern societies, cannot be fully autonomous or closed-off in this sense.[57] At stake, therefore, is not merely the one-sided pursuit of law's autonomy, but rather the discursive management of the necessary co-existence of the formal and substantive dimensions of law. This, as Michelle Everson and Julia Eisner put it, is law's *'proprium'*:[58] 'Law', they write, 'is forever caught on the horns of a dilemma. Law is not of this world, but is, instead, a transcendental force of self-referential reasoning. At the same time, however, law's underlying claim to dispense of social, as well as legal, legitimacy determines that it must engage with a world outside law, in order to bring its abstract formulations into line with an actual realm of social and political contestation'.[59] The intimate connection between these two conflicting goals and the ideal of legitimacy is reflected in a range of tropes common to German and US law, notably in the image of purely individualized judgment that Max Weber and Roscoe Pound shared in their *'Khadi'* judge, and the pictures of a sterile cult of logic decried by Otto von Gierke's 'lifeless abstractions' and Pound's 'mechanical jurisprudence'.[60]

The centrality of this dilemma was acknowledged particularly clearly in legal theoretical writing of the late 1950s and early 1960s: the period during which German and US courts first began to refer to balancing.[61] Gerhard Leibholz, for example, who was a Justice of the *Bundesverfassungsgericht* from its foundation in 1951 until his retirement in 1971, wrote that the task of constitutional lawyers was to 'reconcile rules of law and constitutional reality in such a way that the existing dialectical conflict between rule and reality can be removed as far as possible'.[62] Other German authors noted a permanent struggle to mediate between a *'Gerechtigkeitspostulat'* and a *'Rechtssicherheitspostulat'* – the commands of individual justice and of legal certainty.[63] In the US, meanwhile, Henry Hart, arguably the leading commentator on the work of the Supreme Court during this period, wrote in 1959 of the imperative of keeping the body of constitutional law

---

[57]  See, e.g., Summers & Atiyah (1987), pp. 1ff; Summers (1992).
[58]  Everson & Eisner (2007), p. 9.
[59]  *Ibid.* See also, e.g., Habermas (1996), p. 9 ('immanent tension' in law).
[60]  On Weber and Pound, see further Chapter 2. For von Gierke, see Whitman (1990), pp. 230–31.
[61]  See Chapter 1, Section 5.
[62]  Cited in Brügger (1994), pp. 410–11
[63]  Schneider (1963), p. 30.

simultaneously 'rationally consistent with itself' and 'rationally related to the purposes which the social order exists to serve'.[64]

## 2.   Formal how? Substantive how?

This problem of how to manage law's relative formality, then, in all its different manifestations, pervades legal discourse in Western legal systems. Its status as a common problem to be solved according to local standards and using local means, makes it a useful point of reference for the comparative analysis of legal discourse. Two leading examples of studies taking just such an approach are Summers and Atiyah's *Form and Substance in Anglo-American Law* and Mitchel Lasser's account of judicial reasoning at the French *Cour de cassation*, the Court of Justice of the European Union and the US Supreme Court.[65]

Based on wide ranging observations of familiar features of English and US law, Summers and Atiyah's principal conclusion is that 'the mix of the formal and the substantive in the two systems is very different'. The English legal system, in their view, is highly 'formal', while the American is highly 'substantive'.[66] This contrast, they argue, 'reflects a deep difference in legal style, legal culture, and more generally, the visions of law which prevail in the two countries'.[67]

Where Summers and Atiyah's main interest is in qualifying legal systems as more or less formal, Lasser's path breaking studies tackle two further related issues. First, Lasser looks at differences in local understandings of what counts as substantive or formal reasoning in the first place. It is not at all clear, Lasser argues, that contingent, potentially parochial, terms such as 'formalism', 'nondeductive argument' or 'policy' will have the same meaning in different settings.[68] Finding out what exactly the relevant audience *does* understand by formality and its opposites, and why they think these qualifications matter, should therefore allow for 'a thicker description of the foreign legal system'.[69] Lasser's second main project, then, is to look at the ways in which the formal and the substantive are combined, integrated or juxtaposed in each system. 'What really matters', he writes, 'is not so much *that* both [the French and the American]

---

[64] Cited in Friedmann (1961), pp. 835–36. For an earlier account in similar terms, and with continued influence during this period, see Cardozo (1921), pp. 102ff.

[65] Summers & Atiyah (1987); Lasser (1995); Lasser (1998); Lasser (2001); Lasser (2004).

[66] Summers & Atiyah (1987), pp. 1ff, 410.

[67] *Ibid.*     [68] Lasser (2001), pp. 896ff.

[69] *Ibid.*

systems deploy both types of discourse (can one even really imagine a contemporary, Western democratic legal system that would not?), but *how* they do so.'[70] Lasser's central claim is that 'the American judicial system *combines* the two discourses [of formality and substance] in one and the same place, while the French system *bifurcates* them, doing all in its power to segregate them into separate discursive spheres'.[71] These different forms of co-existence – 'combination', 'bifurcation', perhaps others – in turn correspond to an underlying problematic that typifies the relevant system. As Lasser writes of the American system: its 'formalization of the pragmatic', his terminology for describing its peculiar habit of combining formal and substantive modes of reasoning in one place, 'may well be *the defining trait of American judicial discourse in general*'.[72]

That is quite a claim. But this line of inquiry does hold enormous potential for a comparative study of the discourse of balancing. In particular, it opens up the possibility that the same language may, in different settings, be the manifestation of very different kinds of encounters between legal formality and its opposites. Those different modes of interaction, in turn, could be emblematic for the system concerned, in ways similar to those suggested by Lasser.

Part of the argument this book seeks to develop runs along these lines. While American balancing discourse of the 1950s and 1960s was characterized by pervasive antinomies, balancing in the German constitutional landscape of the time was the principal embodiment one of modern constitutionalism's most significant and successful efforts at overcoming these same basic oppositions. American constitutional jurisprudence continuously draws fundamental distinctions between pragmatic action and reasoned deliberation, between policy and principle and between the substantive and the formal – always relegating balancing firmly to one side of these dichotomies. German constitutional law, on the other hand, has managed, to a large extent, to fuse these elements, adopting balancing as the main vehicle of a jurisprudence that casts the pragmatic as reasoned, policy as principle and the substantive as formal.

In Chapter 5, this argument will be developed by way of a comparative analysis of paradigmatic German and US conceptions of the formal versus substantive opposition. This opposition can be specified along four dimensions: those of the formal, the substantive, of the nature of their

---

[70] Lasser (2004), p. 155 (emphasis added).
[71] *Ibid.* (emphasis in original); Lasser (2001), p. 894.
[72] Lasser (2004), p. 251 (emphasis added).

interaction and of the attitudes adopted towards their co-existence.[73] The first two of these concern the character of, first, 'the formal', and second 'the substantive'. Both elements can be shown to be contingent in various ways. Chapter 5 examines this contingency, analysing among other things the ways local legal actors typically describe legal formality and its opposites. Would it matter, for example, if in one setting formality were typically equated with rules and 'ruleness', whereas in another context the typical references are the ideas of 'system' and conceptual refinement? Broader associations could also be highly revealing, as where in one system formality is habitually related to a particular canonical court decision, or to a particular era in constitutional law, while such associations might be absent in other systems. The crucial point is that these associations may tell the comparative lawyer at least as much about local understandings of legal formality and its opposites as they might about the decisions or eras concerned.

The third and fourth dimensions examine the character ascribed to the interaction between the formal and the substantive in law, and the nature of the attitudes typically adopted towards these encounters. Do the formal and the substantive, for example, relate to each other in a state of 'unsynthesized co-existence' – a state of permanent conflict and paradox? Or do local legal actors believe some form of synthesis could be possible? Is the conflict between rule and reality inescapable, or can it, in the words of Justice Leibholz quoted earlier, be to some extent 'removed'? And finally, is this dilemma of form and substance something lawyers tend to approach sceptically and with trepidation, or embrace with ambition, as a societal challenge only they can really handle?

## E.    Origins: two sets of debates

For all its present day global pervasiveness, the discourse of balancing in constitutional rights adjudication has remarkably concentrated origins. It exploded onto the constitutional scene, as it were, in very similar circumstances, and at almost exactly the same time. Balancing first explicitly surfaced in a handful of major decisions of the German *Bundesverfassungsgericht* and of the US Supreme Court of the late 1950s and early 1960s. The synchronicity is striking. The *Bundesverfassungsgericht*'s first seminal balancing decision, in the *Lüth* case, dates from January 1958, while a balancing war erupted on the US

---

[73] See Chapter 5, Sections B–E.

Supreme Court mainly over cases decided between 1959 and 1961.[74] In both settings, balancing was first referred to and discussed in the area of free speech adjudication. But it quickly spread – as lens, if not quite so clearly as doctrine – to other areas of constitutional law.[75] A further point of commonality is that in both settings, these first discussions of balancing in constitutional law self-consciously and explicitly relied on earlier theoretical work on balancing. This earlier work was again carried out virtually contemporaneously, in the first decades of the twentieth century, by scholars of the *Interessenjurisprudenz* in Germany and by adherents of Sociological Jurisprudence in the US.

These two great parallel debates on the nature, virtues and flaws of balancing that ensued from the early Supreme Court and *Bundesverfassungsgericht* cases of the late 1950s and early 1960s form the main subject of comparative investigation in this book, in Chapters 3 and 4. This account will, in Chapter 2, be grounded, just as in these original debates themselves, in a comparative study of the earlier phase in balancing's genealogy in the *Interessenjurisprudenz* and Sociological Jurisprudence. For both sets of debates, every effort will be made to present balancing as it was discussed – whether as free speech law, constitutional rights law, constitutional law generally or even law as a whole – and in the terms and analytical categories adhered to by participants at the time.

There are a number of reasons for taking a historical approach to the discourse of balancing, and for taking this particular approach specifically. In general terms, a historical investigation fits well with the aim of trying to unpack the meaning of balancing. All legal language comes with baggage from its earlier uses. Even if we are now convinced that earlier debates were unfortunate and misconceived, they still influence what this language stands for today, informing the associations made – wittingly and unwittingly – by contemporary actors.[76] From that perspective, the German and US debates on balancing are still without doubt

---

[74] Kalven (1967), p. 444. See further Chapter 4.

[75] See Chapters 3 and 4.

[76] Cf. Schauer (1984), p. 1285. Schauer argues with regard to the American balancing debate of the 1950s and 1960s that '[t]he language [of balancing] has acquired so much baggage from its previous usages that it blocks us from appreciating the ways in which today is different from yesterday'. That may very well be true, and it may be that an excessive focus on the intricacies of balancing may block real progress when it comes to the important and messy business of understanding what is at stake in constitutional rights adjudication. At the same time, however, this baggage is still real, and its present-day impact cannot safely be ignored.

the most influential historical sources for the contemporary meaning of balancing.[77]

More particularly, though, this book deliberately relies on narrowly focused case studies, as part of an effort to pierce the veil of similarity that shrouds contemporary balancing discourse. The idea that language of balancing will always mean more or less the same thing *itself* originates in the earlier discussions canvassed here. All throughout the twentieth century, commentators have pointed out 'basic similarities' between first *Interessenjurisprudenz* and Sociological Jurisprudence, and later the *Bundesverfassungsgericht*'s and the US Supreme Court's uses of balancing in constitutional rights decisions.[78] Those impressions also sustain the persistent attraction of broad, similarity-focused comparative accounts of balancing and proportionality. Showing how, in fact, both these earlier episodes, for all their remarkable similarities, were also characterized by crucial differences, should be an important step towards dismantling overbroad claims for a global age of balancing today.

---

[77] See, e.g., Mattei (2003); Stone Sweet & Mathews (2008); Tushnet (2008), p. 18. See also Kennedy (2003), p. 635 (referring to the US as the 'hegemonic site of production' of global legal consciousness from 1950 onwards). Kennedy sees the period between 1900 and the 1930s as dominated by French legal thinking. In Chapter 2, I briefly discuss the debt of both the German *Interessenjurisprudenz* and Sociological Jurisprudence to earlier French ideas.

[78] For references, see Chapter 2, Section A. See also, e.g., Häberle (1962), p. 39; Scheuner (1965), p. 55.

# 2

## Balancing's beginnings: concepts and interests

### A.  Introduction

Between roughly 1900 and 1930, academic lawyers and judges in the US and in Europe first began to describe law and lawmaking in terms of balancing and weighing of interests. In these two settings, the new language first appeared as part of a critique of late-nineteenth-century ideas and sensibilities now often called 'classical orthodoxy' or 'classical legal thought'. In Europe, this orthodoxy was the '*Pandektenwissenschaft*' of Puchta and Windscheid in private law, and what the critics labelled as '*Begriffsjurisprudenz*', the 'jurisprudence of concepts', in private and public law more generally. In the US, the classical model was thought to consist of an uneasy amalgam of a distinctive conception of legal science in private law – associated in particular with the work of Dean Langdell at Harvard Law School – and a broadly laissez-faire approach to constitutional review in the courts.[1] The first and most significant alternative approaches invoking the language of balancing were developed by François Gény in France, by Philipp Heck and his fellow members of the school of *Interessenjurisprudenz* ('Jurisprudence of Interests') in Germany and by Roscoe Pound and other 'Sociological Jurisprudes' in the US.

Both in criticizing classical orthodoxy and in developing alternative visions, including those turning on balancing, American scholars drew extensively upon European ideas. These interrelationships have since lent further force to a common impression that these American and European orthodoxies, their critiques and their replacement projects were all, in essential respects, similar. Lon Fuller, for example, writing in the late 1940s, was impressed by how Dean Langdell's thought and method had resembled 'in striking measure those of his German

---

[1]  See, e.g., Summers (1982), p. 27; Grey (1983); Duxbury (1995), pp. 11ff.

counterpart, Windscheid'.[2] Both, he noted, 'practiced a peculiar geomet-
ric brand of legal reasoning' and 'postulated a gapless system of pre-exist-
ing law, from which the solution for every new case could be obtained by
deduction'.[3] As to the critique of this classical heritage, Roscoe Pound
himself by 1913 wrote of a 'reaction from the [...] jurisprudence of conceptions' that had been 'in progress the world over'.[4] And with regard
to the balancing-based replacement projects, finally, the German *émigré*
professor Wolfgang Friedmann early on observed a 'strikingly similar
development of an *Interessenjurisprudenz* by American lawyers against
the background of a very different legal system'.[5] It is this long tradition of emphasis on similarities that forms the backdrop to the analysis
undertaken in this book.

This chapter uncovers balancing's beginnings, or its intellectual origins and early critiques. It presents a comparative historical analysis
of the emergence of one mode of legal discourse – the 'free scientific
research' of Gény and the balancing of interests of Heck, Pound and
others – as part of a critique of, and as an effort to replace, another –
the discourse of classical orthodoxy. In summary form, the argument is
that American lawyers took the methods of French and German private
law scholarly critique and turned it into a critique of American constitutional adjudication. This process of appropriation resulted in three
early meanings for the balancing of interests: as a modest element in
a modest project of methodological adaptation (Gény); as the centrepiece of a 'purely juristic', legal-practice-oriented theory of adjudication (Heck); and as a 'Progressive device' for reform, in which the idea
of 'interests' was central, and 'balancing' appeared almost as an after-
thought (Pound). It also laid the foundations, in US jurisprudence, for
intellectual associations between method and politics – and more specifically: between form and substance – that have exercised a pervasive
influence on legal thinking throughout the twentieth century. These
associations, and their absence in European law, continue to affect the
meanings of balancing today.

The chapter proceeds as follows. Section B discusses the images of late-
nineteenth-century legal thought and its associated methods adopted

---

[2] Fuller (1948), p. xix.    [3] *Ibid.*
[4] Pound (1913), p. 708; Kennedy & Belleau (2000), p. 304.
[5] Friedmann (1967, 1944), p. 336. See also Friedmann (1961), p. 828 ('A comparative analysis
of the thought of common law jurists such as Pound and Cardozo with that of Continental
jurists such as Gény or the German representatives of "*Interessenjurisprudenz*" [...]
reveals striking similarities'); Antieau (1985), pp. 123ff.

by the twentieth-century critics. Section C does the same for the earliest projects of legal-methodological reform, in particular those invoking the imagery of weighing. The focus here, as throughout this book, will be on Germany and the US, but some attention will also be paid to the work of François Gény in France, as a precursor – and to some extent source of inspiration – to both settings. Section D offers some concluding observations, setting the stage for the analysis of balancing in postwar constitutional rights jurisprudence in Chapters 3 and 4.

## B.   The jurisprudence of concepts: classical orthodoxy and the non-balancing past

### 1.   Introduction

At its origins, in both Europe and the US, the jurisprudence of the balancing of interests was a jurisprudence of critique and replacement. Heck, Pound and others explicitly formulated their jurisprudence of interests by way of opposition with an allegedly theretofore dominant and fundamentally flawed alternative model: the 'jurisprudence of concepts', or '*Begriffsjurisprudenz*'. One early meaning of the jurisprudence of balancing, then, has to be, in a deceptively simple phrase, '*not* the jurisprudence of concepts'.

This earlier mode of jurisprudential discourse has been analysed before and in great depth, both for the US and for Europe, especially Germany.[6] These studies commonly emphasize how difficult it is to capture the prevailing legal consciousness of a period of more than a century ago. Late-nineteenth-century American legal thought, Robert Gordon notes, 'has proved maddeningly elusive to historians' attempts to chase it down, especially since we are used to seeing it through the eyes of Progressive critics inclined to hostile caricature'.[7] The same is true in Europe, where the derisory term *Begriffsjurisprudenz* and the tradition of caricature originate with von Jhering himself.[8] With this rich and complex background in mind, the exploration of the jurisprudence of concepts in this section is circumscribed in three ways.

---

[6] See, e.g., Kennedy (1975); Kennedy (1980); Grey (1983); Larenz (1991); Horwitz (1992); Stolleis (1992); Wieacker (1995); Grey (1996b); Duxbury (1995); Gordon (1997); Haferkamp (2004); Kennedy (2006).

[7] Gordon (1997), p. 155.

[8] Von Jhering (1884), pp. 337ff. See also Haferkamp (2004), p. 463; Larenz (1991), p. 49.

First, it is an investigation specifically of what could be called 'the balancer's account' of classical orthodoxy. This is precisely the anti-image Heck, Pound and their contemporaries had in mind when developing their alternative visions. That image is important as it formed part of the meaning of balancing at its inception, in a negative sense, as a reminder of all that the new methods should seek to avoid. Especially in the case of the US, it is also an image that remains relevant to this day, as 'the thesis to which modern American legal thought has been the antithesis'.[9] One argument I make in this chapter and in Chapter 5, is that this 'pendulum swing' narrative of thesis–antithesis which is pervasive in American legal thinking,[10] does not adequately capture the nature of the continued relevance of classical legal thought, neither in Europe nor in the US, although for very different reasons.

Second, one aspect of this received account of classical orthodoxy that deserves special attention is its association with the conceptual vocabulary of legal formality and its opposites. In particular since Max Weber took the German Pandectists as the source and illustration for his ideal type of formal rationality in law, the legal worldview ascribed to mid- and late-nineteenth-century lawyers and the terminology of legal formality and formalism have been inseparably linked.[11] Of course, as Weber's own account makes abundantly clear, it is far from easy to identify the precise ways in which classical legal thought can be said to have been formal or formalist.[12] But since the vocabulary of legal formality and its opposites has become the dominant framework for the description and analysis of balancing specifically,[13] these ambiguities also directly affect our ability to make sense of that language. Understanding how and why these early critics thought classical orthodoxy was formal – and what they thought was wrong about this formality – is, therefore, an important step towards understanding the meanings of balancing.

And third, for both these topics – of the balancer's view of classical orthodoxy generally, and of the association with legal formality specifically – this account is particularly interested in the question of local differences. Here, two further questions are relevant. First: is there anything that distinguishes European critiques of the work of Puchta and

[9]  Grey (1983), p. 3 (making this point about the US).
[10]  See, critically, Duxbury (1995), p. 2. Here I am interested in the persistence of this view as itself culturally significant. See also Chapter 5, Sections D and E.
[11]  See Weber (1925), p. 64.
[12]  'As everyone knows', Weber writes in his *Critique of Stammler*, 'there is no expression more ambiguous than the word "formal"'. Weber (1907), p. 79.
[13]  See Chapter 1, Section D.

Windscheid from American attacks on Langdellian legal science, despite all their undeniable similarities? And second: does it matter that classical orthodoxy in the US has come to be seen as encompassing more than just these rather narrow scholarly and educational projects, and also includes its perceived impact on the practice of constitutional adjudication?

In what follows, I argue 'yes' in response to both these questions. Although the European and the American critics were undoubtedly part of the same broad movement responding to nineteenth-century sensibilities, they had different preoccupations. They were concerned, in other words, with *two orthodoxies*. These orthodoxies, importantly, did not only prompt two different replacement projects, each with a different role for balancing, but also two different conceptions of legal formality and its opposites; conceptions that still haunt the way we understand balancing today.

## 2.    'Scientific law' and legal formality

First, though, the basic contours of the received, shared, image of classical orthodoxy and of its association to legal formality require some further exposition.

In both settings, the traditional view of classical orthodoxy is that of a closed, gapless, system within which it was possible, in every concrete case, 'to derive the decision from abstract legal propositions by means of legal logic'.[14] Its adherents gave this ideal the label of 'scientific law'.[15] Several dynamics came together to promote its ascendancy.[16] Germany, France and the US all faced somewhat similar institutional demands related to the advent of systematic academic legal instruction.[17] Shared too, was a strong desire on the part of legal scholars for their field to be seen as on a par with other academic disciplines.[18] But probably the dominant impetus in all three settings was the ideal of lawyers and judges as a political actors.[19] The upheavals of industrialization and urbanization

---

[14] Weber (1925), p. 64; Frankfurter (1930), p. 665; Pound (1959), pp. I-91ff; Wieacker (1995), pp. 343ff.

[15] Grey (1983), p. 5.

[16] See, e.g., Rümelin (1930), pp. 14ff; Grey (1983), p. 39.

[17] See, e.g., Rümelin (1930); Grey (1983); Wieacker (1995), pp. 346ff; Duxbury (1995), pp. 14ff.

[18] See, e.g., Rümelin (1930), p. 7 (alternative approaches seen as 'unscholarly amateurism and subjectivism'); Llewellyn (1942), p. 228 (describing the 'esthetic goal' of 'structured beauty' common to the German civil code and the work of Dean Langdell); Horwitz (1992), pp. 13ff; Stolleis (1992), p. 331; Wieacker (1995), pp. 295ff; Duxbury (1995), p. 15.

[19] See, e.g., Rümelin (1930), p. 14 (openly pronounced value judgments 'invite the criticism of the interested parties or groups to a much higher degree than do genuinely or apparently logical deductions').

ensured that the second half of the nineteenth century was a period of extraordinary rapid change in Europe and in America.[20] It was in these unsettled times that expectations arose in the US that law could perhaps 'provide a non-political cushion or buffer between state and society',[21] and in Germany, that the creation of a 'strictly juristic method' could mediate 'the tension between reactionism and liberalism' after the 1848 Revolutions in Europe.[22] Both in Europe and in the US, the elaboration of a 'scientific' legal sphere that would be separate from politics thus became a principal preoccupation of legal scholars.

Legal thinkers sought 'an autonomous legal culture', 'a system of legal thought free from politics',[23] the idea being that if little else could be agreed upon, law at least could provide an objective, apolitical, neutral – in short: scientific – way of solving conflicts.[24] Law had to be 'a sophisticated scheme for the coordination of increasingly complex private affairs' that would obviate the need to get 'involved in the political battles of its time'.[25]

Standard depictions of the ideal character of 'scientific law' in Europe and the US, then, do indeed show striking similarities. In particular, they commonly invoke the same more abstract vocabulary to generalize earlier beliefs and habits. This vocabulary is the language of legal formality. On both counts, these similarities owe much to the transatlantic influence of early German analyses. For the general depiction of conceptual jurisprudence this is true notably of the work of Rudolph von Jhering.[26] For the terminology of legal formality specifically, it is the work of Max Weber that has become the standard template.[27]

---

[20] See, e.g., Belleau (1997), p. 381; Kennedy (1980), pp. 7ff; McCloskey (2005), pp. 68ff.

[21] Goetsch (1980), pp. 254ff; Horwitz (1992), p. 9.

[22] Arnaud (1975); Belleau (1997), p. 379; Stolleis (2001), p. 266.

[23] Horwitz (1992), p. 10; Stolleis (1992) p. 331 (the '*konsequente Reinigung des juristischen Denkens von nichtjuristischen Elementen*'). This purported autonomy soon became an important object of critique. See, e.g., Pound (1959), p. I-91.

[24] *Ibid.*, pp. 119ff.

[25] Reimann (1990), p. 893. See also Gordon (1997), p. 140.

[26] See, e.g., Pound (1908), p. 610. But see, famously, Holmes (1879), p. 631 for a virtually simultaneous description, in almost the same wording.

[27] Holmes and Pound are notable partial exceptions. For Holmes, see *ibid.* Pound's case is complex. Pound was invoking the label 'formal' before Weber, in a very similar range of meanings, under reference to an eclectic array of sources drawn mostly from classic English writings on the common law, from English and German studies of Roman law and from social psychology. At the same time though, there is no real attempt in Pound's early work to use this language in the critique of the 'jurisprudence of conceptions', in

Weber's famous, if enigmatic, ideal-typical categories of formal and substantive rationality and irrationality in law appear in Chapter 8 of *Economy and Society*. This general catalogue is followed immediately by an elaboration of the 'formal qualities' of 'present day' German legal science.[28] Its formality, Weber argued, stemmed from its adherence to five postulates:

> first, that every concrete legal decision be the 'application' of an abstract legal proposition to a concrete 'fact situation'; second, that it must be possible in every concrete case to derive the decision from abstract legal propositions by means of legal logic; third, that the law must actually or virtually constitute a 'gapless' system of legal propositions, or must, at least, be treated as if it were such a gapless system; fourth, that whatever cannot be 'construed' legally in rational terms is also legally irrelevant; and fifth, that every social action of human beings must always be visualized as either an 'application' or 'execution' of legal propositions, or as an 'infringement' thereof.[29]

Weber's language quickly became the standard frame of reference for describing the ideas animating the jurisprudence of concepts. In Germany, Philipp Heck invoked Weber explicitly when he identified adherence to '*formallogische Subsumption*' as emblematic for the *Begriffsjurisprudenz*.[30] Later studies continue to invoke the same terminology. In the US, for example, Thomas Grey has described the core of classical theory as the aspiration 'that the legal system be made complete through universal formality, and universally formal through conceptual order'.[31] And in Germany, Franz Wieacker has summarized the nineteenth-century conception of 'law as a positive science', as adhering to the assumptions that a legal system is necessarily 'a closed system of institutions and rules, independent of social reality', within which all that would be needed to make a correct decision in any case would be 'the logical operation of subsuming the case' under a 'general doctrinal principle'.[32]

---

either Pound (1908), Pound (1910) or Pound (1911) (there are just passing references to a 'desire for formal perfection', in Pound (1910), at p. 23, and in Pound (1911a), at p. 596). For a historical overview see also Morris (1958).

[28]  Weber (1925), p. 64.

[29]  *Ibid.*

[30]  Heck (1932a), p. 91. In the US, Realists such as Karl Llewellyn and Walter Wheeler Cook regularly noted their reliance on Weber's sociology.

[31]  Grey (1983), p. 11. For Grey's indebtedness to Weber, see p. 6.

[32]  Wieacker (1995), pp. 342–44. See also Stolleis (1992), p. 331.

### 3.  Conceptual jurisprudence in Germany: Heck's
### Begriffsjurisprudenz

What, then, was the precise nature of the critique of conceptualism that Philipp Heck and other German authors invoked as the background to their proposals for a jurisprudence of interests? To begin with, Heck did not actually invent the term '*Begriffsjurisprudenz*'.[33] And other European writers had criticized the 'obsession of abstract concepts' and ignorance of the 'requirements of practical life' before: most famously, François Gény in his *Méthode d'Interprétation* of 1899.[34] But, at least in Germany, Heck did more than probably anyone else to expound and popularize these ideas.[35] In particular, he coined the influential term '*Inversion*' to capture what he saw as the heart of the error of conceptual jurisprudence.[36] In his 1909 article 'What Is This Conceptual Jurisprudence Which We Fight Against?' Heck described as '*Inversionsverfahren*', 'that tendency in jurisprudence, which treats general juristic principles as the foundation of those legal propositions of which they themselves are in fact a distillation'.[37] In later work, Heck summarized his critique as follows:

> The older school, the Jurisprudence of Concepts, confined the judge to a function of subsuming facts under legal concepts. Accordingly, the legal order was thought of as a 'complete' system of legal concepts, a system which was conceived as a deductive or analytical system. From general concepts there resulted special concepts; from concepts there resulted, by logical deduction, the legal rules applicable to the facts [...] Thus the supremacy of logic was a generally recognized principle in jurisprudence.[38]

The 'orthodox school', Heck wrote, upheld the theory of the 'dogma of cognition', which confined judges to a purely cognitive – that is to say, not evaluative – role.[39] Echoing Roscoe Pound, Heck noted that the judge was 'regarded as an automaton [...] not concerned with the question whether his decision was just from the point of view of its effects on human affairs'.[40]

---

[33]  See von Jhering (1884), p. 337 (using inverted commas).
[34]  Gény (1899), pp. 23, 26. (Page number references are to the English translation by Bruncken & Register.)
[35]  See especially Heck (1909); Heck (1912). On Heck's role, see Haferkamp (2004), pp. 84ff.
[36]  *Ibid.*, p. 84. See also Edelmann (1967), pp. 31ff.
[37]  Heck (1909), cited in Edelmann (1967), pp. 31–32. See also Heck (1932b), p. 107.
[38]  Heck (1932b), pp. 102–3. At p. 103 Heck cites Weber's depiction of formal legal science.
[39]  Rümelin (1930), p. 9; Heck (1933), pp. 33–34.
[40]  Heck (1933), p. 37.

### (a)    A scholarly, private law critique

It is important to note that in criticizing conceptual jurisprudence, Heck and his fellow *Interessenjurisprudenz* writers were primarily targeting a jurisprudential school. They decried a scholarly tendency to promote a particular vision of legal reasoning and adjudication, rather than the form and content of actual judicial decisions. This can easily be observed from the overwhelming predominance of scholarly – rather than case law – examples in the *Interessenjurisprudenz* scholars' work.[41]

Even more narrowly, the *Begriffsjurisprudenz* was seen by its critics primarily as a private law phenomenon, associated with the Pandectist scholarship of Georg Friedrich Puchta, Rudolph von Jhering (until his famous conversion) and Bernhard Windscheid.[42] To be sure, Heck does note by the early 1930s that '[a]t present it is the sphere of public law in which the old controversy [over conceptual jurisprudence] is discussed most heatedly'.[43] And public law did have its influential proponents of conceptual jurisprudence in Carl Friedrich von Gerber and Paul Laband, who, it should be said, first made their mark in private law and legal history respectively.[44] But notwithstanding Heck's passing references to the relevance of the public law context, his focus, and that of other *Interessenjurisprudenz* writers like Max Rümelin, Heinrich Stoll and Rudolf Müller-Erzbach is very firmly on conceptual jurisprudence in the field of private law.[45] Taking these first two points together, the typical target for dismissal as *Begriffsjurisprudenz* appears as an academic, dogmatic exposition of a technical private law problem.[46]

### (b)    System, subsumption, idealism

When looking at the content of *Begriffsjurisprudenz* beliefs as envisaged by its critics, and especially through the lens of a comparison with American understandings of classical orthodoxy, the German critics emerge as principally concerned with the elements of *system, subsumption*

---

[41]  *Ibid.*, p. 40 (commenting favourably on the *Reichgericht*'s performance). See further Speiger (1984), pp. 12ff. Speiger mentions Müller-Erzbach's 1929 article 'Reichsgericht und Interessenjurisprudenz' as the first 'intensive' examination of the role of the jurisprudence of interests in the case law of the German Supreme Court.

[42]  Wieacker (1995), pp. 279ff, 341ff.

[43]  Heck (1932b), p. 104.

[44]  See Stolleis (1992), pp. 330ff, 341ff.

[45]  Heck (1932b), p. 105 (announcing a focus on private law, and claiming that, in any event, 'the problem of public law method cannot be isolated from the problem of private-law method'). On *Interessenjurisprudenz* in constitutional theory, see Stolleis (1999), p. 172.

[46]  See, e.g., Heck (1889); Heck (1890); Heck (1932b), p. 128.

and an *idealist conceptualism*. The emphasis on the idea of systematicity
in law is evident from the way in which the clash between the conceptual jurisprudes' 'dogma of the gaplessness of the legal order' on the one
hand,[47] and the critics' insistent focus on the problem of legislative gaps,
*'Gesetzeslücken'*, and judicial systematic gap-filling, *'Lückenergänzung aus
dem System'*, on the other became a central site of controversy.[48] The role of
subsumption, or syllogistic reasoning, is clear from the contrast between
the conceptual jurisprudes' faith in the power of deductive logic,[49] and
the *Interessenjurisprudenz* scholars' relentless framing of their critique in
terms of a logical error of reasoning. Heck, to be sure, blames the con-
ceptualists for doing something he thought was *wrong* (they ignored 'the
requirements of practical life').[50] But his critique assumes special vigour
when he accuses his opponents of trying something he presents as *logically
impossible*.[51] This somewhat haughty focus on faulty logic fits well with
the nature of the critique as directed primarily at fellow legal academics, rather than judges and practitioners. It also coheres with the importance of system-thinking just alluded to. Finally, the label of an idealist
conceptualism is meant to evoke the extent to which the positions of the
*Begriffsjurisprudenz* were philosophically grounded in broader German
intellectual currents.[52] Conceptual jurisprudence had its foundations in
the Historical School in German legal thought, of which the main figures
were von Savigny and Puchta himself. Von Savigny's work advocated a
philosophical and logical treatment of law as a 'system', drawing on Kant's
formalist epistemology.[53] Puchta elaborated his 'genealogy of concepts',
to a large extent the foundation of conceptual jurisprudence in Germany,
under the influence of Hegel's theory of history.[54]

---

[47] See, e.g., Stampe (1905); Reimann (1990), p. 882.
[48] See, e.g., Heck (1933), p. 37; Heck (1932b), p. 125. See further Coing (1962), p. 28; Edelmann
(1967), pp. 35ff; Canaris (1969); Wieacker (1995), pp. 344ff.
[49] See, e.g., von Gerber (1869), p. viii (referring to the primordial value of *'sichere juristische
Deduktion'*, secure juristic deduction); von Jhering (1884), pp. 339 (attack on Puchta's
*'Kultus des Logischen'*, cult of logic).
[50] Heck (1932b), p. 103.
[51] See, e.g., Heck (1933), pp. 39–40 ('The formula which condenses a certain number of
existing legal rules cannot be made to yield new rules [...] The method of operating with
formulas is a magic charm which helps only those who believe in it'.); Wieacker (1995),
p. 345 (referring to Heck's contempt for 'subsumption machines').
[52] See Pound (1959), p. I-63 (contrasting German 'metaphysical' and English 'analytical'
jurisprudential foundations).
[53] See Wieacker (1995), pp. 293ff, 343ff.
[54] *Ibid.*, pp. 316ff; Rümelin (1930), p. 9; Haferkamp (2004), p. 88.

## 4.  *Conceptual jurisprudence in the US: responding to Langdell and Lochner*

In formulating his critique of the jurisprudence of conceptions – or 'mechanical jurisprudence', as he came to call it – Roscoe Pound drew upon the work of European writers, notably Gény and Raymond Saleilles in France and von Jhering and a host of later authors in Germany.[55] An important question, raised but not answered in the literature, is the extent to which Pound and other American critics 'distorted' the French and German critiques, and, more broadly, whether the attack on conceptualism had the same meaning in the American context as it had in Germany and France.[56] Answering that question requires a closer look at these critics' image of conceptual jurisprudence in American law.

In that regard, it is important to repeat an observation made earlier: legal formalism in late-nineteenth-century America, in its received understanding, consisted of an amalgam of two components. On the one hand, there was the Langdellian legal science in the university law schools. But in addition, Pound and others specifically attacked a form of constitutional law practice: what they saw as a laissez-faire constitutionalism in the courts.[57] And while this first element was, in very broad terms, similar to scholarly tendencies in German jurisprudence, it is in particular, though not exclusively, with regard to the laissez-faire component that significant differences as between Europe and the US begin to appear.

### (a)    Langdellian legal science and legal education

Langdellian legal science refers to a professional and educational project epitomized in the propagation of the case method at Harvard Law School. Dean Langdell's methodological proposals were based on the idea that the study of law could be rendered more 'scientific', and therefore appropriate to a law school embedded in a university, if it were approached through the identification, classification and arrangement of a limited number of overarching basic principles.[58] Thomas Grey's influential 1980s account summarizes the enterprise as follows:

> [T]he heart of classical theory was its aspiration that the legal system be made complete through universal formality, and universally formal

---

[55] Extensively: Pound (1959), pp. I-91ff; Pound (1908), p. 610.
[56] See Belleau (1997), p. 424.
[57] See Duxbury (1995), p. 11.
[58] *Ibid.*, p. 14; Kennedy (1980), pp. 8ff; Horwitz (1992), pp. 12ff.

through conceptual order. A few basic top-level categories and principles formed a conceptually ordered system above a large number of bottom-level rules. The rules themselves were, ideally, the holdings of established precedents, which upon analysis could be seen to be derivable from the principles. When a new case arose to which no existing rule applied, it could be categorized and the correct rule for it could be inferred by use of the general concepts and principles [...].[59]

Even this short description makes clear the great extent to which Pandectist scholarship and Langdellian legal science overlapped in the eyes of their critics, notwithstanding the vast differences in legal source materials in the two legal systems concerned.[60] Appraising Langdell's work and its influence is difficult. On the one hand, Langdell could be seen as one individual law professor, promoting a pet vision of legal education, in somewhat polemical language. At the same time, though, Langdell clearly was not simply just another law professor. He was, from 1870 to 1895, Dean of the nation's premier law school; the country's foremost expert on the most commercially significant area of law (contract); and a writer who, through his own work and that of a number of prominent acolytes, 'had an enormous influence upon the whole atmosphere and temper of American education, not merely legal education'.[61]

What is clear is that Langdell's educational project has come to be read as only the most prominent manifestation of a more general tendency – of a scholarly 'reorganization of legal architecture' intended to 'erect an abstract set of legal categories that would subordinate particular legal relationships to a general system of classification'.[62] What is also clear is that Langdell's polemical language – he famously described 'the purposes of substantial justice' as 'irrelevant' – provided an irresistible target for critique and ridicule by writers like Holmes, Pound, Frankfurter and Llewellyn, who otherwise often found much to admire in the substance of his work.[63] But while Holmes would still write in

---

[59]  Grey (1983), p. 11.
[60]  See, e.g., Frankfurter (1930), p. 664 ('Langdell [...] still conceived of law as a self-contained system, the logical unfolding of relatively few principles whose history and meaning and direction were all imminent [*sic*] in the cases.')
[61]  *Ibid*. On this ambivalence, see also Llewellyn (1942), p. 229 ('The history of the Langdell conception [in contract law] is one of a delighted welcome by law-teachers, which continues still, while piece after piece of the integrated whole continues to be junked.')
[62]  Horwitz (1992), pp. 12, 14ff; Hull (1997), p. 33.
[63]  Oliver Wendell Holmes famously described Langdell as 'the world's greatest living theologian' in his review of his case book on contract; a qualification later repeated almost verbatim by Felix Frankfurter. See Frankfurter (1930), p. 665.

1879 that regardless of such scholarly tendencies to abstraction, the law was generally administered 'by able and experienced men, who know too much *to sacrifice good sense to the syllogism*',[64] it is Roscoe Pound's much less charitable view, voiced thirty years later, that has since dominated received wisdom.

### (b)   Pound's 'mechanical jurisprudence'

Formalism in American law at the turn of the nineteenth century has come to be seen as encompassing more than just this scientification of legal education and scholarship, and it is here, in part, that major differences with German developments originate. In a highly creative and extremely influential intellectual move, Roscoe Pound, building on the views of Supreme Court Justice Oliver Wendell Holmes, aligned the legal doctrinal critique of the formalism of classical orthodoxy along the lines of Langdell's legal science, with a substantive, political or ideological critique of the content of court decisions in constitutional law.[65] This alignment was not obvious, and it did not come about at once. But it resulted in a new understanding of the relation between legal doctrine and political ideology that has influenced American law ever since.

Pound's critique of the uses of classical orthodoxy in the courts started out in terms broadly similar to those of his German and French counterparts. In a 1905 *Columbia Law Review* article, for example, he complained that formerly flexible equitable principles were 'becoming hard and fast and legal' and that the common law, as a result, was in danger of losing its 'quality of elasticity'.[66] Pound's examples may have been predominantly court decisions rather than scholarly writings,[67] but they did concern the same private law problems that preoccupied his European colleagues. Later that same year, however, Pound's critique took on a new focus. 'It cannot be denied that there is a growing popular dissatisfaction with our legal system', he wrote, adding: '[t]here is a feeling that it prevents everything and does nothing'.[68] A fundamental reason for this growing public unease, in Pound's view, was the fact that the legal system exhibited 'too great a respect for the individual, and for the intrenched [*sic*] position in which our legal and political history has put him, and too little respect

---

[64] Holmes (1879), p. 671 (emphasis added).
[65] Cf. Grey (2003), p. 477.     [66] Pound (1905a), pp. 24, 33.
[67] This difference will be important in what follows. See also Kennedy & Belleau (2000), p. 309.
[68] Pound (1905b), p. 344.

for the needs of society, when they come in conflict with the individual, to be in touch with the present age'.[69] This general complaint was also raised in the work of European writers, who called it '*la question sociale*' and who also linked it to questions of legal method. This happened notably in France, where the need for a new approach was felt earlier than in Germany due to the advancing age of the *code Napoléon*.[70] But while in Europe writers took their main examples from private law doctrine such as employment contracts and liability for industrial accidents, the institutional set-up in the US furnished striking illustrations also in constitutional law. Pound relegated typical private law examples to his footnotes, and took the most contentious contemporary issue in constitutional law as his prime example. As he wrote in the article just cited: 'A glance at one of the [case law] digests will show us where the courts find themselves to-day. Take the one subheading under constitutional law, "interference with the right of free contract," and notice the decisions.'[71] Pound went on to cite a series of cases striking down on constitutional grounds various pieces of legislation intended to protect employees. He did not yet include the case decided in the US Supreme Court on 17 April that year that would shortly afterwards become the main focus for the critique of classical orthodoxy: *Lochner* v. *New York*.

In *Lochner*, the Supreme Court invoked the constitutional right of freedom of contract to invalidate legislation enacted by the State of New York on the maximum working hours for bakers.[72] The line of decisions culminating in *Lochner*, which included such famous earlier decisions as *Allgeyer* v. *Louisiana* (1897), was criticized at the time by other scholars for its obstruction of progressive legislation. It was Roscoe Pound, however, building on Justice Holmes, who added a decisive new element: these decisions were not simply wrong, they were wrong *because* they were overly conceptualistic. The steps by which Pound came to frame his critique of these constitutional law decisions in the terms of a critique of conceptual jurisprudence can be traced through his writings, where a critique of an individualistic bias in the common law gradually becomes aligned with an attack of excess abstraction and reliance on deductive reasoning. The two themes are joined only in very loose terms at first, in the 1905 article just

---

[69]  *Ibid.*
[70]  See, e.g., Wieacker (1995), p. 456; Stolleis (2001), pp. 359ff; Jamin (2006).
[71]  Pound (1905b), p. 344.
[72]  198 US 45, 75 (1905).

cited, when Pound wrote: 'the common law knows individuals only [...] But today the isolated individual is no longer taken for the center of the universe. We see now that he is an abstraction ...'[73] By 1908, both the references to the individual and abstraction are discussed in somewhat more depth, in his famous article on 'Mechanical Jurisprudence', of which the title by itself clearly shows a desire to emphasize conceptualist flaws in juristic reasoning:

> The manner in which [the relevant constitutional clause] is applied affords a striking instance of the workings to-day of a jurisprudence of conceptions. *Starting with the conception* that it was intended to incorporate [the social Darwinist text] Spencer's Social Statics in the fundamental law of the United States, *rules have been deduced that obstruct the way of social progress.* The conception of liberty of contract, in particular, has given rise to rules and decisions which, tested by their practical operation, defeat liberty.[74]

Pound's reference to Herbert Spencer's book *Social Statics* is easy to understand: Justice Holmes had used precisely this reference in his landmark dissenting opinion in the then very recent *Lochner* case, which Pound now cites. But Pound's effort to merge Holmes' critique of social-Darwinism and his own anti-conceptualist argument then requires some really rather strained use of legal language. The quoted passage is replete with references to 'conception', 'deduction' and disregard for 'practical operation', so that, on the surface, Pound's argument reads like a standard denunciation of *Begriffsjurisprudenz* as found in German literature. But on closer inspection the real role of each of these terms and, especially, of the connections between them, is peculiarly rhetorical. Pound's continued use of the term 'conceptions', rather than 'concepts' as a translation for '*Begriff*', may have had a special significance here. Spencer's social-Darwinist logic, and the laissez-faire attitude more broadly, can meaningfully be qualified as rigidly held conceptions, from which particular positions might be, in some meaningful sense, 'deduced'. But this usage is a long way from 'concepts' and deduction in the sense used by German authors referring to a 'heaven of juristic concepts' or to '*Begriffsjurisprudenz*'. It is different, too, from Langdell's emphasis on reasoning from a few top-level private law categories.

---

[73] Pound (1905b), p. 346.
[74] Pound (1908), pp. 615–16 (footnotes omitted, emphases added).

It is perhaps not surprising therefore, that Pound appears to backtrack somewhat shortly afterwards in his efforts of trying to connect his critiques of excess individualism and abstraction, or conceptualism. In his major article on 'Liberty of Contract' (1909), the two strands are simply presented alongside each other, without any real effort to work through any connections:

> In my opinion, the causes to which we must attribute the course of American constitutional decisions upon liberty of contract are [...]:
>
> (1) The currency in juristic thought of *an individualistic conception of justice*, which ... exaggerates private right at the expense of public right [...];
>
> (2) what I have ventured to call on another occasion a condition of *mechanical jurisprudence*, a condition of juristic thought and judicial action in which deduction from conceptions has produced a cloud of rules that obscures the principles from which they are drawn, in which conceptions are developed logically at the expense of practical results and in which the artificiality characteristic of legal reasoning is exaggerated;
>
> (3) the survival of purely juristic notions of the state and economics and politics as against the social conceptions of the present [...][75]

Conceptualism is here framed, once again, in terms familiar to Pound's European contemporaries, and presented *alongside* individualism as one of the main causes of dissatisfaction with constitutional decisions. By then, however, the genie of conceptualism *as* conservative politics, and therefore of judicial method as political ideology more generally, was already out of the bottle.[76]

## 5.   *Two orthodoxies and their critiques*

For all their visible similarities and traces of intellectual indebtedness, the European and American received understandings of classical legal orthodoxy diverged on at least two significant points. These can be summarized as follows. First, there were real differences in the nature of the dominant manifestations of classical orthodoxy, with categorization being the principal conceptual operation in the US, while subsumption

---

[75] Pound (1909), p. 457 (emphasis added). Crucially, Pound does not comment on the relationship between, or the relative importance among, these several factors.

[76] See, e.g., Frankfurter (1930), p. 665 (linking Langdell to Darwin); Llewellyn (1942), p. 249 (describing similar 'esthetics' in Langdell and Spencer).

occupied a central position in Europe. And second, there is the legacy of Roscoe Pound's imaginative explicit linking of the methods of classical orthodoxy to conservative politics, when compared to the absence of this connection in German legal thought.

These differences are discussed below. They are important primarily because they continue to affect the way we think about the nature and role of legal formality. In short, while the supposedly neutral ground rules of classical orthodoxy have also been found to imply substantive preferences, for individualism, stability and legal certainty, in Europe,[77] the association between legal method and politics, and therefore indirectly between legal formality and politics, has been both much stronger and more durable in the US.

(a)    The uses and manifestations of orthodoxy (I):
subsumption and categorization

Classical orthodoxy, in the mind of its critics, adhered to an ideal of adjudication as a neutral, objective process carried out by judges bound to the law. Conceptual reasoning was essential to upholding this image. As Philipp Heck wrote, this type of reasoning allowed the judge to feel, falsely, 'relieved of all responsibility. Like Pilate he may wash his hands and calmly declare: "It is not my fault, it is the fault of the concepts"'.[78] But while this general depiction of conceptual reasoning is pervasive both in Europe and the US, there were important differences in operation and impact as between the two versions.

One of these differences relates to the distinction between subsumption and categorization as manifestations of conceptual jurisprudence. Subsumption, or reasoning by deduction from abstract concepts, was the primary target of German and French critics of conceptual jurisprudence, who disparaged the classical jurists' efforts to uphold the image of gapless pyramidal systems of law. In the US, by contrast, in the absence of any major codification of private law, questions of system, deduction and gaplessness were much less pressing. Instead, the main emphasis was on a second main tool in classical orthodoxy's arsenal. That tool was 'categorization' – the technique of drawing firm, principled boundaries around spheres of competence.[79]

---

[77]  See, e.g., Kennedy (1980); Kennedy (2003), pp. 1033ff.
[78]  Heck (1933), p. 40.
[79]  See, e.g., Cushman (2000), p. 1099.

This difference is, of course, one only of emphasis and of relative prominence. Subsumption and categorization both turn on the idea of rigorous definition and invoke a reasoning process that classifies cases as lying either within or outside the scope of a particular concept, rule or category. Categorization and bright-line demarcation clearly also played a significant role in European legal thought, alongside deduction or syllogistic reasoning. As Marie-Claire Belleau has written, '[b]inary, on/off structures' were favoured in French jurisprudence 'because such structures helped maintain the illusion of the complete logical determination of the system'.[80] Meanwhile, subsumption *did* play an important role in the American context, where nineteenth-century legal thinking had gradually become more systematic and abstract, even in the absence of codification.[81] In particular, Pound's critique of the Supreme Court's constitutional right jurisprudence, discussed earlier and revisited in the next section, was principally a critique of the abuse of deduction, very much along French and German lines.

But these important caveats notwithstanding, it does seem fair to identify syllogistic reasoning and the idea of the system as typical European manifestations of conceptual jurisprudence, and categorical reasoning and the bright-line rule as their US counterparts.[82] This difference in emphasis is important for at least two reasons. One of these relates to the specific way in which categorization has been used in US constitutional adjudication. As discussed in the next paragraph, on this point the argument will simply be that the greater prominence of categorization in US law generally also made this specific use more likely. The other reason, however, relates directly to the difference between syllogistic reasoning and categorical reasoning. On this second issue, the argument runs as follows.

While subsumption and categorization have much in common, they can also implicate and sustain subtly different understandings of legal formality.[83] Categorization can rely upon, and be the manifestation of, what may be called a 'formality of choice'. A judge, or a lawyer more generally, may choose to take a categorical approach to a particular legal problem or an area of the law, for reasons familiarly linked to legal formality, such as legal certainty, predictability or the demand for principle. This idea of

---

[80]  Belleau (1997), p. 409.
[81]  Horwitz (1992), pp. 12ff. See also Grey (1983), pp. 5, 36; Hull (1997), p. 33.
[82]  For the US see, e.g., Horwitz (1992), p. 17 (the idea of 'clear, distinct, bright-line classifications of legal phenomena', better than anything else, 'captures the essential differences between the typical legal minds of nineteenth- and twentieth-century America').
[83]  See also Chapter 5, Section D.

formality of choice is significant in two ways. First, if resort to legal formality is itself understood in consequentialist terms, attention is bound to turn to these underlying substantive reasons.[84] As discussed in more detail in Chapter 5, this idea of formalism as strategy is highly typical for American legal thought, where it has even occasioned its own distinctive branch of legal theory: 'the jurisprudence of form'.[85]

Categorization as the manifestation of a formality of choice has a second implication. This is the idea that categorical approaches can easily co-exist with more gradualist, non-categorical, informal approaches to neighbouring problems or doctrinal areas. On this view, a particular area could be 'rulefied' over time. Categorization and gradualism may even be combined within one overarching, multi-part 'test'.[86] By contrast, syllogistic reasoning and system building rely upon, and are the expressions of, an understanding of legal formality that is much more comprehensive and less open to strategic deployment. Reasoning by deduction and system building are not as easily seen as conceptual tools available for use and for combination with other approaches. To sustain jurists' commitment to system building, the system they are working towards has to be, at a minimum, reasonably comprehensive and complete, at least in aspiration. If 'less systematic' parts of the law were to persist, that would likely be seen as a case of neglect or conceptual failure – 'blemishes' in Justice Story's evocative depiction[87] – rather than as products of design. Similarly, syllogistic reasoning either *is* or *is not* able to sustain faith in the outcomes of legal decision making. This is not to say that, as an empirical matter, legal systems will either be fully systematized and exclusively reliant on syllogistic reasoning, or accord no place at all to system and subsumption. That would be an entirely unrealistic claim. The argument is rather that the kind of faith, sensibility or commitment, involved in system building and in deductive reasoning from concepts, is less easily conceived of as a commitment that can be turned on or off at will. Categorization as a legal technique, by contrast, seems much more easily able to sustain such

---

[84] See, e.g., Cushman (2000), p. 1099 ('it is necessary to recognize that formalism was itself rooted in consequentialist concerns [...] The division of the world into local and national spheres [...] was itself a conscious strategy for circumscribing the boundaries of national and local competence in a principled fashion').

[85] *Ibid.*, ('Formalism as consequentialism'). See also, e.g., Kennedy (1976); Sunstein (1999).

[86] The difficult question of the extent to which nineteenth-century lawyers *themselves* experienced this possibility of choice is not relevant for this argument. What matters is the legacy this particular operationalization of legal formality has enabled or made more likely.

[87] In his inaugural address, cited in Frankfurter (1930), p. 664.

a partial commitment, even if it is used selectively, openly instrumentally, and in conjunction with other approaches. Put simply, it is much easier to believe in categorization only some of the time than in reasoning by deduction only some of the time.[88] Chapter 5 elaborates upon this difference and claims that such a choice-based, instrumentalist understanding of legal formality is characteristic for American legal thought more broadly. At the same time, a more comprehensive, all-or-nothing conception of legal formality is emblematic for legal thought in Europe.

### (b)    The uses and manifestations of orthodoxy (II): public and private power

Categorization may have been more prominent in US jurisprudence than in Europe, but categorical, binary solutions of course played a significant role on both sides of the Atlantic. Categorical, approaches found favour because of their proximity to prevailing worldviews and views on the function of law. Mathias Reimann has this succinct summary of prevailing views of law and society in Germany:

> Law served only to limit *private spheres of freedom* in such a way that these spheres could coexist in a society. Its concern was not to find the true idea of justice, or to be fair to the parties under the particular circumstances of the case. It drew only the 'invisible line' at which one individual's freedom had to end because another one's began.[89]

This worldview allowed classical jurists to view adjudication as 'an objective task of drawing lines or categorizing actions as though they were objects to be located in the spatial map of spheres of power'.[90] This relationship between categories and boundaries of power assumed a dramatically different meaning as between Europe and the US. In the former, the boundaries of power envisaged were boundaries to the power of private individuals, asserted against their neighbours through regimes of contact, property or tort law. German examples of demarcation issues typically concern questions such as the right of the owner of a business to enjoin a private individual interfering with his trade or business.[91] In France, Gény

---

[88]  There is a revealing stylistic difference as well. As depictions of analytical processes, 'categorization' foregrounds agency ('the categorizer') in a way that 'syllogistic reasoning' ('the syllogizer'?) and 'subsumption' (the 'subsumer'?) do not.

[89]  Reimann (1983), p. 857 (emphasis added). Reimann invokes von Savigny's notion of 'unsichtbare Gränze', 'invisible boundaries'.

[90]  Kennedy (1980), p. 12.

[91]  See, e.g., Müller-Erzbach (1929), pp. 163ff (example of rights of third parties under a contract); Rümelin (1930), pp. 12ff; Heck (1933), pp. 42ff.

called for a more flexible approach to the determination of the 'meeting of wills' requirement as a boundary to the freedom of contract,[92] so that in some cases one-sided promises might be held binding – an innovation conceptually unthinkable in classical legal orthodoxy, but of practical value for business.[93] In the US, however, it was not only the power of individuals that had to be demarcated, but crucially also *public power* – the power of government institutions. Here, the salient question was: '[t]o what extent may occupations or businesses [...] be made *subject of [governmental] regulation* under our American constitutions?'[94] The answers to this type of question may have been familiarly categorical in nature. Businesses that were 'purely and exclusively private' could not be regulated, whereas businesses that were 'affected with a public interest' could, for example.[95] But the implications of this type of public/private boundary-drawing were much more politically sensitive than the French or German fine-tuning of the law of obligations, significant as those innovations were. The same is true of the kinds of public/public demarcations that were pervasive in American constitutional adjudication, but which judiciaries in other countries never really had to deal with – at least certainly not on anywhere near the same scale.[96]

Studies of classical orthodoxy tend to conflate these two very different questions of the demarcation of private and of public power. This, for example, is Duncan Kennedy's influential early depiction of such classical legal thought:

> The premise of Classicism was that the legal system consisted of a set of institutions, each of which had the traits of a legal actor. Each institution had been delegated by the sovereign people a power to carry out its will, which was absolute within but void outside its sphere. The justification of the judicial role was the existence of a peculiar legal technique

---

[92] Gény (1899), pp. 23, 26.
[93] *Ibid.*, p. 32.     [94] Cheadle (1920), p. 558.
[95] *Munn* v. *Illinois* (1876) 94 US 113, 124–25. ('This brings us to inquire as to the principles upon which this power of regulation rests, in order that we may determine what is within and what without its operative effect.') The *Munn*-criterion was also operative in *Lochner* v. *New York.*
[96] This was especially so for both Federal/State relations in relation to the Commerce Clause and the fact/law distinction in the judicial review of administrative action. See, e.g., Albertsworth (1921), p. 128 ('what the Court is really doing, consciously or unconsciously, and what it should do, is balancing the various individual and social interests involved. For the problem is far too deep to be solved by stating that a particular case involves a question of fact or one of law'). See also Cushman (2000).

rendering the task of policing the boundaries of spheres an objective, quasi-scientific one.[97]

The 'institutions' Kennedy refers to here are individuals and corporations as well as governmental actors. Each of these institutions was thought to possess a power that was 'absolute within but void outside' a certain sphere of action. But while this view is very useful in stressing similarities between European and US classical orthodoxies, it risks obscuring the crucial difference between the demarcation of private power among individuals and that of the limits to public power. Or, put differently: between demarcating the liberty of individuals vis-à-vis other individuals, and in relation to their government, or the power of government branches amongst themselves. Even questions familiar to European critics of classical orthodoxy in private law, such as the inequality of bargaining power between employees and employers, quickly assumed an explicitly public dimension in the US, simply because they arose in the context of judicial review of legislation.[98] This added dimension of 'public power' means that categorization, as a cornerstone of classical orthodoxy, had a very different, much more political, meaning in the US than it had in Europe, and this from the outset.

This original significance is of continued relevance for modern invocations of categorical or rule-based approaches to constitutional law. This historical background, in which demarcation of public power and the protection of individual liberty from government have always been important functions of categorization, shines a new light on pervasive American fears of 'balancing away' fundamental rights protection, on the repeated efforts to create 'bright-line rules' as alternatives to balancing in many different areas of constitutional law,[99] and on explicit calls to 'reclaim the methodology of late nineteenth-century legal thought' as a way to get out of 'the conundrums of balancing'.[100]

---

[97]  Kennedy (1980), p. 7. See also Gordon (1997), pp. 142ff.
[98]  See, e.g., *Adair* v. *United States*, 208 US 161, 175 (1908) (per Justice Harlan) ('In all [...] particulars, the employer and the employee have equality of right, and any legislation that disturbs that equality is an arbitrary interference with the liberty of contract, which no government can legally justify in a free land.') Harlan's approach prompted Roscoe Pound to remark: 'Jurisprudence is the last in the march of the sciences away from the method of deduction from predetermined conceptions.' Pound (1909), p. 464.
[99]  See further Chapters 4 and 5.
[100]  Pildes (1994), p. 712.

### (c)    Roscoe Pound and the linking of method and politics

In German and in French legal thought, the critique of classical orthodoxy was predominantly a private law project. In the US, this critique
quickly assumed constitutional significance through the guarantee of
the 'freedom of contract' in the Bill of Rights, and its interpretation by
the US Supreme Court. In addition, in German and French law, the critique of classical orthodoxy was primarily an academic project, while
in the US the main target of criticism was the judiciary, in particular
for its constitutional decisions of the kind just mentioned. The general
background to these differences is easy to see. A highly visible political role was thrust upon law and adjudication in the US much earlier
than anywhere else. Law and legal method in the US had to face questions concerning constitutional judicial review, of rights clauses and of
federation-state relationships, that were virtually unknown in Europe at
the time. As Thomas Grey has written: 'The most distinctive feature of
American law has been its deep involvement with American government
and politics, and as a result, legal theory in America has always had inescapable political implications'.[101]

The idea that such implications are indeed 'inescapable' has a long tradition in American academic legal writing. In his article on 'The Scope and
Purpose of Sociological Jurisprudence', Roscoe Pound observed that 'the
jurists of whom Jhering made fun [in Europe] [...] have their counterpart in American judges'.[102] In retrospect, a crucial but commonly over-
looked theme in this remark is not the similarity between Europe and
the US that Pound focused on, but the difference between 'jurists' (ivory
tower scholars) on the Continent and 'judges' (officials with real power),
in the US.[103] This difference matters, because it is through these judicial
decisions, notably those of *Lochner*, the bakers' working hours case, and
its progeny, that the perceived vices of classical orthodoxy have become
part of received constitutional law wisdom in American legal thought.

---

[101]  Grey (1996b), p. 510.
[102]  Pound (1911b), p. 146. See also Pound (1912a), p. 502 ('[I]t is true of the codes of
     Continental Europe, as of our Anglo-American common law, that their abstractions,
     proceeding upon a theoretical equality, do not fit at all points a society divided into
     classes by conditions of industry. Much of what has been written in Europe from this
     standpoint might have been written by American social workers.')
[103]  Although it should be said that one difference between law in Europe and the US does lie
     in the greater influence the legal academy has on legal development in countries such as
     France or Germany. To that extent these scholars too wield 'real power'. I am grateful to
     Jan Komárek for drawing my attention to this point.

The need to avoid '*Lochner*'s error', it has often been noted, is a 'central obsession' in American legal thought.[104] It was Roscoe Pound, building on Justice Holmes' dissent, who first identified this 'error' as stemming directly from the conceptualism and formalism of classical orthodoxy.[105] Construing this connection between the *Lochner*-Court's political conservatism and conceptualist jurisprudence was a creative act; the conceptualist or formalist nature of this decision and many other similar ones is not obvious. The *Lochner* decision itself can serve as an example. There are statements in Justice Peckham's majority opinion that sound very different from what might be expected on the basis of Pound's critique. In fact, much of the reasoning reads virtually like a form of proportionality analysis, familiar nowadays in Europe and elsewhere, with its references to appropriateness and necessity.[106] Justice Harlan's reminder, in dissent, that 'liberty' under the Constitution does not import 'an absolute right', is matched by Justice Peckham's aside that 'of course [...] there is a limit to the valid exercise of the police power by the State'.[107] Meanwhile, Justice Holmes' major argument in dissent was that the majority had decided the case 'upon an economic theory which a large part of the country does not entertain'.[108] This is where he added the reference to 'Mr. Herbert Spencer's Social Statics' that Pound later also invoked. It is true that a few lines later in his opinion Justice Holmes offers his famous anti-formalist aphorism that '[g]eneral propositions do not decide concrete cases'; again setting up the point nicely for Pound's subsequent critique. But, intriguingly, this maxim appears *not* as part of Holmes' attack on the majority's reasoning, but by way of a caveat to accompany his own alternative approach to this area of the law. 'General propositions do not decide concrete cases', Holmes writes; adding: 'But I think that the proposition just stated, if it is accepted, will carry us far toward the end.'[109]

It is perhaps not surprising that relative outsiders to American law were among the first to argue that this supposed connection between method and politics was less than convincing. For this claim there are striking

---

[104] Rowe (1999), p. 223. See also Sunstein (1987), p. 873; Grey (1996b), pp. 495ff; Bernstein (2003).

[105] See Chapter 2, Section B.4 above.

[106] See, e.g., 198 US 45, 56 ('In every case [...] the question necessarily arises: is this a fair, reasonable and appropriate exercise of the police power of the State, or is it an unreasonable, unnecessary and arbitrary interference with the right of the individual.'); and at 57 ('The act must have a more direct relation, as a means to an end, and the end itself must be appropriate and legitimate [...]')

[107] *Ibid.*, at 56, 67.    [108] *Ibid.*, at 75.    [109] *Ibid.*, at 76.

implicit and explicit illustrations. One is Edouard Lambert's blockbuster 1921 book *Le Gouvernement des Juges et la Lutte contre la Législation Sociale aux États-Unis*. Lambert, a law professor at Lyon, analysed and criticized exactly the same conservative anti-regulatory case law that Pound had been concerned with. He wrote his book largely as warning to a French audience newly enamoured of the idea of constitutional review.[110] But Lambert's critique does not in any way single out 'formalism' or 'conceptualism' as culprits. Rather, the 'instruments of judicial supremacy', as Lambert labels them, are flexible methods of interpretation, the 'humble' stature of legislation in common law America, and the review of 'rationality', 'opportuneness', 'reasonableness' and 'expediency' of legislation under the Due Process clause.[111] Excessive judicial flexibility and insufficient respect for legislation, then, appear as the foundations of Lambert's critique, rather than any supposed deduction from timeless principles.[112] And it was another foreign visitor, H.L.A. Hart, who offered an early explicit critique of the connection, writing that while *Lochner* might have been 'a wrongheaded piece of conservatism', there simply was 'nothing mechanical about it'.[113]

Regardless of the merits of Pound's assimilation of *Lochner* and the perceived vices of classical orthodoxy, the connection quickly assumed canonical status. It allowed Progressive jurists and other critics to point out a single 'Demon of Formalism' at which to aim all their arrows.[114] The *Lochner* line of decisions is thought to have culminated in the crisis over New Deal legislation and Roosevelt's infamous court-packing plan. Since that time, much of American constitutional scholarship can be structured around the basic question of why *Lochner* was wrong and certain later controversial decisions – *Brown* v. *Board of Education*, *Roe* v. *Wade* – were

---

[110]  On Lambert's influence see further Stone Sweet (2003).

[111]  Lambert (1921), pp. 7, 18ff, 23, 51ff. The term '*formalisme*' does not seem to figure in Lambert's work. There is one mention of '*conceptualisme*' (p. 56) as part of an extended quote from Thomas Reed Powell denouncing the judicial practice of 'hiding behind' concepts. But this quote, curiously, merely serves to set up a typical civil law analysis of the common law judicial practice of leaving the definition of key concepts, like 'due process of law', open for future decisions. Lambert also mentions the Harvard case method, but only as one of the explanations for the weak status of legislation as a source of law (pp. 24ff).

[112]  Lambert does mention the 'individualistic conceptions inherited from English law and fortified on American soil during colonial times' (*ibid.*, p. 54), but, crucially, this line of analysis is not integrated with the critique of 'conceptualism' as in Pound's work.

[113]  Hart (1957), p. 611.

[114]  Cardozo (1921), pp. 66–67.

right.[115] In this way, the *Lochner* episode has perpetuated the relevance of classical orthodoxy to understandings of modern American constitutional law in general.[116] But if '[t]he basic plot line of American legal modernity has been drawn from the responses to Langdell and *Lochner*',[117] Hart and Lambert's work are useful reminders of the precarious and contingent nature of the connection between these two original sins. And when 'Langdell' and '*Lochner*' begin to drift apart, so too do formalism and conservatism, legal method and politics.

## C.   The jurisprudence of interests: Gény, Heck, Pound

### 1.  *Introduction*

This section traces the intellectual history of the rise of balancing of interests in German and American jurisprudence during the first decades of the twentieth century. While the general intellectual and legal trends of the period have often been studied before, a comparative analysis of the specific role of balancing-based reasoning within this broader context appears to be lacking. In addition, although this early history of balancing is a prominent theme in the US, where the idea of a twentieth-century 'triumph of the balancing test',[118] is part of mainstream contemporary constitutional legal thought, this standard American history accords little or no attention to its European precursors and analogues.

The focus in this section is on the German *Interessenjurisprudenz* and Roscoe Pound's Sociological Jurisprudence. As between these two movements, there is very little direct acknowledgment of influence. The German scholars did not cite Holmes or Pound, and Pound's work contains only very few references to Heck and other *Interessenjurisprudenz* scholars. They were, as one reviewer of the seminal 1948 translation of their work put it, among those foreign authors 'almost completely ignored in English and American jurisprudence'.[119] By contrast, Pound seems to have relied heavily on the work of François Gény.[120] Because of this influence, and

---

[115]  See, e.g., Ely (1980), p. 65.

[116]  See, e.g., Bernstein (2003), pp. 18, 60ff (linkage is 'historically inaccurate' but still part of a 'longstanding tradition going back to Progressive-era critics').

[117]  Grey (1996b), p. 495. See also the critical view assessment in Bernstein (2003), p. 18.

[118]  Horwitz (1992), p. 131.

[119]  Ehrenzweig (1948), p. 502.

[120]  Kennedy & Belleau (2000), p. 306 (noting the 'probable' influence of Gény on Roscoe Pound). But see Fikentscher (1975), p. 234 (German *Zweck-* and *Interessenjurisprudenz* more influential in the US).

because Gény was in fact one of the very first, perhaps even *the* first, major European jurist to invoke language and ideas associated with balancing, this section begins with a short description of his work.[121]

## 2.   *Balancing and the critique of classical orthodoxy in France:* libre recherche scientifique *and juridical modesty*

European legal thinkers were preoccupied at the turn of the nineteenth century with the question of 'gap-filling' – making sure written law could maintain its coherent and complete character in the face of new problems. Because French law was based on an ageing civil code, the problem of gap-filling was felt there earlier and more acutely than elsewhere.[122] One of the earliest, and certainly one of the most prominent, writers to engage with this problem was François Gény in his book *Méthode d'Interprétation* (1899).[123] Gény acknowledged that, due to the inherently incomplete nature of the written law contained in the *code civil*, there would always come a point 'where the Court can no longer rest secure on a formal rule but must trust to his [*sic*] own skill in finding the proper decision'.[124] The method to be applied by the judge, according to Gény's famous label, would have to be 'free decision on the basis of scientific investigation' ('*libre recherche scientifique*').[125] Announcing themes that would be echoed by Roscoe Pound a decade later, Gény asked lawyers to 'study social phenomena', called for judicial decisions according to the 'actual facts of social life' and warned against letting the 'needs of actual life' be sacrificed 'to mere concepts'.[126]

In addition to these well-known general themes of the critique of conceptualism and formalism, Gény specifically invokes balancing language where he sets out his method of free scientific research. In a section on 'The Principle of Equilibrium of Interests',[127] Gény writes:

---

[121]  The question of whether *Interessenjurisprudenz* scholars like Heck also leaned on Gény appears to be an open one. There seem to be no direct references, either in the main contemporary German works, nor in later assessments of the School. Some of Heck's early writing in fact predates Gény's work by more than a decade.

[122]  See, e.g., Wieacker (1995), p. 456.

[123]  On Gény's stature see Arnaud (1975), pp. 121–22.

[124]  Gény (1899), p. 2.    [125]  *Ibid.*, p. 5 (no. 155 in the original).

[126]  *Ibid.*, pp. 9, 11, 15. See also p. 26.

[127]  *Ibid.*, pp. 35.

the science of administrating the law could not do better than frankly to adopt, where the formal sources of law are silent, this method: to seek the solution of all legal questions, which necessarily grow out of the conflict of various interests, by means of an accurate estimating of the relative importance and a judicious comparison of all the interests involved, with a view to balancing them against each other in conformity with the interests of society.[128]

Given these general critical themes and this specific methodological proposal, what position does Gény's work occupy in the genealogy of balancing?

It is important to note, first of all, that Gény sought the examples for the application of his new method in private law. In a typical passage, he would for example ask 'how can the legal maxims applicable to such matters as the secrecy of confidential letters, the ownership of letters sent, or the right to use a family name [...] be satisfactorily and equitably applied except by balancing all the interests involved one with the other?'[129] Only at the very end of his discussion of 'free decision on a scientific basis' does Gény suggest that his method could be more broadly applicable to 'certain other problems that cannot be solved along traditional lines' and that 'bring into play even more directly certain moral and economic interests which our written laws do but very little to balance against each other'.[130] Gény mentions the regulation of industrial production and mining laws as examples of areas to which his method could profitably be applied. But by the time these regulatory, public law, subjects are introduced, Gény modestly notes that it is time for him to 'make an end of [his] observations'.[131] In this aspect, Gény's work closely resembles that of the German critics of conceptual jurisprudence.

Secondly, within this private law context, there clearly was a distinctive substantive edge to Gény's methodological critique and proposals.[132] Gény can be situated among a group of contemporaries later labelled '*les juristes inquiets*' or '*les vigiles*': a number of scholars concerned to adapt private law legal doctrines and techniques to rapidly evolving social conditions.[133] What Gény and these other writers were interested in was mainly the safeguarding of the '*édifice juridique*' ('the overall structural

---

[128]  *Ibid.*, p. 38 ('*une judicieuse comparaison des intérêts en presence, en visant à les équilibrer conformément aux fins sociales*', no. 173 in the original). See also pp. 24–25, 35–36, 42.

[129]  *Ibid.*, p. 37.    [130]  *Ibid.*, p. 46.    [131]  *Ibid.*

[132]  Cf. Kennedy & Belleau (2000).

[133]  Arnaud (1975), pp. 122–24; Belleau (1997), pp. 381ff.

integrity of the classical system') in the face of social pressures.[134] Their aim was not so much social 'reform', and certainly not socialist reform,[135] but rather to 'preserve the existing social equilibrium by adapting, and in some cases abandoning, legal classicism'.[136]

These last quotations lead to a third observation which is that, although these methodological innovations did have a substantive, or even political, edge to them, these implications were at the same time rather limited in scope and ambition. This is true in particular in comparison to Roscoe Pound's *Gény*-inspired proposals, as will be argued later.[137] One manifestation of this modesty is what has been called '*le compromis Gény*': the idea that the new flexibility allowed to judges under Gény's method would go hand in hand with a denial of the formal status of 'source of law' to judicial decisions and academic writing.[138] In this way, the structural impact of these methodological innovations on the underlying body of '*le droit*' could remain minimal. Another way in which the work of Gény – and of similar writers, notably Raymond Saleilles – was comparatively modest, was its reliance on non-ideological, 'naturalist', points of reference.[139] When Gény called for law to pay more attention to its social effects, he meant having regard for the actual 'requirements of practical life' and for the concrete 'conditions under which modern society lives'.[140] These factors are introduced in a neutral, dispassionate way, as '*données*' (literally, 'givens'), not as ideals to be worked towards.[141] And while Gény writes that 'one must obviously take into account both the social and the individual interests involved' in any particular case, he simultaneously makes it clear that, when it comes to public order, there can be no question of 'a set of interests really distinct from [...] what are properly private interests'.[142] As will be seen later, this was diametrically opposite to Pound's later attack on the excessive individualism of the common law. In fact, the principal kind of substantive reform that the *Méthode* advocates is simply more flexibility in business transactions.[143] It is no wonder, then, that Wolfgang Fikentscher, in his monumental comparative study of legal

---

[134]  See Arnaud (1975), p. 122, translated in Belleau (1997), pp. 383ff.
[135]  See Arnaud (1975), p. 122.
[136]  Belleau (1997), p. 383.
[137]  *Ibid.*, pp. 383–85; Fikentscher (1975), p. 212. See Chapter 2, Section C.4.
[138]  See Kennedy & Belleau (2000), p. 297.
[139]  *Ibid.*, pp. 300–1. See also Wieacker (1995), p. 456.
[140]  Gény (1899), pp. 26, 45.
[141]  See Arnaud (1975) p. 125; Jamin (2006), pp. 9–10.
[142]  Gény (1899), p. 25 (no. 171 in the original).
[143]  *Ibid.*, pp. 26–27 (no. 171, in the original).

method, calls Gény the 'least politically interested' and the 'purest jurist' out of the group Gény, Holmes and von Jhering.[144]

Finally, all three of the foregoing observations can be related to the topic of balancing. While the methodological and substantive elements in Gény's critique appear closely connected,[145] it is not so clear that this is the case specifically for the 'balancing' element in his proposals. On an even more general note, the status of balancing itself within Gény's overall project is not entirely clear. The *Méthode* is, in its critical aspect, concerned above all with the identification of the 'abuse' of deductive reasoning and of the fallacies of exclusive reliance on literal readings of the antiquated provisions of the *Code civil*.[146] Its constructive contributions consist principally of a plea for the toleration of a wider range of sources for judicial lawfinding and of greater flexibility in legal reasoning generally.[147] But neither the idea of 'balancing' nor of 'interests' seems particularly central to what Gény was criticizing and proposing. Despite its prime position in the general statement of his methodological ideals – Gény's 'simple and glorious formula for handling the Code', in Karl Llewellyn's words[148] – the language of balancing of interests hardly figures at all in the many concrete examples given throughout the *Méthode*.

Balancing of interests then, in Gény's work, appears as a relatively modest component of a relatively modest project of renewal in legal method. As will be seen later, this is in stark contrast with the way jurists in America, where Gény was widely admired, would frame their own proposals only a few years later.

### 3.   *The jurisprudence of interests in Germany: the Interessenjurisprudenz as 'a pure theory of method'*

In Germany, 'balancing of interests' was the principal theme of the School of *Interessenjurisprudenz*, of which Philipp Heck, Ernst Stampe, Max Rümelin, Heinrich Stoll and Rudolf Müller-Erzbach were the main figures. As many of these figures taught at the University of Tübingen, the inner core of the *Interessenjurisprudenz* movement is sometimes also called the 'Tübingen School'.[149] Here, I focus on Philipp Heck, whose

---

[144]   Fikentscher (1975), p. 212.
[145]   Cf. Jamin (2006), pp. 7ff.
[146]   *Ibid.*, p. 13.
[147]   Cf. Belleau (1997), p. 411.
[148]   Quoted in Herman (1979), p. 732.
[149]   See, e.g., Edelmann (1967), pp. 91ff; Wieacker (1995), p. 453.

influence on the science of legal method, Karl Larenz has said, 'is almost impossible to overestimate'.[150]

The School of *Interessenjurisprudenz* has to be situated as an extension of von Jhering's emphasis on teleology in legal method, and as a critique of both the orthodoxy of the *Begriffsjurisprudenz* and of the contemporaneous, more radical attacks on conceptual jurisprudence voiced within the so-called '*Freirechtsschule*'.[151] For the *Interessenjurisprudenz*, judicial freedom of decision was, and had to remain, strictly limited.[152] Heck's favourite image was of the judge as a '*denkender Gehorsam*', a judge who approaches the law thoughtfully and obediently.[153] It is significant that the first mention of the term *Interessenjurisprudenz* is in an article by Heck in 1905 of which the full title is '*Interessenjurisprudenz und Gesetzestreue*' ('The Jurisprudence of Interests and Obedience to the Law').

### (a)    'Gap-filling' through 'sensible weighing'

As for Gény, the point of departure for the German *Interessenjurisprudenz* was the problem of 'gap-filling' in law.[154] Against the 'dogma of the gaplessness of the legal order' and its associated method of 'inversion', the critics proposed 'sensible lawfinding by judges' through 'social weighing' and 'comparative valuation of colliding interests', Ernst Stampe wrote in 1905.[155] Heck even defined *Interessenjurisprudenz* as 'the methodical use of the analysis of interests in order to fill gaps in the law'.[156]

In order to distinguish his own project from von Jhering's teleological revolution and to carve out a distinct place for the *Interessenjurisprudenz*, Heck made a distinction between what he called the 'genetic' and the 'productive' theories of interests. The first was the recognition that diverse interests lay at the basis of existing legal rules. This was the idea already developed by von Jhering. The 'productive' theory of interests, on the other hand, turned on the active use of the analysis of interests in the

---

[150]  Larenz (1991), p. 49. See also Cahn (1948), p. 921.

[151]  See, e.g., Heck (1932a), pp. 108–9 ('The fight against the Jurisprudence of Concepts is the starting point and one of the main contents of our doctrine [...] Our second front is directed against the theory of "Free Law"').

[152]  See, e.g., Heck (1932b), p. 180 (whenever there is a 'gap' in the law, the judge must 'be guided primarily by the value judgments of the legislator and secondarily by an evaluation of his own').

[153]  Heck (1932a), p. 107. Translated as 'intelligent obedience' in Heck (1932b), p. 178.

[154]  See, e.g., Heck (1912); Heck (1914); Heck (1932a), pp. 91ff; Heck (1933), p. 40. See also Heck (1899), p. 589, cited in Edelmann (1967), p. 73.

[155]  Stampe (1905), pp. 24–26.

[156]  Heck (1932b), p. 125.

judicial development of the law. It was this theory that Heck felt was his own innovation.[157]

The *Interessenjurisprudenz* scholars propagated a humble image of what they were trying to do. Their primary concern was to offer practical guidance to judges on how to make a *'vernünftige Interessenabwägung'*, a reasonable, sensible balancing of interests.[158] They saw their work as a contribution to 'the practical art of decision-making', rather than as a 'philosophy of law'.[159] As Franz Wieacker has noted, it was precisely because of this 'unassuming stance' that the jurisprudence of interests was able to enlist 'a major following among both writers and practitioners'.[160]

Both the elements of 'balancing', or 'weighing', and of 'interests' were important in this practical contribution. The idea of weighing up two competing claims was the practical embodiment of the suggestion that what judges really should be doing was to give expression to precisely such trade-offs already contained in legislation. 'Our starting-point', Heck wrote, 'is the consideration that the legislator intends to delimit human interests according to value judgments, and that it is the function of the judge to effectuate this ultimate aim by his decisions of individual cases'.[161] Whenever these original value judgments do not explicitly cover a given case, 'the judge must proceed to fill the gap by weighing the interests concerned'.[162] As for 'interests', Heck favoured this concept over that of alternatives such as *'Rechtsgut'* ('legally protected good or interest') and *'Wert'* ('value') because he thought it permitted 'the finest dissection' in conceptual terms, and because of its clear recognition in social life and everyday parlance.[163]

### (b)   Autonomy and neutrality

Of paramount importance to the *Interessenjurisprudenz* scholars was the affirmation of the strict neutrality of their methods. Heck wrote:

> The method of the Jurisprudence of Interests derives its principles solely from the experience and needs of legal research. It is not based on any philosophy nor modelled after any of the other sciences. This is what I term 'juridical autonomy',[164]

[157]   *Ibid.*, pp. 125–26.
[158]   Edelmann (1967), p. 73.
[159]   Wieacker (1995), p. 455.
[160]   *Ibid.*
[161]   Heck (1932b), p. 178.
[162]   *Ibid.*, p. 180.
[163]   Heck (1932a), pp. 130ff, 136, 138.
[164]   Heck (1932b), p. 120.

This assertion of neutrality, or autonomy, is a dominant theme in the writings of the *Interessenjurisprudenz* scholars. Their jurisprudence was a 'pure theory of method', 'not a theory of substantive values', and 'entirely independent of any ideology'.[165] In this sense, the school of *Interessenjurisprudenz* remained clearly within the traditional European paradigm of 'strictly juristic method'.[166] As Philipp Heck noted in 1932, in words that would soon take on a rather more ominous hue:

> We do not dream of dictating to the legal community which interests it must protect in preference to others. We want to serve all the interests which the legal community holds worthy of protection at a given time.[167]

In part, the *Interessenjurisprudenz* took its valuations from the same naturalistic perspective that Gény and his contemporaries invoked in France.[168] But, more than for these French writers, Heck's main aim was in fact to bring out valuations already inherent in the body of the law. This meant reliance on 'the radiating effect of legislative value judgments' (the '*Fernwirkung gesetzlicher Werturteile*') laid down by the legislator for other cases to which the situation under review could be seen as in some way analogous.[169]

This asserted neutrality assumed special significance in the context of the *Rechtserneuerung* ('legal renewal') under National Socialism after 1933. Heck thought that his method would be ideally suited to support the implementation of the new National-Socialist ideals into German law. He presented his case in a 1936 article '*Die Interessenjurisprudenz und ihre neuen Gegner*' ('The Jurisprudence of Interests and its New Enemies').[170] By 1936, however, the Jurisprudence of Interests had already drawn fire from rival scholars, hence the defensive title of Heck's article. The main charge of critics such as Julius Binder was that Heck's work was tainted by the ideology of classical liberal individualism.[171] As Bernd Rüthers summarized in his seminal *Die unbegrenzte Auslegung*, Heck's critics thought that 'the representatives of the Jurisprudence of Interests would not, as

---

[165] *Ibid.*, pp. 110, 123 (rejecting the characterization of the *Interessenjurisprudenz* as animated by a 'materialistic philosophy of life'), and p. 129 (offering biographical sketches to show that 'neither Jhering nor Rümelin nor myself was subject to any nonlegal influences in developing our theory').

[166] Stolleis (2001), p. 266.

[167] Heck (1932b), p. 123.

[168] See, e.g., Wieacker (1995), pp. 453ff.

[169] Heck (1932a), p. 180. Heck drew an explicit connection between his method of balancing and reasoning by analogy. Cf. Larenz (1960), pp. 129ff; Edelmann (1967), p. 73.

[170] Heck (1936).     [171] *Ibid.*, pp. 173ff.

children of nineteenth-century liberal thought, be able to see the relationship between individual and collective interests in any other way than as in a conflict calling for an equalization'.[172] The whole idea of individual interests as opposed to social or collective interest was alien to the new National-Socialist ideology.[173]

Insistence on the neutrality of this method was of no help. Neutrality itself was seen as 'characteristic for a bygone era'.[174] This is why in his 1936 article, Heck, although careful to maintain his support for the separation between philosophy and legal method he had invested so much in, did suggest that he had always seen individual interests as worthy of protection only because of the fact that they were simultaneously social interests.[175] This substantive adjustment may have amounted to only a limited concession in Heck's own view, but it was a radical reversion when compared to the classical liberal position Gény and others had taken earlier on exactly the same issue. Even this could not, though, much to Heck's evident regret, save his beloved method.

### 4. Balancing of interests in the US: Roscoe Pound's Sociological Jurisprudence

#### (a) Degrees and interconnectedness

The genesis of balancing of interests in the US can to a large extent be told through the figures of Oliver Wendell Holmes and Roscoe Pound. For Holmes, the centrality of balancing came from an acute appreciation of the many new kinds of interdependence and conflict – between economic competitors, between capital and labour, *etc.* – that characterized industrial society. These new configurations precluded traditional all-or-nothing-approaches and called for what Holmes termed 'distinctions of degree'.[176] As early as 1881, for example, in his book *The Common Law*, Holmes found 'the *absolute* protection of property ... hardly consistent with the requirements of modern business'.[177] The same realization, that legal claims in conflict permitted only decisions based on distinctions of

---

[172] Rüthers (1968), p. 271.
[173] Cf. Snyder (2000), p. 55.
[174] Rüthers (1968), p. 271.
[175] Heck (1936), p. 175. Heck also pointed to his work in legal history, in which he had emphasized the position of individuals as members of classes ('*Stände*'). See pp. 174–75.
[176] *Panhandle Oil Co.* v. *Mississippi ex rel. Knox*, 227 US 218, 223 (1928) (Holmes, J., dissenting).
[177] See Horwitz (1992), p. 129 (emphasis added).

degree, led Holmes to formulate, in an 1894 essay on labour law, what Morton Horwitz has called the first 'fully articulated balancing test' in American legal theory.[178]

Holmes was not part of any social progressive movement and his emphasis on the need to balance interests was related to his critique of the inadequacies of prevalent legal methods. It was certainly not part of any substantive program for social reform.[179] That 'balancing of interests' would later be put to this use is foreshadowed in another of the earliest explicit references to balancing in American legal literature. This reference is emblematic for many later discussions to such an extent that it is worthwhile to discuss it at some length.

In an 1895 case comment in the *Yale Law Journal*, an anonymous commentator criticized an 1894 Illinois decision in which the State Supreme Court struck down a law forbidding women in factories to work more than eight hours a day.[180] This decision was representative of numerous state and federal decisions of the period that similarly invoked the right to freedom of contract in order to strike down protective legislation.[181] The Illinois court held that protecting the women themselves could not justify the legislation and that protection of anyone else or of the public interest was not at issue. For the anonymous reviewer, however, the case did not turn on protection of the women themselves, but on protecting society against 'the harm that may be entailed on posterity [a] weakness that may strike at the very life of the State'.[182] This public or social harm was evident, the commentator wrote, from lower birth rates for factory workers. The reviewer concluded: 'The whole question seems to involve a balancing of public policy over against the right to contract, and the court has decided in favor of the latter'.[183]

The alleged laissez-faire constitutionalism of the freedom of contract doctrine, on stark display in this Illinois decision and a range of other decisions leading up to Justice Peckham's majority opinion in *Lochner v. New York* at the Supreme Court in 1905, was Roscoe Pound's main object of attack in the first decades of the twentieth century, in particular in his articles *Mechanical Jurisprudence* and *Liberty of Contract*. Part

---

[178] *Ibid.*, p. 131.    [179] See, e.g., Holmes (1894), p. 3.
[180] Anonymous, (1985), p. 201. The case, *Tilt v. Illinois*, is not discussed in Pound's Liberty of Contract of 1909, even though that article refers to several Illinois decisions on the same topic, from the same period.
[181] But see, e.g., Bernstein (2003); Tamanaha (2009), pp. 27ff, 67ff (disputing the extent of this trend).
[182] Anonymous (1895), p. 201.    [183] *Ibid.*

of this attack echoed the theme of the anonymous *Comment* just cited: if courts would only look at social reality and take all the facts into consideration, they could not possibly come to the conclusions they actually reached. Attention to actual social data – on birth rates for female factory workers in the Illinois case, for example, or on the quality of bread produced by bakers working overly long hours in *Lochner* – would make it impossible to hold, as courts regularly did, that 'the interest of the public' was not 'in the slightest degree affected' by the practices social legislation sought to outlaw.[184] This theme of attention to real world consequences of judicial rulings led Pound to issue his famous call for a 'Sociological Jurisprudence'. He described this project as a 'movement for the adjustment of principles and doctrines to the human conditions they are to govern rather than to assumed first principles'.[185]

### (b)   Rights, policies, interests

For Roscoe Pound, Sociological Jurisprudence was intimately tied up with both a 'new' worldview and a related 'new' ideal of justice. The new worldview sought to replace 'an abstract and unreal theory of State omnipotence on the one hand, and an atomistic and artificial view of individual independence on the other' with a realistic assessment of 'the facts of the world with its innumerable bonds of association'.[186] This awareness of increased interdependence had to be combined with a transition towards a new form of justice. For the latter, Pound set out the required transformation in his 1912 paper *Social Justice and Legal Justice*:

> It has been said that our *legal idea of justice* is well stated in Spencer's formula: 'The liberty of each limited only by the like liberties of all.' Compare this with Ward's formula of *social justice: the satisfaction of everyone's wants so far as they are not outweighed by others' wants.*[187]

The theme of 'balancing of interests' that Pound was to develop in the 1920s has to be seen fully in function of these ideas on social justice and his project of progressive reform.[188] The bulk of these views are set out in his 1921 paper 'A Theory of Social Interests'.[189] That article begins with

---

[184] *Lochner v. New York*, 198 US 45, 75 (1905).
[185] Pound (1909), p. 464; Pound (1908), pp. 609–10 (citing von Jhering's idea of a '*Wirklichkeitsjurisprudenz*', or 'jurisprudence of results').
[186] *Ibid.*, p. 609.
[187] Pound (1912c), p. 458 (emphases added).
[188] Pound's earlier writings, in particular *Mechanical Jurisprudence* and *Liberty of Contract*, contain little or no reference to balancing of interests.
[189] Reprinted as Pound (1943) *A Survey of Social Interests*. Citations are to the 1943 reprint.

Pound's critique of the individualism of classical method. 'From the seventeenth century to the end of the nineteenth', he wrote, 'juristic theory sought to state all interests in terms of individual natural rights'.[190] During this time, 'social interests were pushed into the background'.[191] This meant that while 'the books are full of schemes of natural rights [...] there are no adequate schemes of public policies'.[192] At the time of writing, however, in Pound's view 'pressure of new social interests' was giving courts pause and leading them to cast doubt upon their traditional methods.[193]

These new difficulties, and the way the defects of the traditional approach played out in Pound's view can be illustrated on the basis of the Illinois decision and the *Comment* cited earlier. The court's decision, on this view, was evidently defective in that it took into account only the individual 'natural right of freedom of contract', entirely neglecting any possible effect on other individuals or on society at large. The reviewer's real-life-aware, data-sensitive, balancing approach was, from this perspective, an important step forward. But even the suggested alternative in the *Comment* still had an important weakness. Merely replacing categorical analysis of the outer limits of natural rights by a relative or relational approach turning on weighing or balancing was not enough. Because, Pound wrote, even if a court were to engage in 'balancing', framing the relevant conflict as between an individual *right* on the one hand and a mere social *policy* on the other was liable to determine the outcome in advance.[194] It was in this context that Pound formulated a crucial warning, often repeated later: 'when it comes to weighing or valuing claims [...] we must be careful to compare them on the same plane'.[195] This 'same plane' Roscoe Pound found in the concept of 'interests'.

The central role that 'balancing of interests' played in Progressive jurisprudence can now be assessed. On the one hand, *balancing* was the expression of the new worldview, already touched upon by Holmes, which emphasized interdependence over absolutism and individualism, and questions of degree over categorical boundaries. On the other hand, the concept of *interests* was instrumental in mediating between individual 'rights', which had always been judicially protected, and 'policies', which had not. The concept of interests allowed for evaluation and comparison to be carried out 'on the same plane'. This it achieved primarily through

---

[190] *Ibid.*, p. 5.   [191] *Ibid.*   [192] *Ibid.*, p. 7.
[193] *Ibid.*, p. 12.   [194] *Ibid.* pp. 2, 12.
[195] *Ibid.*, p. 2. (emphasis added). See also, e.g., Fried (1963).

a revaluation of the social and a corresponding 'relativization' of the individual.

The analysis in *A Survey of Social Interests* and in Pound's other writings of the same time are revealing for his instrumental use of the new conception of balancing of interests. Once the theme of balancing was introduced, Pound had little interest in elaborating its structure or nature. Pound's papers contain little or no helpful guidance for judges on how to balance.[196] Much more important for him was his project of drawing attention to the multitude of important 'social interests' and to their neglected weight in contemporary case law; the elaboration of 'adequate schemes of public policies' as he had put it. Once these interests were 'listed, labeled, classified, and illustrated', Edmond Cahn observed later, 'Pound and his school seem ready to adjourn'.[197] 'In short', Cahn concluded, 'the Anglo-Saxon school stands halted at the threshold of the theory of values (axiology). Meanwhile, in Germany, the preoccupation of the *Interessenjurisprudenz* was less with listing and taxonomy and more with the techniques of adjudication'.[198]

Pound was certainly no radical reformer, and he became less enamoured with Progressive ideas later in his career. But because the legal orthodoxy he was concerned with in this early period – constitutional adjudication, primarily in the field of health and safety regulation – was, fairly uniformly, so much more socially conservative than what he and other Progressives desired, it was unavoidable that the call for a more reality- or society-aware *sociological* jurisprudence would be read as a call for a more *social* jurisprudence. In this sense, Pound saw balancing of interests as a way to make 'inroads into [...] individualism', in just the way the old equity jurisprudence had done for the common law.[199] And just as Pound and the other proto-Realists had ascribed (conservative) political dimensions to the legal method they criticized, as described above, they also sought to employ the method they suggested as a replacement – balancing of interests – for their own Progressive project. When, by the late 1920s, Pound became much less sympathetic to the cause of reform,[200] his identification of connections between conceptualism/formalism and reactionary politics on the one hand and of sociological jurisprudence/balancing and progressive politics on the other hand was

---

[196] See, e.g., Pound (1943), p. 35 (calling simply for 'a reasoned weighing of the interests involved and a reasoned attempt to reconcile them or adjust them').

[197] Cahn (1948), p. 921.     [198] *Ibid.*

[199] Pound (1909), p. 482.

[200] See Kennedy & Belleau (2000), p. 311.

already available to be taken up by the Legal Realists, with whom Pound famously fell out, and, later, their Critical successors.[201]

## 5.   *Balancing* and *interests*

Balancing's earliest invocations show a wealth of different meanings for very similar language. Almost exactly the same terms figure in the writings of Gény in France, Heck and others in Germany, and Pound in the US. But in French legal thought, the idea of balancing of interests, even though it surfaces at one prominent place in Gény's methodological proposals, was not in fact all that central. For Pound, ideas of balancing and weighing were subordinate to the project of foregrounding 'interests', in particular 'social' interests. In German legal thought, finally, the two elements of balancing and interests were promoted jointly, as the core of a more suitable adjudicatory technique.

These distinct meanings had special implications for the question of the relationship between method and substance in law, which they starkly reveal to be a contingent one. In the US, the connection between legal method and politics, which the critics had attributed to categorization and other elements of classical orthodoxy, continued into the age of 'the triumph of the balancing test'. This time, however, it was a conscious effort on the part of the Progressives to employ legal method for purposes of reform. Pound himself, as G. Edward White has noted, had a conception of 'judicial decision-making as part of [a] larger project of social engineering'.[202] Balancing of interest, in this project, became a Progressive legal 'device'.[203] Its principal purpose was in the metaphorical language he himself helped make so influential, to 'recalibrate the scales' as between individual rights and collective policies.

This connection between balancing as method and substantive preferences was largely absent in Europe. In France, this was probably in part because the reform effort, both in relation to method and to substance,

---

[201] The specific theme of balancing of interests is, intriguingly, a much less prominent theme in Legal Realist writing than might be expected. Karl Llewellyn thought Pound's balancing of interests was deficient in both its 'balancing' and 'interests' dimensions. See Llewellyn (1930), p. 435 ('Pound's work is as striking in its values as in its limitations [...] "Balancing of interests" remains with no indication of how to tell an interest when you see one, much less with any study of how they are or should be balanced'.) There appears to be no extended discussion of balancing in the work of leading Realist writers such as Oliphant, Cook, Bingham or Lorenzen.

[202] White (1972), p. 101.

[203] Gordon (1997), p. 148.

was on the whole less ambitious than in the US. But the main reason was simply that the specific idea of balancing did not play such a central role in whatever substantive and methodological reform was proposed. In German legal thought, the *Interessenjurisprudenz* purposefully sought to present itself as a neutral, apolitical, juridical method. Heck did not settle on the concept of 'interests' in order to recalibrate conflicts between individual constitutional rights and broad social policies. He chose 'interests' as his conceptual category because he felt it offered the greatest scope for juridical precision. In stark contrast with Roscoe Pound's socially-progressive proposals for balancing in the US, Heck and the other members of the *Interessenjurisprudenz* school were later even charged with promoting excessive *individualism* through their use of balancing of interests – a charge that Heck of course vigorously denied. Clearly, the idea that balancing of interests would foster more socially progressive outcomes did not form part of the understanding of the *Interessenjurisprudenz* nor of its critics. This means that three radically different conceptions of the relationship between balancing as method and substantive outcomes can be identified: balancing of interests would promote social values (Pound), balancing would be completely substantively neutral (Heck) and balancing would foster individualism (Heck's critics).

## D.   Balancing and conceptual jurisprudence

The ambition for this chapter was to uncover different original understandings not only for balancing itself, but also for classical orthodoxy – for 'conceptual jurisprudence' – and therefore for legal formality. The following chapters build on this initial account in two ways. First, they tell the story of balancing's meanings for a later era – the period of its arrival in constitutional rights adjudication proper, in the course of the 1950s. But, secondly, they also look in a more direct way than has been possible so far at the specific question of the relationship *between* balancing and conceptual jurisprudence.

Here is one way of showing how that question arises. The original American meaning of legal formality as categorization, with its emphasis on the preservation of individual liberty vis-à-vis governmental regulation, will, in Chapter 4, be shown to lie at the foundations of a highly visible and peculiar feature of contemporary American constitutional law. This is the recurrence of invocations of 'formality' and 'formalism' that are both explicit and positive. It is important to note that this favourable view of legal formality is decidedly an *anti-balancing* perspective.

American jurisprudence frequently demonstrates a pervasive fear of balancing away constitutional rights protection. This balancing-angst is visible in repeated explicit efforts to cast rights as 'absolutes', to protect 'inviolable cores' of rights, or to create 'bright-line rules' in areas as diverse as freedom of expression or search and seizure – moves discussed in more detail in Chapter 4. These efforts are often propagated by self-styled 'neo-Formalists'. They are all presented explicitly as part of a broader endeavour of 'reclaiming the methodology of late nineteenth-century legal thought' as a way to get out of 'the conundrums of balancing', in Richard Pildes' stark phrase, cited earlier. But that project provides a striking contrast with parallel efforts in Germany to develop an understanding of balancing as part of 'the great analytical tradition of conceptual jurisprudence'.[204] Balancing *versus* nineteenth-century legal thought, then, and balancing as nineteenth-century legal thought. Neither of these diametrically opposing labels, of course, captures all that is salient about American and German legal thinking in this field. But they are evocative reminders of the reality of the challenge set out in the Introduction – the challenge of reconciling a 'turn to balancing' and a 'turn to legalism' in contemporary constitutional jurisprudence. And they are useful as guiding images, to keep in mind as the next instalment of balancing's histories gets under way.

---

[204] Alexy (2002), p. 18. The German original uses the loaded historical term '*Begriffsjurisprudenz*', at p. 38.

# 3

# A perfect constitutional order: balancing in German constitutional jurisprudence of the 1950s and 1960s

## A.   Introduction

### 1.   *Two debates*

During a remarkably concentrated period in the late 1950s, the German *Bundesverfassungsgericht* and the US Supreme Court, as well as academic commentators in their two jurisdictions, first began to use the language of balancing in relation to constitutional rights adjudication. In both systems, the new language first surfaced in the area of freedom of expression. In Germany, this development took off abruptly and decisively with the Court's unanimous 1958 *Lüth* decision.[1] In the US, different Justices of the Supreme Court gradually began referring to balancing in their opinions in first amendment cases of this period; from a lone concurrence by Justice Frankfurter in the 1951 case of *Dennis* v. *United States*, to a five-Justice majority in a series of cases between 1959 and 1961.[2]

It is striking how quickly and how completely 'balancing' came to dominate discussions on freedom of expression adjudication, in Germany and in the US.[3] These early debates shared a number of intriguing characteristics. To begin with, judges and commentators quite visibly operated on the basis of a widely shared understanding that balancing actually *'was something'*. That is, they generally seem to have held the view that the language of balancing, in these free speech opinions but also in other contexts, referred to a discrete and in some way coherent set of practices

---

[1] BVerfGE 7, 198 [1958].

[2] *Barenblatt* v. *United States*, 360 US 109 (1959); *Konigsberg* v. *State Bar of California*, 366 US 36 (1961); *Communist Party* v. *Subversive Activities Control Board*, 367 US 1 (1961). For a more comprehensive overview, see Chapter 4, Sections A–B.

[3] 'Dominate the debates' is not the same as 'dominate freedom of expression law'. The extent to which 'balancing' was ever an adequate depiction of the Supreme Court's dominant approach to freedom of expression adjudication is still a controversial topic in the US. See Chapter 4, Section C.

and ideas that could cogently be discussed and contrasted with alternatives. The precise nature of these practices, of course, was a major point of
contention. Second, the courts' balancing language was generally taken
to refer to *something new*. Balancing language denoted the incidence of
doctrines, methods and sensibilities within constitutional jurisprudence
that had not been present in the same way at earlier times. Third, most
of these same judges and commentators apparently believed that different positions on balancing *mattered* in one or more ways. 'The one thing
which appears to emerge with reasonable clarity', said Laurent Frantz in
describing the atmosphere in 1962, 'is that "balancing" has become the
central first amendment issue.'[4] And finally, not only could balancing be
discussed cogently, debates on balancing quickly became *focal points* for
a wide range of constitutional controversies. Not just with regard to freedom of expression, but also with regard constitutional interpretation generally, or the task of courts in democracies. In both settings, particular
takes on balancing rapidly came to be associated with specific views on a
wide range of other topics. The precise nature and extent of these wider
reverberations were some of the central questions in the new balancing
debates.

## 2.   Argument: synthesis and paradox

This chapter and the next chart the rise of balancing language as a
prominent feature within constitutional rights adjudication in postwar
Germany and the US. Their aim is to unearth the '*zugrunde liegende
Vorstellung*', ('the underlying general conception'), the pervasive associations, the aspirations held out for and critiques raised against balancing,
by judges, primarily those of the *Bundesverfassungsgericht* and of the US
Supreme Court, and by their surrounding communities of constitutional
legal scholars and commentators in the US and Germany.

Summarily stated, my argument in these chapters is as follows. While
American balancing discourse is characterized by pervasive antinomies,
balancing in the German constitutional landscape of the time is the principal embodiment of one of the most significant and successful efforts
at overcoming these same basic oppositions in modern constitutional
jurisprudence. While American constitutional jurisprudence continuously draws fundamental distinctions between 'pragmatic action' and

---

[4] Frantz (1962), p. 1432. For Germany, see, e.g., Schlink (1976), p. 13 (balancing seen as 'the
  key to the method and dogmatics of constitutional law'); Ossenbühl (1995), p. 906.

'reasoned deliberation', between 'policy' and 'principle' and between the substantive and the formal, always relegating balancing firmly to one side of these dichotomies, German constitutional jurisprudence has managed, to a large extent, to fuse these elements, adopting balancing as the main vehicle of a jurisprudence that casts the pragmatic as reasoned, policy as principle and the substantive as formal.

This chapter elaborates the first leg of this argument. The German idea of 'balancing as synthesis', I argue, lies at the heart of a conception of 'the perfect constitutional order' that dominated early postwar German legal thinking.[5] The ideas associated with the language of balancing are simultaneously the principal expression of, and a crucial source of support for, this notion of constitutional legal perfection. That concept, in turn, can be disaggregated into the twin postulates that the constitution should be the expression of a constellation of 'material' or 'substantive' values, and that this constellation should somehow encompass as much of the reality of public and private life as possible. Judicial balancing figured at the centre of each of these two related visions, reflecting and sustaining both.

Both these strands, of 'material' and of 'comprehensive' constitutionalism, are pervasive features of early postwar German legal life. They represent particularly influential efforts at transcending traditional oppositions in constitutional thinking, including notably between the formal and the substantive in constitutional law. That specific dichotomy will be taken up again in Chapter 5. 'Material constitutionalism', I will argue there, is a dominant German expression of 'the substantive' in law. This particular German version, however, is in many ways much more heavily formalized than its US counterparts, such as 'policy', 'pragmatism' or 'instrumentalism'. 'Comprehensive constitutionalism', in turn, will be identified as a prominent German expression of legal formality. In this regard, the argument will be that by nudging legal actors towards the pursuit of completeness and 'perfection', comprehensive constitutionalism exercises a compelling and constraining force very similar to the power attributed to expressions of legal formality more familiar in American law, such as per se rules or hard-edged definitions.

These three ideas of 'the formal' as comprehensiveness and perfection, 'the substantive' as material constitutionalism and the formal–substantive interrelationship as synthesis will serve in Chapter 5 to frame a local

---

[5] The label is provisional in the context of this chapter. For a more elaborate development, see Chapter 5, Section B.

German meaning of balancing that is radically different from notions familiar in US legal thought.

### 3.  Balancing and freedom of expression: textual foundations

Before turning to the relevant *Bundesverfassungsgericht* case law and associated commentary, a brief comparative look at the textual foundations for the constitutional protection of freedom of expression in the US and Germany is necessary. This is in order to answer a basic question: to what extent did these written source materials dictate, or at least make more likely, resort to some kind of balancing approach in either system?

A quick glance reveals that the textual foundations for the protection of expression in the US and in Germany are at once highly similar and utterly different. The first amendment to the US Constitution, on its face, famously appears to forbid any kind of limitation of the freedom to speak, providing:

> Congress shall make no law abridging the freedom of speech.

Art. 5 *Grundgesetz* (GG, or Basic Law), on the other hand, in its paragraph 2, would seem to allow virtually any kind of limitation,[6] providing:

1. Every person shall have the right to freely express and disseminate his opinion in speech, writing, and pictures [...] Freedom of the press and the freedom of reporting by means of broadcasts and films shall be guaranteed.
2. These rights shall find their limits in the provisions of general laws, in provisions for the protection of young persons, and in the right to personal honor.[7]

In a sense, both provisions are worded in absolute terms. The first amendment, on its face, providing for unqualified protection of speech, and Art. 5 Basic Law allowing unqualifiedly for limitation by way of 'general laws', in addition to limitations specifically for the protection of youth and personal honour.[8] Neither the US nor the German guarantee, then, offers any clear textual basis for an explicit weighing of competing values or interests. Neither provision in fact offers an indication of *any kind* of relationship or comparison at all – whether expressed in terms of

---

[6] See, e.g., Bernstein (1967), p. 547ff.
[7] Translation in Kommers & Miller (2012), p. 441.
[8] See further Kriele (1967), p. 228. The specific limitations will not figure in what follows.

balancing or otherwise – between the nature or value of expression on the one hand and the nature or value of its limitations on the other. Neither wording on its face suggests that speech may only be limited in favour of goals of a certain weight or importance, or that a particular expression itself needs to attain a certain worth before it can trump competing legislative goals. The text of the first amendment *does not* say 'abridge if you must, but try to keep it reasonable', as early critics of balancing scathingly described the position of their adversaries.[9] And a literal reading of Article 5 Basic Law *does not* make protection of expression dependent on 'a balancing comparison' (*'abwägender Vergleich'*) between the fundamental right and other relevant values or interests.[10] To interpret this provision as seemingly providing 'a set of scales' and thereby necessitating some kind of weighing process would be to read more into the text than appears warranted.[11]

That some form of limitation or qualification had to be attached to these two seemingly absolute provisions was, of course, inevitable. Neither unqualified protection for expression nor the unqualified permission of its abridgement is tenable on any generally accepted theory of this right. What was not inevitable, though, was the resort to nearly identical language in giving shape to these qualifications. And what was *certainly* not inevitable, and what makes a comparative analysis of the work of these two courts during this period so intriguing, is that this language should come to dominate so much of our thinking about constitutional adjudication generally.

### B.　Balancing at the *Bundesverfassungsgericht*: 1958 to c. 1976

The foundations of contemporary German free speech jurisprudence can be found in decisions of the *Bundesverfassungsgericht* from a period of less than two decades, between the *Lüth* decision of January 1958 and, somewhat more arbitrarily, the decision in the *Deutschland Magazin* case of 1976. Leading cases from this period cover such diverse situations as claims in tort between individuals, claims against news organizations for intrusion in private lives and complaints against police interference in the media. The themes the Court was asked to deal with concerned some of the most politically contentious issues of the day, including the country's

---

[9]　Frantz (1962), p. 1449.
[10]　For that view, see, e.g., Klein (1971), pp. 152–53, 162.
[11]　See, e.g., Kommers & Miller (2012), p. 442.

recent Nazi-past, relations to the GDR and military preparedness in the context of the Cold War.

### 1. From Lüth to Schmid-Spiegel

(a) *Lüth* (1958): *'Es wird deshalb eine "Güterabwägung" erforderlich ...'*

Before the *Bundesverfassungsgericht* had even handed down its decision, the *Lüth* case was already set to become a touchstone of German constitutional law. For the first time under the 1949 Basic Law, the Court was asked to rule on the scope of the right to freedom of expression.[12] In addition, the Court was, also for the first time, faced squarely with the issue of the extent to which constitutional rights had an influence on private law relations; the vexing question of '*Drittwirkung*', or 'horizontal effect'. The actual decision, when it came, introduced striking novelties. The Court proclaimed the idea that the Constitution embodied an 'objective value order', emphasized the social dimension in (individual) constitutional rights, and introduced the concept of '*Wertabwägung*' ('a balancing of values') to solve clashes between competing constitutional goods. It is, of course, this last element we are particularly interested in, but it will be seen very quickly that the Court's balancing language can hardly be understood in isolation from these other facets of the *Lüth* decision.

In 1950, Erich Lüth, at the time Chairman of the Publications Office of the City of Hamburg, gave a lecture before members of Germany's motion picture industry. In his lecture, Lüth called for a boycott of a new film by Veit Harlan, a film director who during the fascist era had produced a strongly anti-semitic film ('*Jud Süss*').[13] Lüth was afraid that Harlan's re-emergence as a director would stain Germany's image abroad and would complicate efforts to rebuild relations between Christians and Jews; a cause he himself was particularly closely involved in. The producer and distributor of Harlan's new film brought an action against Lüth on the basis of Art. 826 of the Civil Code, claiming that his call for a boycott was a tortious act; an '*unerlaubte Handlung*'. The civil law courts found against Lüth and ordered him to refrain from promoting any further boycott of

---

[12] See Herzog (1968), nos. 248–49.

[13] Described as 'perhaps the most notoriously anti-Semitic movie ever made, a box office success in Nazi Germany in 1940 that was so effective that it was made required viewing for all members of the SS'. See Larry Rohter, *Nazi Film Still Pains Relatives*, N.Y. Times, 1 March 2010, at C1.

Harlan's film. Lüth then filed a 'Verfassungsbeschwerde', an individual constitutional complaint, with the Bundesverfassungsgericht.

The Court began its decision by noting that 'without a doubt, the primary purpose of the basic rights is to safeguard the sphere of freedom of the individual against interferences by public authorities'.[14] At the same time, however, it had to be recognized that 'the Constitution, which does not want to be a value-neutral order, has, in its Part on Fundamental Rights, erected an objective value order'.[15] The Court continued: 'This value system, at the core of which is the dignity of the personality of the individual developing freely within the social community, has to be understood as a foundational constitutional decision for all areas of law.'[16] This meant that the ordinary courts would have to test, in each case, whether the applicable rules of private law are influenced by constitutional concerns.

Finding freedom of expression to be 'immediately constitutive'[17] ('schlechthin konstituierend') for a liberal-democratic constitutional order, the Court insisted that limitations to this freedom, in the form of the allgemeine Gesetze clause in Art. 5, should be interpreted in such a way as to guarantee that the 'special value' ('besondere Wertgehalt') of the right remained in tact. The way to achieve this was to understand the 'general laws' and the freedom of expression as mutually limiting and constitutive of each other's meaning; a 'Wechselwirkung' ('dialectic') between right and limitations. The Court concluded that 'it has to be' within its competence to uphold the specific value of this right vis-à-vis all public authorities, including the ordinary courts, 'in order to achieve the equilibration that the Constitution desires' ('den verfassungsrechtlich gewollten Ausgleich') between the opposing tendencies of the basic right and the limiting 'general laws'. This brought the Court to the following interpretation of the scope of freedom of expression:

> the expression of opinions is as such, that is: in their purely intellectual effect, free; if however [this expression infringes] another individual's rights, the protection of which deserves precedence over the protection of the freedom of expression, then this interference will not be allowed simply because it was committed through the expression of an opinion. A balancing of values [Güterabwägung] becomes necessary: the right to the expression of opinions must recede when it infringes protection-worthy interests of another of a higher rank. Whether such overbearing

[14]  BVerfGE 7, 198, 204 [1958].
[15]  Ibid., p. 205.     [16]  Ibid.
[17]  As translated in Eberle (2002), p. 209.

interests of another are present, is to be determined on the basis of all the circumstances of the case.[18]

The Court found that the freedom of expression would have to be 'weighed especially heavily' when engaged in 'not for the purpose of a private dispute, but in the first place as a contribution to the formation of public opinion'.[19] In conclusion:

> the private-law judge is required to weigh, in every case, the significance of the right against the value of the interest [*Rechtsgut*] protected by a 'general law'. This decision can only be made upon a comprehensive analysis of the individual case, taking all relevant circumstances into account. An incorrect balancing [*unrichtige Abwägung*] can violate the basic right and sustain a constitutional complaint to the Federal Constitutional Court.[20]

On the merits, the *Bundesverfassungsgericht* decided that the private-law courts had 'misjudged the special significance that attaches to the basic right to freedom also where it comes into conflict with the private interests of others'.[21] Factors that the Court found particularly relevant were the fact that the speech in question concerned a matter of public interest and the suggestion that Lüth had spoken out of 'pure motives'.[22]

(b)   '*Plakaten*' (1958) and *Schmid-Spiegel* (1961)

The *Lüth* opinion quickly became the authoritative point of departure for freedom of expression law generally.[23] The Court decided another case on Art. 5 Basic Law on the same day as *Lüth*, under reference to 'the principles developed there' (the '*Plakaten*' decision),[24] and confirmed *Lüth's* pre-eminence in its 1961 *Schmid-Spiegel* decision.[25] These two decisions quote important elements of *Lüth's* approach to freedom of expression, in particular the idea of relativity or dialectic ('*Wechselwirkung*') between the right and its limitations ('*Plakaten*'), the suggestion that the particular use made of a constitutional right determines that right's 'weight' in relation to competing interests ('*Plakaten*' and *Schmid-Spiegel*),[26] and

---

[18]  BVerfGE 7, 198, 210–11 [1958].    [19]  *Ibid.*, p. 212.
[20]  BVerfGE 7, 198, 229 [1958].    [21]  *Ibid.*, p. 230.
[22]  BVerfGE 7, 219, 229 [1958].
[23]  On *Lüth's* general importance, see, e.g., Böckenförde (1987), p. 87 ('*eine epochemachende Entscheidung*').
[24]  BVerfGE 7, 230; 234 ('*Plakaten*') [1958].
[25]  BVerfGE 12, 113; 124 (*Schmid-Spiegel*) [1961]. See also Bettermann (1964); Bernstein (1967), p. 553; Herzog (1968), nos. 250–51.
[26]  In *Schmid-Spiegel*: with qualifications. See BVerfGE 12, 113; 127–29 [1961].

the insistence that lower courts should take all competing values and interests into consideration (*Schmid-Spiegel*).

In the '*Plakaten*' case, the Court rejected the constitutional complaint of a tenant who had wanted to affix election posters to his apartment's window but had been prevented from doing so by his landlord. Following the *Lüth* model, the Court approached the case both as a conflict between two constitutional rights in the abstract, the right to property and the right to freedom of expression and as a clash between the opposing interests of the individual landlord and tenant in the concrete circumstances of the case. On the side of the tenant, the Court looked at the background to the expression ('not prompted, but out of own volition'), at its form ('unconventional'), and at the possible effects of restraint ('not substantial').[27] A decisive factor in favour of the landlord, the Court found, was that he had acted, not to protect his own 'formal powers as an owner', but in the interest of protecting domestic peace between the tenants.[28]

The *Schmid-Spiegel* case concerned a row, acrimoniously fought out in public, between a judge and the journal *Der Spiegel*. The journal had accused the judge of harbouring communist sympathies. The judge countered by likening *Der Spiegel*'s political reporting to pornography. When convicted of defamation in the lower courts, he filed a constitutional complaint. The *Bundesverfassungsgericht* found that the criminal courts had focused exclusively on the interests of the journal and its editors and had neglected to take into account the 'immanent value' of the expression of opinion. Through this neglect, they had violated the 'value judgment' ('*Wertentscheidung*') incorporated in Art. 5 Basic Law.[29]

Although these decisions did not repeat *Lüth*'s general statements on the need for a balancing, their references to the earlier decision, the overall tone of their language ('*Wertentscheidung*', '*Güterabwägung*', '*Gewicht*'), coupled with an approach explicitly focused on clashes between opposing values and interests, contributed to a perception that *Lüth*'s 'balancing of values and interests' should be read as embodying the Court's overall take on freedom of expression.[30]

---

[27] BVerfGE 7, 230; 236 [1958].
[28] BVerfGE 7, 230; 237 [1958].
[29] BVerfGE 12, 113; 126–28 [1961].
[30] See, e.g., Zippelius (1962), p. 47 (reading both decisions in terms of '*Güter- und Interessenabwägung*'). But see, e.g., Schlink (1976), p. 21 ('*Plakaten*' decided '*ohne eigentliche Abwägung*', 'without a real balancing'), and pp. 25–26 (discussing *Schmid-Spiegel* as in part rejecting and following *Lüth*).

## 2. *From* Der Spiegel *to* Deutschland Magazin

### (a) *Der Spiegel* (1966)

The 1966 *Spiegel* case still is one of the most controversial cases of the Court's early history, not just in the free speech context, producing its first published minority opinion.[31] Beyond the general controversy surrounding the decision the case also marks an important transition point in the genealogy of constitutional balancing. In the published decisions and in commentary of the time, one finds simultaneously a decisive endorsement of the validity of the *Lüth* approach, with an extension of balancing to all areas of freedom of expression adjudication, and clear indications that the *Lüth* vision of balancing was coming under increasing pressure.

In October 1962, the magazine *Der Spiegel* published an article on the German army's preparedness for military conflict with the Soviet Union. The article listed detailed accounts of the military capabilities of Germany and several other NATO member states and concluded that the West-German government was responsible for 'completely inadequate preparations'.[32] The government reacted to the article by instituting criminal proceedings against the editor and several publishers of the journal and by carrying out an extensive search at the journal's premises. During this search a substantial trove of documents was seized. Upon a constitutional complaint by the publisher, the *Bundesverfassungsgericht*, in a split decision, held that this search and seizure did not violate the guarantee of freedom of the press in Art. 5 Basic Law.

The Court observed that the freedom of the press 'carried within it' the possibility of 'conflict with other constitutionally protected values', in the form of rights and interests of other individuals, as well as those of groups and of society as a whole.[33] Both national security and freedom of the press being '*Staatsnotwendigkeiten*', 'constitutional essentials', the task for the Court was to balance, in the individual case, 'the dangers to the security of the country that may arise from publication [...] against the need to be informed of important occurrences even in the area of defense policies'.[34] The Court added that because governmental interference with a particular publication is likely to have a chilling effect on press freedom generally:

---

[31] BVerfGE 20, 162 [1966].
[32] Quoted and translated in Bernstein (1967), p. 555.
[33] BVerfGE 20, 162, 164 [1966].
[34] BVerfGE 20, 162; 185 [1966]. This translation: Bernstein (1967), p. 556.

there exists an inescapable conflict between the interests of criminal
prosecution and the protection of press freedom; a conflict that has to be
solved with the aid of the balancing of values [*Güterabwägung*] developed
in the case law of the Federal Constitutional Court.[35]

Applying these principles to the case at hand, the 'majority',[36] on the basis
of a '*sachliche Wertabwägung im Einzelfall*', a substantive balancing of
values in the individual case, which found that the prosecution and the
lower court had correctly judged the search and seizure to be both a suitable and a necessary response to the threat caused by the publication.[37]

(b)    Entrenchment: '*die gebotene Abwägung ...*'

With its multiple references to the *Lüth* opinion and to the language of
'*Güterabwägung*' and '*Wertabwägung im Einzelfall*', the *Spiegel* decision was an important step in the entrenchment of the *Lüth* balancing
approach to the right of freedom of expression.[38] The fact that the decision
explicitly extended this approach to freedom of the press and the fact that
both majority and dissenters agreed on the centrality of balancing, contributed to a reading of the case as laying down a general method for the
adjudication of all freedom of speech issues.

The entrenchment of the *Lüth* decision's balancing approach in the
course of the 1960s can, in particular, be gleaned from two factors. First,
it became common for the ordinary, that is, criminal and civil, courts
to explicitly formulate their own treatment of free speech issues in
terms of a balancing of values and interests. This was to give effect to the
*Bundesverfassungsgericht*'s general instruction in *Lüth* that the ordinary
courts should balance in each case the value of freedom of expression
against competing values and interests.[39] In *Der Spiegel* itself, for example, the highest criminal court, the *Bundesgerichtshof*, explicitly framed
its decision with respect to the permissibility of the criminal-procedural
measures predominantly in terms of a '*Güterabwägung*'.[40] Second, the

---

[35]  BVerfGE 20, 162; 187 [1966] (now Art. 15, Para. 4).
[36]  The Court was evenly split (4–4). On the basis of Art. 15, Para. 2 of the Law on the Federal
      Constitutional Court, no infringement of the Basic Law could be declared in the case of
      an equal division.
[37]  BVerfGE 20, 162; 213–14 [1966].
[38]  See, e.g., BVerfGE 20, 162; 189 (*Der Spiegel*) [1966] ('*die gebotene Abwägung*'/ 'required bal-
      ancing'); BVerfGE 25, 256; 261 (*Blinkfüer*) [1969] ('*die vorzunehmende Güterabwägung*'/
      'the balancing that needs to be undertaken').
[39]  BVerfGE 7, 198; 229 [1958].
[40]  As summarized in BVerfGE 20, 162; 184–185 [1966].

constitutional complaints of individuals increasingly came to be cast in the form of objections against a 'balancing' undertaken, or omitted, by the ordinary courts.[41] Again, the *Lüth* decision, with its warning to other courts that a 'wrong balancing' in and of itself could infringe the right to freedom of expression, lay at the basis of this development.[42]

Both trends were on display in a 1969 case that, once again, presented the Court with the issue of a call for a boycott; the fact pattern at issue in *Lüth* itself.[43] A major publishing house, the well-known *Springer Verlag*, had called on its distributors to boycott a much smaller journal, *Blinkfüer*, because of this journal's publications of GDR television programming schedules. Springer threatened its non-complying agents and distributors with a 'revision' of their relationship to the publishing house. The discourse of balancing dominated the whole trajectory of the case. The *Bundesgerichtshof* found that it had to balance *Blinkfüer's* interest in carrying on its business with Springer's right to freedom of expression.[44] *Blinkfüer* then specifically complained that the court's balancing was improper; its own right to freedom of the press had been left out of consideration, while interests not relevant to the dispute had been taken into account.[45] The *Bundesverfassungsgericht* agreed, finding that the *Bundesgerichtshof* had both given too much weight to Springer's right to freedom of expression and too little to *Blinkfüer's* right to freedom of the press.[46]

### (c)  Strains and questions

While the *Spiegel* decision may have offered a resounding confirmation of the Court's line on balancing, the decision also clearly showed the first significant limitations to the model announced in *Lüth*.[47] One important question raised by the *Spiegel* case was what to do with the *Lüth* approach in cases that did not principally involve conflicts between two individuals. Both *Lüth* and 'Plakaten' had, of course, concerned claims in tort. And *Schmid-Spiegel*, while a criminal law case, also involved a

[41]  See e.g. BVerfGE 12, 113; 120 (*Schmid-Spiegel*) [1961].
[42]  BVerfGE 7, 198; 229 [1958].
[43]  BVerfGE 25, 256 (*Blinkfüer*) [1969]. See Klein (1971), pp. 145ff.
[44]  BVerfGE 25, 256; 261 [1969]. See also Schlink (1976), p. 25 (noting that the *Bundesgerichtshof* had specifically tried to follow the *Lüth* decision).
[45]  BVerfGE 25, 256; 261 [1969].
[46]  BVerfGE 25, 256; 263ff [1969]. For an English translation of parts of the decision, see Kommers & Miller (2012), pp. 454–58.
[47]  See, e.g., Bernstein (1967), p. 561 ('serious crisis').

defamation-type action.[48] The *Spiegel* decision was the first time the balancing model had to cope directly with predominantly 'public' or societal interests, like public security and criminal procedure.

This new setting had implications not only for the kinds of interests and values the Court's approach was supposed to accommodate, but also for conceptual understandings of that approach itself. Pre-*Spiegel*, commentators could maintain that the 'private' setting of the relevant free speech cases might have contributed to the Court's resort to balancing. Or even that the basis for the Court's balancing did not lie in constitutional law at all, but within the relevant private law norms on defamation (*Lüth*) or on property ('*Plakaten*').[49] After the *Spiegel* decision, maintaining that what the Court did was somehow private law balancing in a constitutional context, rather than apply a principle emanating directly from constitutional law itself, a '*verfassungsimmanentes Prinzip*',[50] became much more difficult. A place now had to be found for balancing within the confines of constitutional law.

Secondly, and most problematically, the *Lüth* line offered very little guidance as to what lower courts actually were to do in concrete cases and as to what the *Bundesverfassungsgericht*'s review of decisions of other courts would look like. If an inferior court did not refer to a balancing of competing interests, would that *by itself* render its decision constitutionally infirm?[51] If a lower court did balance explicitly, how would the *Bundesverfassungsgericht* review its decision? Would the Court undertake a *de novo* weighing of its own, or invalidate only those outcomes that were manifestly unsound? To use the vocabulary of US constitutional law: the *Lüth* line of decisions contained virtually no information as to the appropriate standard of review. It was this last problem that was to trouble the Court in particular in the decade following the *Spiegel* case.

### (d)    '*Mephisto*' (1971), *Lebach* (1973) and *Deutschland Magazin* (1976)

The *Blinkfüer* case takes analysis of the *Bundesverfassungsgericht*'s free speech jurisprudence to the end of the 1960s. The leading cases of the years that followed show both change and continuity relative to the approach set out in *Lüth* and its progeny. In terms of change, the Court

---

[48]  *Ibid.*, p. 560.
[49]  See, e.g., Bettermann (1964), p. 608.
[50]  See, e.g., Müller (1966), p. 211.
[51]  See, e.g., Bernstein (1967), p. 560.

began to insist, in cases of the early 1970s, on the limited nature of its review of the decisions of the ordinary courts. In 'Mephisto', for example, the 'majority' wrote: 'The Federal Constitutional Court, by its nature as a remedial court, is not competent to put its own valuation of the individual case in place of the ordinarily competent judge'.[52] This more deferential approach had as its result, most notably in 'Mephisto' itself and in Lebach, that the decisions of the ordinary courts were upheld. In both these cases, the freedom of expression lost out in a clash with rights of personal integrity and reputation.[53] This approach was not uncontroversial. In the 'Mephisto' case, for example, Judge Stein wrote a dissenting opinion in which he emphasized the duty of the Bundesverfassungsgericht to 'verify independently' whether the civil courts had properly carried out 'the required balancing'.[54]

Much, however, also stayed the same in these cases, with the Court continuing to frame the analytical framework for freedom of expression analysis in terms heavily reliant on the language of balancing. In 'Mephisto', the 'majority' described its task as 'to decide whether the [lower] courts, in the balancing [...] that they have undertaken, have respected the relevant principles'.[55] And in Lebach, the Court was similarly explicit in its references to the need for a 'Güterabwägung im konkreten Fall', a balancing of values in each specific case.[56] In its decision in Deutschland Magazin, the Bundesverfassungsgericht shifted away from the more deferential position taken in 'Mephisto' and Lebach, adopting a flexible position whereby the intensity of review would itself be dependent on 'the severity of the encroachment upon a basic right'.[57] The language of balancing remained dominant throughout this decision, and in those that followed it and that similarly adopted this flexible approach to the intensity of scrutiny.[58] In fact, in now proclaiming that not only the scope of constitutional rights themselves but also the scope of review of infringements of these rights were matters of relative

---

[52] BVerfGE 30, 173; 197 ('Mephisto') [1971]. The decision was 3–3, which meant the ordinary court's decision was upheld. For a discussion in English, see Krotoszynski (2006), pp. 104ff.
[53] Cf. Kommers (1997), pp. 377ff; Quint (1989), pp. 302ff.
[54] BVerfGE 30, 173; 200 [1971].
[55] BVerfGE 30, 173; 195 [1971].
[56] BVerfGE 35, 202; 221 (Lebach) [1973].
[57] BVerfGE 42, 143; 148 (Deutschland Magazin) [1976] ('die Intensität der Grundrechtsbeeinträchtigung'). This translation: Kommers & Miller (2012), p. 461–62.
[58] See, e.g., BVerfGE 66, 116 (Springer/Walraff) [1984].

weight and importance, the *Bundesverfassungsgericht* had arguably even extended the hold of the language and imagery of balancing over free speech law.

## C. Contemporary critiques of the *Lüth* line on balancing

### 1. Introduction

While *Lüth* proved profoundly influential for the development of freedom of expression adjudication and for constitutional rights adjudication more broadly, the decision and the balancing language it employed also quickly came under fire from critics. This section aims to offer a first sense of what the ensuing debates looked like.

It is useful to begin this exploration with the basic question 'what did contemporary commentators think balancing *was*'? Apart from a minority line of scholarship that sought to cast the *Bundesverfassungsgericht*'s balancing language as mere (misleading) rhetoric,[59] commentators predominantly interpreted balancing on two levels: those of constitutional theory and of (constitutional) legal reasoning.[60] The Court itself, of course, clearly saw balancing on the first of these levels, propagating balancing as part and parcel of an overarching constitutional theoretical construct. That construct was the 'objective value order', first announced in *Lüth*. This 'value order' and its relation to balancing will be discussed in more detail in Sections D and E. For now, it is important to note only the striking contrast between the Court's own emphatic commitment to balancing as constitutional theory, and the precarious position of these ideas within scholarly critique. Today, after more than half a century of '*Wertordnungsjudikatur*', the *Lüth* turn to value balancing is seen as simultaneously 'factually irreversible' and 'highly insecure in its dogmatic foundations'.[61] That assessment also seems an adequate description of the early reactions. Perhaps out of a sense of resignation, but probably also for reasons having to do with a widely shared scholarly commitment to *constructive* criticism, there seems to have been less of a sustained, vigorous

---

[59] Notably: Arndt (1966), pp. 869, 872ff. Also, to some extent, Schlink (1976). For these writers, what the Court had actually, and mistakenly, done in the leading cases was to 'valuate the use' made of the freedom of speech (a '*Gebrauchsbewertung*').

[60] Roughly: '*Verfassungsdogmatik*' and '*Grundrechtstheorie*' on the one hand, and '*Methode*', '*Auslegungslehre*' or '*Grundrechtsinterpretation*' on the other.

[61] Rensmann (2007), pp. 1–2.

questioning of this aspect of the Court's balancing approach than might have been expected.[62] The work of those authors that did voice this type of foundational critique – Ernst Forsthoff and Ernst-Wolfgang Böckenförde most notably – is also discussed in the next section.

Most authors, however, chose to discuss the Court's balancing on the level of (constitutional) legal reasoning or method.[63] A sampling of their thinking is presented here. Commentators working on this conceptual level tended to be preoccupied with projects of salvaging and disciplining elements of the Court's work. There were persistent attempts to rescue some basic ideas of balancing from the case law. These efforts often required *recasting* the Court's approach, sometimes in ways that sat distinctly uncomfortably with some of its explicit language. Many authors were also committed to projects of 'disciplining' *Bundesverfassungsgericht* balancing, often under the heading of '*Verwissenschaftlichung*' ('rendering more scientific'). These projects took two principal forms. Some espoused technical suggestions for a more structured form of weighing and evaluating. Others, finally, turned to newly discovered standards for 'good' legal reasoning.

## 2. 'Verwissenschaftlichung' *(I): a more structured balancing*

In a 1959 essay, Ernst Forsthoff, at the time one of Germany's leading administrative and constitutional law scholars, laid down an explosive challenge. The methods of the *Bundesverfassungsgericht*, he wrote, put the decade-old constitutional order in danger of 'dissolution', or even 'decomposition' ('*Auflösung*').[64] The Court's approach, based on 'value analysis and value balancing', was no longer a 'legal method' ('*juristische Methode*'), but had to be located within the realm of the humanities ('*Geisteswissenschaften*').[65] In an oft-quoted admonition that channelled familiar nineteenth-century sensibilities, Forsthoff wrote: 'Legal science destroys itself when it does not adhere stringently to the position that legal

---

[62] For a typical statement, see, e.g., Hesse (1975), p. 4 (the idea of the constitution as a value system 'raises more questions than it can possibly answer'). See also Rensmann (2007), p. 1 (resignation or triumphalism). On the role of constructive criticism as part of a broader 'aspirational constitutional legalism', see Chapter 5, Section E.1.

[63] Even the fundamental Forsthoff and Böckenförde critiques largely played out on this level. See Forsthoff (1959); Böckenförde (1974) (joint discussion of '*Grundrechtstheorie*' and '*Grundrechtsinterpretation*').

[64] Forsthoff (1959), p. 150. The essay was published in a Festschrift dedicated to Carl Schmitt, of whom Forsthoff had been a student. On Schmitt see further Chapter 3, Section D.

[65] Ibid., pp. 135–38. '*Geisteswissenschaftlich*' is sometimes also translated as 'idealist'.

interpretation is the determination of the correct deduction in the sense of syllogistic reasoning'.[66]

Forsthoff's comprehensive critique of the *Bundesverfassungsgericht*'s methods in terms of a perilous 'deformalization of the Constitution' was in many ways an outlier. And most authors clearly thought that his proposed remedy, a return to the classic Savignian rules of interpretation, was anachronistic and impracticable.[67] But, equally, and in a more general sense, Forsthoff's call for methodologically pure, disciplined juristic thinking in constitutional rights law struck a chord with many of his contemporaries.[68]

A first set of responses to Forsthoff's challenge focused on how the Court's balancing could be made more structured and less particularistic.[69] One prominent author taking this line was Roman Herzog, the later President of the *Bundesverfassungsgericht*. Herzog conceded that a balancing between competing goods on some abstract level was generally '*unumgänglich*' ('unavoidable'),[70] but attacked the individualized nature of the Court's balancing. In his leading commentary on Art. 5 Basic Law, Herzog noted how in the *Lüth* case, the Court did not undertake 'a balancing of legal values' ('*Güterabwägung*'), but rather a balancing of the opposing interests of two individuals ('*Interessenabwägung*').[71] This particularized weighing, he argued, posed a threat to legal certainty and enabled an inappropriate arrogation of judicial power to evaluate the merits of State action on an ad hoc basis.[72] Herzog instead pleaded for a more structured approach, to be undertaken in two steps. In a first stage, the Court should only look at the value of the competing '*Rechtsgüter*' ('legally protected values or interests') in the abstract. A second step should then take into account what Herzog called the '*Gefahrenintensität*', the degree to which the abstract value was threatened in the circumstances of a particular

---

[66]  *Ibid.*, p. 135. See also Forsthoff (1963), pp. 178ff. See also Esser (1970), p. 165.

[67]  See, e.g., Larenz (1975), p. 149. Interestingly, Forsthoff himself qualified '*Wertabwägung*' as an anachronistic remnant from the Weimar era. See Forsthoff (1961), p. 169. On the Weimar roots of 'balancing of values', see Chapter 3, Section D.

[68]  See, e.g., Hollerbach (1960), p. 254; Ehmke (1963), p. 64; Kriele (1967).

[69]  See, e.g., Lerche (1961), p. 150; Bettermann (1964), pp. 602ff ('casuistry ... in the place of constitutional interpretation'); Scheuner (1965), p. 82 ('*individualisierende Güterabwägung*'); Klein (1971), p. 151.

[70]  Herzog (1968), no. 252.

[71]  *Ibid.*

[72]  *Ibid.* See also Lerche (1961), p. 150 (the '*Gesetzesvorbehalt*' of Art. 5 GG has become an '*Urteilsvorbehalt*').

case.[73] Such a phased review of '*Schutzgut*' and '*Gefährdungsgrad*', the value to be protected and the severity of the threat, would mean drawing the 'principle of necessity' ('*Erforderlichkeitsprinzip*'), familiar from other areas of constitutional jurisprudence, into the area of free speech.[74]

Herzog's theory, then, entailed a representative effort to discipline, or formalize, judicial balancing through a framework of 'steps' or 'stages'. In this sense, it was a clear precursor to the work of authors who increasingly came to see balancing as related to, or as part of, a comprehensive three-step proportionality model.[75] One delicate problem facing their efforts, of course, was that this reading was difficult to square with what the Court itself had been saying in *Lüth* or in any of the other early freedom of expression cases.

### 3. '*Verwissenschaftlichung*' *(II): dialectical rationality and topical reasoning*

Among writers on balancing of the early 1960s, one widely shared impression was the idea that some form of malaise in constitutional legal scholarship was at least partly to blame for defects in the Court's approach. 'Theoretical scholarship has, until now, hardly offered any truly useful assistance to the courts', wrote Friedrich Müller in 1966, summing-up this sentiment.[76] What was called for, then, was '*hermeneutische Präzisierung*', hermeneutical clarification and sharpening to be offered, naturally, by academics.[77] These two convictions help explain why authors asked for their contributions to be understood 'not as criticism of the Court, but as a call to persevere in efforts to create a consistent, convincing constitutional dogmatics'.[78]

Intriguingly, the quest for such 'hermeneutical sharpening' took an exciting new turn just around the time the *Bundesverfassungsgericht* first began to invoke balancing.

---

[73] Herzog (1968), no. 267. For an earlier effort in this direction in the field of private law, see Hubmann (1956), pp. 110ff ('*Interessennähe*' and '*Interessenintensität*').

[74] *Ibid.* This last element, though not the abstract balancing of Herzog's first stage, is endorsed in Schlink (1976), pp. 198ff.

[75] See, e.g., Ossenbühl (1995), p. 905. On this transformation see also Schlink (1976), pp. 59ff, 143ff.

[76] Müller (1966), p. 211.

[77] *Ibid.*, p. 212. See also Schneider (1963), p. 15 (call for methods that are 'theoretically-scientifically secure'); Kriele (1967), p. 17 ('*Alles, was dazu nötig ist, ist eine Methodenlehre*').

[78] Ehmke (1963), p. 59; Roellecke (1976), pp. 24, 49.

## (a)  New standards for legal reasoning

The advent of balancing in *Bundesverfassungsgericht* case law coincided with the rise of new ways of thinking about what good legal reasoning should look like. By the early 1960s, the classical ideal of formal rationality in law as espoused by Forsthoff was coming under increasing pressure.[79] The classical orthodoxy of the '*Subsumtions positivismus*' presented an unattractive dilemma. Legal reasoning was either fully rational and conclusive, an 'impossible demand', or it was left 'hopelessly in the hands of arbitrariness and convenience'.[80] To escape this dilemma, constitutional lawyers increasingly turned to theories of what was called 'dialectical' or 'topical' reasoning. These theories were first developed by private law scholars and by philosophers in the course of the 1950s.[81] What they had in common was an abject rejection of formal-logical rationality as an appropriate ideal for legal reasoning; an opening-up of legal argumentation to new sources of input beyond merely legal norms; and, most comprehensively, a new emphasis on legal argumentation as a practical discipline aimed at *convincing* rather than at proving.[82] Only a few years after the *Lüth* decision, public lawyers began to tap the work of these private law thinkers and philosophers to develop a new conception for rationality in constitutional legal reasoning. And so, when the German Association of Constitutional Law Scholars met in Freiburg for their 1961 annual assembly to discuss 'Principles of Constitutional Interpretation', the first such plenary discussion since *Lüth*, the ideas of 'dialectical rationality' and 'topical reasoning' stood at the centre of attention.[83]

These theories brought with them at least two perspectival changes highly relevant to the scholarly reception of *Bundesverfassungsgericht* balancing. To begin with, they offered new standards for the evaluation of the Court's work. Out went the Weberian logical formalism of Laband, von

---

[79]  See, e.g., the opening lines of Kriele's *Theorie der Rechtsgewinnung*: 'The classic conception in German constitutional legal thinking of the nature of "juristic method" [...] is so alien to the new realities of constitutional adjudication that it is in real danger of making impossible demands.' Kriele (1967), p. 5.

[80]  *Ibid.*, p. 54.

[81]  See, e.g., Viehweg (1953); Esser (1956); Gadamer (1960); and the 1958 essay in Perelman & Olbrechts-Tyteca (1963). All invoked Aristotle on rhetoric and argumentation. Esser also sought inspiration in common law legal reasoning.

[82]  See, e.g., Viehweg (1953), p. 85; Esser (1956), pp. 48, 53; Larenz (1960), p. 136; Kriele (1967), p. 106; Larenz (1975), p. 139; Di Cesare (2009), p. 112.

[83]  See Schneider (1963); Ehmke (1963). See also von Pestalozza (1963), pp. 427ff (referring to Gadamer, Esser and Viehweg); Scheuner (1965), p. 38.

Gerber and Forsthoff.[84] In came the idea that judicial reasoning had to be 'optimally susceptible to debate', the aim of *'maximale Diskutierbarkeit'*, and 'convincing' according to a 'consensus of all rational and reasonable individuals'.[85] They also suggested a new purpose for legal reasoning generally: the goal of the *'Aktualisierung'* ('actualization') or *'Konkretisierung'* ('concretization') of legal norms.[86] This meant determining the content and 'the reality' of norms anew in each case, 'bound by particular rules of art, certainly, but always with the aim of *actuality'*.[87] Interpreters continuously had to try to bridge gaps between legislative ideals and social reality, and between past, present and future.

### (b)  Balancing and the new standards

Many influential scholars of constitutional law embraced at least some of the new thinking on topical reasoning.[88] Konrad Hesse, a later judge on the *Bundesverfassungsgericht*, noted in his widely used textbook that *'Verfassungsinterpretation ist Konkretisierung'* ('constitutional interpretation *is* concretization').[89] And so the question arises of how the *Bundesverfassungsgericht*'s balancing fared when judged on the new dialectical, or topical, standards.

The short answer is: not very well. There was, to be sure, the odd positive appraisal. Ulrich Scheuner, for example, in a 1963 lecture argued that the critique of 'logical deduction' and the project of 'concretization', when taken together, could only point to 'the importance of balancing the relevant ethical principles as well as the social interests concerned in the interpretation of fundamental rights'.[90] Scheuner was therefore glad to observe 'a clear commitment to the modern methods of interpretation' in the free speech case law of the *Bundesverfassungsgericht*.[91]

But for many authors the Court's balancing simply 'did not convince'.[92] Take Friedrich Müller's wide-ranging 1966 study on the structure of

---

[84] Schneider (1963), pp. 34–35; Ehmke (1963), p. 71. See also Forsthoff (1959), p. 151 (discussion of Weber), and Chapter 2, Section B.

[85] Schneider (1963), p. 35.

[86] See, e.g., von Pestalozza (1963), pp. 427ff. See also Engisch (1953); Gadamer (1960), p. 307; Lerche (1961), pp. 229ff; Müller (1966).

[87] Von Pestalozza (1963), pp. 427ff.

[88] But see Kriele (1967), p. 115 (Freiburg lectures met mostly with *'abwartende Zurückhaltung'*, or reticence).

[89] Hesse (1993), nos. 60, 61ff, 67 (The first edition of Hesse's textbook dates from 1967). See also, e.g., Roellecke (1976), pp. 23, 29.

[90] Scheuner (1965), p. 55.    [91] *Ibid.*, pp. 61ff.

[92] Roellecke (1976), p. 29.

constitutional norms, for example. For Müller, the central question was 'how the goods to be balanced may be rationally described and valuated in a verifiable and truly inter-subjectively debatable way'.[93] Müller's criterion of the 'potential for inter-subjective deliberation' was clearly inspired by the scholarship on new forms of rationality. And it was on this standard that he found the Court's balancing deficient. The *Bundesverfassungsgericht's* balancing, he wrote, was 'virtually unverifiable'; its decisions were pronounced in a way that was '*kaum anders als affirmativ*', scarcely different from merely propositional.[94]

Balancing's cardinal sin was to reduce judicial decision making to a '*Wettlauf*', a shouting match between the parties, with the Court cutting off the formulation of claims by way of an 'abrupt' decision, in direct violation of the rules for forming agreement that were so central to the newer theories.[95] Balancing decisions, in short, did not rest on rational, inter-subjective deliberation, but merely posited '*ein Wort* [...] *gegen ein anderes Wort*'.[96]

This widespread rejection is particularly striking given how easy it is, in the abstract, to think of ways in which balancing and the standards of dialectical rationality could prove an almost ideal match. Balancing might be taken to open up judicial argumentation to the broader range of input that the dialectical scholars were keen on promoting. Balancing could also, again in theory, be a good fit for an understanding of legal reasoning as aimed at convincing rather than proving. These intuitive connections, together with the overwhelmingly constructive stance of German constitutional legal scholarship alluded to earlier, may explain a second important line in the literature: contributions that, while critical, sought to *recast* the Court's balancing in an idealized form to match dialectical or topical standards.[97]

The most influential attempt along these lines came from Konrad Hesse. In his constitutional law textbook, Hesse adopted the basic tenets of 'topical reasoning' as the foundations for his approach to constitutional interpretation – an approach he labelled simply '*Konkretisierung*'.[98] One

---

[93]  Müller (1966), p. 211.

[94]  Müller (1966), pp. 209ff. See also, e.g., Klein (1971), p. 155.

[95]  Schnur (1965), pp. 127ff. See also Müller (1966), pp. 209–11.

[96]  *Ibid.*, p. 209 (roughly translated as 'one person's word against another's').

[97]  See, e.g., Roellecke (1976), pp. 29–30, 38ff (likening the Court's actual balancing approach to nineteenth-century formalism, but considering that the '*Güterabwägungstopos*' could be developed into a '*legitime Argumentationsfigur*').

[98]  See, e.g., Hesse (1975), pp. 22–26.

of the relevant '*topoi*' or '*Konkretisierungselemente*' for the Court to consider was '*das Prinzip praktischer Konkordanz*' ('the principle of mutual
accommodation').[99] This principle required the 'establishment of a proportional correlation between individual rights and community interests' and was aimed at the 'optimization' of competing values.[100] While
much of this was superficially close to the Court's own language, Hesse
was at pains to distinguish his proposal from what he described as the
*Bundesverfassungsgericht*'s 'overly hasty' and 'excessively formal' abstract
balancing of values.[101]

In the end, these various projects to discipline the Court's reasoning
were in important ways similar. Some relied on the analytical constraints
of 'steps' or 'stages' (e.g. Herzog), while others invoked certain rules of art
for rational deliberation (e.g. Hesse). They tended to retain much of the
Court's balancing language, but ignored some of its component elements,
rejected others outright and sought to reframe the remainder in ways
more in keeping with their own theories.

## D.   The material Constitution

A view of the Constitution as a system of substantive values 'commands the
general support of German constitutional theorists, notwithstanding the
intense controversy, on and off the bench, over the application of the theory to specific situations'.[102] Again and again, the *Bundesverfassungsgericht*
has confirmed the value-based nature of the Basic Law, while academic
commentators have incessantly stressed the dependency of the German
constitutional framework on '*inhaltliche Legitimation*' – substantive legitimization.[103] This constitutional 'value order', or the 'material'
Constitution, is one of two elements that make up the idea of the 'perfect
constitutional order'.[104] That idea, in turn, as claimed at the outset of this

---

[99] Hesse (1993), nos. 67, 72.
[100] *Ibid.*, no. 318. This translation: Marauhn & Ruppel (2008), pp. 280ff.
[101] *Ibid.*, no. 72.
[102] Kommers (1997), p. 47. See also Böckenförde (1974); Roellecke (1976), p. 36 (material
    understanding of the Constitution 'forcefully supported by the dominant strands of
    constitutional theory'); Stern (1993), p. 23; Lindner (2005), p. 13.
[103] See, e.g., BVerfGE 2, 1; 12 ('*SRP-Verbot*') [1952]; BVerfGE 5, 85; 134 ('*KPD Verbot*')
    [1956]; BVerfGE 7, 98; 205 (*Lüth*) [1958]; BVerfGE 10, 59; 81 ('*Elterliche Gewalt*') [1959];
    BVerfGE 12, 113; 124 (*Schmid-Spiegel*) [1961]. For commentary, see, e.g., Ehmke (1963),
    p. 72; Badura (1976); Schlink (1976), p. 24.
[104] The other being the 'comprehensive constitutional order'. See Chapter 3, Section E.

chapter, captures much of what is salient about the 'German' meaning of balancing during the late 1950s and the 1960s.

The relationship between material constitutionalism and balancing is of a dual nature. On the one hand, as will be argued in this section, a material understanding of the Constitution informs much of the *Bundesverfassungsgericht*'s balancing discourse. This means that the Court's use of balancing can only really be understood against this particular background.[105] At the same time, the discourse of balancing itself is one of the primary manifestations and instruments of material constitutionalism. That means, in turn, that an account of one of the dominant strands in modern German constitutional legal thought would be incomplete without an examination of balancing discourse.

## 1.   Weimar origins: freedom of expression and the 'allgemeine Gesetze'

There is an intimate historical connection between the very foundations of material constitutionalism generally and the *Bundesverfassungsgericht*'s turn to balancing in *Lüth* specifically. To begin to explore that connection, it may be helpful to recall that Art. 5 of the 1949 Basic Law establishes that the right to freedom of expression may be limited by '*allgemeine Gesetze*', 'general laws'. It was in the specific context of interpreting this limitation clause that the Court first resorted to the language of balancing in *Lüth*.[106]

The wording of Art. 5, acknowledged early on as among the most complicated and controversial provisions of the Basic Law,[107] was taken from the corresponding article on freedom of expression in the Constitution of the Weimar Republic. That earlier provision, Art. 118 of the *Weimarer Reichsverfassung* (WRV), had itself already occasioned 'many scholarly controversies' during the life of the Republic.[108] There were two main approaches in the literature of the time to the meaning of the *allgemeine Gesetze* clause. The contribution on Art. 118 WRV by Kurt Häntzschel to the authoritative Anschütz-Thoma *Handbuch des Deutschen Staatsrechts*

---

[105]  Cf. Roellecke (1976), p. 36.

[106]  See Chapter 3, Section B.1.

[107]  Herzog (1968), no. 234.

[108]  Ridder (1954), p. 281; Schmitt (1928), p. 167 ('unclear and failed wording'). Art. 118 WRV proclaimed: 'Every German has the right, within the limitations of the general laws, to express his opinion.'

is representative of the reigning view.[109] That position was powerfully challenged in a 1927 address by Rudolf Smend, then professor in Berlin.[110]

This section returns to what at first glance may appear as a narrow debate on an arcane issue of Weimar constitutional law. But, for all its technicality, this was also a debate that perhaps more than any other captured the state of constitutional legal thinking right up to 'the moment when darkness came over German thought'.[111] It was to these discussions that the *Bundesverfassungsgericht* turned for inspiration in the *Lüth* decision, where it quoted both Smend and Häntzschel at length. The 'Smend-Häntzschel debate', therefore remains indispensable to any exploration of the foundations of material constitutionalism, and of its deep imprint on postwar legal thinking.

(a)   The reigning view: definitional, categorical, formal

The dominant approach to the interpretation of the *allgemeine Gesetze* clause during the Weimar era was definitional, categorical and, in a sense, absolute. Commentators attempted to develop a precise definition of '*allgemein*' that would allow for a straightforward determination of the boundaries of a category of permissible limiting laws. The main criterion for most writers was whether or not limiting laws had as their objective the limiting of the freedom of expression – whether they were 'directed against the expression of an opinion *as such*'.[112] As long as the purpose of legislative action was not the prevention of the expression of (certain kinds of) opinions, Art. 118 WRV imposed no limitations on the nature and intensity of the effect these laws could have on freedom of expression.[113] There was, in particular, no room for an assessment of the kinds of goals legislatures would be allowed to promote, or of the importance of these goals, either independently or relative to the value of freedom of expression. As Roman Herzog put it later, in somewhat anachronistic language, this meant that 'in all cases of conflict, the fundamental right of freedom of expression had to give way to any other kind of "*Rechtsgut*", no matter how insignificant'.[114]

---

[109]   Häntzschel (1932), no. 105.    [110]   Smend (1928a).

[111]   Ridder (1954), p. 282. See also von Mangoldt-Klein (1957), p. 250; Nipperdey (1964), p. 448; Lerche (1961), pp. 10ff; Bettermann (1964); Schnur (1965), pp. 124ff; Bernstein (1967); Herzog (1968), nos. 241ff; Klein (1971), pp. 150ff.

[112]   Anschütz, cited in von Mangoldt-Klein (1957), p. 250 (emphasis added in translation). See also Rothenbücher (1928), pp. 20ff; Schmitt (1928), p. 167.

[113]   See also *Reichsgericht* (4th Penal Senate) 24 May, 1930, cited in Häntzschel (1932), p. 660.

[114]   Herzog (1968), no. 243.

Starting from a subtly different angle, Kurt Häntzschel came to a very similar result with regard to the scope of protection of Art. 118 WRV. Häntzschel began, not with a definition of the limitations – the *allgemeine Gesetze* – as other mainstream writers had done, but of the right itself: '*das Recht der freien Meinungsäußerung*' ('the right of freedom of expression'). For Häntzschel, the general laws could limit the right to freedom of expression to that which was '*begriffsnotwendig*' ('conceptually indispensable') for an expression of opinion even to exist.[115] The essence of this freedom was to 'work spiritually', by convincing others of the rightness of one's views.[116] The core objective of Art. 118 WRV, then, had to be to ensure that 'the spiritual should not be repressed because of its mere spiritual effects'.[117]

Any form of expression that went beyond this spiritual essence, would assume the character of a '*Handlung*' ('act') rather than a mere '*Äußerung*' ('expression'). In that case, laws to address the 'direct negative material consequences' of such an act without regard to the underlying opinion would be allowed. On such legislation, Art. 118 WRV imposed no further constraints.[118]

### (b)    Smend's challenge: '*materiale Allgemeinheit*'

In his 1927 address, Smend launched a comprehensive assault on the reigning views. He rejected these as being 'individualistic' and absolutistic because of their attempts to compartmentalize social relations into distinct, absolute 'spheres of will' ('*Willenssphären*').[119] Smend, instead, proposed an understanding of the *allgemeine Gesetze* clause that was in important ways 'material' and 'relative'. This proposal emanated from Smend's broader 'integration' theory of the Constitution, described most comprehensively in *Verfassung und Verfassungsrecht* (1928).[120] That theory held that the 'essence' of the State is the constant integration of individuals into a community.[121] The very existence of the State has to be found in the permanent, repeated 'actualization' of the values of such a

---

[115] Häntzschel (1932), p. 659.
[116] *Ibid.*    [117] *Ibid.*
[118] *Ibid.*, pp. 660–61. Häntzschel's theory incorporated elements of what in American law would later be known as the speech/action and the 'content-neutral'/'content-based' dichotomies.
[119] Smend (1928a), pp. 93ff. See also Korioth (2000), p. 246. On 'spheres of will' see also Chapter 2, Section B. 5.
[120] Smend (1928b). Translated (in part) in Korioth (2000).
[121] Korioth (2000), p. 218; Stolleis (2004), p. 165. On similar ideas in the earlier work of Erich Kaufmann, see, e.g., Häberle (1962), p. 161. See also Dani (2009).

community, in what Smend called an 'actualization of meaning'.[122] Smend was very clear that there could be no question of 'integration' in this sense 'without a substantive community of values'.[123]

This value-based conception of the State had important implications for constitutional interpretation generally, and for the meaning of constitutional rights in particular. First, as constitutional law has as its object 'the totality of the State and the totality of its process of integration' all its particulars 'are to be understood not as isolated, by themselves, but only as elements in a universe of meaning'.[124] The task for constitutional interpretation then becomes what Smend called the 'geisteswissenschaftliche Entwicklung dieses Systems als die eines geschichtlich begründeten und bedingten geistigen Ganzen' ('the humanities-inspired, not legalistic-technical, development of the culture system as a historically contingent intellectual whole').[125] Constitutional rights, on this view, should be understood as primarily constitutive of the State and of a particular 'Kultursystem', rather than as mere limitations on State authority, as in the liberal tradition.[126] They embody the 'cultural and moral value judgments of an era'.[127]

In his lecture on freedom of expression Smend argued that terms in constitutional rights clauses such as 'allgemein' and its opposite 'besonder', should not be interpreted in a 'formalistic-technical' way, as 'reciprocally empty negations', but rather as interrelated elements reflective of the underlying value-system.[128] The word 'allgemein' was, he argued, mere shorthand for these underlying values. The 'generality' of the 'general laws', then, in Smend's view had to be, 'selbstverständlich' ('obviously'):

> the substantive universality of the Enlightenment: the values of society, public order and security, the competing rights and freedoms of others [...] 'General' laws in the sense of Art. 118 are those laws that have precedence over Art. 118 because the societal good they protect is more important than the freedom of expression.[129]

[122] Korioth (2000), p. 229.   [123] Ibid., pp. 228ff.
[124] Ibid., pp. 241, 246.
[125] Smend (1928a), p. 92. For Ernst Forsthoff's critique see Chapter 3, Section C.
[126] Ibid., pp. 91ff.   [127] Ibid., p. 98.
[128] Smend (1928a), pp. 96–97. See also Stolleis (2004) p. 164.
[129] Ibid., pp. 97–98 ('die materiale Allgemeinheit der Aufklärung [...] Gesetze im Sinne des Art. 118 sind also Gesetze, die deshalb den Vorrang vor Art. 118 haben, weil das von ihnen geschützte gesellschaftliche Gut wichtiger ist als die Meinungsfreiheit') (emphasis added in translation).

What counted for Smend, was the '*materiale Überwertigkeit*', the greater substantive value, of a particular '*Rechtsgut*' in relation to the freedom of expression.[130] In one example from the lecture, the '*Unkritisiertheit der Regierung*', allowing the government to forbid criticism, was, in the early twentieth century, simply no longer a value that deserved precedence over the freedom of expression.[131] Smend acknowledged that this way of looking at the limitations of freedom of expression could seem unorthodox from the perspective of the prevalent 'habitual formalistic mode of thought'.[132] He even admitted that there was an element of circularity to his approach: '*Rechtsgüter*' receive priority over the freedom of expression because they '*deserve*' this precedence.[133] For Smend however, this conscious, explicit, 'taking position' with regard to the 'value constellations' of public life, was precisely what fundamental rights were all about.[134]

2.  Güterabwägung *and* Interessenabwägung: *dissecting the Weimar background to* Lüth*'s balancing approach*

In the *Lüth* case, the *Bundesverfassungsgericht* referred to Smend's formula of a '*Rechtsgut* [...] *dessen Schutz gegenüber der Meinungsfreiheit den Vorrang verdient*' ('a value the protection of which deserves precedence over the freedom of expression') just before drawing its seminal conclusion that a 'balancing of values' would be necessary.[135] This manifest judicial reliance on Smend's interpretation invites a more detailed examination of his thesis through a 'balancing lens'. Was the Court justified in reading ideas of balancing into Smend's writing? Had his contemporaries done so? And one question of particular salience in this respect: How did Smend's approach relate to the *Bundesverfassungsgericht*'s insistence on both a balancing of values *and* a balancing of interests in individual cases in the *Lüth* decision?

(a)   'Balancing' in Smend's work

There is no direct mention of either '*Güterabwägung*' or of '*Interessenabwägung*' in the 1927 address or in *Verfassung und Verfassungsrecht*. Equally, however, Smend's approach clearly differed from the methodologies of his contemporaries in his insistence on the

---

[130]  *Ibid.*    [131]  *Ibid.*    [132]  *Ibid.*
[133]  *Ibid.*    [134]  *Ibid.*
[135]  See Chapter 3, Section B.1.

necessity, and possibility, of carrying out value trade-offs between fundamental rights and other societal goods. Smend's interpretation of the limitations to freedom of expression hinged on the idea that some values are *'wichtiger'* ('more important') than this freedom.[136] Although Smend relied more on the imagery of 'importance' and 'precedence' than on that of 'weight', it is undeniable that his approach involves the search for some sort of accommodation or equilibrium between competing goods, *'gegenüberstehende Werte'*,[137] of the kind that characterizes most approaches covered by balancing discourse. And Smend does in fact resort to this type of discourse at least once, where he uses the term *'Abwägungsverhältnisse'* ('relations of relative weight') to describe the relevant relationships between values.[138] Although there is little explicit discussion in Smend's work of how these trade-offs are to be effectuated, or by whom, a picture emerges of a form of evaluation to be carried out by 'juridical' means, between 'public' goods, in a more or less durable fashion.

First, Smend emphasizes that the question of 'ranking' elements within constitutional law is a 'legal question'.[139] He also repeatedly uses legal terms of art, such as *'juristische Begriffsbestimmung'*.[140] Equally, though, Smend was clear that these questions were not to be approached by way of 'standard' juridical methods. Repeated references to a need for a *'geisteswissenschaftliche'* reading of constitutional texts make that point. On the second issue, the parameters to be evaluated and compared are consistently described as being of a 'public', or 'social', rather than of a private nature. Smend invariably uses terms such as *'Gemeinschaftswerte'* ('communal values'), *'Allgemeininteresse'* ('the general interest') and *'gesellschaftliches Gut'* ('a societal good').[141] Even where the rights and freedoms of other individuals are referred to, it is clear that these are to be understood as reflections of underlying public goods.[142] Smend also emphasizes the 'social character' of the right to freedom of expression itself.[143] In short, in Smend's conception, the scope the freedom of

---

[136] Early critics seized on this. As Michael Stolleis writes, 'to many [*Verfassung und Verfassungsrecht*] seemed like an alarm bell on the dangerous path towards a jurisprudence of evaluation and weighing that was dissolving the secure foundations of scholarly work'. Stolleis (2004), p. 166.

[137] Smend (1928a), p. 106.      [138] *Ibid.*, p. 98.

[139] Smend (1928b), p. 241 (*'eine Rechtsfrage'*). This, against a background understanding of the 'political' nature of constitutional law. See p. 238, *ibid.*

[140] See, e.g., Smend (1928a), p. 98.

[141] *Ibid.*, pp. 96–98.      [142] *Ibid.*

[143] *Ibid.*, p. 95.

expression depends on a trade-off between competing public goods, rather than between (public and) private interests. Finally, on the third point, there are important indications that the required trade-offs are to be made, not from case to case, but rather in the form of more durable relationships ('*Verhältnisse*') of precedence ('*Vorzug*'). Smend's key concept of the '*Kultursystem*' is made up out of '*Wertkonstellationen*' ('constellations of values') that, while historically contingent, consist of more or less stable complexes of value relations; '*Wertrelationen*'.[144] Smend's writing suggests that the trade-offs between freedom of expression and competing social goods are to be determined, in principle, only once for each relationship between two values, and are supposed to be of a lasting nature, at least for as long as no major shifts in the political or cultural situation occur.

### (b)   'Balancing' and Smend's critics

The *Bundesverfassungsgericht*, in the *Lüth* case, was not the first to read balancing ideas into the work of Rudolf Smend. His early critics, Kurt Häntzschel as well as Carl Schmitt, had done exactly the same. For the former, the key to Smend's approach was the idea that the drafters of the Weimar Constitution had neglected their duty to 'equilibrate the various competing legally protected interests'.[145] They had left it, in Häntzschels' depiction of Smend's views, to the legislative and judicial authorities to determine 'in specific cases, which of several legally protected interests' they would regard as more important.[146] 'Undeniably', however, Häntzschel countered, such decisions would depend entirely on the 'internal disposition and worldview' of the deciders.[147] Instead, what had to be recognized was that although the problem was indeed one of finding the 'the correct relationship between values', this decision was not left to the 'free discretion' of judges and lawmakers, but had already been made by the Constitutional drafters.[148]

   Carl Schmitt's critique of Smend used many of the same arguments. For Schmitt, Smend had mistakenly 'introduced a balancing of interests' into the question of the limitations to the freedom of expression. This was an innovation 'that could easily relativize the absolute worth of the value of freedom of expression', counter to the fundamental principle of the *Rechtsstaat* that individual freedom should be rule and limitation by

---

[144]  *Ibid.*, pp. 98, 106.
[145]  Häntzschel (1932), p. 659.
[146]  *Ibid.*   [147]  *Ibid.*   [148]  *Ibid.*

the State the exception.[149] 'A fundamental liberty', such as the freedom of expression, Schmitt wrote, 'is not a right or a value that can be weighed, in a balancing of interests, with other societal goods'.[150]

That Schmitt and Häntzschel would describe and criticize Smend's theory in terms of a balancing of interests in individual cases is understandable, but also problematic. It is understandable, first of all, in that Smend's rejection of the '*begriffliche Formaljurisprudenz*' of the dominant approach closely tracked similar and contemporaneous attacks by the *Interessenjurisprudenz* scholars.[151] And it should not be forgotten that Smend's call for an explicit judicial evaluation of competing legal goods and his terminology of '*Abwägungsverhältnisse*' and '*Wertrelationen*' were to a large extent novel at the time, in particular in the area of public law.[152] It was only in 1927, the year of Smend's address, that the Weimar Supreme Court first used the term '*Güterabwägung*' to describe an explicit trade-off between values.[153] It is understandable, therefore, that his critics would identify Smend's call for an explicit evaluation of competing legal goods with the closest matching model of the time. And, from their perspective, the theories of the *Interessenjurisprudenz* scholars may well have seemed a close parallel.

But Schmitt and Häntzschel's alignment of Smend's thesis with the balancing of interests of the *Interessenjurisprudenz* also significantly misstated the nature of his views. The balancing of interests of Philipp Heck and others, as discussed in Chapter 2, was a legalistic–technical, value-neutral, private-law-oriented method, focused on private interests and designed primarily to effectuate the will of the legislature.[154] Smend's interpretation of the limits to freedom of expression, by contrast, was a humanities-inspired, anti-positivist approach to limiting legislative discretion that depended on taking an explicit position in relation to value choices concerning public goods. Differences between the two approaches, namely Smend's material constitutionalism and *Interessenjurisprudenz*, are visible on many levels. Smend turned to '*Güter*' and '*Werte*' as part of an anti-positivist effort of 'opening-up' constitutional law to a broader

---

[149]  Schmitt (1928), p. 167.

[150]  *Ibid.*, ('*Ein Freiheitsrecht ist kein Recht oder Gut, das mit andern Gütern in eine Interessenabwägung eintreten könnte*').

[151]  Smend (1928a), p. 98.

[152]  References to 'value judgments' had surfaced earlier in private law. See for discussion Zippelius (1962), pp. 3ff.

[153]  Reichsgericht 11 March 1927, RGSt. 61, 254 ('*Pflichten und Güterabwägung*'). Cited in Zippelius (1962), p. 15, and in BVerfG 39, 1; 26–27 ('*Schwangerschaftsabbruch*') [1975].

[154]  See Chapter 2, Section C.3.

range of input than simply posited norms.[155] The *Interessenjurisprudenz* scholars, on the other hand, relied on 'interests' in order to be able to look *behind*, not beyond, these norms. The *Interessenjurisprudenz* saw itself as value neutral, whereas Smend was vocal in his affirmation of the essentially value-laden nature of constitutional law and constitutional interpretation. And the *Interessenjurisprudenz* aimed for interstitial, particularistic judgments, whereas Smend was interested in durable 'constellations of values'.

In short, while it is easy to see how Smend's work could be invoked in support of the *Lüth* Court's '*Güterabwägung*', establishing connections between Smend and a particularized balancing of interests is much more problematic. In Section E in this chapter, I will argue that *Interessenabwägung* in *Bundesverfassungsgericht* case law is in fact best understood not as related to material constitutionalism, but to the idea of the 'comprehensive' constitutional order.

### 3.   'Material' constitutionalism and balancing

When the *Bundesverfassungsgericht* took up its duties, 'it found before it a Constitution closely resembling the classical ideal-type of a liberal *Rechtsstaat*. It was only through the Court's case law that the Basic Law was transformed from this classical liberal framework to a substantive value order. The key to this transformation lies in the *Lüth* decision'.[156]

Although he is often less directly, or at least less polemically, visible than his contemporary, Carl Schmitt, Rudolf Smend's influence can be felt all throughout German postwar constitutional jurisprudence; from the *Lüth* decision of 1958, to, say, the *Lisbon* decision of 2009 and beyond.[157] In *Lüth* itself, the *Bundesverfassungsgericht* built a bridge over the abyss of the Nazi-years to Smend's Weimar-era work on the freedom of expression. That connection, had it concerned the work of any other theorist, and had it been in any other decision, might have remained a mere footnote. Instead, the combination of Smend's stature, the nature

---

[155] Contemporary scholars also involved in this project were Erich Kaufmann, Heinrich Triepel and Hermann Heller. See, e.g., Ehmke (1963), p. 62. Ehmke sees the work of these scholars as confirming his idea that '*verfassungsrechtliches Denken ist Problemdenken*' (*ibid.*). He therefore appears to read Smend *et al.* through the lens of debates of *his* time on the '*topische Jurisprudenz*', (see Chapter 3, Section C.3) in the same way that Schmitt and Häntzschel read Smend through the lens of the key debate of *their* time on *Interessenjurisprudenz*.

[156] Rensmann (2007), p. 1. See also Lindner (2005), pp. 13ff.

[157] See, e.g., Pernice (1995); Lhotta (2005); Dani (2009).

of his work and the *Lüth* Court's ambition meant that Smend's powerful comprehensive constitutional vision, within which his theory of this one particular constitutional right had been embedded, became emblematic for the whole of *Bundesverfassungsgericht*'s constitutional rights jurisprudence.[158] And '*Güterabwägung*', in turn, became emblematic for this, now officially sanctioned, constitutional understanding: the theory of material constitutionalism.

Balancing and material constitutionalism are intimately intertwined. Material constitutionalism is both dependent on and enables an explicitly normative, value-oriented approach to constitutional questions. In a most basic sense, 'balancing' can simply be shorthand for the process of the mutual accommodation of values within this substantive framework. Once constitutional ordering is conceived in terms of substantive values, it becomes natural to understand the question of how demanding each value should be as a relative issue, to be decided in terms of optimization. In addition, the explicitly substantive nature of material constitutionalism means that legitimacy is likely to become more dependent on both input, identifying the appropriate values, and output, achieving their appropriate mutual accommodation, rather than on process and on questions of institutional competence and boundary maintenance. The portrayal in German constitutional discourse of balancing as a 'necessity', and the comparative neglect of the question of *who* should do this weighing, prove an easy fit with these material-constitutionalist ideas.

### E.   The comprehensive constitutional order

#### 1.   Introduction

Analysing the Weimar-era background to the *Lüth* Court's balancing leaves an intriguing question unanswered. If '*Interessenabwägung*' formed no part of material constitutionalism, at least not as espoused by its main early propagator, why did the *Bundesverfassungsgericht*, without so much as acknowledging any potential issues of compatibility or conflict, resort to *both* 'value balancing' and 'balancing of interests in light of all the circumstances of the case' in its early free speech decisions?

---

[158] Postwar authors frequently referred to Smend as the 'nestor' of German constitutional thought. See Forsthoff (1959), p. 133; Arndt (1963), p. 1273; Böckenförde (1974), p. 1534. See also Korioth (2000), p. 212. Ulrich Scheuner, Konrad Hesse and Peter Häberle were among Smend's most influential students. Their work is discussed in the next section.

That question is especially interesting because doing so exposed the Court to criticism from all directions. From one side, commentators intent on enhancing the formal qualities of constitutional jurisprudence accused the Court of going beyond what even Smend had suggested. Where Smend had at least argued for an 'objective comparison of values', the Court practised 'casuistry', replacing a '*Smendian* weighing of values' ('*Smendsche Güterabwägung*') with 'a balancing of interests on the model of private law'.[159] But at the same time, the Court's continued references to '*Güterabwägung*' exposed it to more general critiques of its underlying value-based vision of the Constitution, in ways that a more modest, Heck-style, 'balancing of interests' might not have.[160]

I argue in this section that understanding the Court's continued joint invocation of both value- and interest-balancing requires drawing on a second strand of perfectionist constitutional legal thought; the idea of the comprehensive constitutional order.

The dogma that the Constitution was, or should be, an '*absolut vollständige Oberrechtsordnung*' ('a fully comprehensive overarching legal order') dominated German constitutional thought of the late 1950s and the 1960s.[161] As the *Bundesverfassungsgericht* put it in a 1965 decision, the Basic Law stood for 'a unified ordering of the political and social life of State and society'.[162] This ideal of constitutional 'comprehensiveness' can be divided into the two components of the 'complete' constitution and the 'perfect fit' constitution. Both are closely related to balancing. The idea of the 'complete' constitution, I argue below, invokes balancing in order to encompass all domains of social life within a gapless, internally coherent system. In the 'perfect fit' constitution, on the other hand, the individualized balancing of opposing interests is essential to ensure that constitutional reality matches constitutional demands as closely as possible, in each individual case.

---

[159] Bettermann (1964), pp. 601ff. See also Nipperdey (1964); Lerche (1961), p. 150; Herzog (1968), no. 251.

[160] See, e.g., Goerlich (1973); Böckenförde (1974); Schlink (1976); Alexy (2002), pp. 96ff; Rensmann (2007), p. 96. There was a poignant irony to Gerd Roellecke's charge that the Court's value balancing resembled the '*Inversionsmethode*' Philipp Heck had railed against. See Roellecke (1976), pp. 27, 38. See further Chapter 2, Section B.3. See also Chapter 3, Sections C.2 and C.3 on these authors' projects of reframing the Court's balancing in ways more closely aligned with their own outlook.

[161] See, e.g., Roellecke (1976), p. 33.

[162] BVerfGE 19, 206; 220 ('*Kirchenbausteuer*') [1965].

## 2. The 'complete' Constitution

Constitutional case law and commentary of the 1950s and 1960s commonly depicted the Basic Law as instituting, or as *aspiring* to institute (the anthromorphism itself being characteristic), a comprehensive arrangement without gaps or openings and without internal contradictions.[163] On this view, there are no 'value-less' domains or constitutional black holes. Constitutional rights and values are never entirely absent from any given case. They will merely be more or less demanding depending on the circumstances. Constitutional rights bind all organs of the State in all their activities, and their sphere of influence extends right into the domain of private relations.[164] Indeed, German scholars of the 1960s spoke, not always affectionately, of the *'Allgegenwart des Verfassungsrechts'* ('the omnipresence of constitutional law').[165]

This conception of complete coverage rested on a particular prevalent image of the constitutional order of the Basic Law. That image held that this order was composed of values, organized into a gapless value 'system', and dedicated to the aim of unifying and harmonizing conflicting values and interests within society.

### (a)    The Constitution as a value system

Notwithstanding widespread scholarly scepticism, and occasional fierce criticism,[166] the general notion of the Constitution as a value system was *'ständige façon de parler'* ('the habitual way of framing matters') in *Bundesverfassungsgericht* case law of the 1960s.[167] As such, it was tremendously influential within German constitutional discourse during the period when constitutional balancing came to the fore.[168] While the traditional liberal vision of constitutional rights as protective of 'spheres of freedom' for individuals remained important, the main innovation of German postwar constitutionalism was to acknowledge, as the Court did in *Lüth*, that the Basic Law embodied an objective value system that

---

[163]   See, e.g., Dürig (1958), no. 12. See also, e.g., Schneider (1963), p. 14; Badura (1976), p. 6; Roellecke (1976), p. 39.
[164]   BVerfGE 7, 198; 209 (*Lüth*) [1958].
[165]   Walter Leisner, cited in Ehmke (1963), p. 70ff. See also Leisner (1997), p. 101.
[166]   Notably from Ernst Forsthoff. See Chapter 3, Section C.2. See also Ehmke (1963), p. 82; von Pestalozza (1963), p. 436.
[167]   Böckenförde (1974), p. 1534.
[168]   Böckenförde (1987), p. 67.

'should count as a foundational constitutional resolution for all domains of law'.[169]

One way in which this notion of the Constitution as value system was used to promote complete constitutional coverage was through the elevation of certain values to a primordial status from which they could 'radiate' throughout this order, filling in any potential gaps that might exist between specific provisions.[170] This strategy was pursued principally through the conceptions of *'Menschenwürde'* ('human dignity') and *'das Recht auf freie Entfaltung seiner Persönlichkeit'* (a general 'personality' right) as overarching constitutional principles. One particularly powerful image to emerge from doctrine and case law was that of human dignity as a *'Grundsatznorm für die gesamte Rechtsordnung'*,[171] or, in Günter Dürig's influential formulation, *'eines obersten Konstitutionsprinzip allen objektiven Rechts'*[172] ('a supreme constitutional principle for all law').[173]

The Court's early freedom of expression case law offers numerous examples of the use of human dignity or the personality right of Art. 2 as *'oberste Werte'* ('supreme values'). In some cases these rights are presented as standing at the apex of the rights order, as in the *'Mephisto'* case of 1971, where the Court spoke of the value of human dignity as 'a supreme value, which controls the entirety of the value system of constitutional rights'.[174] At other times, as in the *Lüth* case for example, these values are presented as constituting the core, the *'Mittelpunkt'*, of the constitutional order.[175] These 'supreme value' or 'core value' approaches were one important component of a vision of the constitution as embodying a rights order in which every constitutional right would always be interpreted in light of an overarching general principle, lending the whole a measure of structural integrity that might otherwise have been unavailable.[176] They allowed interpreters and commentators to go beyond the confines of a historically contingent catalogue of rights and of liberalism's one-dimensional, formal insistence on rights as boundaries for governmental power.

---

[169]  BVerfGE 7, 198; 205 (*Lüth*) [1958].
[170]  Dürig (1958), nos. 3–6.
[171]  Von Mangoldt-Klein (1957), p. 146 ('a foundational norm for the whole legal order'). For a recent variation on this idea of 'gaplessness', see Lindner (2005), pp. 212ff.
[172]  Dürig (1956), pp. 119, 122; Dürig (1958), no. 5.
[173]  See for a recent example BVerfGE 115, 118; 152 ('*Luftsicherheitsgesetz*') [2005].
[174]  BVerfGE 30, 173; 192 ('*Mephisto*') [1971]. See also Eberle (2002), p. 258.
[175]  BVerfGE 7, 198; 205 (*Lüth*) [1958]; BVerfGE 35, 202; 225 (*Lebach*) [1973].
[176]  The idea that general principles could help in the construction of 'legal systems' was a popular perspective in German legal thought at the time. See, e.g., Esser (1956), pp. 47, 224ff, 227, 321ff.

The written Constitution, on the system-of-values view, might be incomplete and the catalogue of rights haphazard, but the '*hinter der Verfassung stehende Wertordnung*' ('the value order behind the Constitution') could still be comprehensive.[177]

A related approach to fostering complete constitutional coverage was by way of emphasis on the *systematic character* of the value order.[178] Conceiving of the constitutional value order as a system, rather than as a mere collection of assorted rights and principles further helped imbue this order with a degree of integrity and coherence; '*innere Zusammenhang*'.[179] Alexander Hollerbach eloquently described the way this might work in constitutional jurisprudence: 'The discourse of the value system, first and foremost, has the following meaning: to overcome individualization, to strengthen and make visible connections and relationships that exist between the manifold individual provisions of the Constitution and the legal order as a whole. Every individual element always refers to the overarching whole; is only an individual element by reference to the whole'.[180]

The systematic quality of the '*Wertsystem*' was itself to a large extent dependent on the *Bundesverfassungsgericht*'s interpretation of human dignity as an overarching constitutional principle. By investing each individual constitutional right with a degree of '*Menschenwürdegehalt*', by relating the content of each specific right to the ultimate right of human dignity, this perspective assisted in viewing the constitutional order as a unity within which a presumption of gaplessness could reign.[181]

### (b)    The unitary, harmonizing Constitution

From its earliest decisions onwards the *Bundesverfassungsgericht* took great pains to emphasize the unitary character and harmonizing function of the constitutional order. In its 1951 '*Southwest*' decision, the Court held that individual constitutional provisions could not be interpreted in isolation, but had to be read in light of other constitutional commands and on the basis of a general principle of the '*Einheit der Verfassung*' ('the unity of the Constitution').[182]

---

[177]  Von Pestalozza (1963), p. 436.
[178]  *Ibid.*, (commenting on a pervasive '*Bestreben nach Systematisierung*').
[179]  Canaris (1969), pp. 11–13.
[180]  Hollerbach (1960), p. 255.
[181]  Cf. Leisner (1960), p. 146.
[182]  BVerfGE 1, 14; 32 ('*Südweststaat*') [1951]. See, e.g., Roellecke (1976), p. 33. Even commentators critical of the idea of a value system agreed that the Constitution contained

Often, the effort to promote the image of the constitutional order as a unity took the form of a command to interpret individual norms in light of certain overarching foundational norms and resolutions to which all other constitutional provisions were subordinated. Constitutional law, as the Court held, did not consist merely of individual clauses, but also of 'certain unifying principles and guiding ideas' tying all provisions together.[183] Constitutional doctrine, in a telling phrase that is difficult to translate, insisted on '*Auslegung der Einzelnorm aus der Totalnorm*' ('interpretation of every individual norm by reference to the Constitution's normative whole').[184]

But the significance of these ideas of unity in German constitutional doctrine of the 1950s and 1960s went beyond an understanding of the Constitution as an organized whole. Court and commentators continuously sought to emphasize the actively harmonizing qualities of the constitutional order set up by the Basic Law. The Constitution, on this view, actively aimed to create and foster unity by overcoming fundamental antinomies in law, politics and society. In language again strongly reflective of Smend's integration theory, the value order of the Basic Law was said to have a '*zusammenordnende und einheitsbildende Wirkung*' ('a coordinating and unifying effect').[185]

The idea of the Constitution as a vehicle for harmonization and unification found expression on all levels of constitutional legal theory. The Basic Law as a whole was seen as a grand compromise between philosophical tenets of liberalism, socialism and Christian-Democracy.[186] In case law and theoretical writing, relationships between specific values, rights and interests were given emphasis over potential conflicts. A particularly popular figure of speech was the idea of 'dialectical' relations between opposing constitutional values.[187] Law and freedom, or individuals and

---

a '*sinnvoll zusammengehörige, materiell aufeinander beziehbare Ordnung*'. See Müller (1966), p. 227. On the contrast with the largely 'clause-bound' nature of constitutional interpretation in the US, see Chapter 5, Section B.2.

[183] BVerfGE 2, 380; 403 ('*Haftentschädigung*') [1953].

[184] Von Pestalozza (1963), p. 438, with references. For an example, see BVerfGE 30, 173; 192 ('*Mephisto*') [1971] ('need to uphold the unity of [the] foundational value system' in conflict between personality right and artistic freedom).

[185] See, e.g., Häberle (1962), p. 6; Hesse (1975), p. 5 (both citing Smend). See also Ehmke (1963), p. 77.

[186] See, e.g., Dürig (1958), no. 47 (individualism and collectivism). Critical: Zippelius (1962), p. 157.

[187] Cf. Schneider (1963), pp. 33ff. For another use of the term 'dialectical' see Chapter 3, Section C.3.

society, commentators would argue, were indissolubly linked, in the form of communicating vessels.[188] The *Bundesverfassungsgericht* itself gave expression to this idea several years before the *Lüth* decision. The image of human identity to which the Basic Law adheres, the Court held, 'is not that of an isolated, sovereign, individual. Instead, with regard to the tension individual/society, the Basic Law is committed to the community-embedded and community-bound nature of persons – "*der Gemeinschaftsbezogenheit und Gemeinschaftsgebundenheit der Person*" – without however diminishing their inherent independent value'.[189] 'Competing constitutional values', Peter Häberle argued in the early 1960s using very similar vocabulary, 'are not related in terms of superiority and inferiority, in the sense that they might be "played out" against each other. They are, rather, matched so that each influences the other.'[190]

### (c)    The judicial role (I): optimization

These views of the nature of the constitutional order of the Basic Law – its systematic, integrated and integrating character – came with a particular conception of the task of courts in deciding constitutional rights cases. Two suggestions were particularly prominent in this respect.

The first of these was the idea that courts should, in every case, 'optimize' all competing values involved. If constitutional interpretation should take account of the harmonizing and integrating character of the Constitution, then the ideal solution for any conflict between values would be a '*nach beide Seiten hin schonendsten Ausgleich*' ('an accommodation that would do optimal justice to both values in play').[191] 'The principle of the unity of the Constitution', Konrad Hesse wrote, invests constitutional interpretation with 'a task of *optimization*: both values must be limited in such a way that both may be optimally effective'.[192]

The early freedom of expression case law shows several examples of these ideas of principled compromise, 'adjustment' and optimization. In *Lüth* itself, for example, the Court spoke of a '*Wechselwirkung*', and of a '*verfassungsrechtlich gewollten Ausgleich*' ('an adjustment demanded by the Constitution') between the 'mutually contradictory expanding and

---

[188]  See, e.g., Häberle (1962), pp. 21, 161, 164 ('*Ineinanderstehen* [...] *von Recht und Freiheit*').

[189]  BVerfGE 4, 7; 15 ('*Investitionshilfe*') [1954]. For use of this formula in the freedom of expression context, see, e.g., BVerfGE 30, 173; 193 ('*Mephisto*') [1971].

[190]  Häberle (1962), p. 38.

[191]  Müller (1966), p. 213. See also Scheuner (1965), p. 52.

[192]  Hesse (1975), p. 28 (emphasis added in translation). See also Chapter 3, Section C.3.

limiting tendencies of the right to freedom of expression and the competing constitutional goods protected by the general laws'.[193] The *Lüth* Court
also referred in more general terms to the necessity of an 'equilibration'
and 'balancing' of rights wherever large numbers of people had to live
together in harmony.[194]

### (d)    The judicial role (II): overcoming conflicts

A second set of techniques for enhancing the harmonizing qualities of
the Basic Law rested on the understanding that many apparent conflicts
between opposing values and interests could be reframed so as to lessen
their impact, or even so as to overcome them entirely.

This view had a distinguished pedigree in German legal thought.
Within constitutional law one important forerunner was, again, Smend's
integration theory, and more specifically in the context of constitutional
rights, his insistence that the right to freedom of expression not only protected individuals, but had a clear 'social function'.[195] Other sources of
inspiration were the writings of Erich Kaufmann on constitutional theory, and of Otto von Gierke on private law.[196]

In the 1960s, prominent scholars propounding these ideas included
Eike von Hippel and, especially, Peter Häberle. Von Hippel invoked
Smend and Kaufmann to argue that any constitutional-rights-norm could
be 'valid only to the extent that the interests it protects are not opposed
by higher ranking legal goods'.[197] Individual, isolated, absolute rights
were a conceptual impossibility, von Hippel argued. This was something
that Carl Schmitt, Smend's contemporary adversary, had failed to understand.[198] Adjustment to countervailing values, instead, formed part of the
very essence of constitutional rights.[199] For his part, Peter Häberle claimed
that constitutional rights were 'equally constitutive' for both individuals
and society.[200] Individual and collective interests would always be intertwined in the exercise and the limitation of constitutional rights. Right
and limitation were inextricable linked. Society as a whole would always
be affected by an infringement of a fundamental right of any individual.[201] But also, limitations to individual rights were in fact in the interest

---

[193] BVerfGE 7, 198; 209 [1958].
[194] *Ibid.*, p. 220. See also BVerfGE 35, 202; 225 ('*Lebach*') [1973]; Scheuner (1965), p. 58.
[195] See Chapter 3, Section D.1.
[196] See, e.g., Häberle (1962), pp. 9, 23, 180.
[197] Von Hippel (1965), pp. 25ff.
[198] *Ibid.*, p. 27.      [199] Schnur (1965), pp. 103ff.
[200] Häberle (1962), pp. 8, 21ff.      [201] *Ibid.*

of the concerned individuals *themselves*, as much as they served the public interest.[202]

Again, contemporary *Bundesverfassungsgericht* case law furnishes numerous examples of efforts at overcoming antinomies in this way; between individuals and society, individuals and the State or individuals *inter se*. On a most general level, there was the Court's vision of society as a 'community of free individuals', in which 'the opportunity for individual development' would itself be 'a community-building value'.[203] In the context of freedom of expression, a striking instance of this type of view can be found in the *Spiegel* case. Recall that this case concerned the publication in the magazine *Der Spiegel* of secret material and critical commentary on the readiness of West Germany's defence forces.[204] After reciting *Lüth's* demand for a balancing of opposing values in case of conflict, the Court went on to *deny* the existence of such a conflict altogether. The security of the State and freedom of the press were not in fact contradictory propositions. The two values instead had to be seen as connected to each other, and united in their common higher goal of preserving the Federal Republic and its basic order of freedom and democracy.[205] Without freedom of the press no Republic worth saving; without a secure Republic no freedom of the press, the Court could be read as saying.

### (e) The complete Constitution and balancing

In case law and literature of the 1950s and 1960s, the idea of the Constitution as a comprehensive value system was used to bring all domains of public life, including famously that regulated by private law, within the sphere of influence of fundamental rights. The idea of this value-based Constitution as a framework for harmonization and unification – or integration, in Smend's terminology – served as the foundation

---

[202] *Ibid.*, pp. 12, 28 (a '*Wechselwirkung*' between individuals and society). Häberle was concerned that an excessively wide interpretation of constitutional rights would undermine their societal acceptance.

[203] BVerfGE 12, 45; 54 ('*Kriegsdienstverweigerung*') [1960], cited in Badura (1976), p. 6. See also, ambivalently, Schneider (1963), pp. 31ff ('*gemeinschaftsbezogenheit des Menschen*'); Schnur (1965), p. 104 ('*gleiche Legimitation*' of individual freedom and the interests of society).

[204] See Chapter 3, Section B.2. For a recent discussion of this line of thinking, see Rusteberg (2009), pp. 44ff.

[205] BVerfGE 20, 162, 178 [1966]. Translation in Kommers & Miller (2012), p. 506 ('[S]tate security and the freedom of the press are not mutually exclusive principles. Rather, they are complementary, in that both are meant to preserve the Federal Republic'.)

for a range of attempts to overcome basic antinomies within the Basic Law's '*freiheitliche demokratische Grundordnung*'.[206]

This idea of the complete constitutional order informed the meaning of the discourse of balancing, which, in turn, was one of the prime manifestations and operationalizations of 'complete' constitutionalism itself. Contemporary constitutional rights jurisprudence furnishes abundant evidence for the connection between these two themes, both in endorsement and in critique. Peter Häberle, who was broadly supportive of the *Bundesverfassungsgericht*'s approach, saw the *Lüth* Court's balancing exactly in these terms. 'The balancing of values', he wrote, 'produces an equilibration [*Ausgleich*] between colliding values, through which both are given a place within the constitutional whole'.[207] 'Seen this way', Häberle concluded, 'balancing is both equilibration and ordering within an overarching whole'.[208] Peter Lerche, who was much more critical, used very similar language. 'The balancing of values', he noted sceptically, is now touted as a catch-all solution [*Patentlösung*] for the clash between the principle of the '*Sozialstaat*' and the sphere of constitutional rights'.[209]

### 3.   The 'perfect-fit' Constitution

A second dimension of the comprehensive constitutional order was the ideal of a 'perfect fit' between constitutional normativity and social reality. As Peter Häberle argued in his influential 1962 book: 'Every constitutional right wants to be "rule". Law is rule-conform reality. The Constitution intends, through its guarantees of constitutional rights, *to make sure that normativity and normality run "parallel"*'.[210]

In this section, I look in more detail at this ideal of 'perfect fit' and at its relationship to constitutional balancing. In a very general sense, the discourse of 'perfect fit' constitutionalism pervades literature and case law of the late 1950s and early 1960s. Here, two of its more concrete manifestations are singled out. They concern the aforementioned ideal of legal interpretation as 'actualization', and the idea of the Basic Law as an 'aspirational' constitution.

---

[206]  BVerfGE 20, 162, 178 (*Der Spiegel*) [1966].
[207]  Häberle (1962), p. 38. See also *ibid.*: 'The Constitution wants "*Sozialstaat*" and fundamental rights [...] individual rights and penal law [...] property and expropriation'.
[208]  *Ibid.*, p. 39.
[209]  Lerche (1961), p. 129.
[210]  Häberle (1962), p. 44 (emphasis added in translation).

## (a)    Interpretation as 'actualization'

The idea of the 'actualization' or 'concretization' of norms as an interpretative ideal has been encountered before in this chapter, in a discussion of dialectical reasoning – the newer theories of legal interpretation that gained prominence during the late 1950s and early 1960s.[211] This striving for the *'Ziel der Aktualität'*('the goal of actuality') in the interpretation of norms is particularly closely related to the 'perfect fit' ideal. In contradistinction to classical models of interpretation, from an actualization perspective 'there is no separation between the meaning of a norm and its application'.[212] Writers such as Christian von Pestalozza went so far as to suggest that the choice of interpretative method should be dependent on the circumstances: 'That method of interpretation should be chosen [...] that most accurately captures the meaning of the relevant constitutional norm in the concrete case.'[213] The objectivism – some might say circularity – evident from this quotation, is revealing for the attraction of an approach to constitutional rights adjudication that adhered to the idea of a 'meaning before interpretation', and that imposed a duty on interpreters to seek out that precise meaning – the one interpretation that would ensure a perfect fit between abstract meaning and application in the individual case.

German writers were keenly aware of the possibly anti-democratic nature of this approach. Specifically, the charge that more respect should be shown for meanings intended at the time of the framing of the Basic Law, could have been a potent one. But instead of deference to a constitutional founders' moment along 'originalist' lines familiar in American jurisprudence, they would point out that any 'original meaning' approach would tie the meaning of the Basic Law to the 'highly contingent situation' of its birth in a way that would not be legitimate.[214] Instead, both drafting and application had to be seen as equally constitutive moments for the meaning of constitutional norms, and interpretation should consist of a 'continuous dialectic' between general statements and concrete

---

[211]  See Chapter 3, Section C.3.

[212]  Von Pestalozza (1963), p. 427. Critically: von Mangoldt-Klein (1957), pp. 7ff. For an application in the context of freedom of expression, see BVerfGE 42, 143; 147 (*Deutschland Magazin*) [1976] ('*Die* [...] *Feststellung eines Verstoßes gegen die Bestimmungen zum Schutz der Ehre aktualisiert die verfassungsrechtliche Grenze der Meinungsfreiheit im Einzelfall*'.)

[213]  *Ibid.*, p. 433 ('*die im Einzelfall den aktualen Sinn der Grundrechtsnorm am besten verwirklicht*'). Critically: Roellecke (1976), pp. 36ff.

[214]  *Ibid.*, pp. 428ff.

situations.[215] What this mode of interpretation sought to achieve, then, was an elimination of any possible clash between the potentially conflicting ideas of the meaning of norms at the time of their drafting, their abstract meaning at the time of their operation and their concrete meaning in any given case.

### (b)    An aspirational Constitution

In an influential 1929 commentary on the Weimar Constitution, Richard Thoma had at one point written that where traditional legal methods yielded multiple acceptable interpretations, 'preference should be given to the meaning that gives maximal legal effectiveness [*juristische Wirkungskraft*] to the relevant norm'.[216] Although the relevant passage concerned only one very specific question of Weimar-era constitutional law, some postwar writers broadened Thoma's maxim into a principle favouring optimal protection for individual rights under the Basic Law generally.[217] This principle, variously known by terms such as '*in dubio pro libertate*', the '*Freiheitsvermutung*' or the principle of '*Grundrechtseffektivität*',[218] was hotly contested, and never became a stable part of *Bundesverfassungsgericht* doctrine.[219] But these debates themselves are one further manifestation of the contemporary attraction of an only vaguely circumscribed desire to make constitutional rights protection as comprehensive as possible. They can be read, together with many of the tendencies discussed previously, as further contributions to a broader ideal; that of the Basic Law as an 'aspirational' constitution.[220]

This aspirational quality was reflected, for example, in the *Bundesverfassungsgericht*'s insistence that the constitutional order of the Basic Law should not merely guarantee individual liberty in a negative sense, but that it should actively aim to realize the conditions for the meaningful enjoyment of rights.[221] Constitutional rights were understood

---

[215] *Ibid.*, p. 427.

[216] See Rusteberg (2009), p. 168; Stolleis (2004), p. 74.

[217] See, e.g., Schneider (1960), pp. 263ff; Ehmke (1963), pp. 87ff; von Pestalozza (1963), p. 443; Roellecke (1976), pp. 43ff. See also Unruh (2002), p. 310.

[218] Schneider, Roellecke and Ehmke, respectively.

[219] For a recent supportive assessment of a '*Prinzip der Ausgangsvermutung zugunsten der Freiheit*' ('a principled assumption in favour of fundamental freedoms') as a '*Denk – und Rechtfertigungsmodell*' ('a model for thinking about constitutional rights questions and for justifying decisions') see Lindner (2005), pp. 213ff.

[220] For a slightly different use of the term 'aspirational' see Lane Scheppele (2003), p. 299 ('forward-looking' constitutional drafting, rather than interpretation).

[221] See, e.g., BVerfGE 33, 303; 330ff ('*Numerus Clausus*') [1972].

to have a double character: as *'Verbot'* ('prohibition') on certain types of public action, but also as a *'Gebot'* ('a positive obligation, or injunction') on the legislature to realize rights.[222] More generally, in the legal litera-ture of the period there are numerous references to the idea that the con-stitutional order set out by the Basic Law demands action by the State, and to the Basic Law's ambition to actively create desirable forms of social ordering.[223]

### (c)  Balancing and the 'perfect-fit' Constitution

Balancing, in the *Lüth* line of cases, comprised both a balancing of values *and* a balancing of interests. Simplifying somewhat, where weighing values was an expression principally of the idea of the material Constitution, the balancing of interests was particularly closely related to that of the 'per-fect fit' Constitution. It was through a heavily particularized balancing of interests in each individual case that the *Bundesverfassungsgericht*, and the courts it mandated to follow this approach, intended to make sure that social reality would always match the constitutional order as closely as possible. Constitutional doctrine, then, demanded not merely the dur-able constellations of values along Smendian lines, but also the precise and individualized adjustment of constitutional rights and obligations. As the dissenting opinion of Judge Stein in the *'Mephisto'* case put it, the *Bundesverfassungsgericht* should not only be 'the guardian of constitu-tional rights in all legal domains' (the ideal of the complete Constitution) but should also make sure that each and every 'concrete balancing of interests [...] should conform to the value judgments contained in the Constitution'.[224] This idea of 'perfect fit' was reflected in, and supported by, a number of elements in German constitutional rights discourse of the late 1950s and early 1960s. Those elements (actualization, maximal effectiveness, and aspirational constitutionalism more broadly) in turn cast light on the meaning of balancing.

One striking aspect of the discourse of 'perfect fit' was its manda-tory tone. There are ceaseless references to obligations imposed, and to the achievement of goals demanded, by a Basic Law that is said, literally, *to want* certain things done. The ideal of 'actualization' as a method of interpretation could, at least in theory, be satisfied by only one particular

---

[222]  Häberle (1962), pp. 182ff.
[223]  See, e.g., von Pestaloza (1963), p. 440; Badura (1976), p. 7; Roellecke (1976), pp. 40ff. See also Eberle (2002), p. 233.
[224]  BVerfGE 30, 173; 202 [1971].

outcome in any rights case. The principle of maximal effectiveness meant, again at least in theory, maximal effectiveness and nothing less. And aspirational constitutionalism in a more general sense made specific positive demands of public institutions that went beyond prohibitions on interferences with individual rights.

This exacting character of 'perfect fit' constitutionalism will figure again in Chapter 5. There, I will argue that this pervasive sense of compulsion or obligation is part of what enables German legal constitutionalism to imbue even the most highly particularized, seemingly open-ended kind of balancing with a degree of legal formality, in ways not always appreciated.

Perhaps the clearest connection between the themes of balancing and of 'perfect fit' constitutionalism in fact lies largely beyond the scope of this book. This is the development of the principle of proportionality in German constitutional law. That vast topic is left largely unexplored here, as this book focuses rather on the language of balancing in the Court's earlier rights jurisprudence; the value-balancing and interest-balancing of *Lüth* and its progeny.[225] What is salient about the principle of proportionality from the perspective of this study is merely the way in which it too can be read to express a desire for the seamless transposition of the abstract meaning of constitutional rights into particularized, individualized instances of rights protection. Proportionality, in a very basic sense, embodies the ideals of a State which goes *no further than strictly necessary* in limiting rights, and which goes *as far as necessary* in order to realize effective rights protection. To this extent certainly, the Court's value- and interest-balancing and its proportionality jurisprudence share the same core meaning.

## 4.   *Explaining constitutional perfectionism*

Although a fuller elaboration of the point will have to wait until after the American leg of this comparative project is in place, provisionally at least

---

[225] *Lüth* itself does in fact contain some ancillary references to the idea of a 'fit' between means and goals. See BVerfGE 7, 198; 229. The principle of proportionality is commonly traced back not to *Lüth*, but to the '*Apotheken Urteil*' of 11 June in the same year (see BVerfGE 7, 377 [1958]), and beyond that, to roots in Prussian administrative law, rather than to Smend's material constitutionalism and Heck's Jurisprudence of Interests. For early accounts, see von Krauss (1955); Lerche (1961). For an influential contemporary assessment of the relationship between balancing and proportionality, see Häberle (1962), p. 67 ('The question of proportionality only becomes relevant when a balancing of values has already taken place. In other words: a balancing of values is a prerequisite for the principle of proportionality'.)

the label 'constitutional legal perfectionism' seems apt to cover much of what has been discussed in this section.[226] With that label in mind, important questions remain as to *why* the judges of the *Bundesverfassungsgericht* and so many of their observers felt that it was important to promote this particular understanding of their constitutional order. And there is also significant uncertainty as to whether and how prevailing social and political conditions in postwar (Western) Germany allowed them to be successful in this project.

While any kind of comprehensive answer to both these types of question would require a different kind of study than the one undertaken here, some of the basic contours appear reasonably clear. To take the latter point first; the German constitutional landscape of the late 1950s and early 1960s was in many ways much less polarized, or even simply politicized, than that in many other places, including notably the US – the main comparative reference in this book.[227] The postwar years saw the disappearance, by and large, of the extremes of both 'the nationalist Right and the Weimar left'.[228] It is no surprise, then, that Ernst Forsthoff, the prominent critic of the Court's general approach to the Basic Law, in 1961 could lament the 'far-reaching *de-politicization* of the era in which we live'.[229] Such a qualification would have been absolutely unthinkable in the US of the early 1960s.

Forsthoff is also helpful on the first type of question: the 'why' of comprehensive constitutionalism. All discussions on the 'correct' way of interpreting the Basic Law, he wrote, had to be viewed in light of Germany's recent past: 'The demise of the Weimar Constitution and the rise to power of National-Socialism have sharpened the sense of responsibility of constitutional jurists.'[230] There was, in Gerd Roellecke's memorable phrase, a 'rabbit-like fear' ('*kaninchenhaften Angst*') of a descent back into barbarity'.[231] In the eyes of many, if constitutional law was to erect a meaningful obstruction to totalitarianism, the Basic Law had to be similarly 'total',

---

[226] See further Chapter 5, Section B.1. See also Bomhoff (2012b).

[227] See, e.g., Schnur (1965), p. 131 (a more 'politicized' debate on freedom of expression in the US and elsewhere).

[228] Müller (2003), pp. 7ff. Perhaps the deepest fault-line in German political and constitutional thought of the time, between the ideas of the '*Rechtsstaat*' and the '*Sozialstaat*' (see *ibid.*, p. 8), was actively addressed through 'complete' constitutionalism and balancing specifically. See above, Chapter 3, Section E.2. On the relationship between balancing and the '*Sozialstaat*', see also Ladeur (1983).

[229] Forsthoff (1961), p. 164.      [230] Forsthoff (1961), p. 163.

[231] Roellecke (1976), p. 49.

or comprehensive, in its aspirations.[232] All areas of social, political and, to a large extent, even private life, should be protected, against any possible kind of encroachment. The case law of the *Bundesverfassungsgericht*, Forsthoff argued, showed how deeply its members were 'conscious of its *comprehensive responsibility for the constitution-conformity of legal life*'.[233]

Of course in Forsthoff's view this overriding sense of responsibility prompted a deplorable degree of casuistry in the Court's case law. That, in turn, was one of the primary manifestations of a more general 'deformalization' of German constitutional law.[234] As noted before, Chapter 5 will return to the relationship between balancing and 'deformalization', to make the argument that the idea of a 'comprehensive responsibility for the constitution-conformity of legal life' can also be read as imposing precisely the kind of disciplinary constraint normally associated with legal formality.

It is impossible, within the confines of this study, to go much beyond these general statements. As in all forms of intellectual history, it is extremely difficult to attribute causality to ideas; to separate causes and effects, modalities and goals. The idea of the Constitution as a value order, for example, may have served contemporary anxieties especially well in the early postwar years. But it also found a ready model in theories elaborated in a very different age, at a time when the Weimar Republic had already come under severe stress. It is literally impossible to tell, of course, what postwar constitutional jurisprudence would have looked like without Smend's '*Das Recht der freien Meinungsäußerung*', or any of the other sources of inspiration for material constitutionalism. The same goes for assigning priority to any particular idea. Was the *Lüth* Court, for example, first attracted to the idea of the value order because it wanted to accomplish the extension of rights protection into the private sphere, or was that extension rather a (desirable) corollary of a value order idea introduced primarily for other reasons?[235]

What is clear, though, is this. If the judges of the *Bundesverfassungsgericht*, in January 1958, were at all motivated by a desire to contribute to 'the rehabilitation of the moral stature of Germany in the world',[236] then

---

[232] See, e.g., Leisner (1960), pp. 128ff.

[233] Forsthoff (1959), p. 151 (emphasis added in translation). See also Stern (1993), p. 21.

[234] *Ibid.* See above, Chapter 3, Section C.2.

[235] See, e.g., Ossenbühl (1995), p. 905 (the need for balancing was the 'consequence' of the acceptance of horizontal effect of constitutional rights).

[236] Rensmann (2007), p. 84.

on the measure of showing that a perfectionist conception of constitutional law – and, therefore, of balancing – might be viable, they have been extraordinarily successful.

## F.   Balancing's German local meaning

Given the language and images discussed in this chapter, and using von Gierke's wonderfully untranslatable term, what can we say so far about the '*deutschrechtliche*' meaning of the discourse of balancing during the period described here? Three observations may serve by way of interim conclusion.

A first point to note is that the discourse of balancing in German constitutional rights jurisprudence of the time clearly was much broader than the mere occurrence of terms like '*Güterabwägung*' and '*Interessenabwägung*'. These terms, I have argued, should be seen as lying at the heart of an expansive family of related conceptual vocabulary, running through Weimar-era constitutional legal thought, case law, contemporary academic writing and constitutional rights doctrine.[237] In many ways, balancing lies at the heart of this collection of terms and concepts, functioning as a bridge between different historical eras (of the Weimar and the Bonn Republic), different understandings of the nature of constitutional interpretation (from '*Geisteswissenschaftlich*' to strictly '*juristisch*'), different understandings of the role of courts, and of the *Bundesverfassungsgericht* in particular (from highly particularized interest balancing to a more abstract weighing of values) and different areas of law (from private law-style interest balancing to the typically constitutional accommodation of values).

This leads to a second observation on the role and meaning of the discourse of balancing, when conceived in this broad sense. In many of its guises, one of the central functions of this discourse was to overcome deep-seated antinomies in legal and social thought. In the discourse of balancing, basic rights are 'equally constitutive' for both individuals and society. Rights encompass their own limitations. They are both programmatic statements and legal principles. The abstract meaning of constitutional clauses is identical to their 'actualized' meaning in concrete cases.

---

[237] Examples would include 'Wertkonstellationen', 'Kultursystem', 'Wechselwirkung', 'verfassungsrechtlich gewollte Ausgleich' 'Aktualisierung', 'maximale Wirkungskraft', and 'Grundsatz der Verhältnismäßigkeit'.

Value-balancing goes hand in hand with interest-balancing. The autonomy of private law co-exists with a constitutional order that claims to be
comprehensive. Concern for judicial deference co-exists with the desire
for intensive scrutiny. And so on. And even though these are all quite different projects, the language of '*Abwägung*', '*Wechselwirkung*', 'dialectical
understanding' or '*Ausgleich*' and similar terms, is in each case central to
these efforts at synthesis or accommodation.

It is this notion of synthesis that leads to a final observation. While the
ideas of overcoming antinomies, or their synthesis or accommodation,
capture much of what is significant in the German discourse of balancing, it would be far less accurate to understand this discourse in terms of
pragmatic compromise.[238] For one, German judicial decisions and academic commentary regard this synthesizing project as very much a 'juristic' project, to be undertaken according to strict standards of scholarly
legal discipline. The shadow of classical legal doctrine and orthodox rules
of interpretation is always present. What is striking also, from an outsid-
er's perspective, is the extent to which achieving accommodation between
ostensibly conflicting values and perspectives often appears in German
constitutional legal theory and doctrine of the time as something that
can and must be *willed*. The *Bundesverfassungsgericht wills* there to be no
conflict between individualized interest balancing and abstract weighing
of values, or between deferential review and intense conformity with constitutional norms. The Basic Law itself, in the anthromorphism that so
clearly characterizes German constitutional jurisprudence of this period,
*wills* there to be no conflict between more social and more individual
dimensions of societal life, or between the State and the individual.

A theme to which Chapter 5 returns is the fact that this 'willing' often
seems to require some suspension of disbelief by outside observers – and
perhaps by German participants themselves. Or, to put the point from
another angle: what seems to be at work is some degree of pervasive 'faith'
in legal doctrine, and in law more broadly. Without such an understanding it becomes very difficult to account for the phenomenal success of the
Basic Law and its interpretation by the *Bundesverfassungsgericht*, including notably the success of its balancing discourse. Peter Lerche, in his
path-breaking 1961 book on proportionality, spoke of the '*unbewiesene*

---

[238]  It is true that one oft-used term '*Ausgleich*' can mean 'compromise' in English. But even
then, for example as in 'the Austro-Hungarian Compromise' of 1867, its meaning is
more accurately captured by 'settlement' (of accounts), 'equilibration' (between claims),
or 'agreement'. Football jargon is helpful here: '*Ausgleich*' is also the German term for
'equalizer'.

*Vorstellung*' ('the unproven conception') of the constitutional value system, as a force sustaining the operation of '*konkurrenzlösende Normen*' ('competition-overcoming norms') in German constitutional law.[239] That image neatly fits the discourse of balancing. That discourse is arguably the most prominent manifestation of a deep tradition of synthesis in German legal thought, whether in tying together potentially conflicting rights, bridging potentially conflicting understandings of the constitutional order as a whole or overcoming potential clashes between that order and social reality. And this discourse is able to fulfil this synthesizing function because of some form of faith in its unproven, but willed capacity to succeed.

The remainder of this book builds on these observations. In the next chapter, I explore a radically different meaning for the discourse of balancing in mid-century US constitutional jurisprudence. In the polemical terms that often seem to characterize that discourse, 'synthesis' will make way for conflict, compromise and paradox, and 'faith' for a much less stable mix of deep conviction and radical scepticism. Chapter 5, finally, relates these two different meanings to different understandings of legal formality and its opposites, using that conceptual vocabulary to frame two contrasting paradigms of balancing.

[239] Lerche (1961), pp. 125ff.

# 4

# A dangerous doctrine: balancing in US constitutional jurisprudence of the 1950s and 1960s

## A.   Introduction

'So much has been written on the subject', Kenneth Karst observed in 1965 with an air of exasperation, that we have been told 'more about balancing than we wanted to know.'[1] But, he added 'there remains some uncertainty about what the very term means'.[2] Karst's observation succinctly captures the mood pervading American scholarly debates on constitutional rights adjudication, especially in the first amendment context, in the early 1960s. 'Balancing' had already come to be a dominant theme in the relatively young area of civil rights adjudication. Its centrality was not wholly welcome. And yet, no one was entirely certain what the label even referred to.

To a large extent, this picture mirrors contemporary developments in Germany, discussed in the previous chapter. In the US too, this period saw an astonishingly rapid rise in prominence of the discourse of balancing. Even if the exact scope, nature and even the actual relevance of 'balancing' in constitutional rights adjudication were far from certain, debates in the field were increasingly conducted in this language. As in Germany, balancing quickly became a focal point for some of the most heated disagreements in all of constitutional rights law.

This chapter takes up the story of balancing discourse in 1950s and 1960s American constitutional rights jurisprudence, in particular in the area of freedom of expression, where it first came to the fore and was debated most heatedly. As in the previous chapters, the aim is to elaborate a local meaning for balancing language in judicial and academic discourse. The setting for this analysis is radically different from, but also essentially connected to, the one discussed in Chapter 2. There, Roscoe Pound's Sociological Jurisprudence had to be situated in the context of a

---

[1] Karst (1965), p. 22.    [2] *Ibid.*

pre-1937 America in the *Lochner* era, in terms of received chronology. The material for this chapter, by contrast, is not only significantly post-*Lochner*, but also very much 'Cold War', and, largely, post-*Brown* v. *Board of Education*, the famous segregation case of 1954. Virtually all the decisions discussed below relate either to efforts to suppress domestic manifestations of communism or to the struggle over civil rights in the southern States. And they were handed down and debated in a context of acutely heightened sensitivity over the proper boundaries of judicial power.

## 1. Argument: contrast and opposition

If balancing in German constitutional jurisprudence fulfilled essential functions of synthesis, integration and harmonization, its local American meaning emerges primarily out of *juxtapositions and contrasts* with other currents of discourse. I discuss two major such contrasts in this chapter.

First, there was a clash between an increasing emphasis on the need for 'realistic' understandings of the processes of adjudication on the one hand and renewed demands for judicial reasoning to satisfy special standards of justification on the other. Judicial reasoning increasingly had to be convincing as a depiction of what judges *actually did*. But this increasingly 'realistic' picture also had to conform to a newly affirmed acceptable ideal image of what judges *should be doing*. This conflict had been some time in the making. But it came to a head at exactly the time of the battle over balancing at the Supreme Court, especially after the publication of seminal critiques of the work of the Court by Henry Hart and Herbert Wechsler in 1959.

Secondly, the language of balancing assumed its meaning through constant opposition with what will be called the 'definitional tradition' in American constitutional legal thought. At each of the various stages of the development of the discourse of balancing in the freedom of expression context, a prominent 'definitional' alternative was being promoted; whether by way of an 'absolute and objective' judicial test, a principled definition of a 'core' of the first amendment or in some other form. Those alternatives were conceived of, by their exponents and critics alike, as diametrically opposed to anything 'balancers' were thought to be doing. The arguments used, on both sides, in the ensuing classic debates have become an integral part of balancing's American local meaning.

As in the case of German jurisprudence, this American local meaning of balancing will ultimately be expressed in terms of the formal/substantive opposition.[3] Most of the work involved in making these connections is for Chapter 5. But the basic relationships can be sketched as follows.

The search for appropriate standards for the justification of judicial decisions was in many ways a struggle over the virtues of, and appropriate role for, legal formality. On the other hand, the intellectual currents that demanded a more 'realistic' depiction of adjudication were prominent expressions of the substantive in law. The first of the two clashes outlined above, between these demands of 'reasoned justification' and 'pragmatic instrumentalism', thus emerges as a proxy for the formal/substantive opposition as a whole.

As for the second contrast outlined earlier, I will argue in Chapter 5 that the definitional tradition in first amendment jurisprudence is a preeminent, distinctive expression of ideals of legal formality in American legal thought. Insofar as the meaning of balancing emerges from its continuous opposition to this tradition, it is imbued with a correspondingly distinctive sense of anti-formality. In Chapter 5, these 'typically American' notions of legal formality and anti-formality will be compared with their 'typically German' and, by extension, Continental-European counterparts.

## 2.   Free speech and balancing in American jurisprudence

In one sense, studying balancing discourse in early postwar German jurisprudence was relatively easy. There, a single *Bundesverfassungsgericht* judgment, *Lüth*, was the obvious starting point from both the free speech and the balancing perspectives. Pre-War developments in academic literature were certainly important in terms of understanding the *Lüth* decision and its aftermath, but could be dealt with in the form of 'flashbacks', as was done in Chapter 3. Earlier case law could largely be left aside.

Matters are not so straightforward in the American context. 'The problem in running one's mind over the American tradition of freedom of speech', Harry Kalven Jr. wrote in the early 1970s, is '*to find some point from which to begin the journey*.'[4] Although Supreme Court pronouncements on the first amendment began only in earnest in 1919, a number of important decisions had already been handed down by the end of the

---

[3] See Chapter 1, Section D.

[4] Kalven (1988), p. 3 (emphasis added). Note: Kalven's book, though written largely in the early 1970s, was only published posthumously. Harry Kalven, therefore, was very much a contemporary contributor to the debates set out in this chapter.

Second World War. These decisions would have significant repercussions on postwar free speech law. Not only is a starting point difficult to identify, it is also impossible to capture the American free speech tradition in a single judgment, or even a series of judgments, in a way that comes close to the sense in which the *Lüth* case and its aftermath are representative for German free speech law.[5] Where the *Bundesverfassungsgericht* in *Lüth* set out to develop an overarching, comprehensive approach to free speech adjudication, even to constitutional rights adjudication as a whole, the picture in the US is largely of a patchwork of doctrines and subdivisions. As another commentator, Thomas Emerson, wrote in 1970, '[t]he outstanding fact about the first amendment today is that the Supreme Court has never developed any comprehensive theory of what that constitutional guarantee means and how it should be applied in concrete cases'.[6]

If the American free speech landscape, then, is significantly more varied and complex than that encountered in Germany, the object of this study specifically – the meaning of the language of balancing – is arguably more elusive as well. In Germany, *Lüth* and subsequent cases set out 'balancing' as an overarching principle of constitutional interpretation. In the US, by contrast, there is no comparable seminal foundational 'balancing' decision. In addition, the significance of balancing, to the extent that it did figure in Supreme Court opinions, has in the American context always been much more severely contested. While it is generally understood that balancing as 'an overarching principle of constitutional construction has never been Supreme Court doctrine',[7] little common ground has ever existed as to what precisely balancing *did*, and does, mean. Some contemporary commentators saw a wide role for balancing in Supreme Court case law. Emerson, for example, whose views on the lack of coherence in the Court's approach were cited above, also wrote that '[i]nsofar as the Supreme Court *has* developed any general theory of the first amendment it is the *ad hoc* balancing formula'.[8] And in *Democracy and Distrust*, John Hart Ely argued that in the 1950s and into the 1960s 'the Court followed [an] approach of [...] essentially balancing

---

[5] Cf. Greenawalt (1992), p. 5.

[6] Emerson (1970), p. 15. A more recent characterization is also illustrative: 'First amendment law now is, if nothing else, a complex set of compromises [...] The Court periodically formulates exquisitely precise rules; it settles at other times for the most generally phrased standards [...] The result is a body of law complicated enough to inspire comparisons with the Internal Revenue Code.' Shiffrin (1990), pp. 2–3.

[7] Henkin (1978), p. 1024.   [8] Emerson (1970), p. 717 (emphasis added).

in *all* First Amendment cases'.[9] For other contemporary observers, however, it remained 'obscure' whether a Supreme Court majority regarded "balancing' as applicable to all first amendment cases, and if not, to what class of cases it applies'.[10] This fragmented landscape, I argue below, does not only affect the search for balancing's meaning; it actually forms an integral part of that meaning itself, by creating constant opportunities for contrast and comparison.

### 3.    Engaging with a 'balancing war'

Engaging with the twin themes of balancing and 1950s-1960s American free speech jurisprudence means engaging with an American constitutional classic. In the eyes of many contemporary observers, explicit disagreement between the Justices over the meaning and merits of 'balancing' became one of *the* key features of Supreme Court first amendment opinions of the era and one of the central battlegrounds of constitutional adjudication more generally. Within a fragmented free speech landscape, '[t]he one thing which appears to emerge with reasonable clarity', Laurent Frantz wrote in 1962, 'is that *"balancing" has become the central first amendment issue*'.[11] A veritable 'balancing war', so labelled by contemporary observers, raged between on the one hand Justices Frankfurter and Harlan and on the other Justices Black and Douglas. This war was fought out in a series of majority, concurring and dissenting opinions of the 1950s and the early 1960s.[12]

In terms of its position within the genealogies of balancing and of free speech law, two features of this controversy between so-called balancers and their opponents, the so-called absolutists, are particularly noteworthy.[13] First, a number of contemporary participants voiced concerns that the 'balancing/absolutism debate', notwithstanding its high public profile, failed to capture anything of real salience in constitutional rights jurisprudence. The debate, for many, was a simple 'verbal shell'[14] that should 'collapse for want of inner substance' – an 'unfortunate' dispute 'shrouded in semantic confusion'.[15] There was, therefore, *a debate on the*

---

[9]  Ely (1980), p. 114 (emphasis in original).
[10]  Frantz (1962), p. 1424. See also Frantz (1963), p. 730; Kalven (1967), p. 444.
[11]  Frantz (1962), p. 1432 (emphasis added). See also Kalven (1967), p. 441.
[12]  *Ibid.*, p. 444. For contextual detail see Mendelson (1961).
[13]  These terms are used here in the meanings they were given in the relevant debates.
[14]  Karst (1960), p. 81.
[15]  Kalven (1967), pp. 441–42.

*debate* over balancing. Secondly, later commentators have often viewed the debate as a discrete historical incident. It was, they thought, a dispute that had, by the time of their writing, already passed.[16] This was generally seen as a positive development. In the late 1970s already, scholars were loath 'to reopen the controversy that agitated the Supreme Court a generation ago',[17] and in the 1980s some were glad that the 'naïve' disputes over the merits of 'balancing' and 'absolutism' of the 1950s and 1960s were over.[18] Others, on the other hand, wondered why the disputes that were 'fashionable' in this earlier period had been left behind, and actively promoted 'a re-opening of the balancing debate'.[19] Balancing, then, appears subject to the same permanent argumentative conflict, and the same pendulum-swing style narrative, that characterizes American jurisprudence as a whole.[20]

### 4. Legacies of pre-1950s first amendment doctrines

One of the arguments this chapter seeks to make is that the rise of balancing discourse in mid-century American constitutional law has to be understood in the context of a pragmatic search for solutions to new problems through the adjustment and modification of existing doctrinal structures. Once introduced as part of the re-interpretation and adaptation of older 'tests' and doctrines, the language of balancing quickly took on a life of its own. Developing that argument requires a short introduction to the main elements of free speech jurisprudence from before the Second World War.

In very broad terms, two general categories of freedom of expression cases can be distinguished in the Supreme Court's pre-1950s case law. First, there were those cases decided mostly in the immediate aftermath of the First World War and concerned with what was called 'seditious speech' or 'subversive advocacy' – expression critical of the government, or expression allegedly aimed at undermining the war effort. A second

---

[16]  See, e.g., Tushnet (1985), p. 1503 (describing as 'the central debate that occupied constitutional theory a generation ago' the debate 'over whether constitutional decisions should rest on a process of balancing or should instead express certain absolute judgments'; writing that 'the debate ended').

[17]  Henkin (1978), p. 1023. See also at p. 1043.

[18]  Schauer (1981), p. 266.

[19]  Aleinikoff (1987), p. 945.

[20]  Cf. Lasser (2004); Duxbury (1995). Duxbury is critical of the salience of this perspective. But his more nuanced 'patterns of thought' also bring over the kind of unresolved tension and paradox intended here. See also below, Chapter 5, Section D.

category concerned principally cases in which curbs on free speech resulted indirectly from general, local or State governments' regulations that were not themselves focused on limiting expression.

### (a)   Subversive advocacy: 'clear and present danger'

The American tradition of protection for freedom of expression is often traced back to the Supreme Court's decisions in the 'Sedition Act' cases of *Schenck* and *Abrams* of 1919.[21] The Sedition Act of 1918 forbade the publication or utterance during wartime of 'disloyal' language or language intended to bring the government or the military of the US into disrepute. In the *Schenck* case, the defendants were convicted under the Act, for writing that army conscription was 'a monstrous wrong' and that conscripts were 'little better' than convicts.[22] Justice Oliver Wendell Holmes announced, in his opinion for the Court upholding the convictions, what would become famous as the clear-and-present-danger test:

> [T]he character of every act depends on the circumstances in which it is done. The most stringent protection of free speech would not protect a man in falsely shouting fire in a theater, and causing a panic [...] The question in every case is whether the words used are used in such circumstances and are of such a nature as to create a clear and present danger that they will bring about the substantive evils that Congress has a right to prevent. It is a question of proximity and degree.[23]

When looked at through the lens of later debates, a number of elements appear as particularly noteworthy in this iconic passage.[24] First, rather than trying to identify a 'basic value' at the heart of what the first amendment should aim to protect, as most later approaches would, Justice Holmes offers a pragmatic exposition of what the Amendment *should not* cover.[25] Secondly, within this pragmatic framework, Holmes focuses in particular on the likely effect of utterances. The clear-and-present-danger formula, by its terms, asks courts to make a prediction. Their task is empirical rather than value-based. Finally, it is important to note Justice Holmes' emphasis on the idea that constitutional protection for expression should be a question of degree, to be answered for individual cases

---

[21]  See, e.g., *Dennis* v. *United States*, 341 US 494, 503 (1951). ('No important case involving free speech was decided by this Court prior to *Schenck* v. *United States*'). But see critically Rabban (1981).

[22]  *Schenck* v. *United States*, 249 US 47 (1919).

[23]  249 US 47, 52.      [24]  See further Rabban (1983).

[25]  Cf. Stone (2004), p. 194. This would be later lamented as 'intellectual poverty' by Harry Kalven. See Kalven (1965), pp. 16ff.

on the basis of their specific circumstances. This is in keeping with his broader philosophical view that 'the whole law depends on *questions of degree* as soon as it is civilized'.[26]

Justice Holmes' opinion has come to occupy a privileged position in the American free speech tradition. Although in *Schenck* itself the test was used to uphold the convictions of anti-War demonstrators, the clear-and-present-danger formula quickly became popular with libertarians as a doctrine thought to be highly protective of free speech, especially after Justice Holmes in his dissent in *Abrams* v. *United States* argued that only a 'present danger of an immediate evil' could warrant a limitation upon the freedom of expression.[27]

### (b) 'Time, place and manner' restrictions; balancing?

When the direct aftermath of the First World War had passed, the focus of the freedom of expression cases to come before the Supreme Court shifted, from issues of 'subversive' speech such as criticism of the US' involvement in the War in *Schenck*, *Abrams* and *Debs*, to other types of free speech claims. In the late 1930s and early 1940s, the Supreme Court decided a number of cases in which claimants asserted that general, non-speech related, municipal or State laws limited their rights of free expression or association. Such laws typically prohibited the distribution of flyers,[28] the use of sound-systems in public spaces[29] or the staging of demonstrations or marches,[30] and were most often challenged by religious groups, mainly Jehovah's Witnesses, and labour organizations.[31] In all these cases, local or State governments claimed that any resulting limitation on speech rights was an indirect, permissible, by-product of non-discriminatory, general measures in defence of non-speech-related public interests.

The Supreme Court never developed a unified, fully coherent approach to this new type of first amendment claims,[32] many of which were labelled as concerning indirect 'time, place and manner' restrictions on speech.[33] In one sense, the familiar 'danger' test clearly did not prove a good fit with the factual situations presented. At the same time, however, the Court was

---

[26] Cited in Henkin (1968), p. 63. See also Chapter 2, Section C.4.

[27] *Abrams* v. *United States*, 250 US 616, 628 (1919) (Holmes, J., dissenting).

[28] *Schneider* v. *State*, 308 US 147 (1939); *Jones* v. *Opelika*, 316 US 584 (1942).

[29] *Cantwell* v. *Connecticut*, 310 US 296 (1940); *Kovacs* v. *Cooper*, 336 US 77 (1949).

[30] *Cox* v. *New Hampshire*, 312 US 569 (1941).

[31] The leading case was *Thornhill* v. *Alabama*, 310 US 88 (1940).

[32] The problems themselves were not entirely new. But older cases had not been presented or decided on free speech grounds.

[33] See, e.g., *Jones* v. *Opelika*, 316 US 584, 605; *Cantwell* v. *Connecticut*, 310 US 296, 304.

sensitive to a need to provide more stringent control over these speech-impeding measures than was possible under the general 'rational basis' test with its 'presumption of constitutionality', that it had come to use for all kinds of governmental interferences with individual freedom of action in the aftermath of the *Lochner* era.[34]

While in many of these cases the language of 'clear and present danger' was still referred to,[35] the Court in fact often adopted some version of a 'means/ends relation' test or 'least restrictive alternative' test to assess the constitutionality of these general regulatory statutes. Intriguingly, in the elaboration of these tests, the Justices sometimes resorted to a form of balancing language. So, for example, in the leading 'handbill', or flyer, decision of *Schneider* v. *State* (1939), Justice Roberts in his opinion for the Court characterized the case as pitting a 'duty' of municipal authorities to keep their streets open, 'which meant they could lawfully regulate the conduct of those using the streets', against a 'personal fundamental right' of freedom of expression.[36] In every case of this kind, where a legislative abridgment of the right of freedom of speech was asserted, Roberts wrote:

> the courts should be astute to examine the effects of the challenged legislation [...] [T]he delicate and difficult task falls upon the courts *to weigh the circumstances* and to appraise the substantiality of the reasons advanced in support of the regulation of the free enjoyment of the rights.[37]

Justice Roberts' description of the Court's task as one of 'weighing the circumstances' and of comparing effects of and reasons for legislative encroachments on the freedom of expression was cited in a number of subsequent handbill and picketing cases.[38] This approach, in the eyes of contemporary commentators, embodied a principled distinction between deferential 'rational basis' review and more stringent, last-resort 'danger' review.[39] As will be seen below, the use of the imagery of 'weighing' in

---

[34] See, e.g., *Schneider* v. *Schneider*, 308 US 147, 161.

[35] See, e.g., *Thornhill* v. *Alabama*, 310 US 88, 105 (1940); *Jones* v. *Opelika*, 316 US 584, 613.

[36] *Schneider* v. *Schneider*, 308 US 147, 160–61.

[37] *Ibid.*, at p. 161 (emphasis added).

[38] See, e.g., *Jones* v. *Jones*, 316 US 584, 595 ('adjustment of interests'); *Thornhill* v. *Alabama*, 310 US 88, 96 (insufficient legislative care 'in balancing [the interests of business] against the interest of the community and that of the individual in freedom of discussion on matters of public concern').

[39] On these efforts to construe a 'bifurcated' system of constitutional review, whereby cases involving economic liberties would only be reviewed deferentially while civil liberties would remain robustly protected, see, e.g., Nizer (1941), p. 588; White (1996), pp. 331ff.

some of these opinions allowed later judges and commentators to view cases like *Schneider* as the 'earliest balancing cases'.[40]

### (c)  Doctrinal legacies: summary

At the beginning of the 1950s, this was, sketched in very broad terms, what American freedom of expression doctrine looked like. The *rhetoric* of 'clear and present danger', stemming from the First World War cases, was dominant in all areas of freedom of expression law, but the precise meaning and scope of application of 'clear and present danger' as a doctrinal test were unclear. In cases involving 'time, place and manner' restrictions, such as *Schneider* and *Cantwell*, the Court had struck down local and State regulations on the basis that they were too intrusive upon the freedom of speech. These cases seemed to strike a middle note between a stringent requirement that State regulation of speech be only ever a measure of last resort to ward off a clear danger, and a minimal 'rational basis' test applicable to governmental interferences with private rights more generally. The theoretical and doctrinal bases for these decisions, however, were largely unclear.

## B.    The 'balancing opinions' at the Supreme Court

### 1.   Introduction

From the beginning of the 1950s onwards, the Supreme Court was asked to decide a rapidly growing number of cases arising out of the new political tensions of the Cold War. Governmental efforts to repress communism in the US took an astonishingly wide range of forms: from blunt, direct repression of propaganda through the criminal law, to 'loyalty oaths', special requirements for 'professional qualifications' and, of course, the infamous Congressional investigations of the House Un-American Activities Committee. It was largely in cases arising out of these measures that clashes over the role and meaning of balancing came to a head.

The starting point for an overview of these clashes has to be the case of *American Communications Association* v. *Douds*, decided in 1950.[41] *Douds* was the first major postwar first amendment case concerning communism.[42] It was also a case in which Chief Justice Vinson wrote an

---

[40]  Cf. Frantz (1962); White (1996); Porat (2006), pp. 1431ff.

[41]  *American Communications Association* v. *Douds*, 339 US 382 (1950).

[42]  See, e.g., Reich (1963), p. 718; Wise (1969), p. 76.

opinion for the Court containing balancing language, taken from the *Schneider* line of cases, that was seized upon in many of the later decisions.[43] Justice Black dissented in *Douds*, as he would in many later communism cases, but his dissent did not yet touch upon the appropriateness of balancing as a method of constitutional adjudication. In *Dennis* v. *United States*, decided a year after *Douds*, balancing language surfaced once more, again in an opinion for the Court by Chief Justice Vinson, but this time in the form of a restatement, reinterpretation or modification of the 'clear and present danger' test. *Dennis* is also significant for a concurrence by Justice Frankfurter that discusses the relationship between balancing and constitutional rights adjudication in very broad terms, and dissents by Justice Black and Douglas that begin to frame their disagreement with the majority in terms of balancing. The two cases in which the conflict over balancing received its fullest exposition were *Barenblatt* and *Konigsberg*; two 'compulsory disclosure' cases of 1959 and 1961, in which the appropriateness of balancing became the central issue for disagreement between majority and dissenters. Taken together, *Douds*, *Dennis*, *Barenblatt* and *Konigsberg* not only frame most of the balancing debate in first amendment law, but also conveniently cover the paradigmatic factual instances of the repression of communist expression and association in 1950s America: prosecution based on thoughts expressed (*Dennis*), and the three main forms of 'refusal to answer' problems.[44] This section discusses the relevant opinions in turn, with particular focus on the roles attributed to balancing language.

## 2.  *The early 'balancing opinions':* Douds *and* Dennis

### (a)  *Douds* (1950)

The case of *American Communications Association* v. *Douds* concerned a 'loyalty oath' requirement in the labour law context. Section 9(h) of the National Labor Relations Act (Amended) 1947 provided that the National Labor Relations Board (NLRB), a governmental organization, would not hear any petitions or complaints from workers' unions, if these unions had not filed with the NLRB affidavits stating that none of their board members was or had been a member of a communist political organization and

---

[43]  Cf. Emerson (1963), p. 912 ('The [balancing] test, first clearly enunciated by Chief Justice Vinson's opinion in the *Douds* case, has been employed by a majority of the Supreme Court in a number of subsequent decisions.')

[44]  Cf. For this typology, see Kalven (1988), p. 549.

that none of them advocated, or even believed in, the overthrow of the US government by force. The constitutionality of Section 9(h) was challenged in federal court by a number of workers' organizations.

At the Supreme Court, Chief Justice Vinson's opinion for the Court rested on the view that the loyalty oath requirement was primarily a regulation of *conduct* in order to protect interstate commerce. These were the so-called 'political strikes' that Congress had determined, as a matter of 'fact', were carried out by labour leaders with communist affiliations. The central question raised by the case, for the Chief Justice, was to what extent any *indirect* limitations on first amendment rights resulting from this regulation of conduct, which was otherwise reasonable and rational, could render Section 9(h) unconstitutional. This way of framing the free speech issue in the case formed the backdrop to an intricate argument rejecting the unions' contention that their claims found support in the 'clear and present danger' test.[45] Seizing upon a disagreement between two of the claimant unions as to what exactly should be counted as the relevant 'danger' for the purposes of the doctrine, Chief Justice Vinson first took aim at the nature of the test itself, warning against attempts to 'apply the term "clear and present danger" as a mechanical test in every case touching First Amendment freedoms', or as a 'mathematical formula'.[46] '[I]t was never the intention of this Court to lay down an absolutist test measured in terms of danger to the Nation', he wrote.[47] This 'clear and present danger' 'test' of diminished stature could not, in Vinson's view, claim any direct force of application. Not only was the limitation on speech rights merely an indirect result of a general governmental regulation aimed at conduct, as discussed above, but also, the Chief Justice wrote, applying 'a rigid test requiring a showing of imminent danger to the security to the Nation [...] when the effect of a statute [...] upon the exercise of First Amendment freedoms is relatively small and the public interest to be protected is substantial' would be 'an absurdity'.[48] On these two grounds, that is the 'indirect' and 'minimal' nature of the limitation on free speech rights, the case had to be seen as in fact more closely related to the *Schneider* line of cases, on flyers and sound-trucks.[49] And for such cases, Vinson distilled the following general approach from the case law:

---

[45] 339 US 382, 393.    [46] *Ibid.*, p. 394.
[47] *Ibid.*, p. 397.    [48] *Ibid.*
[49] The Opinion cites cases involving sound-trucks (*Kovacs* v. *Cooper*), parades (*Cox* v. *New Hampshire*) and flyers, or handbills (*Schneider* v. *State*), among others.

> When particular conduct is regulated in the interest of public order, and the regulation results in an indirect, conditional, partial abridgment of speech, the duty of the court is to determine which of these two conflicting interests demands the greater protection under the particular circumstances presented.[50]

'In essence', the court's approach had to be one of 'weighing the probable effects of the statute upon the free exercise of the right of speech [...] against the congressional determination that political strikes are evils of conduct which cause substantial harm'.[51] The justices, therefore, had to 'undertake the delicate and difficult task [...] to weigh the circumstances and to appraise the substantiality of the reasons advanced in support of the regulation of the free enjoyment of the rights'.[52] This weighing in the *Douds* case led to a rejection of the claim of the unions.[53]

### (b)   *Dennis* (1951)

Petitioners in *Dennis* were convicted under the Smith Act, a 1940 'sedition' statute, for conspiring to organize advocacy of the overthrow of the US government by force.[54] Chief Justice Vinson wrote an opinion for a plurality of four; Justices Frankfurter and Jackson filed concurring opinions; Justices Black and Douglas dissented. For Vinson the criminal convictions of Eugene Dennis and his fellow defendants, as *direct* restrictions upon speech, fell 'squarely' within the ambit of the 'clear and present danger test', which meant that the Court had to revisit 'what that phrase imports'.[55] In Vinson's reading, the 'Holmes-Brandeis' rationale behind the test was that while 'mere "reasonableness"' would not be sufficient to sustain direct limitations on speech rights, free speech was not, on the other hand, itself 'an absolute': '[N]either Justice Holmes nor Justice Brandeis ever envisioned that a shorthand phrase should be crystallized into a rigid rule to be applied inflexibly without regard to the circumstances of each

---

[50]  339 US 382, 399–400.

[51]  *Ibid.*, p. 400.    [52]  *Ibid.* (quoting from *Schneider*).

[53]  Justice Black dissented, arguing that the majority in fact permitted punishment of simple beliefs, and not conduct. Justice Black's writing foreshadows his later anti-balancing dissents in its commitment to an 'absolute' freedom ('Freedom to think is absolute of its own nature'), its categorical distinction between speech and conduct, and a distrust of judicial flexibility (criticizing 'the assumption that individual mental freedom can be constitutionally abridged whenever a majority of this Court finds a satisfactory legislative reason' *ibid.*, pp. 445, 450).

[54]  *Dennis* v. *United States*, 341 US 494 (1951).

[55]  *Ibid.*, p. 508.

case […]'⁵⁶ 'To those who would paralyze our Government in the face of impending threat by encasing it in a semantic straitjacket', Vinson wrote, 'we must reply that all concepts are relative.' 'Nothing is more certain in modern society', he continued, 'than the principle that *there are no absolutes*, that a name, a phrase, a standard has meaning only when associated with considerations which gave birth to the nomenclature.'⁵⁷

With this Realist gloss in place, Vinson went on to revisit, through a 'balancing' lens, two key elements of the Court's 'clear and present danger' tradition. First, he noted that many of the cases in which convictions had been reversed using 'clear and present danger' 'or similar tests', had been instances where 'the interest which the State was attempting to protect was itself too insubstantial to warrant restriction of speech'.⁵⁸ Such an approach, however, could not be taken in *Dennis*, as the governmental interest at issue – national security – had to be considered sufficiently weighty, at least in the abstract. Vinson therefore proceeded to engage with the heart of the 'clear and present danger' formula: the required likelihood and level of immediacy of the relevant 'danger'. 'The situation with which Justices Holmes and Brandeis were concerned', he wrote, had been one of relatively isolated speakers who did not pose any substantial threat to the community. They had never been confronted with an organization like the Communist Party: 'an apparatus […] dedicated to the overthrow of the Government, in the context of world crisis after crisis'.⁵⁹ This new context required a recalibration of the 'clear and present danger' test:

> Chief Judge Learned Hand, writing for the majority [in the Appeals court] below, interpreted the phrase as follows: 'In each case, [courts] must ask whether the gravity of the 'evil', discounted by its improbability, justifies such invasion of free speech as is necessary to avoid the danger'. We adopt this statement of the rule. As articulated by Chief Judge Hand, it is as succinct and inclusive as any other we might devise at this time. It takes into consideration those factors which we deem relevant, and relates their significances. More we cannot expect from words.⁶⁰

Vinson held that on this standard, the court below had been entitled to convict the petitioners.

---

⁵⁶ *Ibid.*    ⁵⁷ *Ibid.*, (emphasis added).
⁵⁸ On this reinterpretation of older case law on indirect limitations in balancing terms, see further Chapter 4, Section D.1.
⁵⁹ 341 US 494, 510.    ⁶⁰ *Ibid.*, p. 510.

Noting that few questions of similar importance had come before the Court in recent years, Justice Frankfurter wrote a lengthy concurring opinion, in which he sought to recast the Courts' role in all of first amendment law along two main axes: *balancing* and *deference* to congressional authority. Frankfurter framed the issue in the case in terms of 'a conflict of interests' between the appellants' right to advocate their political theory so long as their advocacy did not immediately threaten the organization of a free society, and the Government's right to safeguard the security of the Nation by measures such as the Smith Act. Frankfurter maintained that this conflict could not be resolved 'by a dogmatic preference for one or the other, nor by a sonorous formula' – 'clear and present danger' – 'which is, in fact, only a euphemistic disguise for an unresolved conflict'.[61] He framed his own preferred approach in the following terms:

> The demands of free speech in a democratic society, as well as the interest in national security are better served by candid and informed weighing of the competing interests, within the confines of the judicial process, than by announcing dogmas too inflexible for the non-Euclidian problems to be solved. But how are the competing interests to be assessed? Since they are not subject to quantitative assessment, the issue necessarily resolves itself into asking, who is to make the adjustment? – who is to balance the relevant factors and interests and ascertain which interest is in the circumstances to prevail? Full responsibility for the choice cannot be given to the courts. Courts are not representative bodies [...] Primary responsibility for adjusting the interests which compete in the situation before us of necessity belongs to the Congress.[62]

Frankfurter formulated his general approach on the basis of an overview of the different 'types' of cases in which the Court had been faced with 'conflicts between speech and competing interests'. This overview led to two basic propositions. First: free speech cases were not an exception to the principle that the Justices are not legislators. And second: the *results* reached in earlier decisions were 'on the whole those that would ensue from careful weighing of conflicting interests'.[63] Given these two propositions, Frankfurter defined the Court's role in first amendment cases as one of deferentially reviewing the way in which the legislature had struck a balance between 'the interest in security' and 'the interest in free speech'.[64] On such a deferential review, he upheld the convictions, even

---

[61] *Ibid.*, p. 519.    [62] *Ibid.*, pp. 524–25.
[63] *Ibid.*, pp. 539, 542.    [64] *Ibid.*, pp. 544ff.

while expressing doubt about the practical wisdom of jailing communists for speech offences.

Justice Black wrote a dissenting opinion that foreshadowed many of the themes he would elaborate during the height of the balancing debates with Justices Harlan and Frankfurter. Having noted that petitioners in this case had been convicted, not for attempting to overthrow the government, nor for advocating any such attempt, but merely for agreeing to assemble and to 'talk and publish certain ideas at a later date', Black concluded that the authorities had applied a 'virulent form of prior censorship of speech and press', clearly forbidden by the first amendment.[65] As a second line of argument, Black held that the 'clear and present danger' test was the appropriate inquiry for dealing with cases of advocacy. The majority, in Black's view, had repudiated this classic test in a way that, illegitimately, permitted 'laws suppressing freedom of speech and press on the basis of Congress' or our own notions of mere "reasonableness"'. 'Such a doctrine', Black concluded, 'waters down the First Amendment so that it amounts to *little more than an admonition* to Congress.'[66]

### 3.   *The later 'balancing opinions':* Barenblatt *and* Konigsberg

For all their heated rhetoric, *Douds* and *Dennis*, were mere preliminary skirmishes compared to the conflict over balancing that was to erupt between Justice Black and Justice Harlan in the cases of *Barenblatt* and *Konigsberg*. This section deals with these decisions in turn.

#### (a)   *Barenblatt* (1959)

In the course of the 1950s, the investigations into communist associations and activities by Senator McCarthy's House Un-American Activities Committee were regularly challenged in the courts. After having dealt with a number of cases on primarily procedural grounds, in 1959, in *Barenblatt* v. *United States*, the Supreme Court for the first time based its decision on the constitutionality of these investigations squarely on first amendment grounds.[67] The case gave rise to both an authoritative treatment of the speech rights issues involved in legislative investigations, and a 'key engagement' in the balancing debate.[68]

---

[65]  *Ibid.*, pp. 579–80.
[66]  *Ibid.*, p. 580 (emphasis added).
[67]  360 US 109 (1959).
[68]  Kalven (1988), pp. 498, 500, 504.

The case concerned a young university lecturer, Lloyd Barenblatt, who had refused to answer questions from the House Committee on whether he was or had ever been a member of the Communist Party, in particular whilst teaching at the University of Michigan a number of years earlier. Justice Harlan wrote a concise opinion of the Court for a majority of five. He began by noting that unlike the absolute protection against self-incrimination under the fifth amendment, the first amendment did not afford a witness the right to resist inquiry 'in all circumstances'. His proposed method followed directly from this comparison: '[w]here First Amendment rights are asserted to bar governmental interrogation, resolution of the issue *always involves a balancing by the courts of the competing private and public interests at stake in the particular circumstances shown*'.[69] 'The critical element', in Harlan's model of inquiry, was 'the existence of, and the weight to be ascribed to, the interest of the Congress in demanding disclosures from an unwilling witness'.[70] As the legislative competence of Congress in this situation was 'beyond question' and there were no other factors 'which might sometimes lead to the conclusion that the individual interests at stake were not subordinate to those of the state', Harlan's majority opinion concluded 'that the balance between the individual and the governmental interests here at stake must be struck in favor of the latter', and that, therefore, the provisions of the first amendment had not been offended.[71]

For Justice Black, the majority opinion accepted 'a balancing test to decide if First Amendment rights shall be protected'. He voiced strong objections against both balancing in first amendment cases generally, and, in case some form of balancing had to be accepted, against the way the majority had carried out its balancing in the instant case. First, a balancing approach to the first amendment, in Black's view, offended the clear language of the amendment, violated the spirit of a *written* Constitution and went against the notion that 'the Bill of Rights *means what it says* and that [the] Court must enforce that meaning'.[72] Justice Black framed his position on balancing in unequivocal terms: 'I do not agree that laws directly abridging First Amendment freedoms can be justified by a congressional or judicial balancing process.'[73] There had been 'cases suggesting that a law which primarily regulates conduct but which might also

---

[69] 360 US 109, 126 (citing *Douds*) (emphasis added).
[70] *Ibid.*, pp. 126–27.
[71] *Ibid.*, p. 134.
[72] *Ibid.*, pp. 138–44 (emphasis added).
[73] *Ibid.*, p. 141.

indirectly affect speech can be upheld if the effect on speech is minor in relation to the need for control of the conduct'. With the decisions in these 'time, place and manner' cases, like *Schneider* and *Cantwell*, Justice Black agreed. But, he wrote, the Court had not, in *Schneider* or in *Cantwell*, suggested 'even remotely [...] that a law directly aimed at curtailing speech and political persuasion could be saved through a balancing process'.[74] Secondly, even assuming what he could not assume – that 'some balancing' was proper in the case – Black opined that the Court had ignored its own test. At most, the majority had balanced 'the right of the Government to preserve itself' against 'Barenblatt's right to refrain from revealing Communist affiliations'. In framing its enquiry in this way, the majority had completely ignored the more abstract 'interests of society' in the protection of the freedom to remain silent in front of the congressional committee.[75] This form of inquiry, in Black's view, reduced balancing to 'a mere play on words' and was completely inconsistent with the rule the Court had previously, in *Schneider*, given for applying a 'balancing test': that 'the courts should be *astute* to examine the effects of the challenged legislation'.[76]

### (b)   *Konigsberg* (1961)

The case of *Konigsberg*,[77] another 'refusal to answer' case, was Act II of the balancing debate between Justices Harlan and Black.[78] Raphael Konigsberg had been denied admission to the California Bar because he had refused, on constitutional grounds, to answer the question of whether he was or had ever been a member of the Communist Party. As there was no constitutional authority to deny admission to the bar to members of the Communist party per se, this question was ostensibly asked merely to verify indirectly the accuracy of Konigsberg's explicit claims that he did not advocate violent overthrow of government. Such advocacy, on the other hand, *would* constitute a constitutionally valid reason for exclusion.[79]

'At the outset', Justice Harlan began the analysis section of his majority opinion, 'we reject the view that freedom of speech and association, as protected by the [First Amendment], are "absolutes," not only in the undoubted sense that, where the constitutional protection exists it must

---

[74]   *Ibid.*, p. 142.
[75]   *Ibid.*, p. 144.
[76]   *Ibid.*, p. 145, citing *Schneider*. The emphasis on the word 'astute' was Black's.
[77]   *Konigsberg* v. *State Bar of California*, 366 US 36 (1961).
[78]   Cf. Strong (1969), p. 54.
[79]   366 US 36, 60.

prevail, but also in the sense that the scope of that protection must be gathered solely from a literal reading of the First Amendment'.[80] The Court had, he added, always recognized ways in which the constitutional right to freedom of speech was 'narrower than an unlimited license to talk'. In particular, Justice Harlan noted, 'general regulatory statutes, not intended to control the content of speech but incidentally limiting its unfettered exercise' had been upheld whenever they were 'justified by subordinating valid governmental interests'; and this condition of constitutionality always '*necessarily* involved a weighing of the governmental interest involved'.[81] As in this case the limitations on Konigsberg's speech rights had only been the incidental results of the exercise of a public power in order to verify the accuracy of his statements that he did not advocate the violent overthrow of government, his first amendment claim fell within this category of 'general regulatory laws not intended to control the content of speech'. This meant that a balancing enquiry would be both necessary and appropriate. The majority regarded 'the State's interest in having lawyers who are devoted to the law in its broadest sense [...] as clearly sufficient to outweigh the minimal effect upon free association occasioned by compulsory disclosure' in the circumstances of the case.[82]

Justice Black, in his dissent, focused heavily on the majority's reliance on a 'balancing test':

> The recognition that California has subjected 'speech and association to the deterrence of subsequent disclosure' is, under the First Amendment, sufficient in itself to render the action of the State unconstitutional unless one subscribes to the doctrine that permits constitutionally protected rights to be '*balanced*' *away* whenever a majority of the Court thinks that a State might have interest sufficient to justify abridgment of those freedoms. As I have indicated many times before, I do not subscribe to that doctrine for I believe that the First Amendment's unequivocal command that there shall be no abridgment of the rights of free speech and assembly shows that the men who drafted our Bill of Rights did all the 'balancing' that was to be done in this field.[83]

Justice Black reiterated his view, also expressed in *Barenblatt*, that there were essential differences between the kind of 'balancing' that the court had undertaken in cases like *Schneider* 'as a method for insuring the complete protection of First Amendment freedoms even against purely

---

[80] *Ibid.*, p. 49.
[81] *Ibid.*, pp. 49–50 (citing *Schneider* and *Douds*) (emphasis added).
[82] *Ibid.*, p. 52.   [83] *Ibid.*, p. 61.

incidental or inadvertent consequences', and the balancing test now proposed for a governmental regulation 'that is aimed at speech and depends
for its application upon the content of speech'.[84] Balancing in this latter
type of case, for Black, turned the principle of 'Government of the people,
by the people and for the people' into a 'government over the people'.[85] As
in *Barenblatt*, Justice Black went on to argue that even if he would be able
to accept the idea that 'balancing' would be proper in the case, he would
not be able to support the decision. Under the majority's 'penurious balancing test', the interest of the government had been 'inflated out of all
proportion', while the societal interest in free speech had again not been
given its due weight.[86]

#### 4.   Beyond the balancing debate

With *Barenblatt* and *Konigsberg*, the judicial interchange on balancing
in free speech cases had reached its apogee.[87] The Justices did return to
the theme on a few more occasions. In a later major communism case,
*Communist Party v. Subversive Activities Control Board* (1961),[88] Justice
Black rehearsed his by now familiar objections, but in a noticeably more
defeatist tone. Summing up his critique of a majority opinion by Justice
Frankfurter that accorded a role to balancing,[89] he wrote 'I see no possible way to escape the fateful consequences of a return to an era in which
all governmental critics had to face the probability of being sent to jail
except for this Court to abandon what I consider to be *the dangerous constitutional doctrine of "balancing"* to which the Court is at present adhering'.[90] Balancing language was also used in a number of cases involving
not communism, but civil rights activists who had been persecuted in the
South through very similar techniques, such as the compulsory disclosure of membership.[91] Finally, Chief Justice Warren, towards the end of
his tenure, provided a coda to the balancing debate in his 1967 decision

---

[84] *Ibid.*, pp. 68–69.    [85] *Ibid.*, p. 68.
[86] *Ibid.*, pp. 71–75.
[87] Other first amendment cases from this period in which Supreme Court Justices referred
to a balancing of conflicting interests include: *Wieman v. Updegraff*, 344 US 183, 188
(1952); *Sweezy v. New Hampshire*, 354 US 234, 266–67 (1957) (Frankfurter, J., concurring); *Shelton v. Tucker*, 364 US 479, 496 (1960) (Frankfurter, J., dissenting). For a more
extensive list, see Kennedy (1969), p. 842, and Emerson (1964), p. 912.
[88] 367 US 1 (1961).    [89] *Ibid.*, p. 91.
[90] *Ibid.*, p. 164 (emphasis added).
[91] See, e.g., *NAACP v. Button*, 371 US 415, 453 (1963) (Harlan, J., concurring).

in *United States* v. *Robel*.[92] Holding unconstitutional on the ground of first amendment 'overbreadth' a compulsory registration requirement for members of communist organizations, the Chief Justice, in the final footnote of his opinion for the Court, seemed to offer a comprehensive rejection of balancing as a method under the first amendment:

> It has been suggested that this case should be decided by 'balancing' the governmental interest [...] against the First Amendment rights asserted by the appellee. This we decline to do. We recognize that both interests are substantial, but we deem it inappropriate for this Court to label one as being more important or more substantial than the other. Our inquiry is more circumscribed [...] [W]e have confined our analysis to whether Congress has adopted a constitutional means in achieving its concededly legitimate legislative goal. In making this determination, we have found it necessary to measure the validity of the means adopted by Congress against both the goal it has sought to achieve and the specific prohibitions of the First Amendment. *But we have in no way 'balanced' those respective interests.*[93]

Justice Black did not dissent from this statement for a unanimous Court.

The end of this 'balancing war' between the Justices did not, however, mean an end to the discourse of balancing in constitutional rights cases. The Court itself over the following years frequently revisited and developed first amendment doctrine using the language of balancing. In 1968, for example, in the case of *United States* v. *O'Brien*, the Court constructed an explicit balancing test to deal with instances of so-called 'symbolic conduct' – in O'Brien's case: the burning of his military draft card on the steps of the South Boston Court House in violation of a federal law prohibiting the destruction of such cards.[94] And in 1980, the Court developed an explicit 'four-part balancing test' to deal with first amendment cases in which the relevant speech was of a 'commercial' nature.[95]

---

[92] 389 US 258 (1967).

[93] *Ibid.*, fn. 20 (emphasis added).

[94] 391 US 367, 376 (1968).

[95] *Central Hudson Gas & Electric* v. *Public Service Commission of New York*, 447 US 557, 564–66 (1980) ('In commercial speech cases, then, a four-part analysis has developed. At the outset, we must determine whether the expression is protected by the First Amendment. For commercial speech to come within that provision, it at least must concern lawful activity and not be misleading. Next, we ask whether the asserted governmental interest is substantial. If both inquiries yield positive answers, we must determine whether the regulation directly advances the governmental interest asserted, and whether it is not more extensive than is necessary to serve that interest.') For discussion

The conclusion of the Frankfurter/Harlan *v.* Black/Douglas debate also marked the start of a rise of academic interest in the topic of judicial balancing in the constitutional rights context that has continued to this day. From the early-mid 1960s onwards, a growing number of law review articles appeared that focused principally, or even solely, on the theme of judicial balancing, in the free speech context,[96] or with regard to constitutional rights adjudication generally.[97] 'Balancing' rapidly became one of the most prominent frameworks for understanding free speech issues and other problems of constitutional rights adjudication – a position that it still holds today.[98]

### C. Contemporary critiques of balancing in US free speech jurisprudence of the 1950s and 1960s

This section gives an overview of some of the main themes in contemporary critiques of balancing in American constitutional rights jurisprudence, with particular reference to the context of the freedom of speech. The relevant debates are approached from three angles. First, in a subsection on the nature and scope of 'balancing' I look at the questions of what participants thought balancing *was*, in terms of the different familiar categories of legal thought (doctrine, method, theory, etc.), and to what range of problems they thought balancing, so conceived, was relevant. A second subsection analyses the effects the 'use' of balancing was thought to have for the meaning of the first amendment and for the strength of the protection it could offer to speakers of unpopular opinions. A third subsection, finally, examines the supposed consequences of balancing for the institutional position of the judiciary, and in particular for the institution of constitutional rights review.

### 1. Nature and scope

As in Chapter 3, on German balancing discourse, a first way to distinguish among contemporary interpretations and critiques of the Supreme Court balancing decisions is according to the position judges and commentators

---

of *Central Hudson* as imposing a 'balancing test' see, e.g., Sunstein (1996) pp. 82ff. See also Grimm (2007), p. 384 (noting that *Central Hudson* 'was not a trend-setting decision that gained much influence outside commercial speech problems').

[96] Meiklejohn (1961b); Frantz (1962); Mendelson (1964).

[97] Fried (1963); Shapiro (1963a); Henkin (1978).

[98] See, e.g., Emerson (1963); Kennedy (1969); Emerson (1970); Ely (1975); Schauer (1981).

took on the question of what balancing *was*. Before looking at the different relevant views in detail, one comparative observation may be helpful. Simplifying somewhat: while the *Bundesverfassungsgericht* typically
invoked *Güterabwägung* on the level of general constitutional rights theory, at the US Supreme Court the standard reference would be on the
level of constitutional legal doctrine for a – more or less narrowly circumscribed – area of first amendment law. This prevalence of lower levels of
generality in American balancing discourse came with an important corollary, and that was a much more prominent role for the idea of balancing
*as choice*. Balancing as a 'technique', 'tool' or 'test' of first amendment
law was subject to constant comparison with other 'techniques', 'tools'
or 'tests' that would have been equally available.[99] I return to the implications for balancing's meaning of this pervasive contrasting and comparing in Section E in this chapter.

### (a)   Doctrine, technique, theory

On the Supreme Court itself, the balancing debates between the Justices
were mostly confined to discussions of balancing as a form of first amendment doctrine. The precise scope of application of this doctrine of balancing, however, was subject of some uncertainty. Observers could note quite
easily that balancing had 'come to the fore largely in a single type of case',
involving compelled disclosure of connections to communist organizations.[100] But this narrowly circumscribed factual situation-type clearly
did not exhaust the range of balancing language used by the Justices. The
*Dennis* case in particular did not fit this description. Defining in broader
terms the kind of problems to which balancing as doctrine would be
applicable, therefore, was not easy.

The Justices themselves made a number of attempts at demarcation. In
*Douds*, Chief Justice Vinson explicitly limited his discussion of balancing
to cases in which 'particular conduct is regulated in the interest of public order'.[101] And in *Konigsberg*, Justice Harlan spoke of 'general regulatory statutes, not intended to control the content of speech'.[102] Both these
criteria were clearly inspired by an effort to link the incendiary 'loyalty
oath' and 'compulsory disclosure' situations to the more pedestrian pre-
War *Schneider* line of cases on 'time, place, and manner' restrictions.[103]

---

[99]  In a pun not lost on contemporary commentators, this meant that the value of 'balancing' could itself be subjected to a 'balancing' exercise. See, e.g., Frantz (1962), p. 1433.
[100]  Frantz (1962), p. 1429. See also Kalven (1964), p. 216.
[101]  339 US 382, 399 (1950).    [102]  366 US 36, 50 (1961).
[103]  Cf. Frantz (1962), p. 1429 (suggesting that *Douds* 'reformulated' the *Schneider* principle).
See also Henkin (1978), p. 1045.

Further indices as to the scope of application of balancing as a doctrine came from its opponents. In *Barenblatt*, Justice Black wrote that he did not agree that 'laws directly abridging First Amendment freedoms' could be justified by a balancing process.[104] And in *Konigsberg*, he argued against applying a balancing test 'to governmental action that is *aimed at speech* and depends for its application upon the *content of speech*'.[105]

Taken together, these statements suggest that balancing as doctrine should be limited to cases in which the governmental measure at issue was both (a) primarily directed at and – or? – had a primary effect on *conduct* rather than on speech and (b) in which this measure was *neutral as to the content* of expression, in its aims and – or? – in its effects.[106] As the ambiguity in this summary shows, however, these judicial statements clearly do not answer all questions as to the scope of balancing as doctrine.[107] In terms of application, therefore, the scope of balancing as doctrine was far from clear.

On a second set of views, the language of balancing denoted a particular judicial technique, of which first amendment doctrine was merely the most prominent instance.[108] Justice Black's position in particular could be read at least partially in this way. A telling example can be found in his criticism, in *Barenblatt*, of the majority's decision to accept '*a balancing test* to decide if First Amendment rights shall be protected'.[109]

Naturally, such discussions tended to move especially quickly towards the comparison of balancing with alternative judicial techniques. To take a typical example: a contemporary author would distinguish 'two principal approaches' within 'judicial methodology in constitutional cases': (a) 'the "interest-balancing" technique which may be seen in such diverse matters as state power [...] to regulate interstate commerce [...] and First Amendment freedoms' and (b) the 'application of more-or-less rigid rules or standards to factual situations'.[110] By far the most prominent

---

[104]  360 US 109, 141.

[105]  366 US 36, 70 (1961) (emphases added).

[106]  See, e.g., Kalven (1964), p. 216; Kennedy (1969), p. 846.

[107]  Also: The disagreement between Harlan and Black in *Barenblatt* and *Konigsberg* was not so much over these criteria in the abstract as over whether the relevant measures constituted 'indirect' burdens (Harlan) or 'direct', 'content based' restrictions (Black). See also Kennedy (1969), p. 846.

[108]  See, e.g., Fried (1963), p. 757.

[109]  360 US 109, 139 (emphasis added); 366 US 36, 68 (1961) (Black, J., dissenting). See also, e.g., Rice (1967), p. 455; Nimmer (1968), p. 939.

[110]  Miller (1965), p. 254. Miller also argues that the alternative method of 'rule application', 'in its most extreme form', would fall within the category of Roscoe Pound's 'Mechanical Jurisprudence', discussed in Chapter 2, Section B.4. See also Kennedy (1969), p. 852.

juxtaposition in terms of judicial method in the context of first amendment law, hinted at in this example, was the one between 'balancing' and
'classification' – often also called 'categorization'.[111] That opposition will
be discussed in greater detail in Section E of this chapter, as part of the
'definitional tradition' in American constitutional legal thought and as
an important aspect of balancing's American local meaning.

On a third set of views, closely related to the balancing/classification
dichotomy, balancing language was seen as expressive of a normative
theory of constitutional rights protection, either in general terms or for
the first amendment specifically. Justice Black's February 1960 *Madison
Lecture* at New York University is an influential example of the former.
Black sketched a theory according to which 'individual rights must, if
outweighed by the public interest, be subordinated to the Government's
competing interest' as one of two fundamental approaches to the interpretation of the Bill of Rights.[112] That theory, Black argued, rested 'on the
premise that there are no "absolute" prohibitions in the Constitution, and
that all constitutional problems are questions of reasonableness, proximity, and degree'.[113] Black thought the 'clear and present danger' test and the
explicit 'balancing' test were both 'verbal expressions' of this underlying
theory.[114]

Thomas Emerson's work, finally, offers a prominent example of the
view of balancing as a theory of free speech law.[115] The task for the judiciary in maintaining a system of freedom of expression and integrating
it 'into the broader structure of modern society', Emerson argued, was
to develop 'principles of reconciliation' for competing values, 'expressed
in the form of legal doctrine'.[116] Emerson saw a range of difficulties with
the Court's balancing test, which meant that, in his view, the ad hoc balancing test was 'illusory' as 'a legal theory of reconciliation'.[117] Instead, he
argued, the adoption and continued acceptance of the first amendment
signified 'that some fundamental decisions with respect to reconciliation
have been made, that a certain major balancing of interests has already

---

[111] Cf. Ely (1975), p. 1500.
[112] Black (1960), p. 866.
[113] In another formulation, Justice Black describes this as the view that 'liberties admittedly
*covered* by the Bill of Rights can nevertheless *be abridged* on the ground that a superior
public interest justifies the abridgment' (*ibid.*, at p. 867, emphasis added).
[114] *Ibid.*, p. 866.    [115] Emerson (1963).    [116] *Ibid.*, p. 898.
[117] *Ibid.*, p. 914. Intriguingly, Emerson did not see a natural connection between the theme
of 'reconciliation', which he favoured, and judicial balancing, which he did not. On this
connection in the German context, see Chapter 3, Section E.2.

been performed'.[118] The function of courts was not 'to reopen this prior balancing', but to 'define' as precisely as possible 'the key elements in the first amendment'.[119]

Both Black's 'absolutism' and Emerson's 'definitional approach' will be discussed further below, again as part of the 'definitional tradition' in American law.[120]

### (b)   It's all balancing

There was one further, very different, level on which balancing was discussed. This was in terms of the nature of adjudication and of law generally. For a substantial number of commentators, the language of balancing signalled an acknowledgment, on the part of judges, of the unavoidable, inherent qualities of what they were doing. All adjudication, on this view, could sensibly be described as balancing.[121] Using this language merely meant being open about something that was traditionally being concealed. Such views often relied on one or more of Justice Holmes' aphorisms, or on Benjamin Cardozo's admission that he and his judicial colleagues were 'balancing and compromising and adjusting every moment we judge'.[122] For others, adjudication in at least all difficult cases could suitably be described as involving some form of balancing. Lawyers and political scientists interested in the nascent school of 'political jurisprudence',[123] in particular, liked to emphasize 'the more recent thought about the nature of the judicial process', according to which in many cases before the Supreme Court, there would be 'no law to be discovered', leaving the Court to 'make its own law by balancing the interests of competing parties'.[124] On these views, balancing as a process would be inevitable in all or most cases. The appropriateness of using explicit balancing language in turn would depend on the costs and benefits of being open about the nature of judging.

Quite obviously, if this view of the meaning of balancing language is held, the significance of much of the debates between Justices Black,

---

[118]   *Ibid.*   [119]   *Ibid.*

[120]   See Chapter 4, Section E.

[121]   See, e.g., Karst (1960), p. 79 ('All judges balance competing interests in deciding constitutional questions – even those who most vigorously deny their willingness to do so.'); Blasi (1970), p. 1489.

[122]   Cardozo (1928), p. 75.

[123]   Cf. Shapiro (1963a), p. 587; Shapiro (1963b).

[124]   See, e.g., Miller & Howell (1960), p. 686; Shapiro (1963a), p. 595; Shapiro (1963b).

Frankfurter and Harlan changes dramatically.[125] Referring to Black's categorical approach, for example, one observer could note that on a view of 'adjudication as balancing', there was 'really no difference' between what Black proposed 'and the general use of the "balancing" technique'. 'Actually', this commentator concluded, "balancing" is the very essence of judging, because in every case there must be a determination of which of two or more conflicting interests will prevail [...] It seems much more realistic to recognize this to be the case than to rely on formulae which merely conceal'.[126]

### (c)    Balancing on multiple levels

The parallel existence of multiple levels at which balancing was discussed, from 'local' first amendment doctrine, via general normative theory of constitutional rights to descriptive theory of adjudication, is significant in and of itself. The explanation for how a relatively small number of judicial references to balancing could spiral into one of the most heated controversies in all of constitutional law largely lies in the broad range of virtually automatic associations participants made on the basis of simple balancing language.[127] These tendencies of connection and association, and their implications, can be specified a little further.

One noticeable first trend was for support of reliance on balancing to occupy lower levels of generality – the narrower, localized perspectives of balancing as doctrine or judicial technique – than critical assessments. The easiest way to make this point is to look at some typical critiques. Commonly, whenever Justice Black, Charles Reich, Laurent Frantz or other critics referred to some 'general theory' that conceived of civil liberties adjudication as a wholesale balancing of competing interests, they neglected to include references to scholarly or judicial contributions actually advocating such a view. In his *Madison Lecture*, for example, Black cited no adherents of the 'theory' that 'all constitutional problems are questions of reasonableness, proximity, and degree'. Laurent Frantz gave no examples of writers or Justices advocating 'the theory that the first amendment [...] protects not rights

---

[125]  See, e.g., McKay (1963), p. 280.

[126]  Nutting (1961), p. 174; Klein (1968), p. 785 (referring to Justice Black's 'absolutism' as a 'problem solving technique' for conflicts of interests and arguing that Black 'necessarily' engaged in balancing 'albeit under differently labeled devices').

[127]  For a typical escalation along these lines see, e.g., Fried (1963), pp. 755 (taking up the Court's 'so-called "balancing test"' under the First Amendment as the manifestation 'most in need of analysis' of a general theory of adjudication turning on 'the analysis of rights into interests').

but "interests".[128] And when Frantz wrote that '[i]f a balancing test is applied to the first amendment, it is hard to see why it should not be applied to the entire Constitution', he did not cite any real adherents of such a comprehensive approach.[129]

Particularly striking in this respect was the work of Charles Reich, one of Justice Black's principal apologists. Reich claimed that '[d]uring Justice Black's years on the Court its majority has been dominated by a philosophy of constitutional adjudication based upon the weighing of conflicting values', which holds that the judicial task 'is to resolve these conflicts by the exercise of judgment on a case-by-case basis'.[130] But again no explanation of the background or content of this 'philosophy' was offered, nor were references to judicial opinions to substantiate the claim. Balancing on these higher levels of normative theory, then, appeared largely as a straw man.[131]

A second striking trend was for critical discussions of balancing to include some kind of acknowledgment that 'balancing' in some form or other was natural or inevitable, even when the 'balancing' of the Supreme Court decisions was to be vigorously rejected. Sometimes this nod took the form of a – possibly somewhat ironic – reference to an original 'balancing' undertaken by the framers of the Bill of Rights.[132] Most common, however, was an acknowledgment of the unavoidability of 'balancing' on the level of the mental processes of decision making. Thomas Emerson, for example, who advocated a categorical distinction between 'expression' and 'action' as the centrepiece of his theoretical framework, accepted that this definitional approach 'of course' involved 'a weighing of considerations'. That 'weighing', though, was, he argued, 'narrower, taking place within better defined limits, than ad hoc balancing'.[133] Laurent Frantz made a similar concession: '[T]hough the mental process by which a judge determines what rule to adopt can be described

---

[128] Cf. Frantz (1962), p. 1440.

[129] *Ibid.*, pp. 1444–45. Frantz does cite Judge Learned Hand as an advocate of this position ('if I understand him correctly [...]', see p. 1445). It is clear, though, that Learned Hand in no way advocated a general balancing approach to the Bill of Rights in the sense imputed to him by Frantz. See, e.g., Gunther (1975), pp. 720ff. See also below, Chapter 4, Section E.1.

[130] Reich (1963), p. 737.

[131] This is not to say that there were *no* theories of rights protection based on conceptions of 'weighing', 'conflict of interests' and 'clashes between values'. For two early examples, see Nizer (1941) and Richardson (1951).

[132] Cf. Emerson (1963), p. 929; Black (1960), p. 879.

[133] Emerson (1963), pp. 915–17.

as "balancing," this does not make it the same as "balancing," independent of any rule, to determine what is the best disposition to make of a particular case.'[134]

Statements of this type are illustrative of the hold balancing vocabulary exercised, even over its critics. The dominance of the idiom also gives a rather defensive feel to many of the critiques of balancing. This tension between, on the one hand, the impetus to understand and describe adjudication in balancing terms – as a badge of basic Realist sophistication – and, on the other hand, persistent doubts as to the legitimizing capacity of any judicial method denoted by this language, will be discussed in greater detail in Section E.

## 2.   'Balancing away'

Contemporary critics of balancing were concerned, more than anything else, with its implications for the meaning and force of constitutional rights guarantees, in particular with regard to freedom of expression.[135] Three themes within these critiques were particularly prominent.

### (a)   The genius of a written constitution

First, critics argued that balancing was an unsuitable technique for any form of adjudication constrained by written rules of law. Balancing, on this view, as Justice Black wrote, violated 'the genius of our written Constitution'.[136] 'The balancer's thinking processes eliminate the constitutional text so completely that he soon forgets there ever was one', Laurent Frantz wrote.[137] The 'authority of the Constitution' as a whole, on this view, was at risk.[138] Such unbounded balancing undermined the strength of the first amendment. In abandoning constitutional text, this argument ran, balancing assured 'little, if any, more freedom of speech

---

[134]   Frantz (1962), p. 1434. See also, e.g., Dodge (1969), p. 687.

[135]   The overwhelming focus in contemporary debates was on balancing's implications specifically for the freedom of speech. For a wonderfully pithy example of analysis in another context, see Dodge (1969), p. 687 (Summarizing experiences with the 'balancing test' in freedom of religion cases as follows: '(1) the state always wins; (2) courts scarcely notice the religious interest, much less attempt to analyze it; (3) courts do not really analyze the state's interest either; (4) neither courts nor attorneys accurately delineate the real issues; and, (5) judicial opinions proceed in terms of policy rather than more justiciable standards'.)

[136]   360 US 109, 143–44.

[137]   Frantz (1962), p. 1433. See also, e.g., Chase (1960), p. 602.

[138]   Meiklejohn (1953), p. 479. See also Frantz (1962), pp. 1438, 1445; Reich (1963), p. 721.

than [would have been the case] if the first amendment had never been adopted'.[139] The balancing text 'watered down' the 'unequivocal command' of the Bill of Rights 'into a quavering "Abridge if you must, but try to keep it reasonable"'.[140]

### (b)   Not just any rule of law

A second line of argument held that balancing threatened a critical loss of meaning for the first amendment specifically. This argument took several different forms. For some, like Alexander Meiklejohn or Justice Black, the first amendment was among a small group of civil liberties that simply could not be 'abridged' (although the scope of their application could be defined more or less broadly). In Meiklejohn's view, for example, the first amendment, as 'the most significant political statement which we Americans have made', was incompatible per se with any theoretical framework that accorded 'equal status' to the freedom of expression as to competing interests, such as public security or even self-preservation (as in Justice Frankfurter's *Dennis* concurrence).[141] Others, while not adhering to Black's and Meiklejohn's 'absolutism', still thought balancing was incompatible with some principle fundamental to their preferred theory of freedom of expression. Thomas Emerson's categorical distinction between 'conduct' and 'expression', or Harry Kalven's view of the 'central meaning' of the first amendment as a prohibition restraints on criticism of governmental authority, were two prominent examples of theories that appeared to ask for something different than a generic balancing exercise.[142] On these views, the first amendment had a distinctive 'positive' meaning that a mere 'negative' conception in terms of conflicting interests could not capture.[143] The first amendment specifically, in one striking formulation, should not be treated as if it were '*just another rule or principle of law*'.[144] The language of balancing, with its connotations of utilitarian calculus and social engineering was simply insufficiently sensitive to

---

[139]  Frantz (1962), p. 1443.

[140]  Frantz (1962), p. 1449. Cf. 341 US 494, 558, 580 (Black, J., dissenting); See also Emerson (1963), p. 913.

[141]  Meiklejohn (1953), pp. 461, 479.

[142]  On Emerson, see further below Chapter 4, Section E.2. See also Kalven (1964); Karst (1965), p. 22; DuVal (1972).

[143]  Cf. Frantz (1962), p. 1442; Frantz (1963), p. 754.

[144]  Kalven (1967), p. 429 (emphasis added). See also Blasi (1985), pp. 455ff; White (1996), pp. 300ff.

the distinctive and exalted position of freedom of speech in the American constitutional tradition.[145]

## (c)   Slippery slopes

A third critical theme, finally, was the idea that the Supreme Court's 'balancing opinions' failed to offer sufficient protection to the freedom of expression; the idea that balancing, in Justice Black's words, was a 'dangerous doctrine'.[146] Especially between 1950 and 1960, when the 'red scare' had been at its height, the Supreme Court majority's balancing approach was thought to have fallen short in protecting civil liberties.[147] 'The Court's ad hoc balances are on a "slippery slope"', Charles Reich wrote in this vein. 'Each is likely to reflect present-day needs and views [...] The urgencies of the day, like gravity, pull the Court along; there is no counterweight in its formula to maintain a constant level'.[148] The risk of excessive deference to the legislative and executive branches was felt to be especially severe. 'As applied to date', Thomas Emerson concluded in 1963, 'the test gives almost conclusive weight to the legislative judgment'.[149] While it was true, in his view, that the balancing test itself did not 'necessarily compel this excessive deference', 'the operation of the test tends strongly towards that result'.[150]

And even if the Supreme Court itself might be able, against experience and expectation, to withstand these 'urgencies of the day', critics pointed out that its balancing approach, in any event, did not give sufficient guidance to either rights claimants or to those on the frontlines of the first amendment – police officers, civil servants and lower courts. Balancing reduced the protection of civil liberties to guesswork.[151] This unpredictability could only undermine effective protection for rights. It was this concern that was part of the animating force behind Justice Black's insistence on 'firm and easily apprehended constitutional standards', that would 'minimize the vagrant propensities and biases of the

---

[145]   Cf. Shiffrin (1990).
[146]   367 US 1, 164.
[147]   See, e.g., Black (1960), p. 878; Reich (1963), p. 718; Nimmer (1968), p. 940.
[148]   *Ibid.*, p. 743. See also Schauer (1998), p. 111.
[149]   Emerson (1963), p. 913.
[150]   *Ibid.*, Emerson later reiterated his belief that a 'predilection for ad hoc balancing' had made the system of freedom of expression 'less effective at serving its underlying values'. See Emerson (1980), p. 423.
[151]   See, e.g., *Note: HUAC and the Chilling Effect* (1967), p. 705; Emerson (1963), p. 913. See also Justice Black's dissenting opinion in *Barenblatt*, discussed in Chapter 4, Section B.3.

thousands of judges [...] called on to administer our constitutional order'.[152]

### (d)  Weighing and outweighing

In many contemporary discussions of balancing an almost automatic connection was drawn between 'balancing' and 'balancing away', and between 'weighing' civil liberties and allowing them to be 'outweighed'. Justice Black's evocative imagery of civil liberties being 'weighed out of the Constitution' lies at the core of a tradition of associating balancing with diminished protection for constitutional rights.[153] "[B]alancing", or even worse "ad hoc balancing", still carries a bad odor', Frederick Schauer wrote of the first amendment context at the end of the 1990s.[154] That association is, at least partially, 'a legacy of the debates of the 1950s and 1960s, in which "balancing", especially as championed by Justice Frankfurter, was associated with a tendency to take the substance of governmental justification for restricting speech quite seriously and with a tendency to defer to the government's own determinations of the weight of those justifications'.[155] However hard proponents of balancing might argue that such 'balancing away' was not unavoidable and that rights might just as easily be 'defined away', the 'alignment of balancing with scantier free speech protection' has remained strong ever since.[156]

### 3.  The institutional position of the judiciary

A final lens for looking at contemporary discussions of balancing is by way of the question of its implications for the institutional position of the judiciary, in particular with regard to the exercise of constitutional judicial review.[157] Both the 'balancers' and their opponents agreed on the importance of keeping the judicial function distinct from 'politics' – of maintaining some kind of conceptual boundary between adjudication and 'policy-making'.[158] What they disagreed over was how to carve out

---

[152] Freund (1967), p. 472.

[153] Cf. *Cohen v. Hurley*, 366 US 117, 134 (1961) (Black, J., dissenting). This was a due process case, but Black referred to the first amendment. See also his dissent in *Konigsberg v. State Bar of California*, 366 US 36, 61–62 (1961).

[154] Schauer (1998), p. 110.   [155] *Ibid.*, pp. 110–11.

[156] *Ibid.* See also Karst (1965), p. 13.   [157] Cf. Kennedy (1969), p. 852.

[158] Cf. Harlan (1963), p. 944, cited in Poe (1968), p. 662; 341 US 494, 539 (Frankfurter, J., concurring); Cox (1966), p. 95 (on Black's dissent in the seminal 1965 privacy case of *Griswold v. Connecticut*). See also McWhinney (1955); Chase (1960), p. 662.

such a distinct judicial role. For Paul Freund, a long-time observer of the Supreme Court, the approaches of both sides had to be seen as responses to the constitutional crises of the *Lochner* period:

> Different minds, repelled alike by the excesses of the Court, neverthe-less responded in different ways. Some were profoundly confirmed in the view that in a democratic society the judges must defer to the more representative organs of government [...] Justice Black [...] drew a dif-ferent moral from the experience through which we had passed. For him the lesson was that the judges lose the way when they put glosses on the Constitution, that they are safe, and the people secure, only when they follow the mandates of the Framers in their full and natural meaning.[159]

For Justice Frankfurter, safeguarding a distinct domain for the judiciary meant recognizing the inherently political nature of adjudication and lim-iting the judicial function to a highly deferential form of review. '[C]onsti-tutional law [...] is not at all a science, but applied politics', Frankfurter wrote while still a law professor.[160] Because judicial decision making, on this view, was essentially identical to political decision making, the Supreme Court should limit its review of Congressional actions to a bare minimum of reasonableness testing.[161]

This understanding lay at the heart of Justice Frankfurter's conception of balancing. Political reasoning was ultimately concerned with recon-ciling competing values and interests. Judicial reasoning, on any frank assessment, could not be anything else.[162] And because the question of 'how best to reconcile competing interests' was the business of the legisla-tures, the balance they struck had to be respected by the courts, unless it lay 'outside the pale of fair judgment'.[163]

A radically different conception of the nature of constitutional adju-dication, in turn, sustained Justice Black's and others' opposition to bal-ancing. 'Justice Black's theory of judicial review [...] precludes unfettered judicial subjectivity by pinning down constitutional adjudication to the *interpretation* of specific written language', wrote Sanford Kadish.[164] On this view, keeping the judicial function distinct from politics, meant

---

[159]  Freund (1967), p. 467.
[160]  Cited in Mason (1962), p. 1400.
[161]  Cf. McWhinney (1955), p. 843.
[162]  Cf. Mendelson (1954), p. 311 (Frankfurter on deference as a 'price to be paid'); Kennedy (1969), p. 852 (Frankfurter on the Supreme Court as a 'frankly political but deferential participant in the process of government').
[163]  341 US 494, 540.
[164]  Kadish (1957), p. 337 (emphasis added).

recognizing that the text of the Constitution and the Bill of Rights 'means what it says and that [the Supreme Court] must enforce that meaning'.[165] Because what the Supreme Court did, or rather what it ought to be doing, was inherently and qualitatively different from what Congress did, Black thought, there could be no question of the judiciary intruding upon the legislative domain.[166] It was only when judges would begin to engage in the ad hoc weighing of values and interests that this fragile line of demarcation would be breached, with potentially serious consequences for the institutional position of the judiciary.[167]

Both these positions were subject to extensive debate during the late 1950s and the 1960s. Some of these discussions will figure in the next section, which deals with the demand for new standards for judicial reasoning during this period. At this stage, two observations are important. First, it is noteworthy how much of the general controversy over the judicial role came to be played out via the language of balancing. And second, reliance on this form of language often made these debates less productive than they perhaps could have been, in particular because participants tended to conflate, under a single 'balancing' label, theory and practice, rhetoric and substance. Those claiming that balancing came down to 'legislating from the bench' often ignored that both Frankfurter and Harlan adhered to a severely circumscribed view of what such judicial balancing entailed. So, for example, a serious evaluation of alternative means by which Congress could have achieved its objectives – an exercise which intuitively could easily be counted as 'balancing' – was consistently proclaimed to lie largely outside the realm of judicial control by the 'balancing' Justices.[168] On the other hand, balancing's supporters, who claimed that Justice Black's reliance on 'absolutes' and 'literalness' resulted in an unrealistic depiction of the judicial process, often neglected the more symbolic, rhetorical and strategic dimensions of Black's position – the

---

[165] 360 US 109, 143–44.
[166] Cf. Shapiro (1962), p. 177.
[167] Cf. Reich (1963), p. 749. Reich distinguished typical common law adjudication 'where the judicial function is constantly to adjust "law" to "reality"' – and where some form of balancing might be appropriate – from 'constitutional adjudication', 'where the Court has the function of maintaining a particular historical scheme'. See pp. 737–38. See also Fried (1963), pp. 755ff.
[168] *Shelton* v. *Tucker* 364 US 479, 493–94 (Frankfurter, J., dissenting), discussed in *Note: The First Amendment Overbreadth Doctrine* (1970), pp. 916ff., where the author observes: 'Somewhat ironically, it is the interest balancing method [...] advocated by the champions of judicial restraint, that by its logic requires a court to inquire into alternative statutory schemes'.

idea that 'the extremity of Justice Black's absolutist professions' had to be qualified as 'an opposition program' that was 'mainly tactical.'[169] As Alexander Bickel wrote in his 1961 *Harvard Law Review* Foreword: 'Justice Black knows as well as anyone else that free speech cannot be an absolute [...] and that the first amendment does not literally say any such certain thing.'[170] The notion of absolutes, in the eyes of Justice Black's supporters, had to be seen rather as a general 'plea for constitutional adjudication with definite standards', and as an appeal for adjudication to take place 'on a far higher plane of generality than the balancing formula demands'.[171]

Ironically, perhaps, it may have been precisely Black's extreme choice of rhetoric that made it so easy for his critics to undermine his, to some extent rhetorical, project. But then again, much the same could be said for the balancers' choice of language.

## D.  Balancing, the pragmatic and the reasoned

In the course of the 1920s, 1930s and 1940s, American legal thinkers were increasingly concerned with the elaboration of more realistic, truthful understandings of the processes of adjudication.[172] One important strand within this rapidly growing body of work emphasized the pragmatic and instrumental dimensions of judicial decision making.[173] The language of balancing played an important role in these projects of describing adjudication in more convincing terms. In the freedom of expression context, the main illustration of this trend was the way in which the classic clear-and-present danger test of the early 1920s came to be progressively reformulated in, and ultimately replaced by, balancing ideas and language. That process is described in some detail in this section. As will also be shown, however, the influence of pragmatic and instrumentalist ideas went much further than just the reformulation of this specific doctrine.

By the late 1950s, these tendencies of (re-)description ran into a formidable opposing force. At that time, a series of high-profile scholarly

---

[169] Bickel (1961), p. 41; Reich (1963), p. 744 ('The notion of "absolutes" [...] developed as a dissenting position').
[170] Bickel (1961), p. 41.
[171] Cf. Reich (1963), p. 743.
[172] This was a theme common to the work of, first, Roscoe Pound and Benjamin Cardozo, and then the Realists. On Pound see above, Chapter 2, Section C.4.
[173] See, e.g., Harris (1936), p. 464 (pragmatism and instrumentalism as 'the dominant philosophical influence in American law today').

contributions began to express grave concern over the legitimizing qualities of Supreme Court decisions. These contributions came with proposals for new understandings of what adequate legitimization should
entail and for how it might be achieved. This section discusses the work
of arguably the most prominent writer formulating such ideals: Professor
Herbert Wechsler of Columbia Law School.

On many readings, these new, although often in fact rather traditional,
ideals of judicial craftsmanship stood in direct opposition to the ideas
associated with balancing. This section elaborates this contrast and its
implications for the meaning of balancing.

### 1.   'Whatever formula is used...': from 'clear and present danger' to balancing

#### (a)   Zechariah Chafee and Sociological Jurisprudence

The clear-and-present-danger test, as was seen earlier, is commonly traced
back to the opinions of Justices Holmes and Brandeis in the landmark
cases of *Schenck* and *Abrams* (both 1919).[174] But the fact that Holmes' and
Brandeis' phrase has come to be seen as the cornerstone of an expansive
American approach to freedom of expression, owes at least as much to
Zechariah Chafee, a practicing lawyer and professor at Harvard Law
School. It was Chafee who first praised 'clear and present danger' as
an integral element of the American constitutional tradition and as a
strong barrier against government suppression of dissent.[175] Intriguingly,
Chafee's advocacy of 'clear and present danger' rested on a conceptualiza-
tion of the doctrine in terms of balancing.

In his 1920 book *Freedom of Speech*, Chafee wrote:

> The true boundary line of the First Amendment can be fixed only when
> Congress and the courts realize that the principle on which speech is clas-
> sified as lawful or unlawful involves the *balancing against each other of
> two very important social interests*, in public safety and in the search for
> truth. Every reasonable attempt should be made to maintain both inter-
> ests unimpaired, and the great interest in free speech should be sacrificed
> only when the interest in public safety is really imperilled [...].[176]

The language in which Chafee here described and promoted the clear-
and-present-danger test was that of his contemporaries, the Sociological

---

[174]   See above, Chapter 4, Section A.4.
[175]   See, e.g., Gunther (1975); Rabban (1983).
[176]   Chafee (1920), p. 38 (emphasis added).

Jurisprudes. Chafee's freedom of speech balancing was, in other words, the balancing of interests of Roscoe Pound and others, discussed in Chapter 2.[177]

Chafee, first of all, was interested, in the same way that Pound was, in how a jurisprudence of interests could be more true to life, more real-istic, than a jurisprudence of rights. 'To find the boundary line of any right', he wrote using language almost identical to Pound's, 'we must get behind rules of law to human facts'.[178] In the context of freedom of speech this meant looking at the 'desires and needs of the individual human being who wants to speak and those of the great group of human beings among whom he speaks'.[179] Talk about *rights* in the context of civil lib-erties, Chafee thought, could only lead to 'deadlock'.[180] This distinction between rights and interests, which he traced back explicitly to both von Jhering and Pound, Chafee thought could clarify 'almost any constitu-tional controversy'.[181]

This foregrounding of interests over rights functioned as a stepping stone for Chafee's main substantive argument: the idea that freedom of expression was not merely an individual, but a *social* interest. The first amendment, in Chafee's view, served, besides the interest of individuals, a 'social interest in the attainment of truth, so that the country may not only adopt the wisest course of action but carry it out in the wisest way'.[182] The great trouble with standard interpretations of the 'Sedition Act' – the principal piece of federal legislation limiting speech – Chafee wrote, was that 'this social interest has been ignored and free speech has been regarded as merely an individual interest which must readily give way'.[183]

As in Roscoe Pound's work, Chafee's interest analysis was integral to a project of *recalibration* of individual and societal claims in consti-tutional rights cases. On this point, Chafee's argument was very similar

---

[177] On the Sociological Jurisprudence background to the 1919 decisions and their after-math, see also White (1996), p. 314.

[178] Chafee (1920), p. 35. Pound himself discussed freedom of expression in explicit balan-cing terms, in his two-part article on 'Interests of Personality'. See for a description of 'Pound's Balancing Test' as it emerges from this article, Rabban (1981), pp. 517ff. Pound came to a result less protective of speech. See *ibid.*, p. 589.

[179] Chafee (1920), p. 35.

[180] *Ibid.*, p. 34. Chafee's illustration of the point is memorable: *not* to regard interests, he says, would be to claim, vacuously, that 'your right to swing your arms ends just where the other man's nose begins'.

[181] *Ibid.*, p. 35.    [182] *Ibid.*, p. 36.

[183] *Ibid.*, p. 37. See also White (1996), p. 317 (Chafee benefited from 'close contact with Progressives like Roscoe Pound').

to, but also subtly different from, Pound's critique of the *Lochner* case.[184] Pound, as discussed in Chapter 2, was concerned with promoting a view of the constitutional rights of property and contract as (*mere individual*) interests that could be balanced against other (*important social*) interests, in order to overcome the paramount status they had been given by the Supreme Court. Using the same argumentative device to opposite effect, Chafee argued that protecting the freedom of expression was not merely in the interest of individual speakers, but of society at large. This time, however, the 'rights-into-interests' mode of argument was of course designed to result in greater, not less, protection for the constitutional right concerned.

Chafee relied on two related further elements of the Sociological Jurisprudes' argumentative arsenal. First, his invocation of balancing language was inspired by scepticism of deduction and 'literalness', and, more generally, of methods of legal reasoning that obscured difficult underlying policy choices. 'The rights and powers of the Constitution [...] are largely means of protecting important individual and social interests, and because of the necessity of balancing such interests the clauses cannot be construed with absolute literalness', he wrote.[185] Balancing, on this view, was a pragmatic solution for where legal dogmatics left off, or failed. In Chafee's terms, it was not possible to 'define' the right to free speech with any precision, but it was feasible to 'establish a workable principle of classification in this method of balancing and this broad test of certain danger'.[186]

Finally, Chafee's approach to free speech was akin to Pound's methods in its emphasis on empirical evaluations and attention to factual circumstances.[187] The reference to a 'method of balancing *and this broad test of certain danger*' is revealing for the fact that Chafee saw 'clear and present danger' as turning primarily on the prediction of the likely consequences of allowing or suppressing speech.[188] The idea that this inquiry contains a strong factual element is underlined by contemporary suggestions that 'danger' was a matter of fact for juries to decide, and that 'clear

---

[184] See Chapter 2, Section C.4.
[185] Chafee (1920), p. 35.
[186] *Ibid.*, p. 38. For a later iteration of the same point, see Gollub (1942), p. 261 ('two interests must be weighed in the balance: the interest of freedom of speech and the interest of the public welfare. Obviously there is no logical mathematical solution. The solution must be a subjective, intuitive one').
[187] An additional parallel is found in Chafee's view of 'balancing' as relevant to both legislature and courts.
[188] Cf. White (1996), p. 317.

and present' was merely a description of the requisite standard of proof for this determination.[189]

## (b)   Beyond 'clear and present danger': balancing and policy

The phrase 'clear and present danger' had a chequered history after its initial invocation in *Schenck* and *Abrams*.[190] Its status as a doctrinal test for deciding cases was far from settled. 'Clear and present danger' was arguably never consistently endorsed as a first amendment 'test' by a clear majority of the Supreme Court.[191] Some Justices and observers were not convinced it even was a 'test' at all. "Clear and present danger' was never used by Mr. Justice Holmes to express a technical legal doctrine or to convey a formula for adjudicating cases', Justice Frankfurter wrote in a 1946 concurring opinion: 'It was a literary phrase not to be distorted by being taken from its context'.[192]

The uncertainty over its doctrinal status, however, has to be contrasted with the unequivocal dominance of *the rhetoric* of 'clear and present danger' in American free speech law of the 1930s and 1940s. Not only was the language pervasive in discussions on freedom of expression, 'clear and present danger' became the lens through which many of the problems of first amendment adjudication were viewed.

Throughout these discussions, the connection between the ideas and practices behind 'clear and present danger' and those related to the balancing of interests and values, first expounded by Chafee, assumed ever-greater importance. Paul Freund, for example, in words later cited by Justice Frankfurter, wrote in 1949 that the 'clear-and-present-danger test' was 'an oversimplified judgment', and 'no substitute for the weighing of values'.[193] 'Clear and present danger', other commentators began to argue, was merely a 'shorthand description of the balancing process undertaken by the Court'.[194] Whereas the idea of balancing had originally been

---

[189] See, e.g., Richardson (1951), pp. 25–28; Mendelson (1952a), p. 315. In *Dennis*, the Supreme Court held that 'clear and present danger' was 'a judicial rule to be applied as a matter of law by the courts' based on 'a judicial determination of the scope of the First Amendment applied to the circumstances of the case' (341 US 494, 513).

[190] See also Chapter 4, Section A.4.

[191] Mendelson (1952a), p. 313; Rabban (1983), p. 1348.

[192] *Pennekamp v. Florida*, 328 US 331, 353 (1946) (Frankfurter, J., concurring). See also *West Virginia Board of Education* v. *Barnette*, 319 US 624, 663 (1943) (Frankfurter, J., dissenting); Mendelson (1952b), p. 793 (1952) (Holmes's insights transformed into 'sterile dogma').

[193] Freund (1949), p. 27. See also 341 US 494, 542 (Frankfurter, J., concurring).

[194] Donnelly (1950), p. 53. See also Richardson (1951), p. 17.

invoked by Chafee in order to give practical substance to the distinctive ideology of freedom of speech of Justices Holmes and Brandeis, balancing now came to eclipse the original test virtually entirely. By the late 1940s through early 1950s, an increasingly dominant view held that balancing was *all there was* to 'clear and present danger'.

This growing emphasis on balancing meant that the relevance of 'clear and present danger' as an independent idea came increasingly under strain. Balancing had come to make up 'the extent of the utility of the concept'.[195] 'Clear and present danger' could perhaps still be useful in pointing to the 'relevant factors to be balanced', or as expressive of a more general protective 'attitude' towards free speech that should influence the outcome of a balancing process.[196] But beyond that, its distinctive qualities as an approach to deciding cases were seen as limited. 'Qualified commentators have repeatedly noted', wrote William Lockhart and Robert McClure, summarizing the literature, 'that *whatever formula is used*, the Court's function in freedom of expression cases is to balance competing interests'.[197] This balancing itself, in a new development, was increasingly described as being 'legislative' in nature. Judging first amendment claims, on these views, became explicitly a matter of policy.[198] 'Clear and present danger' or not: what courts were actually doing in first amendment cases, it was felt, was carrying out 'judicial review in the fullest legislative sense of the competing values which the particular situation presents'.[199]

The resulting assimilation of 'free speech adjudication', 'balancing', and 'policy', had assumed considerable importance by the time the Supreme Court decided the *Dennis* case in 1951. It is clearly reflected in the majority's approaches.[200] In their eyes, the rise of the balancing perspective

---

[195] Antieau (1950), p. 639. See also Emerson & Helfeld (1948), p. 86; Nimmer (1968), p. 94.
[196] Cf. Lockhart & McClure (1954), p. 368; Antieau (1950), p. 641.
[197] *Ibid.*, p. 368 (emphasis added).
[198] *Ibid.*, p. 367.
[199] Wechsler & Shulman (1941), p. 887. Herbert Wechsler – on whose work more below, in Chapter 4, Section D.2 – qualified 'clear and present danger', seen in balancing terms, as a 'thin disguise for the essentially legislative nature of constitutional adjudication' (at p. 889).
[200] Not everyone succumbed, of course. See, e.g., Mendelson (1952b), p. 794 ('The danger test that Justices Holmes and Brandeis fashioned was not a scale for "balancing" political freedom against other public interests'.) Strikingly, some contemporary German comparative lawyers thought that 'clear and present danger' and 'balancing' were distinct. See, e.g., Schnur (1965), p. 135 (lamenting the way in which US constitutional jurisprudence appeared to be giving up its 'by now sufficiently concretized clear-and-present-

meant that the classic 'clear and present danger' formula no longer captured what was important in first amendment adjudication.[201] For Chief Justice Vinson, as was seen earlier, the solution was an explicit reformulation of 'clear and present danger' in balancing terms, which he undertook following the model set out by Judge Learned Hand in the court below.[202] Justice Frankfurter, for his part, wanted to go further and to replace entirely the 'sonorous formula' of 'clear and present danger' with a 'candid and informed weighing' that no longer obscured the underlying 'unresolved conflict'.[203]

### (c)   Broader impulses: pragmatism and instrumentalism

This transformation of the clear-and-present-danger test has to be read as part of a broader jurisprudential intellectual current: the rise of pragmatism and instrumentalism as central elements of mainstream legal theory during the middle decades of the twentieth century.[204] These two labels refer to complex and sometimes internally contradictory concepts. But it is possible to single out at least three specific impulses emanating from pragmatism and instrumentalism as the 'dominant philosophical influence' of the time that were of particular relevance to balancing.[205]

On a first, very general, level, pragmatism and instrumentalism promoted an emphasis on the role of interest balancing as a technique of public (judicial and legislative) decision making. Pragmatism did so through its abhorrence of fixed rules for broad categories of cases and its insistence on experiment and incremental change. And instrumentalism did so by viewing law as a means to an end – an end described in very general terms as the 'maximization' of wants and interests.

The adherence to such a broadly applicable value theory of 'maximization', secondly, came with a corresponding scepticism of 'more particular notions of value for the resolution of specific issues'.[206] 'Pragmatic instrumentalism', to use Robert Summers's overarching term, made it very difficult to conceive of adjudication in specific areas, like freedom

---

danger formula in favour of a balancing of interests that can readily be manipulated'). But see Häberle (1962), p. 39 ('clear and present danger' *as* a balancing test).

[201] Cf. Meiklejohn (1961a), p. 13 (balancing 'is a fiction which serves to cover the fact that [...] the Court has reinstated as "controlling" the "clear and present danger" test of 1919, but with the words "clear" and "present" left out').

[202] See above, Chapter 4, Section B.2.

[203] 341 US 494, 519 (Frankfurter, J., concurring).

[204] Summers (1981), p. 873.

[205] Cf. Harris (1936), p. 464. See also Kennedy (1925), p. 66.

[206] Summers (1981), p. 915. See also at p. 876.

of expression, in anything else than the terms of 'maximization'. In this way, the scope for any distinctive normative content for doctrinal tests like 'clear and present danger', or for a categorical prohibition on prior restraints, for example, was severely undermined. Put simply: in the pragmatic instrumentalist view, the philosophical foundations of free speech adjudication could be nothing more or less than the localized instantiation of the philosophical foundations of rights adjudication generally. Having *qualitatively different* 'tests' in operation for different areas of free speech law or for different constitutional rights, in the pragmatic instrumentalist view, could only be a sign of misplaced doctrinal traditionalism.

Finally, 'pragmatic instrumentalists' shared with the Realists a distrust of juridical formulas and doctrinal language. Commentators and judges taking this line were particularly concerned that constitutional metaphors or literary phrases, such as 'clear and present danger', could be transformed into 'sterile dogma', in precisely the way Justice Holmes had warned against. This, again, was one of the many instances in which the perceived formalism of the *Lochner* period served as a commonplace image of what was to be avoided.

### (d)   Balancing as liberation

Taken together, these micro-level doctrinal developments and broader intellectual currents exemplify the pressures on the Court to 'liberate' itself from the confines of doctrinal formulas such as 'clear and present danger', and to move towards candidly framing its opinions in the language of a decisional process that was seen as both inevitable and normatively desirable. That process, of course, was a balancing of interests. Justice Harlan's opinion in the *Dennis* case, read in this way, signified 'a declaration of independence by the Court from the tyranny of a phrase'.[207] There had been 'too many opinions that hide the inevitable weighing process by pretending that decisions spring full-blown from the Constitution' or from doctrinal formulas.[208] 'What seems to have brought balancing out of the closet and into the hard light of day', in the eyes of one later writer, 'was the judicial desire for candor, the simple drive to tell the truth about judging regardless of costs'.[209] The pragmatic instrumentalist perspective meant, furthermore, that once 'candid balancing' surfaced in one area,

---

[207] Corwin (1952), p. 358. Corwin agreed with many of the basic ideas of the Realists. See McDowell (1989); Duxbury (1990).

[208] Mendelson (1962), p. 825.

[209] McFadden (1988), pp. 620–21.

there would be significant pressure to similarly 'liberate' other areas of law from obscurantist traditional formulas and to frame decisions there too in terms of balancing. Balancing's march forward, in that sense, was a truly imperial one.

## 2.	A competing perspective: standards of judicial reasoning

The mid to late 1950s were a pivotal time in the history of constitutional adjudication in the US. Major civil rights cases began to come up for decision by the Supreme Court. And the political exigencies of the Cold War were acutely felt, even after the death of Senator McCarthy. In this climate, spurred on in part by precisely the trends discussed just above, one commentator would note that a majority of the Warren Court conceded 'as perhaps no other Supreme Court before it would have, that courts *make* law'.[210] Such avowals, combined with the impact of monumental decisions such as *Brown* v. *Board of Education*, provoked attacks from politicians. During 1957 and 1958, especially, members of Congress proposed bills to strip the Court of part of its jurisdiction and to abolish life tenure for Justices.[211] While none of these proposals were ultimately enacted, these were attacks on the Court on a scale not seen since Roosevelt's court-packing plan in the 1930s.[212]

In the legal academy, unease about the Supreme Court's work manifested itself in two main related categories of critique.[213] The more general of these concerned the lack of an adequate theory of constitutional adjudication to justify the practice of constitutional judicial review. In the narrower context of judicial performance in specific cases, on the other hand, critiques focused on the inadequate justification provided by the opinions of the Justices. One of the most influential examples of the first kind of critique can be found in Judge Learned Hand's 1958 'Holmes Lecture' on 'The Bill of Rights', in which he called for greater self-restraint on the part of the judiciary in the face of the democratically accountable branches of government.[214] An important instance of the second category was Professor Henry M. Hart's 1959 *Harvard Law Review* Foreword, in

---

[210]	Chase (1960), p. 629.

[211]	Murphy (1962), p. 116, cited in Frickey (2005), p. 427.

[212]	Griswold (1960), p. 82 ('In the past six or seven years, there has been strong and frequent public criticism of the court. The reasons for this are obvious when one considers the history of the period'); Mason (1962), p. 1403.

[213]	See, e.g., Kennedy (1969), p. 852; Greenawalt (1978), p. 999.

[214]	Learned Hand (1958). See also Bickel (1962); Deutsch (1968), p. 170.

which he warned that deficiencies in the Court's reasoning were threatening to undermine 'the professional respect of first-rate lawyers for the incumbent Justices of the court'.[215]

As these calls for more attention to 'the importance of judicial rationalization' grew louder in the course of the late 1950s, legal scholars became engaged in projects of formulating 'a new set of ideals and standards for judicial decision-making' in order to better secure the legitimacy of the institution of constitutional judicial review and its exercise in specific cases.[216] What these critiques amounted to was a high profile attempt to restore 'order to the legal world in the aftermath of realism',[217] a call for a 'return to reason in law',[218] at precisely the time when balancing came to play a significant role in Supreme Court decisions. The resulting clash of ideas has had lasting influence on the meaning of balancing in US legal discourse.

### (a)    Process jurisprudence and 'reasoned elaboration'

Thinking about adequate standards for judicial reasoning had important antecedents in American jurisprudence. But it was during the final years of the 1950s that some of the core ideas within this tradition received their most influential expressions and came to dominate debates in constitutional law. The labels most commonly used to describe these ideas are 'Process Jurisprudence' and 'Reasoned Elaboration'.[219] Their core tenets can be described as a faith in reason and, especially, in the reasoned justification of constitutional decisions.[220] Adherents of this tradition defended an image of adjudication as 'a device which gives formal and institutional expression to the influence of reasoned argument in human affairs'. As such, adjudication had to discharge a particularly heavy 'burden of rationality'.[221] The precise nature of the concept of 'reason' remained

---

[215]  Hart (1959), pp. 100–101, citing Bickel and Wellington.

[216]  White (1973), p. 286.

[217]  Duxbury (1993), p. 669, citing Vetter (1983), p. 416.

[218]  Golding (1963), p. 35. See also Fallon (1997a), p. 19.

[219]  Cf. White (1973). These ideas formed part of, or were intimately related to, what has also been called the 'Hart-Wechsler Paradigm', after two of its most influential expositors: Henry M. Hart and Herbert Wechsler. See, e.g., Fallon (1994). The phrase 'reasoned elaboration' originates in the famous 1958 manuscript of course text and materials *The Legal Process* by Henry Hart and Albert Sacks.

[220]  Cf. Greenawalt (1978), p. 983; Duxbury (1993), p. 605; Fallon (1994), p. 966.

[221]  Fuller (1978), pp. 366–67. Neil Duxbury notes that although Fuller's article was published in 1978, a draft of the paper was circulated as early as 1957. That makes it contemporaneous with the debates canvassed here. See Duxbury (1993), p. 631.

unclear, and the standards of legal argument appropriate to its fulfillment contentious. A common theme in many contributions, however, was the insistence on reason as a 'suprapersonal construct', a form of argument that transcended individual predilections.[222] How to give substance to this idea remained a central challenge for contemporary scholars.

(b)    The call for 'neutral principles of constitutional law'

By far the most influential attempt to develop new ideals and standards for constitutional legal reasoning came from Professor Herbert Wechsler of Columbia Law School. It was contained in a lecture delivered in 1959, entitled 'Toward Neutral Principles of Constitutional Law'.[223] The debate over 'the possibility' of such 'neutral principles' has come to characterize the Warren Court era as a whole.[224] It is in this debate that the themes of process jurisprudence, 'reasoned elaboration' and a more general unease with judicial reasoning at the Supreme Court coalesced.

The central issue in Wechsler's lecture was what he called 'the problem of criteria' – standards for the justification of Supreme Court decisions, to be adhered to by the Justices themselves as well as by their critics.[225] Such standards are necessary if the Court is to function not as a 'naked power organ' but as a 'court of law'.[226] The greatest obstacle to the satisfaction of this ideal – 'the deepest problem' of constitutionalism, even – in Wechsler's view, is ad hoc evaluation; judgments turning on the 'immediate result' in a case.[227] Wechsler's opposition to the ad hoc in adjudication is summed up in an oft-cited paragraph:

> [W]hether you are tolerant, perhaps more tolerant than I, of the *ad hoc* in politics, with principle reduced to a manipulative tool, are you not also ready to agree that something else is called for from the courts? I put it to you that the main constituent of the judicial process is precisely that it must be *genuinely principled*, resting with respect to every step that is involved in reaching judgment on analysis and reasons quite transcending the immediate result that is achieved.[228]

---

[222]  White (1973), p. 287. A favourite trope was Hart & Sacks' reference to 'the maturing of collective thought'.

[223]  Wechsler (1959). See also Shapiro (1963a), p. 588 (Wechsler's 'catalytic Holmes Lectures'); Silver (1976), p. 375 (the lecture 'colored the course of the great legal debate of the 1960s'); Greenawalt (1978); Friedman (1997).

[224]  Friedman (2002), p. 241.     [225]  Wechsler (1959), p. 11.

[226]  *Ibid.*, p. 12.     [227]  *Ibid.*, pp. 12, 19.

[228]  *Ibid.*, p. 15 (emphasis added).

In Wechsler's depiction of the standards for judicial reasoning, ideas of justification, reason, principle, and law come together. A 'court of law' should take decisions that are 'entirely principled'. A 'principled decision' is one that rests on 'reasons' with respect to all the issues in the case. And adequate 'reasons' are those that in their generality and their neutrality transcend any immediate result that is involved.[229]

Despite the enigmatic, 'tantalizing' even,[230] nature of his argument, Wechsler's basic position can be summarized in two simple general statements: Judicial decisions must be *reasoned*, and the reasons supporting these decisions must be *of a special kind*. 'The call for neutral principles in its mildest form is a plea for reasoned elaboration rather than *ipse dixits* in Supreme Court opinions', Wechsler's critic Martin Shapiro wrote approvingly.[231] The difficulty, of course, would be to determine what kinds of reasoning might justify judicial decisions. Within the large body of literature responding to Wechsler's 'neutral principles' suggestion, two trends are particularly striking. On the one hand, the idea of any kind of 'neutrality' in Supreme Court decision making was from the outset greeted with intense scepticism and criticism. At the same time though, to the extent Wechsler's work was read as a broader call for *general* principles' in judicial reasoning, it found widespread resonance. 'I fail to grasp Professor Wechsler's position if it consists in the statement that one ought to, or even can, supply "neutral principles" for "choosing" between competing values', one early critic wrote. However, 'we may still require that the tribunal formulate a standard or criterion that shall function as *a principle of decision in this and other cases of its type*. This principle is general in the sense that it covers but also transcends the instant case'.[232] A 'neutral principle', therefore, came to be largely equated with a 'principle' as such, which in turn was taken to mean a 'rule of general application, logically and consistently applied'.[233]

### 3.   *Principled reasoning and balancing*

We can now frame our central question. How did Wechsler and his contemporaries view the relationship between principled reasoning and judicial balancing?

---

[229] *Ibid.*, p. 19.    [230] Sunstein (1986), p. 590.
[231] Shapiro (1963a), p. 591.
[232] Golding (1963), p. 48. See futher Greenawalt (1978), p. 991.
[233] Henkin (1961), p. 653; Bickel (1961), p. 48 ('[A] neutral principle [...] is one that the Court must be prepared to apply across the board, without compromise').

Wechsler's article was published just before the balancing debate erupted on the Supreme Court and his article does not address the theme in any direct way.[234] A later commentator, Kent Greenawalt, has observed that Wechsler's original lecture left 'some doubt' as to whether the Supreme Court's 'open-ended standards that indicate some kind of weighing of factors or balancing but that do not unambiguously yield results in many of the cases to which they apply' could qualify as 'neutral principles'.[235] Greenawalt also notes that in a later article, Wechsler openly wondered whether constitutional-law questions of the format 'How much is too much?' might not simply be 'beyond the possibility of principled decision'.[236]

Reading Wechsler's original article in light of later interpretations, it is possible, however, to piece together a likely contemporary understanding of the balancing/principled reasoning relationship, along three axes. These concern opposition to types of reasoning that were seen as mechanical, results-based, and legislative, or not appropriate to a 'court of law'. In each case, what is striking is the paradoxical nature of the positions held. It is not surprising, then, that American legal scholars have come to label the discourse of neutral principles and its opposites a 'schizophrenic' discourse.[237]

### (a)   Candour versus 'mechanistic reasoning'

The first of these axes concerns the value attributed to judicial candour and openness. Using a freedom of speech example, Wechsler argued that as 'some ordering' of values would be essential to maintaining a functioning Bill of Rights, judges should be very careful not to take 'a mechanistic approach to determining priorities of values'.[238] This warning demonstrates that Wechsler was taking aim at *unacknowledged* judicial choices as much as at choices that were acknowledged but unprincipled. The 'mechanistic' label, an obvious throwback to Pound's early-twentieth-century attack on the Supreme Court's *Lochner* line of decisions, was invoked to convey the exact opposite of the openness that was demanded of courts.[239]

---

[234]  One further reason for this is that Wechsler was primarily interested in the Supreme Court's segregation decisions. These decisions were not generally seen as raising issues of balancing in the same way the first amendment cases were.

[235]  Greenawalt (1978), p. 988.

[236]  Wechsler (1964), p. 299, cited in Greenawalt (1978), p. 989.

[237]  See, e.g., Redish (1983), p. 1046.

[238]  Wechsler (1959), p. 25.

[239]  In another demonstration of the conflicted nature of the relevant discourse: Wechsler's thesis has itself been rejected as formalistic in the sense of Roscoe Pound's 'mechanical

Wechsler himself did not raise the question of whether the Supreme Court's 'balancing opinions' should be seen as examples of such 'mechanistic reasoning', or rather as manifestations of judicial candour. Other commentators, however, took up precisely this issue. And they came to diametrically opposing conclusions. On one side, writers argued that the open articulation of competing interests was precisely one of the main strengths of balancing-based adjudication.[240] They thought that narrow, 'virtually *ad hoc*', but 'articulated and undisguised' decisions, were all that could realistically be expected from the Supreme Court in difficult areas of constitutional rights adjudication.[241] Not to balance explicitly would be to take an unreasoned, 'mechanistic' approach to constitutional adjudication.[242] On this view, it was precisely the vehement anti-balancing rhetoric of Justice Black and others which most risked to 'deprecate and damage' the process and image of judicial decision making, which had to be 'as deliberate and conscious as men can make it'.[243] For others, on the other hand, the Supreme Court's balancing decisions consisted of no more than 'a declaration of result accompanied by the simple announcement that the Court has balanced the competing interests'.[244] Such opinions clearly did not qualify as 'reasoned decisions' in Wechslerian terms.[245]

Both sides, then, invoked the horrors of 'mechanistic reasoning' – the familiar shorthand for the vices of formalism discussed earlier, in Chapter 2 – and claimed the virtue of candour. That they did so, in the words of one contemporary overview, 'perhaps equally unconvincingly',[246] only serves to underline the continuous tension and ambivalence that lies at the heart of balancing's American local meaning.

---

jurisprudence'. See, e.g., Sunstein (1986), p. 624 ('*Lochner*-like quality'); Friedman (1997), pp. 519–20 ('Wechsler's approach, to those critical of it, bore too much similarity to the now bad old days of arid legal formalism.') See also Chapter 2, Section B. 4.

[240] Karst (1960), p. 81.

[241] Bickel (1970), p. 77. See also Wright (1971), p. 779. Wright also writes: 'Bickel is by no means alone in his conclusion that candid case-by-case balancing of particular elements of particular fact situations is the best that can be done'. *Ibid.* See also Gunther (1968), p. 1148 (claiming that there might be value in the 'relatively unobscured acknowledgment' that Courts 'balance values').

[242] See, e.g., Miller & Howell (1960), p. 671 ('Any reference to neutral [...] principles is [...] little more than a call for a return to a mechanistic jurisprudence and to a jurisprudence of nondisclosure.'); Mendelson (1964), p. 481.

[243] Bickel (1962), p. 96, cited in Powe (1989), p. 281.

[244] See, e.g., Kent (1961), p. 484.

[245] See also Emerson (1963), p. 877 (balancing reduced the first amendment to a 'limp and lifeless formality').

[246] Kennedy (1969), p. 851.

## (b)   Ad hoc-, result-oriented reasoning

In whatever precise way Wechsler's notions of generality and neutrality are understood, a key underlying theme clearly was the opposition to ad hoc decision making focused on results in individual cases.[247] On a most basic level, Wechsler called for decisions based on 'analysis and reasons [...] transcending the immediate result' of the case at hand.[248] The desirability of this criterion was hotly contested. Many commentators felt that attention to the real-world impact of individual judicial decisions had been one of the great contributions of, first, Sociological Jurisprudence and, then, Realism. 'Professor Wechsler's lecture [...] represents a repudiation of all we have learned about law since Holmes published his Common Law in 1881, and Roscoe Pound followed [...] with his pathbreaking pleas for a result-oriented, sociological jurisprudence, rather than a mechanical one', Dean Eugene Rostow of the Yale Law School wrote acidly in 1962.[249] Another writer summarized the debate on 'result-oriented jurisprudence' a year later as follows: 'To some, the label connotes subjectivism pure and simple [...] To others, a "result-oriented" court signifies a welcome innovation, a "belated recognition" of the limitations of logic and tradition'.[250] In addition, the idea of 'narrow' decisions, tailored to the individual case, not only fit well with traditional common law conceptions of the judicial role, but also seemed especially appropriate in an era in which courts were called upon to solve civil rights claims that were seen as both new and difficult.[251] As Kenneth Karst observed, 'the phrase "ad hoc" should not disturb anyone who recognizes that we are concerned with *cases*, decided by courts'.[252]

The Supreme Court's 'balancing opinions' of the late 1950s and early 1960s were widely seen as espousing a kind of ad hoc decision making – or, in more favourable terminology: a 'case-by-case' approach. Justice Harlan, for example, unambiguously described his preferred solution for first amendment cases, in his *Barenblatt* opinion for the Court, as a process of 'balancing [...] the competing private and public interests at stake *in the particular circumstances shown*'.[253] And in *Konigsberg*, Justice Black's dissenting opinion specifically chided Harlan for taking an

---

[247] Cf. Deutsch (1968), p. 178; Wechsler (1959), p. 12.
[248] *Ibid.*, p. 15. Cf. Shapiro (1963a), p. 592 (describing the plea for neutral principles as 'shading into a broad attack on result-oriented jurisprudence').
[249] Cited in Friedman (1997), pp. 519–20.
[250] Rohan (1963), p. 53.
[251] See, e.g., Friedman (1997), p. 525.
[252] Karst (1965), p. 22.
[253] *Barenblatt* v. *United States*, 360 US 109, 126 (1959) (emphasis added).

overly narrow, particularistic view of the interests concerned.[254] Justice Frankfurter's position, on the other hand, was much more ambiguous. In his *Dennis* concurrence, Frankfurter had warned explicitly against the dangers of '*ad hoc* judgment'.[255] And the presentation of his deferential balancing approach proceeds in distinctly general, even 'legislative', terms. A generalized 'interest in security' seen to be threatened by the Communist party[256] was to be weighed against a similarly generalized, social 'interest in free speech'.[257] At the same time however, Frankfurter's comments on the legacy of the clear-and-present-danger test, in particular his reference to its requirement of 'immediate peril' and his appreciation for Paul Freund's multiple-variable understanding of the test,[258] reveal a sensitivity for the need for a more situated judgment.[259]

Notwithstanding these ambiguities, balancing at the Supreme Court predominantly came to be associated with some form of ad hoc decision making. In academic commentary, 'balancing' was routinely referred to as 'ad hoc balancing', and the Court's 'balancing test' was perceived to lie 'very close to the ad hoc end of the continuum' of possible judicial decisional techniques.[260] The great balancing debate between the Justices, in short, was understood to be about not just balancing per se, but about ad hoc balancing.[261]

As Martin Redish observed in a later retrospective study, 1960s attitudes towards the ad hoc in constitutional judicial decision making, both within the balancing context and beyond, revealed a distinct 'schizophrenic' quality.[262] Much of the Supreme Court's reasoning on this issue seemed trapped between on the one hand 'perceptions about the dangers to constitutional rights of anything approaching a detailed case-by-case balancing process', and on the other hand apprehension about 'the Court's institutional incompetence to perform [the] "legislative" function' of reviewing potentially offending legislation in any way that would transcend the boundaries of the immediate case at hand.[263]

---

[254] *Konigsberg* v. *State Bar of California*, 366 US 36, 74–75 (1961).

[255] *Dennis* v. *United States*, 341 US 494, 529 (1951).

[256] Frankfurter writes of the need to go beyond the findings of the jury, and to approach the case 'in the light of whatever is relevant to a *legislative* judgment' (emphasis added), *ibid.*, at p. 547.

[257] *Ibid.*, pp. 546–52.    [258] *Ibid.*, pp. 527, 542.

[259] See also *ibid.*, p. 519 (arguing against a 'dogmatic preference' for either speech or its limitation, and for a 'candid examination of the conflicting claims').

[260] Kennedy (1969), p. 844.

[261] See, e.g., Reich (1963), p. 749; Redish (1983), p. 1046.

[262] *Ibid.*    [263] *Ibid.*, pp. 1045–46.

## (c)   Courts of law

If Wechsler's opposition to 'mechanistic' reasoning, ad hoc decision making and result-oriented reasoning are difficult to interpret in any precise
way, the most enigmatic element of his, and others', proposals surely was
their broad call for courts to behave like '*courts of law*'.[264] But this demand
for judges to behave 'judicially', in both its negative and positive aspects,
arguably formed the core of the new proposals for the standards for judicial reasoning.[265] Negatively speaking, judges were exhorted *not* to behave
like legislators or policy makers. Wechsler and others, notably those scholars associated with 'process jurisprudence', were profoundly attached to
a principle of 'institutional settlement'.[266] The question of 'who should
decide what'[267] was of fundamental importance to these writers because
of their conviction that the Supreme Court's prestige could only be pre-
served if it could be ensured that the Court 'did not overstep the limits of
its function'.[268] Viewed from a positive angle, these same commentators
were interested in promoting the importance of 'traditional standards of
judicial performance';[269] of the relevance of doctrine, legal method and
'craftsmanship' to the exercise of the judicial function, as distinct from
other forms of decision making.[270]

These aspirations for judicial reasoning are coupled with, or translated
into, critiques of judicial balancing throughout the literature and case law
of the period. Balancing, it was argued, was 'not law'; carrying out balancing exercises was not appropriate 'judicial behaviour'; and balancing
opinions forced or incited judges to intrude upon the sphere of competence of the legislative branch. Louis Henkin, in a seminal 1978 article,
gave the following summary of the critique:

> Wechsler's most famous demand of the Court, that it decide cases on
> the basis of neutral principles, is at bottom a demand *that the Court
> act according to law*, not caprice. Some have seen a tendency towards

[264]   Cf. Wechsler (1959), p. 19.

[265]   *Ibid.*, pp. 15–16 ('reasoned explanation' as 'intrinsic to judicial action' and 'the province
of the courts').

[266]   See, e.g., Fallon (1994), p. 964.

[267]   See Duxbury (1993), p. 633 (on the 'discovery', in the late 1950s, of this issue as a 'fundamental question of modern jurisprudence' by writers such as Lon Fuller, Albert Sacks
and Henry Hart).

[268]   White (1973), p. 290. See further Chapter 5, Section B for a contrast with a German
image of constitutional legal perfection.

[269]   Cf. Greenawalt (1978), p. 1005.

[270]   See, e.g., White (1973), p. 290 (perceived need for 'professional expertise' in opinion
writing); Duxbury (1993), p. 641 ('good lawyership'). See also Fallon (1994), p. 966.

judicial 'lawlessness,' or at least a straining at the restraints of legal process, method and doctrine, and an exaltation of judicial reinlessness and improvisation, in *the growing resort by the courts to 'balancing'* in constitutional adjudication.[271]

Henkin here describes a diametrical opposition between balancing and 'legal method and doctrine', that, he writes, 'some' commentators and judges had drawn earlier.[272] One of the most prominent of the participants in these earlier debates was Thomas Emerson, who had formulated many of his central objections to balancing in the first amendment context in precisely these terms. 'The principal difficulty with the ad hoc balancing test', he wrote, 'is that it frames the issues in such a broad and undefined way, …, that *it can hardly be described as a rule of law at all*'.[273] Commenting on the Supreme Court's use of a balancing test for cases of indirect regulation of speech (the *Douds*-type of conflict),[274] for example, he wondered whether it might be possible 'to frame a more satisfactory interpretation of the first amendment in this area', one that would be less 'open-ended', and that would 'permit the courts to function more like judicial institutions?'[275]

In criticizing balancing's 'open-ended' nature, Emerson was primarily focused on safeguarding the 'law-like' character of Supreme Court first amendment doctrine – the positive dimension of the argument outlined above. The negative side of that argument was given voice by other judges and commentators who argued that balancing, as practiced by the courts, was primarily a *legislative*, rather than a judicial, activity.[276] Justice Frankfurter's position on the inevitably legislative nature of balancing has been discussed earlier.[277] Many commentators raised very similar concerns. Judicial balancing was felt to be 'too insensitive to the special competencies of legislatures and the judiciary'.[278] Interest balancing tended to lead courts 'into regions better known to legislatures', hampering 'strictly

---

[271] Henkin (1978), p. 1022 (emphases added).
[272] See also Henkin (1961), p. 653. Henkin does not identify any proponents of this view.
[273] Emerson (1963), p. 912 (emphasis added).
[274] See Chapter 4, Section B.2.
[275] Emerson (1963), p. 940.
[276] See, e.g., BeVier (1978), p. 329 ('[B]ecause many of the Court's first amendment decisions rest on highly particularized analyses of […] many variables, they tend to be more suggestive of the legislative mode of compromise and interest-balancing than the judicial mode of delineation of principle and precedent'.)
[277] See Chapter 4, Section B.2.
[278] Dodge (1969), p. 687.

principled decisionmaking'.[279] The perceived similarity between balancing by courts and 'legislative judgment' was problematic, as it might suggest that courts 'were in a better position than legislatures to make decisions about social questions'.[280]

While the 'balancing ≠ judicial behaviour' critique was widespread, there were also commentators who took a diametrically opposed viewpoint, arguing that it was not balancing but the idea of 'neutral principles' itself which was 'too legislative'.[281] These opposing perspectives again exemplify Martin Redish's argument about the 'schizophrenic' attitude towards the particular and the general, the ad hoc and the rule-based, and the substantive and the formal, in constitutional adjudication at the time.[282]

### (d)  'The best that can be done'

The notion of a discourse with schizophrenic characteristics, if use of this term may be forgiven, is possibly the best way to sum-up the intersection of discussions on balancing and on standards for constitutional legal reasoning. The extent to which these two debates were intertwined deserves special emphasis. On the one hand, the clash over balancing to a great extent was seen to turn on 'large issues about [...] the proper role of judicial review', i.e. the question of standards.[283] At the same time, discussions on these 'large questions', on the proper role for the judiciary and on the standards for carrying out that role, very often took the problem of balancing as their central concern. Looking at constitutional discourse in the US in the early 1960s either from the angle of 'balancing', or from the angle of 'standards of reasoning', then, a very similar set of questions and problems emerges. To a large extent, these problems center on the question of the virtues of legal formality and of its opposites. A conceptual framework thus appears in the form of a triangle of balancing, standards of reasoning and formal versus substantive.

The debates that arose at the intersection of these three perspectives were marked by ironies, contradictions blatant and subtle, and aspirations and exhortations to judges and writers that were avowedly unrealistic but which were passionately adhered to nonetheless. These ambiguities

---

[279] Note: The First Amendment Overbreadth Doctrine (1970), p. 913.
[280] White (1996), p. 322. As White notes, ironically, 'this was the very suggestion that Progressives had deplored in decisions such as Lochner'.
[281] See, e.g., Karst (1960), p. 110.
[282] Redish (1983), p. 1046.    [283] Kalven (1964), p. 215.

pervaded everything: the nature of the desired standards of reasoning, the meaning of the terminology of formal and substantive and the meaning of balancing. It was recognized that commentators and the public at large made 'complex and often conflicting demands' upon the federal courts; 'demands for adherence to logic, to neutrality, and to experience'.[284] At work was a 'nostalgic yearning' for an avowedly impossible 'pre-political jurisprudence' or a 'return to doctrine'. What is significant is that this yearning itself and the recognition of its impossibility were both seen as 'an existential reality – a fact of American political life'.[285]

Contradictions, then, abounded on all levels of the standards, balancing, and legal formality debates, and their interrelations. Within the discussions on standards, there was a foundational tension in that the call for adjudication based on 'neutral principles' contained elements of, and was intended as, both a defense of the institution of judicial review and a limitation on its exercise.[286] In terms of legal formality, there was the irony that Wechsler's and others' attempts to provide an ideal for the reasoned justification of decisions were often seen as steps on a road leading straight back to the archetype of faulty judicial decisions: the allegedly 'mechanistic' reasoning of the *Lochner* era.[287] Others observed that even Wechsler's own followers 'when forced to adjust [his] rules to the realities of constitutional adjudication' wound up 'abandoning those rules'.[288] Out of this resignation to reality arose an important idea: 'the conclusion that candid case-by-case balancing of particular elements of particular fact situations' might be *'the best that can be done'*.[289]

Such contradictions and tensions remain in view when the lens of balancing is used to look at some of the same issues. On the one hand, it was recognized that if 'neutral principles' were to mean anything more than 'minimal rationality', then their position would have to be 'at *the opposite extreme* from a resolutely ad hoc weighing of a welter of conflicting interests to produce a one-time-only result'.[290] At the same time, however, there was the irony that some high profile 'enthusiastic balancers' were seen also to be 'strong advocates of principled decision making'.[291] There

---

[284] Deutsch (1968), p. 243 (difficulty of reconciling 'craft pressures' with the Court's 'symbolic role').

[285] Cf. Shapiro (1963a), p. 605.     [286] *Ibid.*, p. 598.

[287] See, e.g., Dean Rostow's remark on Wechsler, Holmes and Pound, cited above. See also Miller & Howell (1961), p. 671.

[288] Wright (1971), p. 779.     [289] *Ibid.*, (emphasis added).

[290] Kennedy (1969), p. 852.

[291] *Ibid.*, (referring to Gerald Gunther and Dean Griswold).

were balancers who did not give up their search for principle,[292] and there were those who recognized that 'devotion to principle' did not preclude a 'balancing approach'.[293]

To sum up; both sides in the debates over both standards of reasoning and balancing proclaimed the virtues of candour and the vices of mechanistic reasoning. Both were caught between the dangers of the ad hoc and the attractions of situated, 'realistic judgment', and both seemed trapped between the promises of the rule of law and the haunting spectre of excessive formalism. The resulting unease over the standards for legal reasoning and apprehension over balancing were not merely aspects of mid-century American legal life. They were emblematic of it.

## E.   Balancing and the definitional tradition

From its very beginnings, the debate over balancing in American constitutional jurisprudence has been understood by participants as a dispute between balancing and alternatives. No single, uniformly agreed upon label covers all of these perceived alternatives during the period under consideration. But among the various terms used most often, namely 'categorization', 'classification' and 'absolutism', there is much continuity and overlap, despite significant differences in emphasis and focus. This continuity will be referred to here as the 'definitional tradition' in American constitutional legal thought.[294]

This section shows how for every 'episode' in the genealogy of free speech balancing discussed earlier, from 'clear and present danger' through to the communism cases of the 1950s and 1960s, a corresponding alternative from within this definitional tradition was available. Balancing's local meaning, I will argue, has to be seen at least partly as a function of its perennial contest with these alternatives.

---

[292] Alexander Meiklejohn so classified Zechariah Chafee. See Meiklejohn (1961b), pp. 252–53. On Chafee, see above, Chapter 4, Section D.1.

[293] Karst (1965), p. 17. The reference was to Alexander Bickel.

[294] The term 'definitional tradition' is not commonplace in US scholarly literature. For a succinct overview of the conceptual and rhetorical style intended, see Pierre Schlag's depiction of the 'grid aesthetic' in American law. See Schlag (2002), p. 1051 ('In the grid aesthetic, law is pictured as a two-dimensional area divided into contiguous, well-bounded legal spaces [...] The resulting structure – the grid – feels solid, sound, determinate [...] The grid aesthetic is the aesthetic of *bright-line rules, absolutist approaches, and categorical definitions*)' [definitions',] (emphasis added).

### 1.   An 'absolute and objective test': Learned Hand's opinion in Masses Publishing Co. v. Patten (1917)

Earlier, this chapter presented the genesis of the clear-and-present-danger test in the Supreme Court's early post-First World War case law as an important precursor to the Court's later balancing cases. In that same earlier period, an alternative test to 'clear and present danger' was discussed among judges and scholars. This alternative was Judge Learned Hand's test in the case of *Masses Publishing Co. v. Patten*.[295] The *Masses* case was one of the first judicial decisions to examine the Espionage Act of 1917, the Act at issue also in *Schenck* and *Abrams* (both 1919). At the time, as Gerald Gunther has written, according to prevalent thinking on the first amendment, 'the punishability of speech turned on an evaluation of its likelihood to cause forbidden consequences'.[296] Holmes' and Brandeis' clear-and-present-danger test was, as its name indicates, at heart an application of this line of reasoning, turning on an assessment of the probable immediate consequences of expression. Learned Hand, an influential Federal District Court judge, by contrast, thought this evaluative characteristic of the prevalent formulas 'too slippery, too dangerous to free expression'.[297] Instead, he advocated, in his *Masses* Opinion and in later writings, 'the adoption of a strict, "hard," "objective" test focusing on the speaker's words'.[298] Only when speech had the character of direct incitement to unlawful action, in Learned Hand's view, could it be constitutionally proscribed.[299] Gerald Gunther's summary of Learned Hand's correspondence with Zechariah Chafee, the main advocate for 'clear and present danger', makes clear the vital differences between his approach and the prevalent wisdom:

> Instead of asking in the circumstances of each case whether the words had a tendency or even a probability of producing unlawful conduct, he sought a more 'absolute and objective test' focusing on 'language' – 'a qualitative formula, hard, conventional, difficult to evade' as he said in his letters. What he urged was essentially an incitement test, 'a test based

---

[295]   244 F. 535 (S.D.N.Y.). Billings Learned Hand (1872–1961) was probably the most prominent American judge in the twentieth century never to have sat on the Supreme Court.

[296]   Gunther (1975), p. 720.

[297]   *Ibid.*, p. 721.      [298]   *Ibid.*

[299]   See, e.g., Learned Hand's letter to Chafee cited in Gunther, *ibid.*, at p. 749 ('[N]othing short of counsel to violate law should be itself illegal').

upon the nature of the utterance itself': [only] if the words constituted solely a counsel to law violation, they could be forbidden.[300]

The vocabulary chosen by Learned Hand to describe his test – *qualitative, absolute, objective* – is, of course, the vocabulary of legal formality. These terms are invoked in direct opposition to the vocabulary of balancing: *quantitative, relative,* and, at least in the eyes of its critics, *subjective* and personal. Learned Hand's preferred solution is a 'largely definitional' model; an interpretation and classification of the 'nature of the utterance' concerned, which eschews analysis of 'case circumstances' and of the 'probability of consequences'.[301] A brilliant passage from one of Learned Hand's letters to Zechariah Chafee, in which he discussed Justice Holmes' clear-and-present-danger test, presents the intended contrast in stark form:

> I am not wholly in love with Holmesy's test and the reason is this. Once you admit that the matter is one of degree […] you so obviously make it a matter of administration, i.e. you give to Tomdickandharry, D.J. [a fictional lower court judge], so much latitude that the jig is at once up. Besides even their Ineffabilities, the Nine Elder Statesmen [the Supreme Court Justices], have not shown themselves wholly immune from the 'herd instinct' and what seems 'immediate and direct' today may seem very remote next year.[302]

All of this, it is worth emphasizing, was written before balancing itself became a significant first amendment theme, or even before the clear-and-present-danger test had come to be seen as a balancing test.[303] And yet all the characterizations and oppositions familiar from the later balancing debates are already in evidence. 'Clear and present danger' is too much a matter of 'degree', giving too much discretion ('latitude') to judges and juries. Not surprisingly, the spectre of formalism and 'mechanical jurisprudence', familiar from Pound's writing and from the later balancing debates, is also present. Learned Hand's references to the 'character' and the 'nature' of utterances have a distinct essentialist undertone. The Judge himself was concerned to make clear that his distinction between direct incitement to illegal action and 'legitimate agitation' was 'not a scholastic subterfuge, but a hard-bought acquisition in the fight

---

[300] *Ibid.*, p. 725.
[301] Cf. Karst, (1965), p. 10.
[302] Learned Hand letter to Zechariah Chafee, cited in Gunther (1975), pp. 749–50.
[303] The story of that development is recounted in Chapter 4, Section D.1.

for freedom'.[304] To the extent, however, that Learned Hand's approach was an 'all or nothing proposition' that failed to 'adjust the [...] meaning of words to the context of their utterance',[305] a charge of formalism and mechanical reasoning could easily be made.

As it was, Learned Hand's contribution in the *Masses* case was 'obliterated' by the ascendancy of the clear-and-present-danger test set out in *Schenck* and *Abrams* and as interpreted by Chafee and others.[306] But the difference between the Holmes/Brandeis/Chafee approach, focused on context, consequences and questions of degree, and Learned Hand's proposal of a hard, qualitative distinction based on the 'nature' of the speech at issue, provides an early glimpse of the definitional tradition in American free speech law. It is important to note the potential scope of the differences between this definitional approach and the alternative of 'clear and present danger', reinterpreted later in balancing terms. Learned Hand searched for a limiting principle to define the appropriate scope of the freedom of expression, much like his German contemporaries Häntzschel and Schmitt.[307] Such a limiting principle – in Hand's case the principle of 'seditious libel', or the idea that the advocacy of unlawful conduct should be prohibited but that all other forms of speech should be unrestricted – would provide the foundations for free speech law, but not for adjudication on other constitutional rights. The courts were meant to proceed on the basis of such principle and of an understanding of its core application, and then to decide cases further removed from this core instance by way of analogy, allowing the principle to radiate outwards. By contrast, the process of restating the clear-and-present-danger approach in balancing terms, outlined earlier, was seen to replace such localized, i.e. speech-specific, considerations of principle with a generalist, pragmatic, balancing assessment of interests and potential consequences that could be invoked in all areas of constitutional adjudication.[308] This opposition between 'principle' and 'balancing' was to become a staple of debates on balancing, and an important element of its American local meaning.[309]

---

[304] 244 F. 535, 540 (S.D.N.Y.), cited in Gunther (1975), p. 725.

[305] BeVier (1978), p. 337. See also Schwartz (1994), p. 243.

[306] Cf. Kalven (1965), p. 16.

[307] See Chapter 3, Section D.1.

[308] See, e.g., Karst (1965), p. 9.

[309] See, e.g., Baker (1976), pp. 44–47 (critical of balancing and in favour of a 'principled' approach).

## 2.  Categories and the first amendment

The early 1940s saw the first appearances of what would become the most prominent manifestation of the definitional tradition in American free speech law: the rhetoric and practice of categories and categorization. It is in the debates on the attractions and vices of 'categorization', that the opposition between balancing and the definitional tradition – and, by association, between balancing and the attractions and vices of legal formality – became most starkly visible; even more clearly than in the discussions on Learned Hand's test in respect of balancing and the attractions and vices of legal formality.

### (a)    Early Supreme Court categories: *Chaplinsky* v. *New Hampshire* (1942) and onwards

In a series of cases that began with *Chaplinsky* v. *New Hampshire* (1942) and continued through *Beauharnais* v. *Illinois* (1952) and *Roth* v. *United States* (1957), the Supreme Court held that particular kinds of utterances were categorically unworthy of first amendment protection. Although many of the specific assessments made in these cases have since been reversed or modified,[310] the basic analytical structure and rhetorical form inaugurated in *Chaplinsky* retain an important place in the landscape of American constitutional thinking, even to this day.[311]

Walter Chaplinsky was a Jehovah's Witness who was convicted of shouting 'you are a God damned racketeer' and 'a damned Fascist' at a local police officer during a demonstration in Rochester, New Hampshire. In a unanimous decision for the Supreme Court upholding his conviction, Justice Murphy wrote:

> [I]t is well understood that the right of free speech is not absolute at all times and under all circumstances. There are *certain well-defined and narrowly limited classes of speech*, the prevention and punishment of which has never been thought to raise any Constitutional problem. These include the lewd and obscene, the profane, the libelous, and the insulting or 'fighting' words – those which by their very utterance inflict injury or

---

[310]  See, e.g., Schauer (2004), pp. 1774–77. *Chaplinsky* itself was revised and significantly narrowed down in *R.A.V.* v. *City of St. Paul*, 505 US 377, 383ff (1992). But Justice Scalia's opinion for the Court notes: 'Our decisions since the 1960s have narrowed the scope of the traditional categorical exceptions for defamation [...] and for obscenity [...] but a limited categorical approach has remained an important part of our First Amendment jurisprudence'.

[311]  See, e.g., *Virginia* v. *Black*, 538 US 343, 358 (2003) (reference to *Chaplinsky*'s categories).

tend to incite an immediate breach of the peace. It has been well observed that such utterances are no essential part of any exposition of ideas, and are of such slight social value as a step to truth that any benefit that may be derived from them is clearly outweighed by the social interest in order and morality.[312]

Because Chaplinsky's 'fighting words' lay outside the scope of coverage of the first amendment, it was unnecessary for the State of New Hampshire to show that his arrest and conviction served any societal interest that could override any right to freedom of expression in this specific case.[313] A few weeks after *Chaplinsky* was decided, the Court adopted a very similar approach in the case of *Valentine* v. *Chrestensen*, when it held that the first amendment did not protect 'purely commercial advertising'.[314]

The quoted passage from *Chaplinsky* came to be cited as authority for the proposition that particular kinds of speech – libel, obscenity, 'fighting words', etc. – lay outside the coverage of the first amendment. *Chaplinsky*, in this sense, introduced what Harry Kalven later called a 'two-level theory' of freedom of expression, according to which some forms of speech are entirely 'beneath First Amendment concerns'.[315] The most famous applications of this two-level model concerned (group)-libel and obscenity. In *Beauharnais* v. *Illinois* (1952), the Court quoted *Chaplinsky* to support its conclusion that 'libelous utterances' were not 'within the area of constitutionally protected speech', which meant that it was not necessary to consider whether they represented any 'clear and present danger'.[316] And in *Roth United States* (1957), it was stated, again under reference to *Chaplinsky*, that the Court had always assumed that 'obscenity' was outside 'the area of protected speech and press'.[317]

In the wake of *Chaplinsky* and *Valentine*, a 'categorization' approach came to signify a determination of first amendment cases based 'solely

---

[312]  315 US 568, 571–72 (1942) (emphasis added).

[313]  As others have noted, the Court's original statement in *Chaplinsky*, with its reference to the benefits of speech being 'outweighed' by competing social interests, was ambiguous. Nevertheless, *Chaplinsky* came to stand for an approach to the first amendment that *does not* consider possible countervailing interests. See, e.g., Schauer (2004), p. 1777.

[314]  316 US 52, 54 (1942). The Court did not cite *Chaplinsky* in *Valentine*, but the 'commercial speech' line of cases has generally been read as espousing the same logic. See, e.g., Redish (1971), p. 431.

[315]  Kalven (1964), p. 217. See also Kalven (1960), p. 10.

[316]  343 US 250, 266 (1952). *Beauharnais* was distinguished, and largely abandoned, in *New York Times* v. *Sullivan*, 376 US 254, 268ff (1964). But that case itself retained a categorical, definitional, element in the key criterion of whether the target of expression was a 'public' official.

[317]  354 US 476, 481 (1957).

on the basis of the first amendment value of the utterance itself, without regard to possible justifications for restriction'.[318] In such a categorization model, questions as to the likely consequences of speech or as to the relative importance of possible countervailing social interests were simply irrelevant. 'What distinguishes a categorization approach from clear-and-present-danger and similar tests', John Hart Ely wrote, 'is that *context* is considered only to determine *the message* the defendant was transmitting.' Whereas a categorization approach 'asks only "What was he saying?" [...] A clear and present danger or ad hoc balancing approach, in contrast, would regard that question as nondispositive: a given message will sometimes be protected and sometimes not'.[319]

(b)   Categories and definitions: the first amendment theories
      of Thomas Emerson and Alexander Meiklejohn

In the course of the late 1950s and early 1960s, the theme of categories and categorization within first amendment law assumed a new, expanded meaning. No longer confined to *Chaplinsky's* traditional set of 'well defined and narrowly limited classes of speech', categorization – or classification, as it was now also sometimes called – came to refer to any doctrinal method that approached freedom of speech in a binary, 'in-or-out' way. The two most prominent propagators of such methods were Yale Law School's Thomas I. Emerson and Alexander Meiklejohn, who was not a lawyer but a well-known professor of philosophy.

The core of Emerson's theory of freedom of expression was a dichotomy between 'expression' and 'action'.[320] Expression would be entitled to 'complete protection against government infringement', while action would be subject to 'reasonable and non-discriminatory regulation designed to achieve a legitimate social objective'.[321] Emerson summarized his proposed 'doctrinal structure' for first amendment analysis as follows:

> [M]aintenance of a system of freedom of expression requires recognition of the distinction between those forms of conduct which should be classified as 'expression' and those which should be classified as 'action' [...] Translated into legal doctrine based upon the first amendment, this theory requires the court to determine in every case whether the conduct

---

[318]   Schauer (1982), p. 303.

[319]   Ely (1975), p. 1493 (emphasis added). See also *R.A.V.* v. *City of St. Paul*, 505 US 377, 426 (Stevens, J., concurring) ('the categorical approach does not take seriously the importance of *context*') (emphasis in original).

[320]   Ely (1975), p. 1495.

[321]   Emerson (1964), p. 21.

involved is 'expression' and whether it has been infringed by an exercise
of governmental authority [...] The test is not one of clear and present
danger, or [...] balancing interests. The balance of interests was made
when the first amendment was put into the Constitution. The function of
a court in applying the first amendment is to define the key terms of that
provision – 'freedom of speech,' 'abridge,' and 'law.'[322]

Emerson's approach relies heavily on a conceptual apparatus and on
imagery developed as a direct opposite to 'balancing of interests' or a flexible judicial assessment of proximate consequences in the circumstances
of each case. His interest is in the construction of a hard, coherent 'system'
of freedom of expression, in which the courts' task is to classify and to
'define', not to weigh.[323]

The same emphasis on definition and categorical boundaries can be
found in the work of Alexander Meiklejohn. Meiklejohn was the foremost
advocate of the idea that speech was to be protected because of its relation
to self-government.[324] The first amendment, in his view, did not forbid the
abridging of speech per se, but it did categorically forbid the abridging
of the 'freedom of public discussion'.[325] Meiklejohn's theory, therefore,
depended upon a clear definition of this narrower freedom; a definition
that was to proceed through a binary distinction between expression relevant to the project of self-government, and expression not so relevant. At
various points in his work, Meiklejohn made clear the centrality of this
definitional enterprise to his theory. 'There is a desperate need', he wrote
in the early 1950s, that the Supreme Court 'should *define* much more
accurately, and with more careful consideration, what is that "Freedom"
which the First Amendment intends to secure'.[326] By the time "balancing"
became an important aspect of the Supreme Court's case law, Meiklejohn
was quick to point out the differences between the Court's approach and
his own theory. 'The theory that asserts that constitutional values may be
"balanced" by the appellate courts', he wrote in response to the *Barenblatt*
decision, 'is radically hostile, not only to the first amendment, but also to
the intent and provisions of the Constitution as a whole.'[327]

---

[322] *Ibid.*
[323] See, e.g., Kennedy (1969), p. 844 (Emerson as one of 'the classifiers', together with Justice
  Black); *Note: The First Amendment Overbreadth Doctrine* (1970), p. 883.
[324] See, e.g., Meiklejohn (1948), p. 26.
[325] *Ibid.*, p. 54.
[326] Meiklejohn (1953), p. 462 (emphasis added) (calling on the Supreme Court to 'clarify
  [...] the most significant principle of our American plan of government').
[327] Meiklejohn (1961a), p. 7.

While their underlying substantive principles were very different, in terms of analytical structure and style, the Emerson and Meiklejohn perspectives on freedom of expression adjudication were highly similar. Both approached the question of protection for speech as a matter of defining the coverage of the first amendment, rather than as a matter of assessing the relative strengths of competing values or interests.[328] That assessment, they argued, had been carried out by the framers when they decided to give absolute protection to the freedom of speech properly defined: insofar as distinguished from action (Emerson), or insofar as related to the project of self-government (Meiklejohn).

The stature of Emerson, Meiklejohn and their theories meant that prominent alternative conceptual and discursive frameworks were available precisely at the time balancing came to the fore in first amendment law. These alternative frameworks were emphatic expressions of an underlying belief in the virtues of legal formality – of the attractions of hard definitions and of not leaving matters to the discretion of 'Tomdickandharry, D.J.' By implication, this meant that these theories contributed to a jurisprudential climate in which balancing and legal formality were seen as radical opposites.

On a comparative law aside, the prominence of the Emerson and Meiklejohn theories also made for an important difference with German jurisprudence of the time. German free speech law had known its share of proposals for definitional approaches, in the Weimar-era theories of Häntzschel and Schmitt and others.[329] But none of these were given any serious traction when the *Bundesverfassungsgericht* came to decide its first major free speech cases in the late 1950s. The *Lüth* decision 'obliterated' all definitional opposition to Rudolf Smend's 'material constitutionalism'. In the US, by contrast, although 'clear and present danger' and balancing were enormously successful, they did not conquer all.

### (c)    'Absolutes': the first amendment of Justices Black and Douglas

The fact that balancing did not conquer everything before it, was demonstrated most starkly in the position taken by Justices Black and Douglas. It was in their first amendment opinions that the definitional tradition received its most high profile exposition in mid-twentieth-century

---

[328]  See, e.g., Schauer (1981), p. 270 ('Taking the "freedom of speech" as the appropriate unit of coverage has traditionally been the opening move of the "definers."')

[329]  See Chapter 3, Section D.1.

American jurisprudence, not just within the area of free speech law, but within all of constitutional law.

For Justices Black and Douglas, just as for Professors Meiklejohn and Emerson, questions of substantive principle and doctrinal structure were closely intertwined. Like Thomas Emerson, Black and Douglas espoused a principled 'speech'/'conduct' dichotomy. 'A "bright line" distinction between speech and conduct', Morton Horwitz wrote, was 'a staple of Justice Black's effort to develop an absolutist conception of the First Amendment that would nevertheless contain a clear limiting principle'.[330] Justice Black's dissent in *Barenblatt* and Justice Douglas' dissent in *Dennis*, to mention two of the cases discussed earlier, both contain prominent references to the speech/conduct distinction.[331] In a later dissent, Justice Black explained his famous 'I take 'no law abridging' to mean *"no law abridging"*' reading of the first amendment[332] in terms of specifically this distinction, when he wrote 'I think the Founders of our Nation in adopting the First Amendment meant precisely that the Federal Government should pass "no law" regulating speech and press but should confine its legislation to the regulation of conduct'.[333]

The label used by both critics and the Justices themselves to frame this position on the freedom of expression was 'first amendment absolutism'. This term was used inconsistently, 'by both friend and foe'.[334] What is clear though, is that its core meaning places it both squarely within the definitional tradition and in diametrical opposition to balancing. Dean Ely himself, for example, drew a contrast between balancers on the one hand and 'categorizers, or 'absolutists'' on the other.[335] G. Edward White's description similarly makes clear the basic dichotomy. 'Absolutism in First Amendment jurisprudence', he writes, 'refers to a jurisprudential perspective that ostensibly rejects balancing in free speech cases for an analysis that treats some, or even all, forms of expression as presumptively protected'.[336] I should emphasize once again, however, that just as

---

[330] Horwitz (1993), p. 111.
[331] *Dennis v. United States*, 341 US 494, 584 (Douglas, J., dissenting); *Barenblatt v. United States*, 360 US 109, 141 (Black J. dissenting).
[332] Black (1960), pp. 874, 879, 882.
[333] *Mishkin v. New York*, 383 US 502, 518 (1966) (Black, J., dissenting) cited in Horwitz (1993), p. 112 (emphasis added).
[334] Ely (1975), p. 1500. See also Meiklejohn (1961a), p. 246 (referring to different varieties of 'absolutism', including his own).
[335] *Ibid.*, p. 1500. See also Ely (1980), pp. 108ff (contrasting balancing and different forms of 'absolutism').
[336] White (1996), p. 351.

with other manifestations of the definitional tradition – and, of course, as with balancing itself! – the meaning of 'absolutism' cannot fully be captured in terms of merely an analytical device. There was an important rhetorical dimension to the two Justices' position. Absolutism, for them, was at least in part 'a rhetorical device to express an attitude about how first amendment adjudication should be approached'.[337] In this way, absolutism symbolized their condemnation of 'how the balance worked out after a decade of deciding cases growing out of [Anti-Communist] hysteria'.[338] Dean Ely, in *Democracy and Distrust* recognized that 'a case can be made [...] that even though a Justice must know deep down that no one can really mean there can be no restrictions on free speech, there is value in his putting it that way nonetheless'.[339]

Justices Black and Douglas' first amendment absolutism was by no means the last manifestation of the definitional tradition in American free speech law. The tradition continues to play a crucial role, through such doctrines as the prohibition on 'content-based' restrictions,[340] and in the way different classes of expression such as commercial speech,[341] hate speech,[342] and expressive conduct,[343] attract differing standards of review. But within the period with which we are concerned, their opinions constituted the high-water mark of the hold of the definitional tradition on the American constitutional legal imagination.

### (d)    Balancing as 'not definition'

By the early 1960s these various strands of the definitional tradition in American constitutional legal thought (Judge Hand's incitement test, the *Chaplinsky* and *Chrestensen* categories, the theories of Emerson and Meiklejohn and the first amendment 'absolutism' of Justices Black and Douglas) coalesced into a powerful set of ideas, the primary focus of which was to challenge the theory, practice and rhetoric of balancing. The definitional tradition grew into a *definitional school*.[344] Its main tenet was opposition to judging the constitutionality of laws by way of

---

[337]  Powe (1989), p. 281.    [338]  *Ibid.*, p. 280.
[339]  Ely (1980), p. 109.
[340]  See, e.g., Stephan (1982); Stone (1983).
[341]  *Central Hudson Gas & Electric* v. *Public Service Commission*, 447 US 557 (1980).
[342]  *Brandenburg* v. *Ohio*, 395 US 444 (1969).
[343]  *United States* v. *O'Brien*, 391 US 367 (1968).
[344]  *Note: The First Amendment Overbreadth Doctrine* (1970), p. 883 (referring to Emerson, Meiklejohn and Laurent Frantz as members of a 'definitional school of commentary' united in opposition to balancing).

'an interest-balancing technique', and its principal flag bearers were the two Justices.[345] Categorization now became more than just a particular analytical device to be used with regard to particular forms of speech, or a specific conceptual tool for theories of freedom of expression. It became the centrepiece of a 'style' in constitutional legal reasoning; a style that competed for dominance with the style of balancing.[346]

Both the content and the mere existence, and persistence, of a set of ideas presented as diametrically opposite to balancing are deeply significant for the local meaning of balancing in US constitutional legal discourse.

First, as to content, it is in the opposition between balancing and its definitional alternatives that some of the perceived core attributes of balancing are most clearly expressed. The main theme to come out of this opposition is that of attention to context and consequences, which balancing was thought to offer and definitional approaches were seen to avoid. This particular aspect of balancing's meaning can be traced all the way along the definitional tradition.[347]

But beyond their specific content, the mere existence, and persistence, of a high profile set of ideas alternative to balancing, had important implications for balancing's local meaning. It meant that balancing came to be understood, to a large extent, *by way of* this opposition. Balancing really was, to an important degree, *not* categorization, or *not* definition – just as categorization and definition were understood to be *not* balancing. This pervasive opposition cast balancing as a prime instance of the 'not formal' in constitutional law – of constitutional legal *anti*-formality.[348]

These two mutually exclusive styles (definitional and balancing, formal and anti-formal) came to dominate debate on freedom of expression to such an extent that they were thought by many to cover much of what first amendment adjudication was all about. Dean Ely, in the mid 1970s remarked how debate in this area had 'traditionally proceeded on the assumption that categorization and balancing [...] are mutually exclusive approaches to the various problems that arise under the first amendment'.[349] Many contemporary contributions similarly framed key issues

---

[345] *Ibid.*     [346] Sullivan (1992b), p. 293.

[347] See, e.g., Learned Hand's rejection of 'clear and present danger' as 'too slippery', or the *Chaplinsky* and *Valentine* categories as attempts at avoiding the difficult assessments of 'gravity, probability, and proximity' of 'clear and present danger'. Cf. Gunther (1979), pp. 720ff; Kalven (1964), p. 218; Karst (1965), p. 5; *Note: The First Amendment Overbreadth Doctrine* (1970), p. 887.

[348] Cf. Tushnet (1985).

[349] Ely, (1975), p. 1500.

in free speech law, or even in constitutional rights law generally, in terms of the opposition between balancing and its definitional alternatives.[350] Most famously perhaps: Ronald Dworkin's 1970 essay *Taking Rights Seriously* is centrally concerned with the dichotomy between a model of 'striking a balance between the rights of the individual and the demands of society at large' and a principled search for 'grounds that can consistently be used to limit the definition of a particular right'.[351]

## F.   Balancing's US local meaning

Given the language and images described in this chapter, what was the US American meaning of the discourse of balancing during the period portrayed here? By way of interim observations, here are a number of distinctive features that emerge particularly clearly when compared to the German meaning of balancing discussed in Chapters 3.

One important conclusion must be that the discourse of balancing in the US was so much narrower than that in Germany. Balancing in Germany was the cornerstone of a comprehensive constitutional vision: that of the 'perfect constitutional order'. In the US, balancing was largely a feature of first amendment law. This first amendment balancing, in addition, was the product of a much more gradual process: Not the proverbial big bang of one seminal decision like *Lüth*, but the incremental modification and replacement of familiar older concepts and doctrines lay at the heart of balancing's rise in the US.

Within this narrower, more incrementally developing discourse, it was much less clear in the US context than it was in German jurisprudence what the language of balancing was supposed to stand for. Assessments of balancing ranged from 'mere rhetoric', through a narrow doctrine for certain well-defined categories of first amendment cases, to a description of the judicial function more generally. In addition, many of these different meanings came loaded with (contradictory) assumptions as to how 'balancing courts' were likely to behave, and to what results 'balancing decisions' were likely to lead. As a result, many of the participants in the relevant debates were often talking *to* each other – and to easily debunked straw men – rather than *with* each other. Their contributions remain col-

---

[350] For an overview, see Kennedy (1969).
[351] Reprinted in Dworkin (1977), pp. 197–200. See also Ely (1980), pp. 108ff (contrasting balancing and absolutism).

ourful and sometimes wonderfully insightful even for readers today. But they were and are also often frustratingly opaque.

Amidst all this uncertainty, one aspect of balancing's meaning does emerge with great clarity. This is the fact that balancing in US jurisprudence was, to a very large extent, understood by way of opposition and contrast. In part, this occurred in the course of the struggle over appropriate standards for judicial reasoning. These were the clashes between the values of judicial honesty and legal craftsmanship, between the attractions of situated, realistic decision making and the virtues of the rule of law. Most comprehensively, these were the conflicts over what it meant for courts to be acting as 'courts of law'. A second main contrast opposed the discourse of balancing to that of the definitional tradition in American jurisprudence, mainly in its contemporary guises of categorization and 'absolutism'.

That latter opposition in particular, I argue in the next chapter, remains central to balancing's contemporary meaning in the US. Many later debates, such as the 'rules versus standards' dichotomy pervasive in the late 1980s and early 1990s, self-consciously trace their roots to the classic disputes in early 1960s first amendment law. The repeated resurgence and disappearance of these questions supports two related conclusions. First, the basic American meaning of balancing is still strongly connected to its 1950s and 1960s intellectual foundations. And second, the theme of opposition, contrast and tension, that was so important during this foundational period, continues to play out also *over time*, as 'revisitings' are revisited, and spectres are brought back to haunt again.

# Two paradigms of balancing

## A.  Introduction

Balancing, I have argued throughout this book, is capable of having, and does in fact have, multiple, radically different meanings. Chapter 3 gave an account of balancing in German constitutional jurisprudence as both sustaining and reflective of ideas of 'material constitutionalism' and of the 'comprehensive constitutional order'. These ideas were themselves in turn identified as aspects of what was there called, in provisional terms, an underlying constitutional legal 'perfectionism'. Balancing, in all these various senses, was central to the foundations of postwar German constitutionalism. In US constitutional jurisprudence, by contrast, as discussed in Chapter 4, judicial balancing was seen rather as a pragmatic, incremental solution for when doctrinal frameworks no longer 'worked', because they were no longer capable of generating commitment among legal actors, or because new fact patterns arose for which they were thought not to offer acceptable outcomes. This pragmatic form of balancing was generally viewed with suspicion rather than aspiration, and stood in a constant dialectic of opposition with elements of alternative modes of thinking; those of 'reasoned justification' and of the 'definitional tradition' in American law.

This final chapter aggregates these different meanings encountered so far into two paradigms of balancing discourse. These paradigms are condensed, abstracted depictions of characteristic elements of the 'German' and 'US' meanings of balancing for the period studied.[1] In the definition adhered to here, legal paradigms have four distinctive interrelated features. First, their propositions generally remain implicit, which means that they must normally be gleaned indirectly from the discursive practice of participants in the relevant system.[2] Second, they

---

[1]  See further van Hoecke & Warrington (1998); Michaels (2006b), p. 1022.
[2]  *Ibid.* See also Gordon (1984), p. 59.

are ideal typical in the sense that they are abstractions typifying locally held ideas. Paradigms are implicit analytical constructs of which it is expected that, if they were to be made explicit, most local legal actors would accept most elements most of the time.[3] A third distinguishing feature of paradigms is the way they exercise a real hold on the thought and practice of those within their reach. Paradigms are not theories or principles that can simply be adhered to or not. They constitute a framework within which even opposing theories are formulated.[4] In the context of adjudication, paradigmatic understandings of law 'influence judges collectively', by stabilizing interpretive practices over time and across different areas of law.[5] Finally, paradigms are, within their area of operation, comprehensive in coverage. Paradigms 'contain not just the meaning of a particular institution [...] but rather the whole set of instruments, argumentative modes, and theories connected with this institution, as well as other, related institutions'.[6] Paradigms of balancing, as defined here, are comprehensive in their coverage of the use of the language of balancing and its related vocabulary, ideas and practices; that is, of the discourse of balancing in a broad sense. No further validity is claimed for them here.[7]

The two paradigms of balancing discourse will be elaborated using the common conceptual grid of the formal versus substantive opposition, set out in Chapter 1, and illustrated at the end of the chapter in a table that contrasts elements of the German and US approaches. In the course of the chapter, three successive sections discuss different ideal typical local understandings for each of the elements of 'the formal', 'the substantive', and their interrelationship. The formal will be shown to refer to ideas of perfection in German constitutional jurisprudence and of limitation in the US. 'The substantive' will be identified as 'material constitutionalism' (Germany) and as policy and pragmatism (US). And where German constitutional jurisprudence tends to think of the relationship between these elements in terms of synthesis, the co-existence of formality and its opposites in American jurisprudence is marked rather by conflict and paradox.

---

[3] *Ibid.* See also Fallon (1997a), pp. 10–11.
[4] Cf. Michaels (2006b), pp. 1023ff. In this specific sense, paradigms are akin to ideologies. See, e.g., van Wezel Stone (1981), p. 1515.
[5] Dyzenhaus (1996), p. 159. See also Bell (1986), p. 62.
[6] Michaels (2006b), p. 1023.
[7] But see the Conclusion to this book.

Section E in this chapter then broadens these accounts by looking at the question of the nature of the attitude held by local legal audiences toward the formal versus substantive dilemma. This, as discussed in the Introduction and in Chapter 1, is the question of the nature of their legalism. These attitudes will then be used to distinguish German and US ways of balancing in terms of faith in, and scepticism over, law. The same language of balancing, I argue in conclusion, can be the expression of both an aspirational legalism and of a sceptical-pragmatic approach to law.

## B.    The formal: perfection and limitation

Constitutional rights balancing in German and European jurisprudence is persistently depicted by American observers as a radically open-ended and informal practice, at odds with the formalist heritage of European legal culture. This section brings together ideas of legal formality and of constitutional legal perfectionism in order to present a case for the hidden formal dimensions of German, and by extension European, judicial balancing.

At the heart of the concept of legal formality lies the idea of juridical autonomy. Formality, as Laura Kalman puts it in admirable defiance of lexicographical strictures, simply means '*autonomousness*'.[8] This idea of autonomy, in turn, is commonly equated with the notion of constraint.[9] Autonomy for the juridical then comes to evoke the image of a bounded legal sphere; a closed domain, strictly separated from the outside world.[10] But juridical autonomy, and thus legal formality, can also be read in a broader sense, to refer to any instance where legal ideas or concepts are thought to exercise any kind of independent force. That independent – autonomous – force, in turn, need not necessarily come in the shape of constraint, understood as limitation. It can also manifest itself in a more positive way, as a form of compulsion – the compulsion to maximize and intensify, to make the constitutional legal order, in different senses, the best it can be. This is the compelling force of a constitutional legal perfectionism.

---

[8]  Kalman (1986), p. 36. See also, e.g., Teubner (1983), pp. 247ff.

[9]  See, e.g., Schauer (1988); Eskridge (1990), p. 646; p. 530; Jackson (1999), p. 621; Schauer (2010).

[10]  For the archetype, see Weber (1925), pp. 63ff.

## 1. Constitutional legal perfectionism

German constitutional legal discourse of the 1950s and 1960s is striking for its incessant references to the ideals of the expansion, intensification and other forms of what could, at least intuitively, be called the *betterment* of the constitutional order. Typically, these references employ the vocabulary of 'perfection'. Take this characterization by the preeminent English-language analyst of modern German constitutionalism. The 'German legal mind', Donald Kommers writes, has a tendency 'to envision the Constitution as an almost perfect – and gapless – unity'.[11] 'Every provision of the Constitution', he adds, 'is a legally binding norm requiring full and unambiguous implementation.'[12] The function of the *Bundesverfassungsgericht* in this vision is, in Kommers' view, 'the preservation of the constitutional state in *all* of its particulars'.[13] Many further examples of such language can be found in Chapter 3.

There is some way to go, however, between identifying instances of perfectionist rhetoric, however pervasive, to the elaboration of 'perfectionism' as a conceptual category appropriate to German constitutional jurisprudence.[14] This section is concerned with making the argument for that transition. It derives such a conceptual category by way of comparative analysis that draws from the broad contours of American scholarly debates in which constitutional 'perfectionism' figures as an explicit label.[15] That label, in those discussions, does not come with anything approaching a comprehensive or even internally coherent definition of 'perfection' in constitutional law. But the debates do reveal a number of recurrent and related characteristics of what could be called a 'perfectionist' style in constitutional jurisprudence. These may be summarized as follows.

(1) Constitutional legal perfectionism is *aspirational*. It exhorts legal actors to honour their legal order's 'aspirational principles' rather than

---

[11] Kommers (1991), p. 848.    [12] *Ibid.*
[13] *Ibid.*, p. 851 (emphasis in original). See also Forsthoff (1959), p. 151.
[14] Especially since 'perfectionism' is not a standard term of art in German or European constitutional jurisprudence itself. See also Bomhoff (2012b).
[15] See in particular Monaghan (1981); Fleming (1993); Sunstein (2005); Tushnet (2005); Fleming (2006); Fleming (2007); Greene (2007); Sunstein (2007); Sunstein (2008). The work of the late Ronald Dworkin, who does not use the explicit label of 'perfectionism', but who does address the same themes and who uses related vocabulary should be included in this list. See further Bomhoff (2012b). Although they do not address the question, most of these authors would probably qualify 'perfectionism' as a form of *constitutionalism* manifested in legal doctrines and theories. Here, 'perfectionism' is seen rather as a *legalism* with particular salience in the constitutional context.

merely follow 'historical practices and concrete original understanding'.[16]
(2) Perfectionism is *substantive*. References to the 'substantive' in law
are notoriously vague, but what is intended here is the (doubly negative)
idea that the function of constitutional law and courts is not limited to
merely securing a procedural framework for effective self-government.[17]
(3) Perfectionism is *constructivist*, in that it emphasizes the virtues of
coherence over more localized forms of reasoning and interpretation.[18]
(4) Perfectionism strives for *maximally intense* rights protection.[19]
(5) Perfectionism aims for *maximally comprehensive* coverage of societal
domains through law and legal processes.[20] (6) Perfectionism demands
*maximal effectiveness* in rights protection, by way of a 'perfect' system
of remedies. (7) And finally, perfectionism is *maximally particular*. It
demands 'perfect justice' on the circumstances of each individual case.[21]

These characteristics, although derived from a debate in American constitutional legal theory, show a striking degree of overlap with the components of the German vision of the 'perfect constitutional order' discussed
in Chapter 3. 'Material constitutionalism' was an overtly substantive,
value-based approach to constitutional jurisprudence. The 'complete'
constitutional order turned on the idea that the value system enacted in
the Basic Law 'should lay claim to an absolute validity extending to all
spheres of social life'.[22] And the 'perfect fit' constitution demanded an as-
close-as-possible congruence between the abstract meaning of constitutional rights provisions and their effectuation in concrete cases.

The discourse of balancing, as was also shown in Chapter 3, is the most
prominent manifestation of this German constitutional legal perfectionism. There is a direct link between Smend's material (substantive) constitutionalism and the value balancing of the *Lüth* court. The extension of
the sphere of rights protection to the private sphere, also initiated in *Lüth*,
relied on value- and interest-balancing as a key instrument for avoiding
inconsistencies in the operation of rights protection in this new set-up,

---

[16] Fleming (2006), pp. 211, 227.
[17] For this contrast, see, e.g., Tribe (1980); Fleming (1993); Fleming (2007). On the substantive in law see further Chapter 5, Section C.
[18] See, e.g., Fleming (2006), p. 230. This is akin to Mitchel Lasser's concept of 'meta-
teleological' reasoning in European Union law. In a thicker sense, it approximates
Dworkin's notion of law as integrity. See Dworkin (1998), pp. 230ff; Lasser (2004),
p. 288.
[19] Fleming (2007), p. 2890.
[20] See, e.g., Sunstein (2008), p. 825 ('minimalism' – Sunstein's opposite for 'perfectionism' –
as protective of 'space for self-governance').
[21] See, in mocking terms, Scalia (1989), p. 1178.
[22] Ernst Böckenförde, cited in Kommers (1997), p. 37. See also, e.g., Kumm (2004), p. 587.

with its vastly increased potential for conflict. 'Perfect fit' constitutionalism found expressions in the conception of constitutional interpretation as the 'actualization' of rights clauses and in the principle of the 'optimization' of constitutional rights and values.[23]

One illuminating example of the influence of this idea of 'optimization' and its relation to balancing, not yet discussed because it fell outside the time frame adopted in Chapter 3, is Robert Alexy's seminal *Theorie der Grundrechte*, of 1986. In that book and in later work, Alexy presents fundamental rights norms, understood as 'principles', in terms of '*Optimierungsgebote*' ('optimization requirements' or, more strikingly, 'injunctions'). They are 'norms which require that something be realized to the greatest extent possible given the legal and factual possibilities'.[24] Balancing and optimization are closely connected in Alexy's theory. In empirical terms, the *Bundesverfassungsgericht*'s balancing is taken as 'the clearest sign the Federal Constitutional Court understands constitutional rights norms [...] as principles', in the sense intended by Alexy. And on a conceptual level, Alexy argues that conflicts between these principles 'are played out in the dimension of weight', by way of the operation of the proportionality principle and its inherent 'law of balancing'.[25]

### 2. Anti-perfectionism in US constitutional jurisprudence: formality as constraint and limitation

If German constitutional jurisprudence can be seen as perfection-seeking, at least on the American definitional fragments adopted earlier, American constitutional jurisprudence itself is, on these same criteria, emphatically *non-* or even *anti*-perfectionist. Dominant strands within American constitutional legal thought and practice manifest an underlying negative, limiting, form of constitutional legalism, rather than a desire to construct any kind of comprehensive or perfect constitutional legal order. It is important to note that the claim here is not that this anti-perfectionism in American jurisprudence is related to balancing in any similar way as perfectionism is in the German setting.[26] The purpose of this discussion is

---

[23] See Chapter 3, Section E.3.
[24] Alexy (2002), p. 47.
[25] *Ibid.*, p. 50. Julian Rivers translates '*Güterabwägung*' in the German original (at p. 79) as 'balancing of interests'. On the confusion between these terms, and on the Court's simultaneous reliance on both elements, see Chapter 3, Sections D.2 and E.
[26] In fact, the relationship between balancing and anti-perfectionism in the US setting varies widely, ranging from the supportive, through the absent, to the antagonistic.

rather to examine the extent to which constitutional perfectionism could be in any way distinctive for German theory and practice, by way of a contrast with experiences in the US. This will be a stepping stone for the main project of relating this distinctive German idea, and balancing as one of its main expressions, to the topic of legal formality.

### (a)    Facets of American constitutional anti-perfectionism

Examples of anti-perfectionist tendencies in American constitutional jurisprudence abound. Instead of gazing 'outwards' or 'forwards' to values and principles, as aspirational and substantive constitutional legalisms would, there is a pervasive tendency to look 'backwards', to original meaning and precedent. In place of a 'substantive' constitution, comes a longstanding preoccupation with questions of process and institutional competence, described as 'flights from substance'.[27] The rights contained in the Bill of Rights are commonly seen as essentially negative limitations on governmental authority, rather than as positive building blocks for the realization of some overarching value, such as individual autonomy or human dignity.[28] Instead of pursuing comprehensive constitutional rights coverage of the private domain, American jurisprudence is so anxious and conflicted over the 'spooky' idea of 'horizontal effect' that its equivalent doctrines are widely seen as a 'conceptual disaster area'.[29] And instead of striving for coherence, American rights jurisprudence is often 'unreflexively *clause-bound*' – a term not even known in German or European law.[30]

A more circumscribed search among the materials discussed in Chapter 4 reveals some more specific examples. It is striking, first of all, how many of the principal figures in the history of first amendment law had unambitious, or even downright pessimistic, views of what constitutional rights adjudication might be able to accomplish. Zechariah Chafee, for instance, one of the founders of the modern tradition of free speech protection, was said to be 'acutely aware of the limitations of law and the legal process', and to have felt strongly that law 'must be tolerant of many evils that morality condemns'.[31] Judge Learned Hand, who advocated the definitional alternative to 'clear and present danger', and Justice Black,

---

[27] Fleming (1993), p. 213.
[28] See, e.g., Bandes (1990) (critique of the 'negative constitution'). For a comparative German–US assessment, see Rensmann (2007), pp. 245ff.
[29] Cf. Black (1967), p. 95; Hershkoff (2011). See also Gardbaum (2003); Gardbaum (2006); Bomhoff (2008).
[30] Amar (1998), p. 29 (American rights jurisprudence 'ignores the ways in which the Bill [of Rights] is, well, a *bill* – a set of interconnected provisions').
[31] Angell (1957), p. 1343.

who stridently opposed balancing on the Supreme Court, espoused similarly limited conceptions of what judges could, and legitimately should, do.[32] So too, of course, did Justices Frankfurter and Harlan, who advocated balancing on the Supreme Court, in part precisely on this ground.[33]

Some of this jurisprudential reticence can be traced to the influence of the two main traditions in first amendment thinking, which may be labelled the 'common law' and the 'principled foundations' approaches.[34] In the first of these two, first amendment adjudication is viewed through a classic common law lens. The resulting approaches, exemplified in the scholarly work of Harry Kalven and Kenneth Karst, is limited or modest in its ambitions in the same basic sense that common law adjudication as a whole purports to be modest; through its incremental and pragmatic nature and its focus on incidental problem-solving rather than comprehensive system-building. Balancing, as was seen earlier, *can* play a positive role in these approaches, but only if it is taken as an expression of such particularist and incrementalist tendencies.

In the 'principled foundations' tradition, on the other hand, first amendment adjudication is approached by way of the construction of general theories concerning the value or values that the first amendment is supposed to protect, or the kinds of harm it is meant to guard against. The main early representatives of this tradition were Alexander Meiklejohn and Thomas Emerson, both discussed earlier as part of the definitional tradition in American free speech law.[35] The 'principled foundations' approach became especially prominent during the 1970s and 1980s.[36] 'Principled foundations' first amendment thinking is also likely to be anti-perfectionist, in several ways. For one, these theories often focus on one single fundamental value underlying the freedom of expression. In that way, they obviously limit the possibilities for the consideration of alternative values and interests in order to achieve a more comprehensive appraisal.[37] But more generally, any approach seeking to *define* the freedom of speech will treat the question of the coverage of first amendment protection to some extent in a rule-like, categorical and therefore exclusionary fashion. On such views, cases are either within or outside the area covered by the amendment, depending on

---

[32]  See, e.g., Black (1960). For Learned Hand, see, e.g., Richardson (1951), pp. 52–54.
[33]  See Chapter 4, Section B.
[34]  Cf. Cass (1987), pp. 1406ff.
[35]  See Chapter 4, Section E.
[36]  See, e.g., Scanlon (1972); Baker (1978); Redish (1984). But see Shiffrin (1984).
[37]  Cf. Greenawalt (1989), p. 126; Cass (1987), p. 1413.

their proximity to the core(s) of its underlying value(s).[38] The resulting categorical or rule-like conception of first amendment doctrine is often seen as integral to its ability to adequately protect the freedom of individuals expressing unpopular opinions against the vagaries of public sentiment.[39] But it comes with an important corollary in terms of the perfectionism / anti-perfectionism distinction. The 'rule-like nature of the first amendment', as Frederick Schauer has written, shows that it '*is not* the reflection of a society's highest aspirations, but rather of its fears'. It is 'the pessimistic and necessary manifestation of the fact that, in practice, neither a population nor its authoritative decisionmakers *can even approach* their society's most ideal theoretical aspirations'.[40] The result, in Schauer's striking terminology, is a first amendment that is, appropriately, '*second-best*'.[41]

### (b)   Anti-perfectionism and legal formality

A major theme underlying and unifying these different strands of anti-perfectionism in US constitutional jurisprudence is the idea of legal formality. In a variety of ways, these strands are expressive of a basic equation: anti-perfectionism = formality = constraint and limitation. Legal formality and anti-perfectionism both express and serve to uphold law's autonomy. They do so by strictly enforcing the boundaries of the juridical sphere. This is true, in different ways, for 'originalism', 'clause-bound' reasoning, or the denial of horizontal effect. It is especially visible in the more general way formality is interpreted as '*ruleness*'.[42] Decision making according to rule blocks consideration of 'the felt necessities of particular cases' – of 'factors that a sensitive decisionmaker would otherwise take into account'.[43] For such rule-based conceptions of adjudication, obtaining 'the "perfect" answer is nice – but it is just one of a number of competing values'.[44]

---

[38]  Or, in more nuanced models: within or outside areas of 'higher' or 'lower' speech protection. See also Chapter 4, Section E.2.

[39]  See, e.g., Ely (1975), p. 1501 ('The categorizers were right: where messages are proscribed because they are dangerous, balancing tests inevitably become intertwined with the ideological predispositions of those doing the balancing.') But see Schlag (1983).

[40]  Schauer (1989), p. 2 (emphases added).

[41]  *Ibid.*, (emphasis added). See also Blasi (1985); Cass (1987).

[42]  Schauer (1989), p. 22.

[43]  Schauer (1988), p. 510; Jackson (1999), p. 621. The proverbial '*Khadi*' judge, conversely, is the fictional archetype of radical *informality* understood as extreme decisional *freedom*.

[44]  Scalia (1989), p. 1178.

Legal formality and constraint in the American context, then, are seen as essentially connected. Formality means juridical constraint; and constraint in turn requires legal formality for its operationalization. This intimate relationship sets up a fascinating question of comparative law. If American *anti*-perfectionism is, in so many ways, supported by and reflective of formalizing tendencies, is German constitutional legal perfectionism *anti*-formalizing in any comparable way? That, certainly, is the prevailing American view, as discussed in the Introduction to this book. But there is an intriguing alternative. And that is the idea that German perfectionism might instead be formal, in a way analogous to the formality of American anti-perfectionism. If that were the case, then the meaning of the discourse of balancing, as a key component and manifestation of this German perfectionism, might also be revealed as formal in a sense difficult to square with prevalent (American) conceptions.

### 3. Perfectionism and balancing in German constitutional jurisprudence: formality as compulsion and optimization

#### (a) Embedded informality

At first sight, the idea that perfectionism and balancing might be related to formalism is counterintuitive. After all, important elements of perfectionist constitutional legal thought and of rights balancing specifically, such as maximal particularity and reliance on open-ended constitutional norms capable of constitutionalizing large areas of social life, seem radically at odds with core dimensions of legal formality.

And yet, manifestations of formalizing tendencies are not all that difficult to find. German balancing, and German constitutional legal perfectionism more broadly, are formalizing, first of all, in they way they combine maximal particularity with case-transcending, stabilizing elements. Among the most important of these stabilizing elements are various conceptions of a 'value system' within the Basic Law and the view of the Basic Law as a 'logical-teleological whole'.[45] Another important case-transcending element in the *Bundesverfassungsgericht*'s approach is its simultaneous invocation of *both* interest-balancing and value-balancing – what German commentators call 'value balancing in the individual case'. These specific elements are, moreover, embedded within a scholarly culture that continuously makes explicit and implicit efforts to

---

[45] See Chapter 3, Section E.2.

formalize judicial technique, by way of the '*Verwissenschaftlichung*' of legal doctrine.[46] These elements support at least an initial case that constitutional rights balancing might be *something more* – something rather more constraining, especially – than mere '*Khadi*'-like, ad hoc, maximal particularism.

### (b)    Formality as optimization: of 'baselines' and the 'fully realized constitutional order'

Uncovering the full extent of the formalizing potential of constitutional perfectionism and balancing in German jurisprudence, though, requires going beyond these instances where particularity and legal informality are simply embedded among formalizing supports. It demands instead a more radical reappraisal of the character of legal formality itself, starting from its basic definition as faith in, and commitment to, the possibility of juridical autonomy. There are two ways in which this idea of autonomy may produce an overly narrow understanding of the ways in which law could be formal.

First, faith in juridical autonomy is, at heart, a form of belief in the agency of legal ideas; a belief that legal doctrines, concepts, theories, etc. can exercise some kind of independent force. That independent force has traditionally been conceived of in constraining, limiting terms. Legal formality then stands for the idea that legal decision makers are *prevented* from doing certain things; from taking into account factors they would otherwise have considered, for example. But a similar sense of constraint could also come from an *obligation* to do certain things. Legal formality would then mean compulsion instead of limitation. It would compel legal actors to take *all* relevant factors into account, for example, obliging them to take seriously the 'maximal' in 'maximal particularity'.

The idea of autonomy may also be misleading in a second way, in that it tends to suggest some form of bounded, limited domain for law. But the autonomous, independent force of the juridical could also find expression in the form of a *totalizing* pretension – a mode of thinking in which all other societal domains or modes of knowledge are first framed by law, before they can assert any remaining independent identity.

Probably the clearest illustration of this alternative reading of legal formality can be found in the operation of the idea of 'optimization' in German constitutional jurisprudence.[47] The mandatory and totalizing qualities of this idea can be brought out in several related senses.

---

[46]  See Chapter 3, Section C and Chapter 5, Section C.2.
[47]  See also Chapter 3, Section E.2.

First, optimization as a principle in German constitutional jurisprudence has distinctive 'rule-like' qualities. By way of illustration:
Alexy's 'law of balancing' referred to earlier and his framing of rights as
'*Optimierungsgebote*' ('injunctions to optimize'), are clear expressions
of compulsion. So too, albeit to a lesser extent, are older concepts such
as '*praktische Konkordanz*', or the presumption in favour of individual
rights, which is now largely discarded but was earlier fervently discussed.
These may sound like pragmatic and open-ended concepts, but they come
with powerful preconceptions of the kinds of 'optimal' solutions to be
achieved.[48] The image of constitutional justice that they convey is not that
of a pragmatic tweaking of interests, but of a finely calibrated balance,
perched on the one narrow ridge where all values and interests in play can
receive their exact due.

But optimization is also formal in a more complex sense, analogous to a
leading tradition of interpreting the formality of the *Lochner* line of decisions in American constitutional law.[49] *Lochner* and its canonical, albeit
troubled, association with formality and formalism in American jurisprudence have already been discussed, in Chapter 2. *Lochner*'s formality,
in one major line of thinking, lay in the Supreme Court's adherence to
some particular conception of neutrality.[50] It was the Court's 'yearning
to believe in an idealized oasis of neutrality' that allegedly informed its
rejection of regulatory measures such as limitations on working hours
for bakers.[51] Views differ as to the precise nature of this conception of
neutrality and its jurisprudential implementation. Some interpretations
emphasize the neutrality of the State in terms of the idealized liberal
'night-watchman' State of nineteenth-century political thought. Others
emphasize the neutrality of 'self-executing and prepolitical' markets,
and others still the neutrality of a common law 'state of nature'.[52] This
neutrality was implemented by way of a distinction between (legitimate)
intervention for the general good and (illegitimate) 'class legislation', or
through an array of 'fixed categories of legitimate police power [derived
from] the common law of nuisance'.[53] In Cass Sunstein's hugely influential reading, the Court took 'the existing distribution of wealth and

[48] See Chapter 3, Sections E.2 and E.3.
[49] See Chapter 2, Section B.4.
[50] See, e.g., Les Benedict (1985); Sunstein (1987); Horwitz (1992); Sunstein (1992); Cushman
(2005). But see Bernstein (2003) for critique of the 'neutrality' reading.
[51] Cf. Rowe (1999), p. 233.
[52] See Sunstein(1990), p. 19; Rowe (1999), pp. 226–33 (discussion of the views of Owen Fiss,
Howard Gillman and Morton Horwitz).
[53] Rowe (1999), p. 232.

entitlements' as a neutral '*baseline*' from which the constitutionality of governmental action would be judged.[54] '[M]arket ordering under the common law' was, he wrote, 'a part of nature rather than a legal construct'.[55] Sunstein's 'baseline' notion and his depiction of common law doctrines as 'part of nature', rather than as legal constructs, have been forcefully criticized for being anachronistic.[56] But in broader terms, his reading of *Lochner* as emblematic for a categorical distinction between (some forms of) intervention and (some forms of) maintenance of the status quo clearly resonates with more historically grounded work. On this reading, governmental *action*, for example to enhance the working conditions of the *Lochner* bakers, requires special justification in a way that governmental *inaction* would not.

This comparison with *Lochner*-style formality in its dominant, received understanding (still the archetype of legal formality in American law), brings out parallels with the formal character of optimization in German constitutional jurisprudence. *Lochner's* neutrality, its status quo, or its 'baseline', has its counterpart in the German vision of the fully realized optimum of constitutional rights protection. Where in *Lochner* formalism, any deviation from the status quo is subject to a high burden of justification, so in the German context is any detraction from fundamental rights' 'full effectiveness', in terms of scope and intensity.[57] The way that in *Lochner*-type reasoning, existing common law arrangements or patterns of distribution are 'natural' or uncontroversial has its equivalent in the German view of the full effectuation of the value order of the Basic Law as a natural, uncontroversial state of affairs.

The quest for neutrality and 'naturalness' in *Lochner* jurisprudence has been read as part of a (formalist) strategy of de-politicization. The *Lochner*-court's doctrinal categories and modes of justification, on this view, served to keep judicial ideological preferences out of the

---

[54] Sunstein (1987), p. 874. Cf. also, in somewhat different terms, Les Benedict (1985), pp. 304ff. On the formalism of 'baselines' in legal thought outside this specific context see, e.g., Singer & Beerman (1989), pp. 914ff.

[55] *Ibid.*

[56] See White (2000), pp. 24; Bernstein (2003), pp. 18ff. The vocabulary of 'naturalness' is widely shared, though. See Rowe (1999), pp. 236, 239 (references in the work of Horwitz and Fiss).

[57] For an evocative reference in German constitutional rights theory to the idea of a '*status naturalis libertatis fictivus*', presented as a principle demanding justification of all actions and omissions that detract from the optimal realization of individual fundamental rights under the Basic Law, see Lindner (2005), pp. 212ff.

adjudication process. Such attempts at de-politicization through legal form are generally treated with suspicion and are often seen as incorporating an individualist bias.[58] Intriguingly, a very similar form of de-politicization can be observed in the early *Bundesverfassungsgericht's* pursuit of optimization and maximization. That project, though, as I will argue below in Section E, was not so much directed at keeping ideology out of constitutional adjudication, but at enforcing a uniform, all-encompassing, semi-official ideology – a public ideology that integrated democracy, social welfare and individual rights. And the Court's balancing played a central role in the judicial effectuation and safeguarding of this judicial synthesis between the main currents in early postwar German political thought.[59]

## C.   The substantive: materiality and policy

One of the central themes in *Economy and Society* is what Max Weber identified as the 'anti-formalistic tendencies of modern legal development', or the materialization of law.[60] In Weber's view, contemporary demands for 'social' law and for 'judicial creativity' engendered a new understanding of adjudication as turning on 'concrete evaluations', rather than on the formally rational 'logical analysis of meaning'.[61] The hallmark of this new mode of lawmaking, as Weber described it, was *balancing*: 'the expediential balancing of concrete interests' and 'the free balancing of values in each individual case'.[62] This way of proceeding, Weber thought, was 'not only *nonformal* but *irrational*'.[63]

The processes of the materialization of law are widely understood as having intensified with the rise of the welfare state and the dawn of the 'Age of Rights' after the Second World War.[64] The enunciation of 'broad social goals' in legislation, and the implementation of judicial review of broadly formulated constitutional rights clauses are thought to have promoted 'judicial methods that are informal, compared [...] to the traditional civil-

---

[58] See, e.g., Zumbansen (2007), p. 207. Weber himself, already, noted a likely pro-capitalist, individualist bias in formal legal rationality, based on its tendency to favour the status quo.

[59] See below, Chapter 5, Section D.2.

[60] Weber (1925), pp. 303ff.     [61] *Ibid.*, pp. 311, 63.

[62] *Ibid.*, p. 312–13.

[63] *Ibid.*, p. 311 (emphasis added).

[64] Cf. Teubner (1983), p. 240; Habermas (1996), pp. 190, 240ff, 392ff; McCormick (1997), p. 327; Wiethölter (1986), p. 221.

law conceptual approach'.[65] The spread of these 'informal' methods has brought about a crisis of formal legal rationality,[66] necessitating a quest for new types of legal rationality.[67]

The materialization thesis is broadly accepted for legal systems in all Western democracies, including those in Europe and the US.[68] And in accounts for both settings, since Weber, judicial balancing is seen as the prime manifestation of a new materialized, deformalized, mode of legal thought and practice. It is interesting to note, however, that accounts of legal materialization typically spend little energy on trying to identify what 'the material' in law might mean. Weber's own typology is a case in point. His definition of legal formality, while certainly ambiguous, is considerably more precise than the casual list of factors given to describe 'substantive rationality'.[69] This neglect is curious. After all, the question of the identity of the substantive in law is not an easy one. By way of illustration, think of the list of possible opposites for 'formal' and its derivations. Along with 'substantive', a list of leading candidates would have to include at least 'instrumental', 'pragmatic', 'contextual' and 'particular'.[70] It is worth asking, therefore, whether this façade of uniformity might not hide different understandings of the substantive in law operative in

---

[65] Grey (2003). Cf. Dyzenhaus (1996).

[66] Teubner (1983), p. 242.

[67] Friedman (1966), p. 164 ('What judicial reasoning is tending toward is, in Weber's terms, substantive rationality [...] The move toward this type of rationality has been moderately controversial'.); Teubner (1983), pp. 267ff (in process of (re)materialization, law is thought to develop 'a substantive rationality characterized by particularism, result-orientation, an instrumentalist social policy approach, and ... increasing legalization').

[68] See, e.g., Maduro (1998), p. 17; Kennedy (2003b).

[69] Weber (1925), pp. 63ff. Lists and negative definitions – by way of opposition to legal formality – are typical. Summers (1978), p. 710 mentions appeals to 'moral, economic, political, institutional, or other social considerations' as instances of 'substantive reasons' in law, before noting: 'Although a more precise definition could be formulated, there is no need to do so here. Judges already have a working familiarity with the notion of a substantive reason *as distinguished from* a reason based on prior legal authority' (emphasis added).

[70] Other, even more obviously contingent, candidates exist, notably: 'realism'. Intriguingly, not all of these opposites exist in all forms. Pragmatism, contextualism, particularism and instrumentalism are all commonly used opposites for 'formalism'. But *'substantivism'* is only used in limited contexts (conflict of laws and legal ethics, mainly). Contextualizing, particularizing and instrumentalizing are common opposites for 'formalizing', but *'substantivizing'* and *'pragmatizing'* are rarely encountered. Instrumentality and particularity are common opposites for 'formality', but neither *'substantivity'* nor *'substantiveness'*, or *'pragmaticality'* and *'contextuality'* are recognized terms of art. These gaps only serve to underline the basic ambiguities in the meaning of 'substantive', and, of course, of 'formal', in law.

different legal settings. Such different 'substantives' might imply different 'materializations' of law. And different 'materializations', Weber would probably have agreed, could mean different forms of balancing.

## 1. US: pragmatism, instrumentalism and policy

In postwar American constitutional jurisprudence, the substantive in law is associated with pragmatism, instrumentalism and 'policy' reasoning.[71] American commentators often attest to the pervasive influence of these ideas. 'Pragmatic instrumentalism', a combination of 'philosophical pragmatism, sociological jurisprudence, and certain tenets of legal realism', is seen as 'America's only indigenous theory of law'.[72] During the middle decades of the twentieth century, 'this body of ideas' was, according to Robert Summers, 'our most influential theory of law in jurisprudential circles, in the faculties of major law schools, and in important realms of the bench and bar'.[73] Pragmatism has long been 'the working theory of most good lawyers',[74] and American judges are described as 'practicing pragmatists'.[75] A similar story can be told for 'policy', which is a 'standard category in everyday American lawyer-talk'.[76] 'Policy argument' or 'policy analysis' – whether these terms are understood in the narrower sense of a specific form of utilitarian argument or in the broad sense of an 'everything that is not deductive argument' – exemplify the 'utilitarian and other expediential rules, and political maxims' that Weber saw as defining elements of the substantive in law.[77]

## 2. The substantive in law: US versus German legal thought

Are these 'typically American' versions of the substantive in law any different from their 'typically German', or even 'European', counterparts? This is a difficult question, not least because demonstrating the absence of any 'typically American' ideas in the German context would require

---

[71] See, e.g., Summers (1981); Grey (1996a); Leiter (1997); Grey (2003), p. 478 ('Weber's substantively rational mode of legal thought matches up with pragmatism as I describe it'); Vermeule (2007).

[72] Summers (1981), p. 862.    [73] Summers (1982), p. 35.

[74] Grey (1990), p. 1590.    [75] Posner (1990), p. 1566.

[76] See, e.g., Shubert (1965); Chayes (1976); Kennedy (1997), p. 109.

[77] Cf. Dworkin (1977), p. 222; Kennedy (1997), p. 109; Weber (1925), pp. 63ff. See also Friedman (1966), p. 151 ('In Weber's terms, decisions [built on considerations of] "political or social policy" would be substantively (as opposed to formally) rational').

proving a negative. Even so, there are many indications that subtle but significant differences do exist.

To begin with, the claim that pragmatism, instrumentalism and policy reasoning are in some way distinctive for American legal thought and practice has a distinguished pedigree in comparative legal studies. While instrumental views of law have also spread in other systems, it is commonly noted that the US has somehow 'moved furthest in this direction'.[78] 'Although European judges may becoming more policy-oriented', Robert Kagan wrote in the late 1990s, 'they still are profoundly uncomfortable with the unbridled instrumentalism of many American judges'.[79] A first distinction, then, may simply be that even if very similar ideas are in operation, their influence is more intense and more pervasive in the US than in Germany.

Terminological differences offer a second set of clues. Mitchel Lasser has highlighted the potential significance of the fact that one legal culture, like the American, 'uses a single term such as "policy" to express several different meanings whereas another legal culture, which apparently has no such overarching term, divides the concept into multiple subparts, such as "equity" or "legal adaptation"'.[80] The conceptual categories used in the two settings to describe the substantive in law do indeed differ markedly. Most notably, the term 'policy' as used in American legal writing has no direct equivalent in German (or in French, it might be added).[81] The term 'pragmatic' and its derivations are not commonly encountered in German academic legal writing. The German word 'Pragmatismus' is in fact generally reserved for discussions of Anglo-American legal thought and philosophy.[82] Differences also go the other way. While more specific terms, like 'pragmatism', are rarely used in the German context, the overarching concept of 'the substantive' or 'the material' is, by contrast, rarely referred to in US jurisprudence. The general idea of the 'materialization' of law, for example, is, at least on this high level of abstraction, not nearly as important a theme in American legal writing as it is in

---

[78] Tamanaha (2006), p. 1.     [79] Kagan (1997), p. 180.
[80] Lasser (2001), p. 899.     [81] Cf. Kennedy (1997), p. 109.
[82] See, e.g., Esser (1956), pp. 183ff; Fikentscher (1975), pp. 275ff); Lege (1998). An important exception is the generally accepted qualification of von Jhering's later work as 'pragmatische Jurisprudenz'. Von Jhering's writing is of such basic, foundational importance for *all* of mainstream modern, European and American, legal thinking, however, that it could be said that his pragmatism is no longer pragmatic in any distinctive sense. 'Pragmatisch' is also sometimes used in the context of discussions on 'Topik' and 'topische Jurisprudenz'. See, e.g., Esser (1956), p. 44, and above Chapter 3, Section C.3.

Europe.[83] Similarly, the idea of a 'substantive' constitution, or a 'substantive' ideal for the rule of law, though by no means nonexistent, are still 'relatively rare' in American constitutional jurisprudence.[84] Not surprisingly, Smend's terminology of 'material constitutionalism' does not have an obvious analogue in the US.

A third set of differences is related to these terminological points. Very often, when substantive elements surface in German constitutional jurisprudence, they are hemmed in by other ideas, doctrines or frameworks, or pulled up towards higher level of abstraction. As a result, they often lack much of the unequivocally instrumentalist, pragmatist or even ideological dimensions of American policy reasoning. In part, these background frameworks are themselves substantive in nature. Conflicts over social and economic issues in the first decades after the Second World War, for example, played out in Germany against a political–economic ideological background far more broadly agreed upon than any set of socio-economic ideas prevalent in the US at the time.[85] Other pervasive background understandings during this period were rather more methodological in their focus. Time and again, German legal scholars called for the '*Verwissenschaftlichung*' ('the rendering scientifically acceptable') of substantive evaluations, by scholars and judges.[86] '*Verwissenschaftlichung*' is of course by nature a mode of formalization, in the sense that scientific standards are invoked to 'discipline' participants. Such 'disciplining' in American jurisprudence has consistently entailed resort to empirical sciences – sociology, psychology, economics.[87] The search for disciplining frameworks looked very different in early postwar German constitutional jurisprudence. There, '*Verwissenschaftlichung*' was sought in the form of a '*Wertungsjurisprudenz*' – a thoroughly theorized jurisprudence

---

[83] See, e.g., Teubner (1983), p. 240 (referring to 'materialization' as an idea held by European scholars). In part, this difference is related to variations in the scope and depth of the welfare state as between the US and Europe.

[84] Cf. Fallon (1997a), p. 32. Fallon's concept of the 'substantive ideal type' of the rule of law is clearly not identical to Smend's material constitutionalism, but it does show some affinities.

[85] See, e.g., Gerber (1994) (on 'Ordoliberalism'); Nicholls (1994), p. 5 (the 'social market economy' as a synthesis of 'market freedom and social responsibility' was 'accepted by all the major parties by the end of the 1950s').

[86] See especially Kriele (1967), pp. 97ff. See also Markesinis (1986), p. 366 (German judges 'pursue relentlessly their scientific approach which (they are taught to believe) is bound to produce the right result and may even lead them into the *Paradise of Legal Ideas*').

[87] See, e.g., McDougal (1947); Schlegel (1995).

of values and valuation.[88] Other influential contemporaneous turns
include those to '*Systemdenken*' ('systematization')[89] and towards the idea
of a '*topische Jurisprudenz*' ('a jurisprudence of topics'), or 'dialectical
jurisprudence'.[90]

Each of these streams of thought contributed ideas on how to discipline, organize and control the materialization of law through abstraction,
situation, systematization, dialogue. Each, also, was very different from
the more direct, unmediated ways that pragmatism, instrumentalism and
policy reasoning influenced US constitutional jurisprudence. Smend's
conception of the substantive as 'value constellations' expressive of all
cumulative learning and experience brought on by the Enlightenment,
for example, is worlds away from the idea of the substantive as economics-
based policy argument. Not all differences, of course, are as dramatic. But
even subtle variations in emphasis can be significant.

By way of example, take this 1969 assessment of the topical jurisprudence of Viehweg and Esser, written for an American audience by the
German *émigré* professor Edgar Bodenheimer.[91] '[I]t might seem reasonable, *at first sight*', Bodenheimer wrote, 'to identify dialectical reasoning
with "policy" reasoning', but he cautioned: 'Upon closer examination,
however, it becomes desirable to enter a caveat against making this identification readily and without substantial qualifications'.[92] Dialectical reasoning in the German mode, in Bodenheimer's view, involved a much
more situated and interstitial form of judicial creativity than American
policy jurisprudence.[93] As he described the German perspective:
'Although it is true that determinations of policy often form elements in
the adjudicatory process, such determinations are incidental to the primary task imposed on the courts [...] This task, must, as a general rule, be
performed within the framework set by the legal and social system and
excludes free-wheeling forms of policy-making designed solely to accomplish objectives of political expediency'.[94]

---

[88] For a discussion of the term '*Wertungsjurisprudenz*' see, e.g., Zippelius (1962); Larenz (1991), pp. 54ff.
[89] See, e.g., Canaris (1969).
[90] See Chapter 3, Section C. 3.
[91] Bodenheimer (1969), p. 273. The article's title is revealing also in the opposite direction. Bodenheimer calls topical jurisprudence 'A Neglected Theory of Legal Reasoning' in the US.
[92] *Ibid.*, p. 394 (emphasis added).
[93] *Ibid.*, p. 395.     [94] *Ibid.*, pp. 395–96.

Bodenheimer's reticence to equate US 'policy argument' with German, or European, 'topical jurisprudence' was, I would argue, entirely justified. But not every comparative analysis has brought out difference in the same careful way. Here, by way of contrast, is an extract from one of the very first commentaries on postwar German constitutional rights adjudication written for an American audience, published even before the *Lüth* decision was handed down. The comments concern the decision of the *Bundesverfassungsgericht* to ban the German Communist Party, or *KPD*, finding it to be *'verfassungswidrig'* – contrary to the Constitution. The Court's opinion in this case, Edward McWhinney wrote, demonstrated that:

> the [German] constitution is not to be regarded as establishing philosophic absolutes, but standards capable of varying application in varying societal conditions, thus opening the way to a pragmatic, balancing-of-interests approach that is quite novel to German public law jurisprudence and clearly owes much to the influence of American legal ideas and techniques during the Allied occupation period.[95]

Everything in this observation betrays an Anglo-American perspective. The binary distinction between 'philosophic absolutes' in the first amendment sense – McWhinney mentions the *Dennis* decision of the US Supreme Court for comparison – and 'pragmatism' in its classical American philosophical meaning, simply does not match up with what the *Bundesverfassungsgericht* set out to do, as would become abundantly clear in *Lüth* and other later decisions.[96] The idea of weighing and adjusting values was not novel, not even in public law, given Smend's influential work on the Weimar Constitution.[97] And on the influence of 'American legal ideas and techniques': while the Allies of course had real sway over the structure and the content of the Basic Law when it was being drafted, there appears to be little or no evidence

---

[95] McWhinney (1957), pp. 308–9.

[96] And for which important hints had already been given in the *Southwest* case. See BVerfGE 1, 14; 32 ('*Südweststaat*') (1951). On 'absolutism' in the first amendment context, see Chapter 4, Section E.

[97] McWhinney does refer to the *Interessenjurispudenz* as a precursor in private law (at p. 309). Note that the *Bundesverfassungsgericht* in the '*KPD*' decision did not purport to be 'balancing' itself; it only mentioned '*Abwägung*' when referring to the nature of the 'political freedom of evaluation for the government' in deciding whether to ban the *KPD*. The Court's role was merely to police the outer boundaries of that 'freedom of evaluation'. See BVerfGE 5, 85, 231 (1956).

for any subsequent American influence on judicial method or scholarly thinking in constitutional law.[98]

### 3.   Categories of the substantive

The ideas of 'the substantive', 'policy reasoning' and 'balancing' are intimately related in American legal thought.[99] Explicit weighing is seen as the surest sign that courts are engaged in (illegitimate) policy-making, rather than (legitimate) 'lawfinding'. Yet, if these same courts neglect or explicitly reject policy argumentation, they stand accused of 'irrealistic' and 'formalistic' judging. Both policy argument and balancing, therefore, are key sites of the 'perpetual argumentative conflict' that characterizes American legal reasoning.[100]

Adopting a comparative perspective on the materialization of law, however, enables a framing of the intrusion – or rather, as it would then become, in more neutral terms: the *inclusion* – of substantive elements in legal reasoning in entirely different terms. Where in the paradigmatic American experience, the substantive has to be policy, politics or unprincipled pragmatism, an entirely different category of substantive prevails elsewhere, notably in German and European constitutional jurisprudence. The substantive, it turns out, can be 'material constitutionalism' with its durable yet evolving constellations of values. It can mean '*topoi*', or the consensual 'common places' of the Aristotelian tradition. And most comprehensively, substantive can mean principled.[101]

---

[98]   The literature on the question of the 'Americanization' of West-German society in the 1950s more generally is immense. See, e.g., Nicholls (1994), pp. 9ff; Schildt & Sywottek (1997), pp. 439ff; Müller (2003), pp. 5ff. In the realm of legal method, however, the overwhelming impression is one of basic continuity with the Weimar era. Indeed, as Chapter 3 argued, both the value- and interest-balancing components of the *Bundesverfassungsgericht*'s postwar approach were to large extent continuations of pre-War practices. Contemporary observers did suggest that in the early years after the War there was 'a general tendency towards paying more regard to foreign views than has been the case in the past' (see Cohn (1953), p. 181). But, while German practitioners were said to be 'deeply impressed in particular by English and American criminal procedure', Cohn found it 'a matter of regret' that *among legal academics* this 'living experience' of foreign law under occupation '*remained unused*, in particular because it would have been able to stimulate self-criticism, a habit which unfortunately has always been sadly underdeveloped in the German legal and non-legal tradition' (at pp. 189–90, emphases added).

[99]   See, e.g., Aleinikoff (1987), p. 949; Tamanaha (2006), p. 96.

[100]   Lasser (2004), p. 15.

[101]   See also Barak (2010).

### D. The formal and the substantive: conflict and synthesis

If the discourse of balancing is one of the primary sites in constitutional jurisprudence where the formal and the substantive, in all their different guises, meet, what is the nature of these meetings? How, in other words, do the formal and the substantive interact in paradigmatic versions of German and US constitutional rights jurisprudence, as exemplified in the discourse of balancing?

Answering that question requires a brief return to two basic approaches to the roles of legal formality and its opposites in comparative studies of legal reasoning outlined earlier.[102] In the first of these, legal reasoning in one system is identified as more formal or less formal than in another. In a second approach, the focus is rather on the way in which formal and other elements are combined or juxtaposed in different settings. As Mitchel Lasser has written in his study of French and American judicial discourse, in a phrase quoted before: '[w]hat really matters is not so much that both systems deploy both types of discourse (can one even really imagine a contemporary, Western democratic legal system that would not?), but *how* they do so'.[103] That, for Germany and the US, is the question this section seeks to answer.

### 1. *The formal and the substantive in US constitutional jurisprudence*

Lasser's studies build towards a striking contrast. On one side stands a French judicial discourse that is 'bifurcated' between an open-ended but hidden dialogue among magistrates and a public, official, judicial discourse that is formal in the extreme. On the other side, an American judicial discourse that integrates its formalist and policy-oriented discourses in one space: the individually signed published opinion.[104] In these American opinions, the informal elements of judicial reasoning are then hemmed in by the formal strictures and categorical frameworks of so-called 'multi-part tests', schemes of 'tiered scrutiny' and other structuring devices.[105] What this means, in Lasser's view, is that 'the composite character of American judicial discourse produces and/or is constituted by a certain formalization of purpose/effect/policy discourse'.[106] This

---

[102] See Chapter 1, Section D.
[103] Lasser (2004), p. 155 (emphasis in original).
[104] Lasser (2004), pp. 27ff, 62ff, 245.
[105] *Ibid.*, p. 64. See also, e.g., Nagel (1989); Massey (2004), pp. 980ff.
[106] *Ibid.*, p. 251.

'formalization of the pragmatic', Lasser concludes, might well be 'the defining trait of American judicial discourse as a whole'.[107] That characterization seems widely shared among American observers.[108]

These ideas of 'integration' and of a 'formalization of the pragmatic' capture much of what is salient about the character of American judicial discourse, and of American legal discourse more broadly, certainly in the area of constitutional law. But when the comparative point of reference switches from France to Germany, some limitations on their capacity to fully convey American distinctiveness begin to appear. German constitutional legal discourse too, is 'integrated', rather than 'bifurcated' in the French sense.[109] And there are many elements in German constitutional legal discourse that can also validly be described in terms of a 'formalization of the substantive', even if both these formal and substantive dimensions themselves differ in character from their American equivalents, as argued earlier.[110]

The material covered in Chapters 2 and 4 suggests ways to complement and nuance this picture of how formal and substantive elements co-exist in US constitutional legal discourse. What is distinctive about this discourse, on this view, is not only that the formal and the substantive are commonly combined in one place, but also the fact that, in those combinations, formal and substantive remain distinct entities. They exist in a relationship of combination and juxtaposition rather than of integration or synthesis. This is exemplified in the side-by-side existence of categorical and more open-ended 'steps' in the typical American 'multi-part' doctrinal test. What is striking is that in those tests, as elsewhere in American jurisprudence, formality is optional. It is a matter of strategic choice by participants. This strategic dimension of legal formality is informed by, and does itself sustain, the idea that legal formality has inherent substantive implications. The formalization of the pragmatic (the substantive), in other words, goes hand in hand with an 'instrumentalization' ('substantivization') of the formal, and, ultimately, a conception of the formal *as a*

---

[107] *Ibid.*

[108] For expressions of similar views in otherwise very different projects, see Nagel (1989) (on the 'formulaic' nature of constitutional jurisprudence) and Kennedy (2003b), p. 1073 (on the 'ritualization' of policy argument).

[109] The Court of Justice of the European Union, Lasser's other principal comparative point of reference, is not helpful here: its institutional model is too obviously derived from the French example (not, though, the substance of its jurisprudence, which is much more clearly inspired by German understandings).

[110] See Chapter 5, Sections B and C.

particular brand of substantive.[111] The following paragraphs expound on these characteristics in turn.

### (a)    Formal and substantive: combined but separate

In American constitutional legal discourse, formal and substantive elements appear side by side. Open-ended analysis of circumstances and interests, typically framed in terms of balancing, is combined with highly formal, analytical and rhetorical, structures of 'steps', 'stages' and 'tiers'. These elements can all, of course, be seen as part of what Chapter 4 identified as the 'definitional tradition' in American constitutional jurisprudence. The typical multi-part American 'balancing test', or scheme of tiered analysis, is an intricate, deliberate effort by judges 'to create impersonal, formal rules that can constrain the Court'.[112] The resulting tests and frameworks have been described as 'an attempted synthesis of formalism and realism'.[113] But despite the intricately interwoven character of these tests and formulas, despite these attempts at synthesis, the formal and the substantive remain two separate categories. They may be integrated within overarching jurisprudential constructs, but they have not lost their respective distinctive natures, enduring in a condition described in mild terms as one of 'not always peaceful coexistence',[114] and in starker language as a 'perpetual state of argumentative conflict' generating 'significant argumentative tensions and distrust'.[115]

Examples abound of this intertwined-but-separate relationship between the formal and the substantive. Two particularly illustrative instances from among the material covered in Chapter 4 can be found in the work of John Hart Ely and Melville B. Nimmer. Both these authors wrote in reaction to the ostensibly all-or-nothing balancing versus absolutism controversy of the late 1950s and early 1960s. In Ely's view, 'what the decisions of the late Warren era began to recognize is that categorization and balancing need not be regarded as competing general theories of the first amendment, but are more helpfully *employed in tandem*, each with its own legitimate and indispensable role in protecting expression'.[116]

---

[111] This does not contradict the depiction of formal and substantive as distinct entities. On the contrary: a 'substantivization of the formal' implies that there is a formal element to be substantivized. On the difference with the 'German' idea of 'the substantive as formal', see the next section.

[112] Nagel (1985), p. 181.

[113] *Ibid.*, p. 182; Lasser (2004), pp. 15ff.

[114] Friedman (1966), p. 151.    [115] Lasser (2004), p. 15.

[116] Ely (1975), p. 1501 (emphasis added). See also at p. 1483 (referring to 'distinct and quite sensible roles' for balancing and categorization); Tushnet (1985), p. 1531.

Nimmer, for his part, aimed to construct a 'third approach' to free speech adjudication, situated in between what he saw as the 'equally unacceptable' alternatives of literal interpretation and ad hoc interest balancing in first amendment cases.[117] '*Definitional balancing*', as Nimmer labelled this middle way, aimed to combine the virtues of balancing and of more formal approaches, without falling into the alleged excesses of either.[118]

(b)   The formal as substantive: the instrumentalization
of legal formality

This idea of the formal and the informal as separate but combinable produces, sustains and is constituted by a conception of legal formality as a matter of choice for participants. The Nimmer and Ely projects are typical examples of this stance. They see the formal, in first amendment jurisprudence, as something that can be resorted to at will. An initially amorphous balancing test can be '*rulefied*': another term with no obvious German or French counterpart. Balancing can be made 'definitional', or not, or only in part. This conception makes for interpretations of formal, substantive and their interrelationship that are very different from those commonly encountered in Continental-European legal literature. Formalism in American jurisprudence is '*an interpretive strategy*'.[119] A pragmatic judge 'might think the pragmatic thing to do would be a formalist course of action'.[120] Formalism is simply one weapon among others in the juristic arsenal.[121]

When legal formality and its opposites are seen as a matter of choice and strategy, the question of the reasons for this choice will quickly come up for scrutiny. That question has given rise to a type of jurisprudential enquiry that is far more pervasive in American legal thought than, it would seem, anywhere else. This 'jurisprudence of form' is premised on the notion that the choice between the tools of legal formality (e.g. rules) and of informality (e.g. standards) 'can be analyzed in isolation from the substantive issues' that these tools respond to.[122] Once legal formality is a

---

[117]  Nimmer (1968), pp. 941–42.
[118]  *Ibid.*, pp. 944ff (emphasis added). On Ely see further Schauer (1981), pp. 266ff. For an extensive overview of Nimmer-inspired literature, see Deutsch (2006).
[119]  Sunstein (1999), p. 638 (emphasis in original). See also Posner (2003), p. 59 (legal formality as part of a 'pragmatic strategy').
[120]  Vermeule (2007), p. 2116.
[121]  Cf. Friedman (1966), p. 169.
[122]  Kennedy (1976), p. 1687. Intriguingly, even Kennedy's 'jurisprudence of form' – later mostly developed in the private law context – appears to have had its origins in the

matter of choice, however, and once the reasons for this choice are seen to be the ordinary reasons of policy, politics and ideology, this position of course translates into nothing less than the instrumentalization of legal formality.

This instrumentalization of legal formality has a long history in American jurisprudence. At the beginning of the twentieth century, as described in Chapter 2, it was the Supreme Court's alleged adherence to formal methods of interpretation that took the blame for its rejection of socially progressive legislation. Roscoe Pound and others denounced the Court's method of 'logical deduction' as producing judgments which were 'wholly inadequate' for industrialized society.[123] The invention of this 'Demon of Formalism' – the attribution of substantive implications to questions of form – has been an astoundingly successful jurisprudential innovation.[124] Just as Pound decried the false belief of formalist judges in the necessity and neutrality of their methods, he and his fellow critics managed to instill another belief, at once entirely similar and radically opposite, among wider legal academic and judicial circles: a belief in the hidden political motivations for, and disastrous substantive implications of, legal formality.[125]

Comparable inventions of connections between legal form and substantive outcomes could be observed in the period discussed in Chapter 4. This time, the critics' favoured target was what they saw as the excessive *in*formality of the Supreme Court's first amendment balancing. Balancing 'got a bad name with liberals from the speech and association cases of the McCarthy era'.[126] For these liberals, balancing was inherently government-friendly. But balancing was not the only methodological aspect of constitutional adjudication that was politicized. 'Reasoned elaboration', for example – the newer standards for good judicial reasoning also discussed in Chapter 4 – 'was at first largely methodological' in its critique.[127] But, as G. Edward White has written, these methodological critiques '*inevitably*

---

1950s–1960s constitutional law 'balancing debates' canvased in Chapter 4. See his 1969 *Yale Law Journal* Student Note on 'Civil Disabilities and the First Amendment'. For another influential project, also discussing balancing, see Sullivan (1992a) and Sullivan (1992b).

[123] Pound (1908), p. 616.

[124] Cf. Grey (2003), p. 477. The debate over the formalism of the *Lochner* era continues. See, e.g., Phillips (2001) and, more recently, Tamanaha (2009). There is, of course, a paradox here: the possibility of a 'jurisprudence of form' depends on form and substance being separate; its meaningfulness depends on their connection.

[125] Pound (1908), p. 608.     [126] See, e.g., Sullivan (1992b), p. 294.

[127] White (1973), pp. 279–80.

took on substantive content with the explosive loss of social consensus on first principles in the 1960s'.[128] Again and again, American constitutional jurisprudence shows the imprint of a powerful shared intuition, or suspicion, that the formal and the substantive must somehow be connected, that methodological choices must have ideological implications, even if the nature of these connections remains highly contested.[129]

This instrumentalization of formality has surprising implications. In US law, the very setting where formalism was supposed to have been virtually annihilated, first by Pound and then by the Realists and those who followed them, legal formality remains available as a powerful jurisprudential weapon. The use of this weapon is, however, subject to two important paradoxes. First, legal formality as choice sits uneasily, to put it mildly, with the basic idea of legal formality as constraint. The constraining power of post-Realist versions of legal formality, therefore, has to rely heavily on notions of active judicial *self*-restraint. Second, however, the power of the weapon of legal formality is thought to reside at least partly in the *actual* constraining force of formulas, tests and categories. The formality of multi-part tests, per se rules, and categorization devices depends on the perception that these jurisprudential tools are in fact able to constrain judicial power. John Hart Ely's retrospective analysis of the balancing debates is revealing:

> The categorizers were right: [...] balancing tests *inevitably* become intertwined with the ideological predispositions of those doing the balancing – or if not that, at least with the relative confidence or paranoia of the age in which they are doing it – and we must build barriers as secure as words are able to make them. *That means rigorous definition* of the limited categories of expression that are unprotected by the first amendment.[130]

Of course, neither of these paradoxes is insoluble. Judicial self-restraint is both widely observed as an empirical phenomenon and commonly advocated as a normative position.[131] And the power of tests and categories could lie merely in their appeal to such judicial self-limitation, even if that appeal is mainly or even purely rhetorical. But the impression given by

---

[128]  *Ibid.*, (emphasis added).
[129]  See, e.g., Sullivan (1992b), p. 294 ('[n]either the categorization/conservative nor the balancing/liberal connection is borne out'); Gordon (1984), p. 66 (discussing the possibility of a 'radical formalism' and a 'conservative Realism').
[130]  Ely (1975), p. 1501 (emphasis added). Ely did add the eloquent caveat that these barriers could only be 'as secure as words are able to make them'. For a more recent account along similar lines, see Schauer (2010), pp. 41ff.
[131]  See, e.g., Kavanagh (2009).

much of the American legal literature is that this is not how formality and formalism are actually understood. Legal form *can* constrain; hard and fast rules *do* bind; 'rigorous definition' *is* able to prevent the ideological bias of balancing.[132] And balancing, quite simply, is *'nothing like rule-application'*.[133]

## 2. *The formal and the substantive in German constitutional jurisprudence*

In German legal thought, and in Continental-European legal thought more broadly (although that claim cannot be fully substantiated here), legal formality is not a matter of choice or strategy. Formality, rather, is always present, even in the most seemingly open-ended, apparently informal legal settings, such as constitutional rights balancing. In contrast to the American context, where formality is simply a different kind of substance, in German constitutional jurisprudence, the substantive has always remained formal.

Reference has been made before to standard American observations on the alleged extreme informality of German and European constitutional rights balancing, exemplified in references to European rights case law as '*Khadi*'-like. Clearly, the type of balancing engaged in by the German courts is not formal in the paradigmatic American understanding of rules and categories. But the argument developed here is that this type of discourse is not only formal by other means, but also that it integrates formal and substantive elements in ways quite unlike those seen in US jurisprudence. To this end, this section presents the following three argumentative steps, all designed to highlight differences with paradigmatic US understandings.

First, in the German setting, legal formality is achieved primarily through conceptualization and systematization, rather than by way of constraint through doctrinal rules. This 'conceptual formality' then allows for the infusion of substantive values into law in a way that is very different from the 'rule formality' found more typically in US jurisprudence. Secondly, within German constitutional jurisprudence unremitting efforts are made to synthesize formal and material elements. This 'synthesis tradition' in constitutional law goes back to at least the Weimar era, and has maintained its strength both through law under fascism

---

[132] See, e.g., Ely (1975).　　[133] Tamanaha (2006), p. 96.

and in the era of the Basic Law. These fusions and amalgamations, incidentally, are much easier to achieve with a conceptual, or system-based, understanding of legal formality, than with any understanding emphasizing rules. Thirdly, in US constitutional jurisprudence, the typical way of framing the relationship between form and substance in constitutional law is by way of a 'blaming method': a search for undesirable substantive consequences of formal choices. That particular argument is dramatically less common in German jurisprudence. This, even despite the obvious elephant-in-the-room-candidate of law under fascism.

### (a)    Conceptual formality versus rule formality

Where in US constitutional jurisprudence legal formality is vested primarily in *rules, categories* and *definitions*, formality in the German tradition is seen to lie in *concepts, system* and *deduction.* All these elements go back to nineteenth-century understandings of the nature of law and 'legal science'.[134] 'The idea of a science of German private law', Franz Wieacker has noted, was founded on a 'juristic formalism' that transferred 'the systematics and concept-building of Pandecticism to substantive German private law'.[135] Its formalism, therefore, was first and foremost a '*conceptual* formalism',[136] based on the 'assumption of the perfection and inherent completeness of the system',[137] and on a powerful faith in deductive logic.[138]

Notwithstanding the radical critique levelled at this conceptual formalism during the late nineteenth and early twentieth century, all these ideas retain their relevance for postwar German legal thought, both in private and in public law. This is how Gunther Teubner, for example, characterizes the role of the principle of 'good faith' in Continental European private law:

> [T]he specific way in which continental lawyers deal with such a 'general clause' is abstract, open-ended, principle-oriented, but at the same time strongly systematised and dogmatised. This is clearly at odds with the

---

[134] These ideas were important in nineteenth-century American legal thought as well. Their legacy has been very different, however. See Chapter 2, Section B.5, and below, Chapter 5, Section E.

[135] Wieacker (1995), pp. 320ff.

[136] *Ibid.*, p. 292 (emphasis added).

[137] Reimann (1990), p. 882.

[138] *Ibid.*, p. 894. For public law, see, e.g., von Gerber (1869), p. viii (referring to the primordial value of '*sichere juristische Deduktion*', 'secure juristic deduction').

more rule-oriented, technical, concrete, but loosely systematised British style of legal reasoning.[139]

'Conceptual systematisation', Teubner writes, is still 'close to the heart of German law'.[140] But this conceptual formality, with its roots in the nineteenth-century ideas just mentioned, is now combined with open-endedness and orientation to principle in a synthesis of form and substance that is largely unthinkable in Anglo-American jurisprudence. Intriguingly, however, Teubner's study also shows that Anglo-American reasoning, in foregoing systematization, dogmatism and conceptualism, is not necessarily less formal than its German counterpart. In its reliance on rule-orientation and technicality, it is simply formal by other means.

The leading example of conceptual formalism in public law, certainly in relation to balancing, has to be the work of Robert Alexy.[141] As mentioned at the end of Chapter 2, Alexy emphatically locates his theory of constitutional rights within 'the great analytical tradition of conceptual jurisprudence' in German legal thought.[142] His is a theory heavily invested in conceptual dogmatics,[143] for which Alexy cites leading nineteenth-century public lawyers as Laband and von Gerber in support.[144] Most striking is the fact that Alexy's evident concern is not simply to show that constitutional rights balancing might be rational in some generic sense. What is envisaged is not the instrumental rationality of policy reasoning, or even the rule-based rationality of structured legal tests. Rationality, for Alexy, clearly means *formal* rationality in the logical, exacting Weberian sense. Balancing can and must be rational in the way deductive reasoning is rational.[145] That specific project is highly revealing. It shows how the ideal of formal legal rationality remains alive, as a powerful benchmark for the assessment of the legitimizing force of legal reasoning. Why go through the trouble of showing balancing can be formally rational, if formal

---

[139] Teubner (1998), p. 19.

[140] *Ibid.*, p. 21. See also, e.g., Markesinis (1986), pp. 350–52, 366 (decisions of the German *Bundesgerichtshof* [the highest private law court] combine an 'increasing tendency for casuistry' with a 'highly conceptual, even metaphysical' tone, and a 'scientific' search for the 'right result' with pragmatism).

[141] For discussions in English, see Ewald (2004); Menéndez & Eriksen (2006); Schauer (2010).

[142] Alexy (2002), p. 18. The German original uses the loaded term *Begriffsjurisprudenz* (at p. 38).

[143] Cf. Ewald (2004).

[144] Alexy (2002), pp. 14, 16–17. See also Ewald (2004), p. 595.

[145] Although Alexy does not use the term 'formal rationality' or refer to Weber's scheme, it seems clear that this is the kind of rationality envisaged. See, e.g., Alexy (2003).

rationality does not retain any purchase? These connections between balancing and formal rationality may not convince all of German constitutional rights scholarship, but, significantly, they are taken seriously as a possibility, in a way that is difficult to even imagine within mainstream American constitutional jurisprudence.

Of course, none of these differences are in any way absolute. Some aspects of the interaction between legal formality and informality in German jurisprudence really are to some degree similar to American experiences. The way the proportionality assessment has been structured in a number of heavily dogmatized 'steps', for example, does look somewhat like the American judicial 'tests'. Here, German legal formality relies upon rules, in addition to systematization and conceptualization. But even here, differences remain. So, for example, American judicial tests are primarily seen as methods to 'implement' constitutional commands, and not, as proportionality in Germany, as indispensable to uncovering the exact 'meaning' of those commands. Proportionality, in German jurisprudence, is conceived of as a principle, not just a test. And, perhaps most revealingly: proportionality is comprehensive and compulsory; it cannot be put aside in favour of some alternative test. To say, then, that German constitutional jurisprudence formalizes its balancing predominantly by way of the steps of proportionality analysis in the same way as do American balancing 'tests', is to read German law through American eyes. Balancing's formality, in German jurisprudence, is much richer and goes much further.

(b)    The formal and the substantive: the synthesis tradition in German legal thought

Legal formality, in German constitutional jurisprudence, is always present, as a permanent background notion. It is not an option or one available strategy among others. Legal reasoning is always somewhat formal, alongside any material elements it may contain. Formality in German law, unlike in US law, cannot be 'turned off' at will.

But the relationship between legal formality and its opposites in German legal thought is given shape through more complex mechanisms than this mere background presence. There is, in particular, a long and much broader tradition within German legal scholarship of deliberate attempts at overcoming contradictions and tensions, including those between legal formality and its opposites. In the nineteenth century, the most prominent exponent of this tradition, and in some ways its founder, was Friedrich Carl von Savigny. Von Savigny famously attempted to bridge the divide between historical and systematic visions of law. In its fusion of 'the real and the ideal, the historical and the logical, the organic and the systematic', his conception of '*Rechtswissenschaft*' 'promised to resolve conflicts hitherto believed unsolvable'.[146] In the early twentieth century, Philip Heck and Rudolf Smend both, in very different ways, belonged to this same tradition of synthesis. Heck, in his simultaneous defense of conceptual refinement and interest analysis, and Smend, in his elaboration of durable value constellations, intended to mediate between social change and stability. During the fascist era, Karl Larenz propagated the 'complete reciprocal penetration and concrete unity of the individual and the whole', and coined the Orwellian-sounding label of '*konkret–allgemeine Begriffe*' ('specific–general concepts') to capture this idea.[147] Early discussions of the Basic Law, too, often took this form, relying on strikingly similar imagery. Peter Schneider, for example, writing on "Principles of Constitutional Interpretation" in 1963, saw the constitution of the Basic Law as embodying a '*logisch-teleologisches Sinngebilde*' ('a logical–teleological meaningful unity').[148] For Martin Kriele, writing in 1967, there was, despite all apparent tensions, no real contradiction between formal and substantive conceptions of the rule of law: '*Der materiale Rechtsstaat schließt den formalen ein und begrenzt ihn.*'[149] Unsurprisingly, this attempted synthesis also characterizes Alexy's work on balancing. 'Balancing on the facts of a case and universalizability', Alexy postulates, are '*not irreconcilable*'.[150]

It is intriguing to note that, for the era of the balancing debates of the late 1950s and early 1960s, these attempts at overcoming juridical antinomies appear to have been embedded within a much broader intellectual

---

[146] Reimann (1990), p. 894 (*Rechtswissenschaft* as a 'synthesis of history and system').

[147] Larenz (1938), p. 43. See further, e.g., Rüthers (1968), p. 277; Joerges (1994), p. 179.

[148] Schneider (1963), p. 13 (defending a systematic conception of the Basic Law that aimed 'to interpret the specific in light of the general, and *vice-versa*'). See also at p. 33 (calling for a 'dialectical' understanding of individual freedom and its limitations). See further Chapter 3, Section E.2.

[149] Kriele (1967), pp. 225–26 ('the material *Rechtsstaat* incorporates the formal *Rechtsstaat*, and delimits it').

[150] Alexy (2002), p. 107 (emphasis in original). See also Kumm (2009), p. 408 ('The idea of European legal scholarship, then, can be [defined in positive terms] as an attempt to *integrate* the formal/conceptual with the empirical and moral in some way so as to define a distinctly legal perspective. It is precisely the nonreductive nature of jurisprudence that defines it') (emphasis in original). The reconciliation of formal and substantive is also a major theme in Habermas' account of the co-existence of the *Sozialstaat* and the *Rechtsstaat* in postwar Western Germany. See, e.g., McCormick (2003), pp. 64, 65ff, 67.

and social climate that favoured synthesis and reconciliation over contestation and conflict. In terms of political economy, for example, the
Adenauer years were dominated by Ludwig Erhard's conception of the
'social market economy', which sought to reconcile 'market freedom and
social responsibility'.[151] In politics, both the Right and Left underwent a
process of 'deradicalization'. Conservatism was being 'modernized', while
the social sphere was undergoing a 'modernization under a conservative
guardianship'.[152] 'A strong desire to reduce conflict [...] sometimes going
so far as to want to end conflict for good', Jan-Werner Müller has written
of this period, 'has been present in ideologies of the Right and the Left'.[153]
The aim to overcome antinomies may have had deep roots in German
legal thinking, but the idea seems to have resonated particularly strongly
at exactly the time when the *Bundesverfassungsgericht* first spoke of the
need to balance values and interests.[154]

### (c)    Method and substance in German legal thought

One peculiar jurisprudential move often encountered in American legal
writing is 'blame the method'. Mainstream American constitutional
jurisprudence is characterized by persistent efforts to link legal methodological choices to political or ideological substance, as well as by the
equally persistent efforts to contest these same associations. The arche-
typical instance of this move is the critique of *Lochner* as simultaneously
excessively formalist *and therefore* economically conservative. A close
second would be the critique of 1950s and 1960s free speech balancing as
excessively open-ended *and therefore* insufficiently protective of speech.

The canonical familiarity of these arguments in the American context raises an intriguing question. What role does 'blaming method' play
elsewhere? Are German jurists equally interested in developing and con-
testing method/substance associations? And if so, what would be their
typical targets? To begin with that last question: one potential target for
the elaboration of connections between legal method and substantive evil
in the German context, of course, looms larger than any other; the cata-
clysm of law under fascism. It seems no other episode could even come
close to matching this one in terms of historical profile and continued
significance.

---

[151] Nicholls (1994), p. 5.
[152] Müller (2003), pp. 8–10; Schildt & Sywottek (1997), p. 415.
[153] *Ibid.*
[154] On this belief see further Chapter 5, Section E.

The historiography of the method/substance connection as it relates to law under fascism is an extraordinarily complex topic. In the early postwar years, some commentators, including in particular Gustav Radbruch, did attack legal positivism and formalism for having rendered German jurists 'defenseless and powerless against [...] unlawfulness in the form of a statute'.[155] But this rather short episode of 'blaming formalism' remains clearly distinct from experiences in the US, for at least three reasons. First, in the German context, most accusations have in fact been levelled against positivism rather than against formalism. The two concepts obviously overlap, but many of the specific early charges against fascist-era judicial methodology concerned typically positivist themes, such as the acceptance of the validity of legislation without regard to its moral worth and the rejection of any form of higher law as capable of overriding posited legislative commands.[156] Secondly, after initial identification of positivism/formalism as the primary culprit for Nazi-era injustices, legal historians have shifted towards targeting rather excessive judicial freedom, i.e. legal informality, as primarily responsible. As Vivian Grossswald Curran has written, 'the myth of judicial positivism in Germany slowly unraveled' and 'by 1970 numerous German scholars had debunked positivism as a viable culprit theory'. 'Free law', positivism's perceived antithesis soon took over positivism's place to bear the brunt of the blame.[157] This 'post-war about-face', in Grosswald Curran's words, has largely absolved positivism/formalism. Thirdly and lastly, some European writers on the relationship between legal method and fascist injustice have actually identified a positive role for legal formalism. Guido Calabresi, for example, has argued that in Italy, 'for the scholars opposing fascism, the nineteenth-century self-contained formalistic system became a great weapon' in that it helped conserve liberal values in the face of the new 'Functionalist' fascist ideals.[158]

As these examples illustrate, formalism has never been as thoroughly associated with substantive injustice or with the dominance of a particular brand of ideology or politics in Europe as it has been in the US. There has, consequently, never been a method/substance connection in Germany of the nature and intensity commonly found in the US. For many different

---

[155] Cited and translated in Caldwell (1994), p. 273. See further Grosswald Curran (2001).

[156] See Grosswald Curran (2001), pp. 126–7, 147. Despite its title, 'Fear of Formalism', Grosswald Curran's article in fact refers to 'positivism' much more frequently than to 'formalism'. See also Ott & Buob (1993). Positivism was also central to the discussion of Radbruch's position in the Hart-Fuller debate. See Fuller (1958).

[157] *Ibid.*, pp. 151ff, 158, 165.

[158] Calabresi (2000), p. 482.

reasons and in many different ways, law under fascism *is not* 'Germany's *Lochner*'.[159] In comparative terms, then, the formal/substantive relationship in German constitutional jurisprudence really is the mirror image of its US counterpart. Not only is the active attribution of substantive implications to formal choices characteristic for US constitutional jurisprudence, but the *absence* of this connection, the unwillingness or perhaps rather the disinterest to engage in 'blaming method', is also, in many ways, characteristic for German law.

### (d)   Counter-currents: 'materialization' and 'deformalization' in German law?

The claim that legal formality remains an omnipresent background factor in German constitutional jurisprudence needs to confront one obvious and powerful counter-argument: the observation voiced by numerous leading German theorists that their legal order has undergone a radical '*materialization*' in the course of the twentieth century. In Bernard Schlink's summary: '[i]t has often been observed that German law and legal doctrine have, throughout this century, displayed a tendency to turn from formal to material concepts, and from specific to general terms'.[160] The work of one of the leading writers making this argument in the 1950s, Ernst Forsthoff, was discussed in Chapter 3. For Forsthoff, the 'deformalization' ('*Entformalisierung*') of constitutional law signified nothing less than 'the unfolding of the judiciary-State' and the 'dissolution of the Constitution'.[161] And for Forsthoff, as for many other observers of 'materialization', judicial balancing was the prime manifestation of this tendency.

A strong case can be made, however, that materialization has not equalled deformalization in German jurisprudence. In part, this assertion can rest on the many indications of formal elements in German constitutional jurisprudence outlined earlier; from 'system thinking' to deduction and attachment to conceptual rigour.[162] But comparative analysis can

---

[159] That is not to say that fear of a 'descent back into barbarity' is not a powerful animating factor underlying the quest for 'perfection' and 'comprehensiveness' in postwar German constitutionalism. See Chapter 3, Section E.4.

[160] Schlink (1992), p. 1713.

[161] Forsthoff (1959), pp. 145, 151.

[162] See especially McCormick (2003), p. 65 ('formal and substantive modes of law can coexist in the *Sozialstaat* rule of law'). For a similar argument based on a different reading of Habermas, see Dyzenhaus (1996), p. 154 (arguing that Habermas ignores the possibility 'that the materialization of law does not necessarily involve[s] its deformalization'). See also Forsthoff (1959), p. 145 ('The current situation of public law is characterized by

provide further support. One notable dialogue between Duncan Kennedy and Rudolf Wiethölter is particular revealing for the divergence between German and American understandings of materialization. As Kennedy notes, much of Wiethölter's analysis of materialization in German law initially develops very similar themes to those found in American Critical Legal Studies, in particular 'the failure, death or exhaustion of legal reason',[163] and the loss of formal rationality in law. At the same time, however, Wiethölter's initial, apparent 'pure pragmatism, in the mold of William James' is combined with a 'faith in and hope for law' that, to an American, appears 'paradoxical'.[164] In short, Kennedy writes, there appears to be 'a general absence in Western Europe of the particular kind of radicalized critique of law represented by Legal Realism and then Critical Legal Studies in the US'.[165]

As mentioned in Chapter 2, though, the critiques offered by the *Freirecht* scholars in Germany were at least as radical as anything suggested in the US in the early twentieth century.[166] The real question therefore rather seems to be: why did such radical critiques not have the same lasting impact in Germany as they had in the US? Part of the answer to this puzzle has also already been suggested; the fact that American judges had to decide intensely political questions regarding the limitation of public power at a time when such issues rarely if ever came before the judiciaries of Western Europe. As a result, legal method came under early strains in the US that were not as acutely felt elsewhere.[167] Kennedy's response also suggests another explanation. This is the possibility that European experiences of fascism and communism have instilled an attitude among European lawyers that makes American-style radical anti-rationalism, and anti-formalism, simply 'too painful even to listen to'.[168] This last point may have a degree of truth to it, though it must be noted that the *Freirecht*-critique seems to

---

the fact that both these fundamentally different [formal and material] methods of legal interpretation and application coexist, without any logical relationship being present between them; a logical relationship which would be impossible in any event.')

[163] Kennedy (1985), p. 512.

[164] *Ibid.*, p. 516.   [165] *Ibid.*, p. 518.

[166] See Chapter 2, Section C.3. Another example is the work of René Demogue in France, whose work has been rejected as embodying a '*nihilisme juridique*'. See, e.g., Jamin (2006); Kennedy & Belleau (2006).

[167] See Chapter 2, Sections B.5 and C.

[168] Kennedy (2011), p. 522.

have been largely a spent force already *before* the atrocities of the Second World War.[169]

A more comprehensive answer to this puzzle of European/US difference, including discussion of the very real possibility that American legal thought is the atypical case in need of explanation, has to remain outside the scope of this book. The point I have sought to make in this section is simply that the oft-voiced observation that German law, like all Western-European law, has 'materialized', does not fundamentally undermine the claim that it continues to rely on a high degree of background legal formality that sustains even the more seemingly open-ended balancing exercises of the *Bundesverfassungsgericht* and its European sister courts.

## E.    Faith and disenchantment

All Western systems of constitutional rights adjudication continuously grapple with classic dilemmas of logic versus experience, symmetry versus fairness, legal certainty versus correctness or 'historical-institutional' embeddedness versus 'rational–correct' outcomes.[170] In the vocabulary that both European and American jurisprudence traces back to Max Weber, these are the dilemmas of the formal versus substantive opposition. Throughout this chapter, Weber's conceptual framework has been invoked to show that these encounters between the formal and the substantive in law, for which the discourse of balancing is the primary modern site, are contingent in three dimensions and that these elements (the formal, the substantive and the mode of their co-existence or interaction) can all have different meanings in different settings.

Weber's work, though, is not only the seminal point of reference for discussions of legal formality and its opposites. It is also still a classic source for thinking about the basic concern underlying all these formal versus substantive dilemmas. And that is the problem of the legitimacy of the legal order.[171] A central element in Weber's writing is his sociological conception of *legitimacy as a belief* shared by participants in a given order. Legitimacy, for Weber, is 'the belief in the existence of a legitimate

---

[169] In the same way that, in France, Demogue's work was already rejected on the ground of '*nihilisme*' long before the Second World War.

[170] In the formulations of Holmes, Cardozo, Habermas and Alexy respectively. See further the Conclusion in this book.

[171] See also Chapter 1, section C.

order'.[172] This qualification of legitimacy as belief is important in the broader context of his work, which has as one of its leading themes the rationalization and '*Entzauberung*' ('disenchantment') of the world.[173] In Weber's account, formal rationality, was the form that legitimacy took in advanced capitalist democracies when religious or charismatic authority no longer had the capacity to 'enchant'.

As later writers have noted, however, these ideas of belief and enchantment can also be used in ways Weber himself may not have foreseen.[174] In particular, as Duncan Kennedy has argued, they can be applied to the notion of formal legal rationality itself, and to legalism more broadly.[175] If formalism and legalism consist of 'a commitment to, and therefore also a belief in the possibility of' a particular method of legal justification, then, it would seem, that belief might change, evolve or be lost, just like other ideas and convictions.[176] These questions could have important implications for understandings of constitutional rights balancing. If the meaning of balancing is viewed through the lens of the formal versus substantive opposition, and if legal formality, as part of that dichotomy – or legalism as its successful management – is itself seen as a belief, then the nature of that belief will have to make up an important component also of balancing's local meaning.

The question of the nature of formalism and legalism as a matter of faith is a complex one. In part, this is due to our habitual ways of defining legal formality and formalism. Many classic definitions of legal formality and of formalism do rely on some element of 'attitude' or 'commitment', in addition to a list of properties ascribed to legal institutions.[177] But they tend to remain frustratingly vague on the precise nature of that attitude or commitment. In *The Concept of Law*, for example, Hart contrasts formalism with 'rule-scepticism'.[178] Jurisprudential inquiry, especially in

---

[172] In the translation by Henderson and Parsons, cited in, e.g., Hyde (1983), p. 382. The German original uses '*Vorstellung*', which the Rheinstein edition translates rather as 'idea'. See Weber (1925), p. 3.

[173] Weber (1919), p. 155 ('The fate of our times is characterized by rationalization and [...] above all by the "disenchantment of the world").

[174] Most notably by Jürgen Habermas. See for discussion Tamanaha (1999), pp. 990ff.

[175] Kennedy (2003b).

[176] Cf. Unger (1986), p. 1. On formalism as a matter of faith, see also, e.g., Seidman (1987); Singer (1988); Lidsky (1995).

[177] As in Roberto Unger's definition.

[178] Hart (1961), p. 129. Hart also describes formalism (and 'conceptualism') as 'an attitude to verbally formulated rules which both seeks to disguise and minimize the need for

Hart's own analytical tradition, has subsequently been preoccupied with the 'rule' part of that definition. But if its definition is 'rule-*scepticism*', then formalism, quite literally, cannot only be about specific qualities of legal norms (their 'rule-like' or 'non-rule-like nature', in Hart's case). It also has to refer to an attitude that is somehow different from 'scepticism'. And, as is clear even on a purely intuitive level, there are many ways of being *not* sceptical.[179]

It is this kind of more nuanced understanding of formalism as an attitude of faith and commitment that is necessary in order to capture a fourth, and final, dimension of difference between the American and German paradigmatic meanings of balancing. Recall once more the pervasive association, also going back to Weber, between balancing and radical non- or anti-formality. This association sustains qualifications of balancing and proportionality as '*the form that reason will take when there is no longer a faith in formalism*'.[180] But that qualification leaves very little scope for any kind of non-sceptical conception of balancing, as itself a matter of faith in law. It is the possibility of precisely such a conception that this section seeks to explore.

### 1.  *Balancing and aspirational legalism*

The subtle and multifaceted relationship between balancing and legal formality in German jurisprudence has been discussed in Chapter 3. Contemporary views on this relationship ranged from scepticism of both formal legal rationality and balancing, via a critique of the *Bundesverfassungsgericht's* balancing approach as itself overly formalist, to faith in legal formality coupled with a rejection of balancing.[181] But even the more sceptical contributions appear pervaded by a deep commitment to, and therefore belief in, the possibility of rationality, neutrality and objectivity in constitutional adjudication. As in Rudolf Wiethölter's work mentioned earlier, there is a widespread and pervasive 'faith in and hope for law'.[182]

---

[...] choice'). He does not, however, give any more details as to what the nature of this 'attitude' is thought to be.

[179] It is not entirely clear what the conventional disciplinary home might be for this question. For an agenda along similar lines in the anthropology of law, see Riles (2005).

[180] Kahn (2003), pp. 2698–99.

[181] The views of von Pestalozza, Roellecke and Forsthoff respectively. See Chapter 3, Section C.

[182] Kennedy (1985), p. 516. See also Zimmermann (1996), p. 583 (contrasting American scepticism with European – Continental and English – faith in law as an autonomous discipline).

This faith had a range of different intellectual and social sources. One surely was the idealism, or intellectualism, inherited from nineteenth-century German legal thought. This idealism, as Franz Wieacker has noted, should not be understood as 'restricted to the formal ordering of legal science', but also in a broader sense as urging an 'ideologizing of the quest for justice'.[183] It is characteristic for European legal thought, Wieacker writes, 'that the issue of justice has been transmuted from a matter of correct public conduct to one of intellectually cognizable judgments about truth', in a way that ensures that an 'ideology of general justice' remains compatible with, and available as a counterpoint to, more formal legal ideals.[184] Another strand appears to have been the revival of natural law ideas in the aftermath of the Second World War.[185] The prestige of the institution of the *Bundesverfassungsgericht*, too, was intimately tied up with the development and maintenance of a widespread faith in law, as was a more general trust in public institutions.[186] Such is, still, the level of trust in the Court that some observers have warned of a risk that is diametrically opposite to the tenor of American agonizing over the counter-majoritarian dilemma: '[t]he German faith in constitutional jurisdiction must not be allowed to turn into a lack of faith in democracy'.[187]

It is important to caution against an equation of this faith in law and legal reasoning with a naïve, blind acceptance of all that the *Bundesverfassungsgericht* does and all that constitutional legal reasoning stands for, even during the foundational period of the 1950s and early 1960s. What seems most distinctive about German legalism during this period was rather its *aspirational* quality; the pervasive sustaining idea that, for all its imperfections, constitutional jurisprudence was a worthwhile endeavour. As was seen in Chapter 3, the basic tenor of German writings on legal methods of this time evidenced a fundamental commitment to, and a faith in, what the *Bundesverfassungsgericht* was trying to

---

[183] Wieacker (1995), pp. 25–26.
[184] *Ibid.*, pp. 26–27.
[185] See, e.g., Radbruch (1957). For an overview in English, see von der Heydte (1956).
[186] For this point in relation to English and American law, see Atiyah & Summers (1987), pp. 36ff. Atiyah & Summers note that a widespread use of 'formal reasons' in judicial reasoning presupposes that the 'relevant substantive reasons will be, or have been, or at least could have been, more appropriately and more satisfactorily dealt with at some other time […] before some other body'. Such refusals by judges to consider substantive reasons 'requires a degree of confidence […] that the rest of the system is working properly'. See also Forsyth (2007), pp. 332ff.
[187] Häberle (1980), p. 79. Peter Häberle was one of the main participants in the debates canvassed in Chapter 3.

do. German authors *did* ask critical questions such as '[i]s there really no longer any juristic objectivity in constitutional law? Is it no longer possible to distinguish legitimate and illegitimate forms of legal argument?'[188] But these were questions raised, and done away with, at the outset of books and articles, not at their conclusion. 'Insofar as one has not given up all hope entirely', German writers were likely to respond to their own interrogations, realistically but constructively, 'various possible solutions present themselves for discussion'.[189] And that is where they began their efforts at (re-)construction.[190]

It is this aspirational, constructive attitude that makes for a decisive difference with American constitutional jurisprudence. This is the difference between striving for juridical coherence and autonomy, even when fully cognizant of inevitable imperfections, and giving up on these ideals, engaging instead in a form of juridical damage control; a contrast that is still best captured in Hart's depiction of the differences between a nightmare and a noble dream.[191]

Constitutional rights balancing is an integral element, if not the foundation, of this 'aspirationally legalist' German constitutional jurisprudence. Balancing is seen to help preserve the unity and integrity of the constitutional legal order. It sustains this order's comprehensive reach and its attempts to achieve a perfect fit with social reality. It allows for the inclusion, rather than, as American writers would have it, the *intrusion*, of substantive considerations. It integrates case-by-case analysis with principle; harmonizes values and interests, particularism and formal legal doctrine. Constitutional balancing in *Lüth a*nd its progeny is the embodiment of a powerful will to believe that a formal, juridical conception of the judicial weighing of interests and values is possible.

## 2.   *Balancing and sceptical pragmatism*

American law too, once found itself in an 'Age of Faith'.[192] But, so its self-description goes, that age is long past. What remains is a 'pervasive

---

[188]   Kriele (1967), p. 14.
[189]   *Ibid.*
[190]   See also, e.g., von Bogdandy (2009), pp. 377ff (describing a 'positivism' prevalent in Continental-European constitutional legal scholarship that 'systematizes constitutional jurisprudence and, thereby, upholds the original doctrinal agenda in times of balancing-happy constitutional courts'. Von Bogdandy notes the dominance of this line of thinking but also expresses some reservations about its long-term viability).
[191]   Hart (1967). Hart, of course, thought both these elements were present in American legal thought. That, too, has been the argument here.
[192]   Gilmore (1977), p. 41.

'scepticism' with which legal scholars view the work of the judiciary.[193] With belief in formal legal rationality gone, all that seems left is a naked 'type of esoteric legalism' under which some legal theorists are 'willing to promote *a false belief* in the truth of anti-instrumentalism in order to secure the benefits of that belief', in the face of the overwhelming rejection of these beliefs by their peers.[194]

There is, however, a great paradox at the heart of this oft-described loss of faith in American law. Because while mainstream American jurisprudence is highly sceptical of the autonomy or objectivity of law and legal reasoning, some degree of faith clearly remains in the ability of the juridical to constrain. As Annelise Riles, the legal anthropologist, has noted with regard to the so-called 'New Formalism' movement of the 1990s, a continued '*faith in rules*' as constraining doctrinal tools, goes hand-in-hand with '*a realist loss of faith* in the conceptual system that sustained the earlier formalism' of Langdell and *Lochner*.[195] This paradoxical stance has been discussed earlier as the instrumentalization of legal formality in American legal thought.

Judicial balancing is *the* primary site at which this paradox plays out in American constitutional law. American constitutional rights adjudication, as described in Chapter 4, oscillates between the desire for truthful, 'realistic' descriptions of 'what judges actually do', driven by a loss of faith in legal formality, and the construction of elaborate doctrinal frameworks of steps and tests to guide judicial discretion, sustained by the remnants of a belief in the continued effectiveness of precisely that same legal formality.[196] Given these surroundings, balancing is only

---

[193] Tamanaha (2006), p. 96.

[194] Vermeule (2007), p. 2114 (emphasis added). See also, with respect specifically to constitutional adjudication, Kennedy (2003), p. 2778; Sadurski (2005), p. xiii ('In contrast to the United States and Canada, European constitutional adjudication has not developed a tradition of self-doubt, agonising over legitimacy').

[195] Annelise Riles (2000), pp. 11, 60 (emphasis added).

[196] For a discussion in the context of the displacement of the first amendment 'clear and present danger' test by balancing, see Chapter 4, Section D.1. For a retrospective analysis, see, e.g., Powe (1989), p. 270 (Justice Douglas, one of the principal 'balancers' on the Supreme Court, 'drank at the well of legal realism too long and too thoroughly. With the other founders of the movement he stripped away the silly doctrinal shrouds [...] he concluded that doctrine was irrelevant, the explanatory cloak for decisions reached on more significant grounds [...] Perhaps he was right [...] but as Edward White notes, this may have been *an insight too fundamental and vastly too unsettling for others to accept*. Douglas, the legal realist, turns out not to have been much of a judicial realist. He had to know that *almost everyone else believed doctrine to have a part in the legal system*') (emphases added).

ever allowed to play a pragmatic role. Balancing is what judges turn to when legal doctrine runs out. The suspension of doctrinal, categorical, reasoning in favour of a balancing approach, Kathleen Sullivan has written, 'typically comes about from a crisis in analogical reasoning'.[197] That observation covers at least part of the development described in Chapter 4. Balancing is what happens when '[a] set of cases comes along that just can't be steered readily onto [one particular doctrinal track]';[198] when familiar frameworks, such as 'clear and present danger', or the speech/conduct distinction, are confronted with new circumstances for which they are no longer seen to provide an acceptable answer.[199] In those circumstances, balancing emerges as an awkward place-holder. Balancing is a solution that can be accepted on a temporary basis, until, ideally, an area is 'rulefied' and new doctrinal structures are developed; doctrinal structures that will themselves again, just like balancing, be viewed with suspicion.

## 3.  Conclusion: attributes and attitudes

In order to capture balancing's local meaning in terms of the formal versus substantive opposition, then, it is not sufficient to merely look at the attributes of legal formality and its opposites. The *attitudes* local lawyers exhibit towards these attributes are also important. If formalism is, as in H.L.A. Hart's definition, the opposite of 'rule scepticism', then the nature of this scepticism and of its opposites will have to be taken into account. And the opposite of scepticism, it has been argued, has to be some kind of 'faith in, and hope for law'.

The meaning of the discourse of balancing is intimately related to this scepticism versus faith dichotomy. This is because balancing can be a manifestation of both scepticism and of faith, but for very different reasons. In a setting pervaded by a 'material' and 'comprehensive' constitutionalism, balancing is a powerful expression of faith and aspiration; faith in and hope for a constitutional order built on a universally accepted, objective value order, and aiming for perfect constitutional justice in every

---

[197] Sullivan (1992b), p. 297.

[198] *Ibid.*

[199] See, e.g., BeVier (1978), p. 300 (the balancing debate on Supreme Court arose when 'it became increasingly evident that the clear and present danger formulation was an inadequate response to the cases' [new, broader] contextual variety').

Table 5.1 *Two paradigms of the formal and the substantive in law: US and Germany constitutional jurisprudence*

|  | US | Germany |
|---|---|---|
| **Formal** | Autonomy | Autonomy |
|  | Constraint | Compulsion |
|  | Limitation | Optimization |
|  | Status quo | Fully realized rights |
|  | Anti-particular | Maximal particularity |
|  | Definitions and categories | Concepts and system |
|  | 'Conservative' | 'Apolitical' |
|  | Popular | Scholarly[200] |
|  | Anti-perfectionist | Perfectionist |
| **Substantive** | Pragmatism | Material constitutionalism |
|  | Policy | Values |
|  | Intrusion | Inclusion |
| **Formal and substantive** | Conflict, paradox | Synthesis |
|  | Formality as substance | The substantive formalized |
|  | Pragmatic, incremental solutions | Totalization |
| **Balancing** | Compromise | Synthesis |
|  | Breakdown of analogy | Choice |
|  | Policy | Principle |
|  | Anxiety | Ambition |
|  | Scepticism | Faith |

case. This, it is submitted, is the case for the paradigmatic understanding of balancing in German constitutional jurisprudence during its early decades. But where balancing comes to the fore when visibly structured legal doctrines are no longer seen to suffice; where the judicial statement 'I have been weighing' is taken as a confession to be applauded for its candour, but to be rejected as a reflection of any legitimate mode of judicial

---

[200] For this distinction, see the Conclusion.

decision making; where balancing is pervasively seen as *anti*-rules and *anti*-concepts, it will be very difficult to associate balancing with anything else than a deep scepticism of law and adjudication. That, in turn, to a large extent characterizes balancing's paradigmatic local meaning in the US.

~

# Conclusion

It was enormously intriguing and significant, the American legal scholar Richard Pildes observed about ten years ago, that an 'attachment to legalism and judicial institutions' in countries outside the US appeared to be 'reaching a peak' during exactly the period when the US was in thrall to a 'general and increasing scepticism about judicial institutions'.[1] These two very different but parallel periods, I have argued in this book, have *both* been ages of balancing.

The ideas of an 'attachment to legalism' and of its opposite – scepticism – are central to solving this apparent contradiction. The embrace of balancing in German constitutional jurisprudence, I have argued, was possible thanks to, not in spite of, a continued faith in legal formality, simply because balancing was seen as law, not politics or policy. Moreover, balancing was not simply merely acceptable within German constitutional jurisprudence; it in fact played a central role in sustaining a distinctively legalist brand of constitutionalism, helping to garner commitment to and belief in the constitutional legal order. Typical American accounts, because of the background scepticism that tends to pervade them, and because of their association of the 'rise of balancing' with a paradigm shift from 'formalism' to 'realism', often have trouble even seeing this European way of balancing. And they certainly have difficulty believing it. In the paradigmatic American view, the substantive has to be policy; legal formality can only realistically exist in the form of doctrinal rules and categories, and any combination between the two can only ever be a pragmatic and unstable paradox.

This Conclusion is mainly concerned with some of the questions left open by the story told in this book, and with what they reveal about what has been discussed. Two of these questions seem particularly pressing. They are: 'what happened later', and 'what happened elsewhere'?

---

[1] Pildes (2003), p. 147.

## 1.   Continuity and change?

The first of these questions principally asks to what extent the account of German balancing given here is a *pre-1968* account. That date is still by far the most dramatic potential cut-off point between any story told about law in Western Europe in the 1950s and early 1960s, and experiences today; both for histories of law in context, and for more narrowly focused, internal legal–intellectual histories.[2] From the perspective of this question, two elements are particularly noteworthy in the Pildes observation cited earlier: the contrast between an 'attachment to legalism' and a 'general scepticism' is a description claimed to be valid for today – or at least for the first decade of the twenty-first century, and a description that is not confined to legal elites – judicial, scholarly or otherwise. The explanation for this attachment given in this book has been one of a sincere faith in law, and more precisely of a faith in the capacity of law to overcome otherwise apparently insurmountable antinomies.[3] But support for this claim has been drawn almost exclusively from the writings of an elite community of scholars and judges active in the late 1950s and early 1960s.[4] At this point, some difficult questions arise. In particular, was this faith in the possibility of juridical synthesis really such a powerful factor to begin with? And if so, did it survive the social and political upheavals of the later 1960s that affected West-German society more generally?

There certainly are reasons to hesitate over a positive answer on either or both of these questions. Historians have described West Germany during the Adenauer years in terms of the pursuit of a 'policy of concealment';[5] as beholden to a technocratically-minded, post-ideological 'politics of productivity'; and, most evocatively, as an 'ironic Nation', characterized by a 'hardheaded realism' and 'scepticism'.[6] They have also observed a transition, in later years but especially from 1968 onwards, from a 'culture of consensus' to a 'culture of conflict'.[7]

---

[2] Even if only because of a dearth of other clear 'breaks'. The other obvious candidate – 1989/1990 – does not appear as important, at least not in terms of legal intellectual history, and certainly for Western Germany.

[3] See above, Chapter 3, Section E.2 and Chapter 5, Section D.2.

[4] But see also the general high level of popular trust in the *Bundesverfassungsgericht*, mentioned in Chapter 5, Section E.1.

[5] Elias (1996), p. 407.

[6] Müller (2003), pp. 8–9.

[7] *Ibid.*, pp. 14–15; Elias (1996), pp. 405ff. But see Schildt & Sywottek (1997) (stability of the 1950s did to a large extent withstand the 'convulsions' of the 1960s).

These qualifications suggest at least two alternative interpretations of the German turn to constitutional rights balancing in the late 1950s and early 1960s. First, it could be that instead of any kind of faith in the legal, the driving intellectual forces were rather more of a cynical or ironic nature; a hypocritical papering-over of differences, rather than the ambitious and hopeful pursuit of synthesis described earlier. And second, even if some form of belief in law was involved at the time, it is possible that the late 1950s constituted, in retrospect, a golden age of parenthesis; that it was a brief period of juridical ambition very different from what was to follow.

It is impossible to fully assess the significance of these alternative accounts on the basis of the kind of limited, internal legal–intellectual history set out in this book. But there are at least three reasons to doubt that they fatally undermine the claims made here. First, pragmatism and cynicism in the political and social spheres are not necessarily irreconcilable with faith and ambition in law – on the contrary. Much depends on the extent to which the juridical sphere is seen as separate from other fields. This, of course, only appears to lead us in circles: belief in law's autonomy is invoked to explain belief in law's autonomy. But then again, that circularity affects all participation in the juridical sphere, which, in its entirety, rests on an unavoidable, 'essential tautology'.[8] It is a form of circularity therefore, that only troubles non-believers. Much also depends on the sources for this purported faith. And this leads to a second argument: the overwhelming impression of continuity given off by the relevant legal materials. The belief in the possibility of juridical autonomy and in synthesis through law that appears to have characterized 1950s and 1960s contributions proves a striking fit with both earlier and later writing. German balancing debates in constitutional jurisprudence of the 1950s and early 1960s simply *look very much like* German balancing debates in private law theory of the 1920s and 1930s.[9] And more recent contributions, such as notably the work of Robert Alexy, also show remarkable congruity with those of Philipp Heck and other *Interessenjurisprudenz* scholars of the early twentieth century. Alexy's ambition to demonstrate the possibility of a formally rational conception of balancing, for example, fits very neatly with Heck's commitment to a 'pure theory of method'.[10]

---

[8] Cf. Bourdieu (1987), p. 831.

[9] And they resemble each other much more than they do contemporaneous US debates.

[10] On balancing's continued relevance in German constitutional law, see, e.g., Rusteberg (2009), pp. 50ff.

Finally, there is this consideration. Even if the period of the late 1950s and early 1960s *was* special, it was also a period with extraordinary influence on what came afterwards. This is of course true for German law itself, in the sense that this was the time during which the *Bundesverfassungsgericht* laid the foundations for all of its postwar constitutional jurisprudence. But it is also true for Europe more broadly, through the influence that German legal scholars exercised over the early development of European law. Walter Hallstein, the first president of the Commission of the European Economic Community (EEC), was one such German scholar. He brought with him a coterie of jurists who forcefully developed and defended a claim to 'juristic' and 'objective' authority for the Commission.[11] Their systematic, objectivist and constructivist approach to the early Treaties – the efforts, famously, to create 'a new legal order' out of an otherwise unsystematic, rather haphazard assemblage of Treaties – have done much to perpetuate the relevance of 1950s German legal ideas for modern European law.

For the account of balancing in US constitutional jurisprudence, any similarly dramatic potential later cut-off point is even more difficult to see. The evidence suggests rather that the struggle between faith and scepticism that characterized the 1950s and early 1960s debates, has continued unabated. It is true that the 1960s witnessed an 'explosive loss of social consensus on first principles' and, in legal circles, a profound agonizing over the perceived activism of the Warren Court.[12] But the 1980s and early 1990s then saw a resurgence of a self-styled 'New Formalism', and Critical Legal Studies dominated much of the period in between. In American constitutional jurisprudence, then, it is conflict itself that provides the constant.[13]

## 2.   *The broader balancing world*

What, then, about balancing elsewhere, beyond German and US constitutional jurisprudence? The case studies in this book have been deliberately narrow in focus, in order to complement the prominence given in existing

---

[11] On these connections see Vauchez (2013).

[12] Cf. White (1973), pp. 279–80.

[13] Particularly revealing on this point is the continued dominance in legal scholarship of a very particular vocabulary of paradox and especially: *schizophrenia*. The latter term is pervasive in discussions of legal formality and its opposites, of balancing and of first amendment jurisprudence. For a sample see, e.g., Redish (1983), p. 1046; Kalman (1986), p. 14; Shiffrin (1990); Cushman (2000), p. 1091; Friedman (2002), p. 58.

literature to the themes of similarity and convergence. And so, for the wider world – for all those other, national and supranational systems of rights adjudication that have similarly turned to balancing over the past decades – the one claim this book can quite safely support, I would argue, is that the language of balancing *can* have dramatically different meanings, and that comparative studies need to be aware of the likelihood that it may. Beyond that, little is clear.

Does either of the two paradigms of balancing identified in Chapter 5 have any strong claim to broader validity? For the German model, the answer is probably to some extent 'yes'. European human rights adjudication and European law more generally share a distinctly 'German' imprint, in part because of historical connections of the kind identified above. To the extent that it is possible to speak of a 'European legal culture', or a 'European way of law', this must be a legal culture in which German experiences, and in particular the use of balancing and proportionality, form a central pillar. And to that extent, it should not be surprising if it were found that many aspects of balancing's local *German* meaning are of relevance to its local *European* meaning.[14] More generally, as Lorraine Weinrib has argued, to the extent that there is anything like a global, or near-global, 'Post-War Paradigm' in constitutional rights adjudication, it is a paradigm that originates in, and in many ways still strikingly resembles, the German model.[15]

It is also clear that the theme of 'faith in and hope for law', described earlier as sustaining balancing in German jurisprudence, is also a significant factor in other European jurisdictions, both of the West and the former East. Wojciech Sadurski's study of the advent of constitutional rights adjudication in Central and Eastern Europe is particularly revealing on this latter point. Not only was the process of adoption of constitutional review in these countries marked by a striking absence of the kind of agonizing over legitimacy that characterizes US constitutional jurisprudence; one notable legitimizing strategy in the new systems was in fact to explicitly claim the mantle of 'law' and 'judicial activity', even where the new constitutional courts were institutionally quite distinct from the ordinary judiciary.[16] Constitutional courts in Western and Eastern Europe generally, then, have tended to present themselves very much as *judicial* institutions, embedded within established *legal* traditions. That

---

[14] On the role of balancing in European law, see, e.g., Rusteberg (2009), pp. 74ff.
[15] See Weinrib (2006), pp. 89ff.
[16] Sadurski (2005), pp. 27ff.

strategy, it would seem, can be read as evidence for the legalism – the faith in law – that also characterized the balancing case law of the early *Bundesverfassungsgericht*, discussed in Chapter 3.

As for the American model, despite the hegemonic influence often ascribed to US law more generally, neither the institutional set-up of its system of constitutional adjudication nor its specific doctrines in fields like the freedom of expression have been particularly influential elsewhere. The fairly homogeneous rejection, in Central and Eastern Europe, of US-style constitutional review, and the adoption of a radically different model is again a case in point.[17]

But the American 'paradigm' outlined earlier can also be read as typifying in a more abstract sense one set of extreme positions on a series of continuums running from faith to scepticism; pragmatism to principle; social-science input to juridical dogmatics; etc., along the lines of the contrasts drawn in Table 5.1 in Chapter 5. On that reading, it becomes much more difficult to tell whether any of these tendencies will spread to other jurisdictions, or perhaps have already done so. But again, at least for legal systems in Europe, this does not seem to have been the case. Yet.

This book began by taking issue with overly broad claims of convergence. It only seems fair to volunteer, in closing final pages, some account of the developments that I would argue *do* seem probable.

As far as convergence between the two models is concerned, neither the spread of 'European-style' balancing and proportionality to the US nor, conversely, an 'American-style' 'rulefication' of European balancing, seem to me particularly likely.[18] American pragmatic scepticism prevents adoption of the open-ended-but-still-law mode of balancing familiar to Europeans, even if American lawyers may, at some point, give up their resistance to the vocabulary of proportionality. And on the other side, one central argument of this book has been that German and European balancing are *already formal* in ways not captured by the American focus on rules and categories.

But if these trends are not likely, what sorts of developments might be expected instead? On this point, one further difference, not yet discussed, between US and European cultures of adjudication may be significant. This is the nature of the relevant audiences for the courts' projects of legitimization. I have argued that the work of courts in different jurisdictions

---

[17] See, e.g., Sadurski (2005). For developments in Western Europe, see, e.g., Stone Sweet (2003).

[18] For such a 'rulefication' prediction, see Schauer (2005).

is comparable precisely via the angle of their legitimization problematic: the fact that they must publicly justify their exercises of authority, and that they must do so through the use of a range of argument forms considered acceptable by the relevant local legal audience. But little has been said about the precise nature of this audience, apart from the observation that it should at least include participants in 'the higher reaches of the law': principally fellow judges and academic commentators. This, however, may not be enough, given the extent to which judicial reasoning in the US is the object of public debate more generally and the way in which American judicial argumentation is, at least in part, addressed to the population at large more often than is common in Europe. The reasons for this public dimension have been debated at least since Tocqueville and are not especially relevant here. What matters is that *if* legitimization is a distinctly public affair, and if, as has been argued before, legitimization turns upon the interaction of the formal and substantive elements of judicial reasoning, as exemplified in the discourse of balancing, then the judicial expressions of these formal and substantive elements, and of balancing itself, will have to take on a 'popular' appearance.

Legal formality, in such a mode, is very likely to be expressed in the highly visible, rhetorically powerful, easily understandable terms of 'bright-line rules', 'hard and fast tests' and 'black and white categories'. Formality in the much more academic, conceptual and systematic German sense, is less likely to be convincing if the audience is not composed of professors and judges, but of journalists and their readers. Similarly, the substantive is likely to have to be expressed as 'policy', rather than as Smendian 'value constellations' or a 'logical–teleological objective value order'. Balancing itself, finally, in such a setting *simply has to look legal.* To the extent that the broader public is not, and cannot be, convinced of the legality of balancing, such apparently open-ended, flexible modes of reasoning are unlikely to take off in the American context.[19] If these popular expectations were to change, however, the outlook for balancing and proportionality could be different.

This same perspective points to perhaps more troublesome predictions for the influence of the German paradigmatic model of balancing. If, as has been claimed here, the legitimacy of this mode of argumentation is

---

[19] See also, e.g., Vicki Jackson's question on this point: 'Is US legal culture likely to view a less formal, more open-ended approach examining the "proportionality" of legislative means to legitimate legislative goals as an opportunity for invidious biases to affect decision-making?' Jackson (1999), p. 589.

deeply bound-up with a vast network of background understandings largely peculiar to the German context, this raises the worrying question of the stability and continued legitimacy of the balancing approach outside this very specific, highly contingent setting. If the global 'postwar constitutional paradigm is the juridical consequence of the defeat of Nazism', as Lorraine Weinrib has argued, does German and, to some extent European law occupy a special position simply because of their history?[20] It is easy to see how the strident and ambitious character of German constitutionalism might be traced in part to a 'rabbit-like fear "*kaninchenhaften Angst*" of a descent back into barbarity'.[21] Is it not at least somewhat more difficult to make that connection in the case of, say, Canada or India?[22]

It is possible that legal actors in all these different systems see balancing – their own version of balancing – as an answer to their own highly peculiar, largely indigenous, legitimacy problematic. In that case, the fact that similar language features so often would be largely a coincidence. That, though, seems unlikely as an explanation sufficient by itself. It is also possible that the global turn to balancing corresponds to a global rise of a form of universalistic rationalism, in which constitutional adjudication becomes increasingly unmoored from local concerns and juridical constraints.[23] In that case, the language of balancing really would mean more or less similar things everywhere. Intriguingly, though, that is clearly *not* what happened in the two systems this book has looked at in some depth: the two 'original' balancing jurisdictions. It is also not easy to see how any account drawing on a combination of these trajectories could be stable in the longer term. And any explanation, along 'postwar Paradigm' lines, of a spread of German-style constitutionalism, as argued above, has to face the issue of the particularity of German modern history, including the extraordinarily ambitious character of its nineteenth-century legal scholarship, its Weimar-era foundations for material constitutionalism, and its experiences of law under fascism.

---

[20]  Cf. Weinrib (2006), p. 89.

[21]  Roellecke (1976), p. 49. But note also the extent to which postwar German constitutional rights balancing drew on Weimar era thinking. Those ideas, too, were at least to some degree peculiar to the German context. See Chapter 3, Section D.

[22]  The European Court of Human Rights and the Court of Justice of the European Union – in their fundamental rights jurisprudence – may have been able to draw on some similar ideas.

[23]  For recent accounts along these lines see Cohen-Eliya & Porat (2011); Möller (2012).

The explanation for balancing's global pervasiveness most in line with the case studies in this book is the idea that this language is uniquely capable of expressing both our darkest fears and our greatest hopes for law. For the world outside the US, balancing's prominence suggests that the 'hope for and faith in law' so strikingly visible in German jurisprudence, is in fact, not all that characteristic for Germany after all. It appears to be rather an attitude shared far more widely than conventional, American-inspired 'post-Realist' accounts allow for.[24] But if that is true, then explanations for balancing's rise will have to be sought at least as much in a shared paradigm of *legalism*, as in any shared paradigm of *constitutionalism*. Whether this legalism – this faith in law – can endure, and whether it will on the whole be a force for good, are open questions. Giving in to the near-irresistible force exerted by our contemporary discourse, is it even possible to say anything else than that the future of global constitutional rights jurisprudence is fated to remain in the balance?

---

[24] *This* is where US hegemony surfaces: in the historiography of global constitutional law.

# BIBLIOGRAPHY

E.F. Albertsworth (1921), Judicial Review of Administrative Action by the Federal Supreme Court, 55 HARV. L. REV. 127

T. Alexander Aleinikoff (1987), Constitutional Law in the Age of Balancing, 96 YALE L.J. 943

Robert Alexy (1978), THEORIE DER JURISTISCHE ARGUMENTATION (Frankfurt am Main: Suhrkamp)

Robert Alexy (1986), THEORIE DER GRUNDRECHTE (Frankfurt am Main: Suhrkamp)

Robert Alexy (1996), Jürgen Habermas's Theory of Legal Discourse, 17 CARDOZO L. REV. 1027

Robert Alexy (2002), A THEORY OF CONSTITUTIONAL RIGHTS (Translated and with an Introduction by Julian Rivers) (Oxford University Press)

Robert Alexy (2003), Constitutional Rights, Balancing, and Rationality, 16 RATIO JURIS 131

Robert Alexy (2006), Discourse Theory and Fundamental Rights, in ARGUING FUNDAMENTAL RIGHTS 15 (Agustín José Menéndez & Erik Oddvar Eriksen, eds.) (New York, NY: Springer)

Albert W. Alschuler (1987), Failed Pragmatism: Reflections on the Burger Court, 100 HARV. L. REV. 1436

Akhil Reed Amar (1998), THE BILL OF RIGHTS (New Haven CT: Yale University Press)

Ernest Angell (1957), Zechariah Chafee, Jr.: Individual Freedoms, 70 HARV. L. REV. 1341

Anonymous (1895) Comment, 4 YALE L.J. 200

Anonymous (1940) Notes and Comments, 2 WIS. L. REV. 265

Anonymous (1967) Note: HUAC and the Chilling Effect, 21 RUTGERS L. REV. 679

Anonymous (1970) Note: The First Amendment Overbreadth Doctrine, 83 HARV. L. REV. 844

Chester James Antieau (1950), Clear and Present Danger – Its Meaning and Significance, 25 NOTRE DAME L. REV. 603

Chester James Antieau (1977), The Jurisprudence of Interests as a Method of Constitutional Adjudication, 27 CASE WESTERN RES. L. REV. 823

244

Chester James Antieau (1985), ADJUDICATING CONSTITUTIONAL ISSUES (London: Oceana Publications)

André-Jean Arnaud (1975), LES JURISTES FACE À LA SOCIÉTÉ (Paris: Presses Universitaires de France)

Adolf Arndt (1963), Gesetzesrecht und Richterrecht, 1963 NJW 1273

Adolf Arndt (1966), Zur Güterabwägung bei Grundrechten, 1966 NJW 871

P.S. Atiyah & Robert S. Summers (1987), FORM AND SUBSTANCE IN ANGLO-AMERICAN LAW (Oxford University Press)

Peter Badura (1976), Verfassung, Staat und Gesellschaft in der Sicht des Bundesverfassungsgerichts, in: BUNDESVERFASSUNGSGERICHT UND GRUNDGESETZ: FESTGABE AUS ANLASS DES 25 JÄHRIGEN BESTEHENS DES BUNDESVERFASSUNGSGERICHTS II 2 (Christian Starck, ed.) (Tübingen: Mohr Siebeck)

C. Edwin Baker (1976), Commercial Speech: A Problem in the Theory of Freedom, 62 IOWA L. REV. 1

C. Edwin Baker (1978), The Scope of the First Amendment Freedom of Speech, 25 UCLA L. REV. 964

J.M. Balkin (1991), The Promise of Legal Semiotics, 69 TEX. L. REV. 1831

Susan Bandes (1990), The Negative Constitution: A Critique, 88 MICH. L. REV. 2271

Aharon Barak (1999), The Role of the Supreme Court in a Democracy, 33 ISR. L. REV. 1

Aharon Barak (2010), Proportionality and Principled Balancing, 4 LAW & ETHICS OF HUMAN RIGHTS 1

Aharon Barak (2012), PROPORTIONALITY: CONSTITUTIONAL RIGHTS AND THEIR LIMITATIONS (Cambridge University Press)

Katherine T. Bartlett (1990), Feminist Legal Methods, 103 HARV. L. REV. 829

David Beatty (1993), Protecting Constitutional Rights in Japan and Canada, 41 AM. J. COMP. L. 535

David M. Beatty (1995), CONSTITUTIONAL LAW IN THEORY AND PRACTICE (University of Toronto Press)

David M. Beatty (2004), THE ULTIMATE RULE OF LAW (Oxford University Press)

John Bell (1986), The Acceptability of Legal Arguments, in: THE LEGAL MIND: ESSAYS FOR TONY HONORÉ 49 (Neil MacCormick & Peter Birks, eds.) (Oxford University Press)

Marie-Claire Belleau (1997), The 'Juristes Inquiets': Legal Classicism in Early Twentieth-Century France, 1997 UTAH L. REV. 379

Harold J. Berman (1983), LAW AND REVOLUTION: THE FORMATION OF THE WESTERN LEGAL TRADITION (Cambridge, MA: Harvard University Press)

David E. Bernstein (2003), Lochner's Legacy's Legacy, 82 TEX. L. REV. 1

Herbert Bernstein (1967), Free Press and National Security: Reflections on the Spiegel Case, 15 Am. J. Comp. L. 547

Donald L. Beschle (2001), Clearly Canadian? *Hill v. Colorado* and Free Speech Balancing in the United States and Canada, 28 Hastings Const. L.Q. 187

Karl August Bettermann (1964), Die allgemeinen Gesetzen als Schranken der Pressefreiheit, *JZ* 601

Lillian R. BeVier (1978), The First Amendment and Political Speech: An Inquiry into the Substance and Limits of Principle, 30 Stan. L. Rev. 299

Alexander M. Bickel (1961), Foreword: The Passive Virtues, 75 Harv. L. Rev. 40

Alexander M. Bickel (1962), The Least Dangerous Branch: The Supreme Court at the Bar of Politics (New Haven CT: Yale University Press)

Alexander M. Bickel (1970), The Supreme Court and the Idea of Progress (New York, NY: Harper & Row)

Charles Black (1967), Foreword: 'State Action', Equal Protection, and California's Proposition 14, 81 Harv. L. Rev. 69

Hugo L. Black (1960), The Bill of Rights, 35 N.Y.U. L. Rev. 865

Vincent Blasi (1970), Prior Restraints on Demonstrations, 68 Mich. L. Rev. 1481

Vincent Blasi (1985), The Pathological Perspective and the First Amendment, 85 Colum. L. Rev. 449

Philip Bobbitt (1982), Constitutional Fate (New York, NY: Oxford University Press)

Philip Bobbitt (1989), Is Law Politics?, 41 Stan. L. Rev. 1233 (Book Review)

Ernst W. Böckenförde (1974), Grundrechtstheorie und Grundrechtsinterpretation, 27 NJW 1534

Ernst W. Böckenförde (1987), Zur Kritik der Wertbegründung des Rechts, in Recht, Staat, Freiheit 67 (Frankfurt am Main: Suhrkamp)

Edgar Bodenheimer (1969), A Neglected Theory of Legal Reasoning, 21 *J. Legal Educ.* 273

Armin von Bogdandy (2009), The Past and Future of Doctrinal Constructivism: A Strategy for Responding to the Challenges facing Constitutional Scholarship in Europe, 7 I-Con 364

Jacco Bomhoff (2008), The Reach of Rights: 'The Foreign' and 'the Private' in Conflict of Laws, State Action, and Fundamental Rights Cases with Foreign Elements, 71 Law & Contemp. Probs. 39

Jacco Bomhoff (2012a), Comparing Legal Argument, in Practice and Theory in Comparative Law 74 (Maurice Adams & Jacco Bomhoff, eds.) (Cambridge University Press)

Jacco Bomhoff (2012b), Perfectionism in European Law, 14 CYELS 75

Pierre Bourdieu (1987), The Force of Law: Toward a Sociology of the Juridical Field, 38 Hastings L.J. 814

William J. Brennan (1965), The Supreme Court and the Meiklejohn Interpretation of the First Amendment, 79 HARV. L. REV. 1

Winfried Brügger (1994), Legal Interpretation, Schools of Jurisprudence, and Anthropology: Some Remarks from a German Point of View, 42 AM. J. COMP. L. 395

Bundesverfassungsgericht (1963), DAS BUNDESVERFASSUNGSGERICHT, (Celebratory Collection, published by the Federal Constitutional Court) (Karlsruhe: C.F. Müller)

Edmond Cahn (1948), Book Review, 1948 ANN. SURV. AM. L. 915

Guido Calabresi (2000), Two Functions of Formalism, 67 U. CHI. L. REV. 479

Peter Caldwell (1994), Legal Positivism and Weimar Democracy, 39 AM. J. JURIS. 273

Claus-Wilhelm Canaris (1969), SYSTEMDENKEN UND SYSTEMBEGRIFF IN DER JURISPRUDENZ (Berlin: Duncker & Humblot)

Benjamin N. Cardozo (1921), THE NATURE OF THE JUDICIAL PROCESS (New Haven CT: Yale University Press)

Benjamin N. Cardozo (1924), THE GROWTH OF THE LAW (New Haven CT: Yale University Press)

Benjamin N. Cardozo (1928), THE PARADOXES OF LEGAL SCIENCE (New York, NY: Columbia University Press)

Gerhard Casper (2002), Die Karlsruher Republik, in DAS BUNDESVERFAS-SUNGSGERICHT 1951–2001 23 (Hans-Jürgen Papier, ed.) (Heidelberg: C.F. Müller)

Ronald A. Cass (1987), The Perils of Positive Thinking: Constitutional Interpretation and Negative First Amendment Theory, 34 UCLA L. REV. 1405

Donatella Di Cesare (2009), GADAMER: EIN PHILOSOPHISCHES PORTRÄT (Tübingen: Mohr Siebeck)

Zechariah Chafee, Jr. (1919), Freedom of Speech in War Time, 32 HARV. L. REV. 932

Zechariah Chafee (1920), FREEDOM OF SPEECH (New York NY: Harcourt Brace & Howe)

Harold W. Chase (1960), The Warren Court and Congress, 44 MINN. L. REV. 595

Abram Chayes (1976), The Role of the Judge in Public Law Litigation, 89 HARV. L. REV. 1281

John B. Cheadle (1920), Government Control of Business, 20 COLUM. L. REV. 550

Erwin Chemerinsky (1989), Foreword: The Vanishing Constitution, 103 HARV. L. REV. 43

Sujit Choudhry (1999), Globalization in Search of Justification: Toward a Theory of Comparative Constitutional Interpretation, 74 IND. L.J. 819

Elizabeth A. Clark (2004), HISTORY, THEORY, TEXT: HISTORIANS AND THE LINGUISTIC TURN (Cambridge MA: Harvard University Press)

Felix S. Cohen (1935), Transcendental Nonsense and the Functional Approach, 35 COLUM. L. REV. 809

Felix S. Cohen (1964), THE LEGAL CONSCIENCE: SELECTED PAPERS OF FELIX S. COHEN (New Haven, CT: Yale University Press)

Moshe Cohen-Eliya & Iddo Porat (2009), The Hidden Foreign Law Debate in Heller: The Proportionality Approach in American Constitutional Law, 46 SAN DIEGO L. REV. 367

Ronald M. Dworkin (2011), Proportionality and the Culture of Justification, 59 AM. J. COMP. L. 463

E.J. Cohn (1953), German Legal Science Today, 2 ICLQ 169

Helmut Coing (1962), ZUR GESCHICHTE DES PRIVATRECHTSSYSTEMS (Frankfurt am Main: Vittoria Klostermann)

Edward S. Corwin (1952), Bowing Out 'Clear and Present Danger', 27 NOTRE DAME L. REV. 325

Robert M. Cover (1983), Nomos and Narrative, 97 HARV. L. REV. 4

Archibald Cox (1966), Foreword: Constitutional Adjudication and the Promotion of Human Rights, 80 HARV. L. REV. 91

Barry Cushman (2000), Formalism and Realism in Commerce Clause Jurisprudence, 67 U. CHI. L. REV. 1089

Barry Cushman (2005), Some Varieties and Vicissitudes of Lochnerism, 85 B.U. L. REV. 881

Mirjan R. Damaška (1986), THE FACES OF JUSTICE AND STATE AUTHORITY (New Haven, CT: Yale University Press)

Marco Dani (2009), Economic and Social Conflicts, Integration and Constitution-alism in Contemporary Europe, LEQS DISCUSSION PAPER SERIES, available at: http://papers.ssrn.com/sol3/papers.cfm?abstract_id=1518629.

Jan G. Deutsch (1968), Neutrality, Legitimacy and the Supreme Court: Some Intersections between Law and Political Science, 20 STAN. L. REV. 169

Norman T. Deutsch (2006), Professor Nimmer Meets Professor Schauer (and Others): An Analysis of Definitional Balancing as a Methodology for Determining the Visible Boundaries of the First Amendment, 39 AKRON L. REV. 483

Joseph M. Dodge II (1969), The Free Exercise of Religion: A Sociological Approach, 67 MICH. L. REV. 679

Richard C. Donnelly (1950) Government and Freedom of the Press, 45 ILL. L. REV. 31

Günter Dürig (1956), Der Grundsatz von der Menschenwürde, 81 AöR 117

Günter Dürig (1958), Kommentar zu Art. 1; Art. 2, in MAUNZ-DÜRIG-HERZOG-SCHOLZ, GRUNDGESETZ KOMMENTAR (München: C.F. Beck) (Loose-leaf edition)

Benjamin S. DuVal (1972), Free Communication of Ideas and the Quest for Truth: Toward a Teleological Approach to First Amendment Adjudication, 41 GEO. WASH. L. REV. 161

Neil Duxbury (1990), Some Radicalism about Realism: Thurman Arnold and the Politics of Modern Jurisprudence, 10 OXFORD J. LEGAL STUD. 11

Neil Duxbury (1993), Faith in Reason: The Process Tradition in American Jurisprudence, 15 CARDOZO L. REV. 601

Neil Duxbury (1995), PATTERNS OF AMERICAN JURISPRUDENCE (Oxford University Press)

Ronald M. Dworkin (1977), TAKING RIGHTS SERIOUSLY (Cambridge, MA: Harvard University Press)

Ronald M. Dworkin (1985), A MATTER OF PRINCIPLE (Cambridge, MA: Harvard University Press)

Ronald M. Dworkin (1998), LAW'S EMPIRE (Oxford: Hart Publishing)

David Dyzenhaus (1996), The Legitimacy of Legality, 46 U. TORONTO L.J. 129

Edward J. Eberle (2002), DIGNITY AND FREEDOM: CONSTITUTIONAL VISIONS IN GERMANY AND THE UNITED STATES (Westport, CN: Praeger)

Johann Edelmann (1967), DIE ENTWICKLUNG DER INTERESSEN-JURISPRUDENZ (Bad Homburg: Gehlen)

Klaus Eder (1988), Critique of Habermas's Contribution to the Sociology of Law, 22 LAW & SOC'Y REV. 931

Horst Ehmke (1963), Prinzipien der Verfassungsinterpretation, 20 VVDStRL 53

Albert Ehrenzweig (1948), Book Review, 36 CAL. L. REV. 502

Eugen Ehrlich (1913), GRUNDLEGUNG DER SOZIOLOGIE DES RECHTS (München, Leipzig: Duncker & Humblot)

Eugen Ehrlich (1917), Judicial Freedom of Decision: Its Principles and Objects, in SCIENCE OF LEGAL METHOD: SELECT ESSAYS BY VARIOUS AUTHORS 65 (Ernest Bruncken & Layton B. Register, trans.) (Boston Book Company)

Norbert Elias (1996), THE GERMANS: POWER STRUGGLES AND THE DEVELOPMENT OF HABITUS IN THE NINETEENTH AND TWENTIETH CENTURIES (New York, NY: Columbia University Press)

Ferdinand Elsener, ed. (1977), LEBENSBILDER ZUR GESCHICHTE DER TÜBINGER JURISTENFAKULTÄT (Tübingen: Mohr Siebeck)

John H. Ely (1975), Flag Desecration: A Case Study in the Roles of Categorization and Balancing in First Amendment Analysis, 88 HARV. L. REV. 1482

John H. Ely (1980), DEMOCRACY AND DISTRUST (Cambridge, MA: Harvard University Press)

Thomas I. Emerson (1963), Toward a General Theory of the First Amendment, 72 YALE L.J. 877

Thomas I. Emerson (1964), Freedom of Association and Freedom of Expression, 74 YALE L.J. 1

Thomas I. Emerson (1970), THE SYSTEM OF FREEDOM OF EXPRESSION (New York NY: Random House)

Thomas I. Emerson & David M. Helfeld (1948), Loyalty among Government Employees, 58 YALE L.J. 1

Karl Engisch (1953), DIE IDEE DER KONKRETISIERUNG IN RECHT UND
    RECHTSWISSENSCHAFT UNSERER ZEIT (Heidelberg: C. Winter)
Eric Engle (2012), The History of the General Principle of Proportionality: An
    Overview, 10 DARTMOUTH L.J. 1
William N. Eskridge (1990), The New Textualism, 37 UCLA L. REV. 621
Josef Esser (1956), GRUNDSATZ UND NORM IN DER RICHTERLICHEN
    FORTBILDUNG DES PRIVATRECHTS (Tübingen: Mohr Siebeck, 4th
    edn. 1990)
Josef Esser (1970), VORVERSTÄNDNIS UND METHODENWAHL (Frankfurt
    am Main: Athenäum)
Michelle Everson (2002), Adjudicating the Market, 8 EUR. L.J. 152
Michelle Everson & Julia Eisner (2007), THE MAKING OF A EUROPEAN
    CONSTITUTION: JUDGES AND LAW BEYOND CONSTITUTIVE
    POWER (New York NY: Routledge)
William Ewald (1995), Comparative Jurisprudence (I): What was it Like to Try a
    Rat, 143 U. PA. L. REV. 1889
William Ewald (2004), The Conceptual Jurisprudence of the German Constitution,
    21 CONST. COMMENT. 591 (Book Review)
David L. Faigman (1994), Madisonian Balancing: A Theory of Constitutional
    Adjudication, 88 NW. U. L. REV. 641
Richard H. Fallon, Jr. (1994), Reflections on the Hart-Wechsler Paradigm, 47
    VAND. L. REV. 953
Richard H. Fallon, (1997a), The Rule of Law as a Concept in Constitutional
    Discourse, 97 COLUM. L. REV. 1
Richard H. Fallon, (1997b), Implementing the Constitution, 111 HARV. L.
    REV. 54
Richard H. Fallon, (2005), Legitimacy and the Constitution, 118 HARV. L.
    REV. 1787
Richard H. Fallon, (2006), Judicially Manageable Standards and Constitutional
    Meaning, 119 HARV. L. REV. 1275
Wolfgang Fikentscher (1975), METHODEN DES RECHTS IN VER-
    GLEICHENDER DARSTELLUNG, BAND II: ANGLO-
    AMERIKANISCHER RECHTSKREIS (Tübingen: Mohr)
William W. Fisher III (1997), Texts and Contexts: The Application to American
    Legal History of the Methodologies of Intellectual History, 49 STAN. L.
    REV. 1065
James E. Fleming (1993), Constructing the Substantive Constitution, 72 TEX. L.
    REV. 211
James E. Fleming (2006), SECURING CONSTITUTIONAL DEMOCRACY: THE
    CASE OF AUTONOMY (Chicago, IL: University of Chicago Press).
James E. Fleming (2007), The Incredible Shrinking Constitutional Theory: From
    the Partial Constitution to the Minimal Constitution, 75 FORDHAM L.
    REV. 2885

Ernst Forsthoff (1959), Die Umbildung des Verfassungsgesetzes, in RECHTSTAAT IM WANDEL 130 (Stuttgart: W. Kohlhammer, 1964; 2nd edn., 1976)

Ernst Forsthoff (1961), Zur Problematik der Verfassungsauslegung, in RECHTSTAAT IM WANDEL 153 (Stuttgart: W. Kohlhammer, 1964; 2nd edn., 1976)

Ernst Forsthoff (1963), Der introvertierte Rechtsstaat und seine Verortung, in RECHTSTAAT IM WANDEL 175 (Stuttgart: W. Kohlhammer, 1964; 2nd edn., 1976)

Christopher Forsyth (2007), Showing the Fly the way out of the Flybottle: The Value of Formalism and Conceptual Reasoning in Administrative Law, 66 CAMBRIDGE L.J. 325

Jerome Frank (1930), LAW AND THE MODERN MIND (New York, NY: Brentano's)

Jerome Frank (1949), Modern and Ancient Legal Pragmatism, 25 NOTRE DAME L. REV. 460

Günter Frankenberg (1985), Critical Comparisons: Re-thinking Comparative Law, 26 HARV. INT'L L.J. 411

Felix Frankfurter (1930), The Conditions for, and the Aims and Methods of, Legal Research, 6 AM. L. SCH. REV. 663

Felix Frankfurter (1939), Mr. Justice Cardozo and Public Law, 52 HARV. L. REV. 440

Laurent B. Frantz (1962), The First Amendment in the Balance, 71 YALE L.J. 1424

Laurent B. Frantz (1963), Is the First Amendment Law? A Reply to Professor Mendelson, 51 CAL. L. REV. 729

Paul A. Freund (1949), ON UNDERSTANDING THE SUPREME COURT (Boston, MA: Little, Brown)

Paul A. Freund (1967), Mr. Justice Black and the Judicial Function, 14 UCLA L. REV. 467

Philip P. Frickey (2005), Getting from Joe to Gene (McCarthy): The Avoidance Canon, Legal Process Theory, and Narrowing Statutory Interpretation in the Early Warren Court, 93 CAL. L. REV. 397

Charles Fried (1963), Two Concepts of Interests: Some Reflections on the Supreme Court's Balancing Test, 76 HARV. L. REV. 755

Charles Fried (1981), The Artificial Reason of Law or: What Lawyers Know, 60 TEX. L. REV. 35

Barry Friedman (1997), Neutral Principles: A Retrospective, 50 VAND. L. REV. 503

Barry Friedman (2002), The Birth of An Academic Obsession: The History of the Countermajoritarian Difficulty, Part Five, 112 YALE L.J. 153

Lawrence M. Friedman (1966), On Legalistic Reasoning – A Footnote to Weber, 1 WIS. L. REV. 148

Wolfgang Friedmann (1961), Legal Philosphy and Judicial Lawmaking, 61
    COLUM. L. REV. 821
Wolfgang Friedmann (1967), LEGAL THEORY (London: Stevens) (1st edn.
    1944)
Lon L. Fuller (1946), Reason and Fiat in Case Law, 59 HARV. L. REV. 376
Lon L. Fuller (1948), *Introduction*, in The Jurisprudence of Interests (Magdalena
    Schoch, ed.) (Cambridge, MA: Harvard University Press)
Lon L. Fuller (1958), Fidelity to Law: A Reply to Professor Hart, 71 HARV. L.
    REV. 630
Lon L. Fuller (1978), The Forms and Limits of Adjudication, 92 HARV. L.
    REV. 353
Hans-Georg Gadamer (1960), WAHRHEIT UND METHODE (Tübingen: Mohr)
Marc Galanter (1974), Why the Haves Come out Ahead: Speculations on the Limits
    of Legal Change, 9 LAW & SOC'Y REV. 95
Stephen A. Gardbaum (2003), The 'Horizontal Effect' of Constitutional Rights, 102
    MICH. L. REV. 388
Stephen A. Gardbaum (2006), Where the (State) Action is, 4, 760
Manfred Gentz (1968), Zur Verhältnismäßigkeit von Grundrechtseingriffen,
    NJW 1600
François Gény (1899), MÉTHODE D'INTERPRÉTATION ET SOURCES EN
    DROIT PRIVÉ POSITIF (Paris: Librairie Générale); English translation in
    SCIENCE OF LEGAL METHOD (Ernest Bruncken & Layton B. Register,
    trans.) (Boston, MA: Boston Book Company, 1921)
C.F. von Gerber (1869), GRUNDZÜGE EINES SYSTEMS DES DEUTSCHEN
    STAATSRECHTS (Leipzig: Bernard Tauchnitz) (1st edn., 1865)
David J. Gerber (1994), Constitutionalizing the Economy: German Neo-Liberalism,
    Competition Law and the New Europe, 42 AM. J. COMP. L. 25
Walter van Gerven (1999), The Effect of Proportionality on the Actions of Member
    States, in THE PRINCIPLE OF PROPORTIONALITY IN THE LAWS OF
    EUROPE 37 (Evelyn Ellis, ed.) (Oxford: Hart Publishing)
Grant Gilmore (1977), THE AGES OF AMERICAN LAW (New Haven, CT: Yale
    University Press)
Helmut Goerlich (1973), WERTORDNUNG UND GRUNDGESETZ:
    KRITIK EINER ARGUMENTATIONSFIGUR DES BUNDESVER-
    FASSUNGSGERICHTS (Baden-Baden: Nomos)
Charles C. Goetsch (1980), The Future of Legal Formalism, 24 AM. J. LEGAL
    HIST. 221
M. P. Golding (1963), Principled Decision Making and the Supreme Court, 63
    COLUM. L. REV. 35
Myron Gollub (1942), The First Amendment and the N.L.R.A., 27 WASH. U. L.
    Q. 242
Robert W. Gordon (1984), Critical Legal Histories, 36 STAN. L. REV. 57

Robert W. Gordon (1997), The Elusive Transformation, 6 YALE J.L. & HUMANITIES 137 (Book Review)

Kent Greenawalt (1978), The Enduring Significance of Neutral Principles, 78 COLUM. L. REV. 982

Kent Greenawalt (1989), Free Speech Justifications, 89 COLUM. L. REV. 119

Kent Greenawalt (1992), Free Speech in the United States and Canada, 55 LAW & CONTEMP. PROBS. 5

Abner S. Greene (2007), The Fit Dimension, 75 FORDHAM L. REV. 2921

Thomas C. Grey (1983), Langdell's Orthodoxy, 45 U. PITTSBURG L. REV. 1

Thomas C. Grey (1989), Holmes and Legal Pragmatism, 41 STAN. L. REV. 787

Thomas C. Grey (1990), Hear the Other Side: Wallace Stevens and Pragmatist Legal Theory, 63 S. CAL. L. REV. 1569

Thomas C. Grey (1995), Langdell's Orthodoxy, U. PITT. L. REV. 1

Thomas C. Grey (1996a), Freestanding Legal Pragmatism, 18 CARDOZO L. REV. 21

Thomas C. Grey (1996b), Modern American Legal Thought, 106 YALE L.J. 493 (Book Review)

Thomas C. Grey (2003), Judicial Review and Legal Pragmatism, 38 WAKE FOREST L. REV. 473

Dieter Grimm, (2007), Proportionality in Canadian and German Constitutional Jurisprudence, 57 U. TORONTO L.J. 383

Erwin N. Griswold (1960), Foreword: Of Time and Attitudes – Professor Hart and Judge Arnold, 74 HARV. L. REV. 81

Vivian Grosswald Curran (1998), Cultural Immersion, Difference and Categories in U.S. Comparative Law, 46 AM. J. COMP. L. 43

Vivian Grosswald Curran (2001), Fear of Formalism: Indications from the Fascist Period in France and Germany of Judicial Methodology's Impact on Substantive Law, 35 CORNELL INT'L L.J. 101

Gerald Gunther, (1968), Reflections on Robel: It's Not What the Court Did But the Way That it Did it, 20 STAN. L. REV. 1140

Gerald Gunther (1975), Learned Hand and the Origins of Modern First Amendment Doctrine, 27 STAN. L. REV. 719

Peter Häberle (1962), DIE WESENSGEHALTGARANTIE DES ART. 19 ABS. 2 GRUNDGESETZ (München: C.F. Beck)

Peter Häberle (1980), VERFASSUNGSGERICHTSBARKEIT ZWISCHEN POLITIK UND RECHTSWISSENSCHAFT (Frankfurt am Main: Athenäum)

Jürgen Habermas (1979), COMMUNICATION AND THE EVOLUTION OF SOCIETY (Thomas McCarthy, trans.) (Boston, MA: Beacon Press)

Jürgen Habermas (1996), BETWEEN FACTS AND NORMS: CONTRIBUTIONS TO A DISCOURSE THEORY OF LAW AND DEMOCRACY (William Rehg, trans.) (Cambridge: Polity Press)

Hans-Peter Haferkamp (2004), GEORG FRIEDRICH PUCHTA UND DIE 'BEGRIFFSJURISPRUDENZ' (Frankfurt am Main: Vittoria Klostermann)

Kurt Häntzschel (1932), Das Recht der freien Meinungsäußerung in HANDBUCH DES DEUTSCHEN STAATSRECHTS II 105 (Gerhard Anschütz & Richard Thoma, eds.) (Tübingen: Mohr)

Sarah K. Harding (2003), Comparative Reasoning and Judicial Review, 28 YALE J. INT'L L. 409

Rufus C. Harris (1936), What Next in American Law?, 8 AM. L. SCH. REV. 461

H. L. A. Hart (1957), Positivism and the Separation of Law and Morals, 71 HARV. L. REV. 563

H.L.A. Hart (1961), THE CONCEPT OF LAW (Oxford: Clarendon Press)

H. L. A. Hart (1967), American Jurisprudence through English Eyes, 11 GA. L. REV. 969

Henry M. Hart (1959), The Supreme Court 1958 Term: The Time Chart of the Justices, 73 HARV. L. REV. 84

Philipp Heck (1889), DAS RECHT DER GROSSEN HAVEREI (Berlin: H.W. Müller)

Philipp Heck (1890), Die Lebensversicherung zu Gunsten Dritter, eine Schenkung auf den Todesfall, 4 ARCHBÜRGR 17

Philipp Heck (1905), Interessenjurisprudenz und Gesetzestreue, DJZ 1140

Philipp Heck (1909), Was ist diejenige Begriffsjurisprudenz, die wir bekämpfen?, DJZ 1456

Philipp Heck (1912), DAS PROBLEM DER RECHTSGEWINNUNG (Tübingen: Mohr)

Philipp Heck (1914), Gesetzesauslegung und Interessenjurisprudenz, 112 ARCHIV FÜR DIE CIVILISTICHE PRAXIS

Philipp Heck (1932a), BEGRIFFSBILDUNG UND INTERESSENJURIS-PRUDENZ (Tübingen: Mohr)

Philipp Heck (1932b), The Formation of Concepts and the Jurisprudence of Interests, in THE JURISPRUDENCE OF INTERESTS 102 (Magdalena Schoch, trans. ed., 1948) (Cambridge, MA: Harvard University Press)

Philipp Heck (1933), The Jurisprudence of Interests, in THE JURISPRUDENCE OF INTERESTS 31 (Magdalena Schoch, trans. & ed., 1948) (Cambridge, MA: Harvard University Press)

Philipp Heck (1936), Die Interessenjurisprudenz und ihre neuen Gegner, 22 ARCHIV FÜR DIE CIVILISTICHE PRAXIS 129

Thomas C. Heller (1984), Structuralism and Critique, 36 STAN. L. REV. 141

Louis Henkin (1961), Some Reflections on Current Constitutional Controversy, 109 U. PA. L. REV. 637

Louis Henkin (1962), Shelley v. Kramer: Notes for a Revised Opinion, 110 U. PA. L. REV. 473

Louis Henkin (1968), Foreword: On Drawing Lines, 82 HARV. L. REV. 63

Louis Henkin (1978), Infallibility under Law: Constitutional Balancing, 78 COLUM. L. REV. 1022

Shael Herman (1979), Book Review, 27 AM. J. COMP. L. 729

Helen Hershkoff (2011), Horizontality and the Spooky Doctrines of American Law, 59 BUFF. L. REV. 455

Roman Herzog (1968), Kommentar zu Art. 5 Abs. 1–2, in MAUNZ-DÜRIG-HERZO-SCHOLZ, GRUNDGESETZ KOMMENTAR (München: Beck) (Loose-leaf edition)

Konrad Hesse (1993), GRUNDZÜGE DES VERFASSUNGSRECHTS DER BUNDESREPUBLIK DEUTSCHLAND (Karlsruhe: C.F. Müller) (1st edn., 1967; 8th edn. 1975; 19th edn., 1993; 20th edn., 1999)

F.A. von der Heydte (1956), Natural Law Tendencies in Contemporary German Jurisprudence, 1 NATURAL L. F. 115

Eike von Hippel (1956), GRENZEN UND WESENSGEHALT DER GRUNDRECHTE (Berlin: Duncker & Humblot)

Mark van Hoecke & Mark Warrington (1998), Legal Cultures, Legal Paradigms and Legal Doctrine: Towards a New Model for Comparative Law, 47 ICLQ 495

Alexander Hollerbach (1960), Auflösung der rechtsstaatlichen Verfassung?, 85 AöR 241

Oliver Wendell Holmes (1879), Common Carriers and the Common Law, 13 AM. L. REV. 609

Oliver Wendell Holmes (1894), Privilege, Malice and Intent, 8 HARV. L. REV. 1

Morton J. Horwitz (1992), THE TRANSFORMATION OF AMERICAN LAW 1870–1960: THE CRISIS OF LEGAL ORTHODOXY (New York, NY: Oxford University Press)

Morton J. Horwitz (1993), Foreword: The Constitution of Change: Legal Fundamentality without Fundamentalism, 107 HARV. L. REV. 30

Heinrich Hubmann (1956), Grundsätze der Interessenabwägung, 155 ARCHIV FÜR DIE CIVILISTISCHE PRAXIS 85

N. E. H. Hull (1997), ROSCOE POUND AND KARL LLEWELLYN: SEARCHING FOR AN AMERICAN JURISPRUDENCE (Chicago, IL: University of Chicago Press)

Joseph C. Hutcheson, (1928) The Judgment Intuitive: The Function of the Hunch in Judicial Decision, 14 CORNELL L. Q. 274

Allan Hyde (1983), The Concept of Legitimation in the Sociology of Law, 1983 WIS. L. REV. 379

Vicki C. Jackson (1999), Ambivalent Resistance and Comparative Constitutionalism: Opening Up the Conversation on Proportionality, Rights and Federalism, 1 U. PA. J. CONST. L. 583

Vicki C. Jackson, (2004), Being Proportional about Proportionality, 21 CONST. COMMENT. 803

Christophe Jamin (2006), Demogue et son Temps: Réflexions Introductives sur son Nihilisme Juridique, 56 REV. INTERDISCIPLINAIRE D'ETUDES JURIDIQUES

Rudolf von Jhering (1884), SCHERZ UND ERNST IN DER JURISPRUDENZ (Max Leitner, ed.) (Wien: Linde Verlag, 2009)

Christian Joerges (1994), History as Non-History: Points of Divergence and Time Lags Between Friedrich Kessler and German Jurisprudence, 42 AM. J. COMP. L. 163

Sanford H. Kadish (1957), Methodology and Criteria in Due Process Adjudication, 66 YALE L.J. 319

Robert A. Kagan (1997), Should Europe Worry about Adversarial Legalism?, 17 OXFORD J. LEGAL STUD. 165

Robert A. Kagan (2007), European and American Ways of Law: Six Entrenched Differences, in EUROPEAN WAYS OF LAW: TOWARDS A EUROPEAN SOCIOLOGY OF LAW 41 (Volkmar Gessner & David Nelken, eds.) (Oxford: Hart Publishing)

Paul W. Kahn (2001), Freedom, Autonomy, and the Cultural Study of Law, 13 YALE J. L. & HUMANITIES 141

Paul W. Kahn (2003), Comparative Constitutionalism in a New Key, 101 MICH. L. REV. 2677

Otto Kahn-Freund (1966), Comparative Law as an Academic Subject, 82 L.Q.R. 40

Laura Kalman (1986) LEGAL REALISM AT YALE, 1927–1960 (Chapel Hill, NC: University of North Carolina Press)

Harry Kalven, Jr. (1960), The Metaphysics of the Law of Obscenity, 1960 SUP. CT. REV. 1

Harry Kalven, Jr. (1964), The New York Times Case: A Note on the Central Meaning of the First Amendment, 1964 SUP. CT. REV. 191

Harry Kalven, JR. (1965), THE NEGRO AND THE FIRST AMENDMENT (Columbus, OH: Ohio State University Press)

Harry Kalven (1967), Upon Rereading Mr. Justice Black on the First Amendment, 14 UCLA L. REV. 428

Harry Kalven (1988), A WORTHY TRADITION (Jamie Kalven, ed.) (New York, NY: Harper & Row)

Kenneth L. Karst (1960), Legislative Facts in Constitutional Litigation, 1960 SUP. CT. REV. 75

Kenneth L. Karst (1965), The First Amendment and Harry Kalven: An Appreciative Comment on the Advantages of Thinking Small, 13 UCLA L. REV. 1

Aileen Kavanagh (2009), Judicial Restraint in the Pursuit of Justice, 60 U. TORONTO L.J. 23

David Kennedy (1987), INTERNATIONAL LEGAL STRUCTURES (Baden-Baden: Nomos)

David Kennedy (1997), New Approaches to Comparative Law: Comparativism and International Governance, 1997 UTAH L. REV. 545

Duncan Kennedy (1969), Note: Civil Disabilities and the First Amendment, 78 YALE. L.J. 842

Duncan Kennedy (1973), Legal Formality, 2 J. LEG. STUD. 351

Duncan Kennedy (1975), *The Rise and Fall of Classical Legal Thought* (Unpublished manuscript, available at http://duncankennedy.net/legal_history/essays. html#R&F)

Duncan Kennedy (1976), Form and Substance in Private Law Adjudication, 89 HARV. L. REV. 1685

Duncan Kennedy (1979), The Structure of Blackstone's Commentaries, 28 BUFF. L. REV. 205

Duncan Kennedy (1980), Toward an Historical Understanding of Legal Consciousness: The Case of Classical Legal Thought in America, 1850–1940, 3 RESEARCH IN LAW & SOC. 3

Duncan Kennedy (1985), Comment on Rudolf Wiethölter's 'Materialization and Proceduralization in Modern Law', and 'Proceduralization of the Category of Law', 12 GERMAN L.J. 474 2011 (reprint)

Duncan Kennedy (1997), A CRITIQUE OF ADJUDICATION – FIN DE SIÈCLE (Cambridge, MA: Harvard University Press)

Duncan Kennedy (2000), From the Will Theory to the Principle of Private Autonomy: Lon Fuller's Consideration and Form, 100 COLUM. L. REV. 94

Duncan Kennedy (2003a), The Disenchantment of Logically Formal Legal Rationality, or Max Weber's Sociology in the Genealogy of the Contemporary Mode of Western Legal Thought, 55 HASTINGS L.J. 1031

Duncan Kennedy (2003b), Two Globalizations of Law and Legal Thought, 36 SUFFOLK U. L. REV. 631

Duncan Kennedy (2006), Three Globalizations of Law and Legal Thought: 1850–2000, in THE NEW LAW AND ECONOMIC DEVELOPMENT: A CRITICAL APPRAISAL 19 (David Trubek & Alvaro Santos, eds.) (New York, NY: Cambridge University Press)

Duncan Kennedy & Marie-Claire Belleau (2000), François Gény aux États-Unis, in FRANÇOIS GÉNY, MYTHE ET RÉALITÉS (Claude Thomasset, Jacques Vanderlinden & Philippe Jestaz, eds.) (Bruxelles: Bruylant)

Duncan Kennedy & Marie-Claire Belleau (2006), La place de René Demogue dans la généalogie de la pensée juridique contemporaine, 56 REV. INTERDISCIPLINAIRE D'ÉTUDES JURIDIQUES 163

Walter B. Kennedy (1925), Pragmatism as a Philosophy of Law, 9 MARQ. L. REV. 63

Robert B. Kent (1961), Compulsory Disclosure and the First Amendment – The Scope of the Judicial Review, 41 B.U. L. REV. 443

Hans H. Klein (1971), Öffentliche und private Freiheit: Zur Auslegung des Grundrechts der Meinungsfreiheit, 10 DER STAAT 145

Michael R. Klein (1968), Hugo L. Black: A Judicial View of American Constitutional Democracy, 22 U. MIAMI L. REV. 753

Donald P. Kommers (1991), German Constitutionalism: A Prolegomenon, 40 EMORY L.J. 837

Donald P. Kommers (2006), Germany: Balancing Rights and Duties, in INTERPRETING CONSTITUTIONS. A COMPARATIVE STUDY 161 (Jeffrey Goldsworthy, ed.) (Oxford University Press)

Donald P. Kommers & Russel A. Miller (2012), THE CONSTITUTIONAL JURISPRUDENCE OF THE FEDERAL REPUBLIC OF GERMANY (Durham, NC: Duke University Press) (3rd edn., 2012; 2nd edn., Kommers, ed., 1997)

Stefan Korioth (2000), Rudolf Smend, in WEIMAR: A JURISPRUDENCE OF CRISIS 207 (Bernhard Schlink & Arthur J. Jacobson, eds.) (Berkeley, CA: University of California Press)

Martti Koskenniemi (2005), FROM APOLOGY TO UTOPIA: THE STRUCTURE OF INTERNATIONAL LEGAL ARGUMENT (Cambridge University Press) (Originally published 1989)

Ruprecht von Krauss (1955), DER GRUNDSATZ DER VERHÄLT-NISMÄSSIGKEIT (Hamburg: L. Appel)

Martin Kriele (1967), THEORIE DER RECHTSGEWINNUNG (Berlin: Duncker & Humblot)

Anthony M. Kronman (1983), MAX WEBER (Stanford, CA: Stanford University Press)

Ronald Krotoszynski (2006), THE FIRST AMENDMENT IN CROSS-CULTURAL PERSPECTIVE (New York, NY: NYU Press)

Mattias Kumm (2004), Constitutional Rights as Principles: On the Structure and Domain of Constitutional Justice, 2 I-CON 574

Mattias Kumm (2006), Who's Afraid of the Total Constitution?, 7 GERMAN L.J. 341

Aharon Barak (2009), On the Past and Future of European Constitutional Scholarship, 7 I-CON 401

Ming-Sung Kuo (2009), From Myth to Fiction: Why a Legalist-Constructivist Rescue of European Constitutional Ordering Fails, 29 OXFORD J. LEGAL STUD. 579

Karl-Heinz Ladeur (1983), Abwägung als neues Rechtsparadigma? Von der Einheit der Rechtsordnung zur Pluralität der Rechtsdiskurse, 69 ARSP 463

Karl-Heinz Ladeur (2004), KRITIK DER ABWÄGUNG IN DER GRUNDRECHTSDOGMATIK (Tübingen: Mohr Siebeck)

Gérard V. La Forest (1992), The Balancing of Interests under the Charter, 2 NAT'L J. CONST. LAW 113

Edouard Lambert (1921), LE GOUVERNEMENT DES JUGES ET LA LUTTE CONTRE LA LÉGISLATION SOCIALE AUX ÉTATS-UNIS (Paris: M. Giard & Cie.)

Kim Lane Scheppele (2003), Aspirational and aversive constitutionalism: The case for studying cross constitutional influence through negative models, 1 I-CON 296

Karl Larenz (1938), ÜBER GEGENSTAND UND METHODE DES VÖLKISCHEN RECHTSDENKENS (Berlin: Duncker & Jünnhaupt)

Karl Larenz (1991), METHODENLEHRE DER RECHTSWISSENSCHAFT (Berlin: Springer) (1960; 3rd edn., 1975; 6th edn., 1991)

Mitchel de S.-O.-l'E. Lasser (1995), Judicial (Self-Portraits): Judicial Discourse in the French Legal System, 104 YALE L.J. 1325

Mitchel de S.-O.-l'E. Lasser (1998), Lit. Theory Put to the Test: A Comparative Literary Analysis of American Judicial Tests and French Judicial Discourse, 111 HARV. L. REV. 689

Mitchel de S.-O.-l'E. Lasser (2001), Do Judges Deploy Policy?, 22 CARDOZO L. REV. 863

Mitchel de S.-O.-l'E. Lasser (2004), JUDICIAL DELIBERATIONS. A COMPARATIVE ANALYSIS OF JUDICIAL TRANSPARENCY AND LEGITIMACY (Oxford University Press)

David S. Law (2005), Generic Constitutional Law, 89 MINN. L. REV. 652

Learned Hand (1958), THE BILL OF RIGHTS: THE OLIVER WENDELL HOLMES LECTURES (Cambridge, MA: Harvard University Press)

Joachim Lege (1998), PRAGMATISMUS UND JURISPRUDENZ (Tübingen: Mohr Siebeck)

Walter Leisner (1960), GRUNDRECHTE UND PRIVATRECHT (München: Beck)

Walter Leisner (1997), DER ABWÄGUNGSSTAAT (Berlin: Duncker & Humblot)

Brian Leiter (1997), Rethinking Legal Realism: Toward a Naturalized Jurisprudence, 76 TEX. L. REV. 267

Pierre Lepaulle (1922), The Function of Comparative Law, 35 HARV. L. REV. 838

Peter Lerche (1961), ÜBERMAß UND VERFASSUNGSRECHT (Köln: Heymann)

Michael Les Benedict (1985), Laissez-Faire and Liberty: A Re-Evaluation of the Meanings and Origins of Laissez-Faire Constitutionalism, 3 LAW & HIST. REV. 293

Roland Lhotta ed. (2005), DIE INTEGRATION DES MODERNEN STAATES. ZUR AKTUALITÄT DER INTEGRATIONSLEHRE VON RUDOLF SMEND (Baden-Baden: Nomos)

Barnett Lidsky (1995), Defensor Fidei: The Travails of a Post-Realist Formalist, 47 FLA. L. REV. 815

Jutta Limbach (2000), The Effects of Judgments of the German Federal Constitutional Court, 2 EUR. J. L. REF. 1

Josef Franz Lindner (2005), THEORIE DER GRUNDRECHTSDOGMATIK (Tübingen: Mohr Siebeck)

Karl N. Llewellyn (1930), A Realistic Jurisprudence – The Next Step, 30 COLUM. L. REV. 431

Karl N. Llewellyn (1942), On the Good, the True, the Beautiful in Law, 9 U. CHI. L. REV. 224

William B. Lockhart & Robert C. McClure (1954), Literature, the Law of Obscenity, and the Constitution, 38 MINN. L. REV. 295

Neil MacCormick (1978), LEGAL REASONING AND LEGAL THEORY (Oxford: Clarendon Press)

Neil MacCormick & Robert S. Summers (1991), INTERPRETING STATUTES: A COMPARATIVE STUDY (Aldershot: Dartmouth)

Miguel Poiares Maduro (1998), WE THE COURT (Oxford: Hart Publishing)

Hermann von Mangoldt and Friedrich Klein (1957), DAS BONNER GRUNDGESETZ: KOMMENTAR (München: F. Vahlen)

Thilo Marauhn and Nadine Ruppel (2008), Balancing Conflicting Human Rights: Konrad Hesse's Notion of 'Praktische Konkordanz' and the German Federal Constitutional Court, in CONFLICTS BETWEEN FUNDAMENTAL RIGHTS 273 (Eva Brems, ed.) (Antwerp & Oxford: Intersentia)

Basil S. Markesinis (1986), Conceptualism, Pragmatism and Courage: A Common Lawyer Looks at Some Judgments of the German Federal Court, 34 AM. J. COMP. L. 349

Alpheus Thomas Mason (1962), Myth and Reality in Supreme Court Decisions, 48 VA. L. REV. 1385

Calvin R. Massey (2004), The New Formalism: Requiem for Tiered Scrutiny, 6 U. PA. J. CONST. L. 945

Ugo Mattei (2003), A Theory of Imperial Law: A Study on U.S. Hegemony and the Latin Resistance, 10 IND. J. GLOB. L. ST. 383

Robert G. McCloskey (2005), THE AMERICAN SUPREME COURT (4th edn., revised by Sanford Levinson) (Chicago, IL: University of Chicago Press) (Originally published 1960)

John P. McCormick (1997), Max Weber and Jürgen Habermas: The Sociology and Philosophy of Law during Crises of the State, 9 YALE J.L. & HUMANITIES 297

John P. McCormick (2003), Habermas' Reconstruction of West German Post-War Law and the Sozialstaat, in GERMAN IDEOLOGIES SINCE 1945 65 (J-W Müller, ed.) (Basingstoke: Palgrave Macmillan)

Myres S. McDougal (1947), The Law School of the Future: From Legal Realism to Policy Science in the World Community, 56 YALE L.J. 1345

Gary L. McDowell (1989), The Corrosive Constitutionalism of Edward S. Corwin, 14 LAW & SOC. INQUIRY 603

Patrick M. McFadden (1988), The Balancing Test, 29 B.C. L. REV. 585

Robert B. McKay (1963), Congressional Investigations and the Supreme Court, 51 CAL. L. REV. 267

Edward McWhinney (1955), The Supreme Court and the Dilemma of Judicial Policy-Making, 39 MINN. L. REV. 837

Edward McWhinney (1957), The German Federal Constitutional Court and the Communist Party Decision, 32 INDIANA L.J. 295

Alexander Meiklejohn (1948), FREE SPEECH AND ITS RELATION TO SELF-GOVERNMENT (New York, NY: Harper)

Alexander Meiklejohn (1953), What does the First Amendment Mean?, 20 U. CHI. L. REV. 461

Alexander Meiklejohn (1961a), The Balancing of Self-Preservation against Political Freedom, 49 CAL. L. REV. 4

Alexander Meiklejohn (1961b), The First Amendment is an Absolute, 1961 SUP. CT. REV. 245

Wallace Mendelson (1952a), Clear and Present Danger – From Schenck to Dennis, 52 COLUM. L. REV. 313

Wallace Mendelson (1952b), The Clear And Present Danger Test – A Reply to Mr. Meiklejohn, 5 VAND. L. REV. 792

Wallace Mendelson (1954), Mr. Justice Frankfurter and the Process of Judicial Review, 103 U. PA. L. REV. 295

Wallace Mendelson (1961), JUSTICES BLACK AND FRANKFURTER: CONFLICT IN THE COURT (Chicago, IL: University of Chicago Press)

Wallace Mendelson (1962), On the Meaning of the First Amendment: Absolutes in the Balance, 50 CAL. L. REV. 821

Wallace Mendelson (1964), The First Amendment and the Judicial Process: A Reply to Mr. Frantz, 17 VAND. L. REV. 479

Augustin Menéndez & Erik O. Eriksen (2006), ARGUING FUNDAMENTAL RIGHTS (Dordrecht: Springer)

Ralf Michaels (2006a), The Functional Method, in THE OXFORD HANDBOOK OF COMPARATIVE LAW 339 (Mathias Reimann & Reinhard Zimmermann, eds.) (Oxford University Press)

Ralf Michaels (2006b), Two Paradigms of Jurisdiction, 27 MICH. J. INT'L L. 1003

Frank I. Michelman (1986), Foreword: Traces of Self-Government, 100 HARV. L. REV. 4

Arthur Selwyn Miller (1965), On the Choice of Major Premises in Supreme Court Opinions, 14 J. PUB. L. 251

Arthur Selwyn Miller & Ronald F. Howell (1960), The Myth of Neutrality in Constitutional Adjudication, 27 U. CHI. L. REV. 661

Kai Möller (2012), THE GLOBAL MODEL OF CONSTITUTIONAL RIGHTS (Oxford University Press)

Henry P. Monaghan (1981), Our Perfect Constitution, 56 N.Y.U. L. REV. 353

Clarence Morris (1958), Law, Reason and Sociology, 107 U. PENN. L. REV. 147

Friedrich Müller (1966), NORMSTRUKTUR UND NORMATIVITÄT (Berlin: Duncker & Humblot)

Jan-Werner Müller (ed.) (2003), GERMAN IDEOLOGIES SINCE 1945 (New York, NY: Palgrave Macmillan)

Rudolf Müller-Erzbach (1929), Reichsgericht und Interessenjurisprudenz, in DIE
    REICHSGERICHTSPRAXIS IM DEUTSCHEN RECHTSLEBEN II 161
    (Otto Schreiber, ed.) (Berlin: Walter de Gruyter)
Walter F. Murphy (1962), CONGRESS AND THE COURT: A CASE STUDY
    IN THE AMERICAN POLITICAL PROCESS (Chicago, IL: University of
    Chicago Press)
Robert F. Nagel (1985), The Formulaic Constitution, 84 MICH. L. REV. 165
Robert F. Nagel (1989), CONSTITUTIONAL CULTURES: THE MENTALITY
    AND CONSEQUENCES OF JUDICIAL REVIEW (Berkeley, CA: University
    of California Press)
Anthony J. Nicholls (1994), FREEDOM WITH RESPONSIBILITY: THE SOCIAL
    MARKET ECONOMY IN GERMANY, 1918–1963 (Oxford: Clarendon
    Press)
Melville B. Nimmer (1968), The Right to Speak from Times to Time: First Amendment
    Theory Applied to Libel and Misapplied to Privacy, 56 CAL. L. REV. 935
Hans Carl Nipperdey (1964), Boykott und freie Meinungsäußerung, DVBl 445
Louis Nizer (1941), Right of Privacy – A Half Century's Developments, 39 MICH.
    L. REV. 526
Georg Nolte (2005), European and US Constitutionalism: Comparing Essential
    Elements, in EUROPEAN AND US CONSTITUTIONALISM 3 (Georg
    Nolte, ed.) (Cambridge University Press)
Charles B. Nutting (1961), Is the First Amendment Obsolete?, 30 GEO. WASH. L.
    REV. 167
Fritz Ossenbühl (1995), Abwägung im Verfassungsrecht, DVBl 904
Walter Ott & Franziska Buob (1993), Did Legal Positivism Render German Jurists
    Defenceless During the Third Reich?, 2 SOC. & LEGAL STUD. 91
Jeremy Paul (1991), The Politics of Legal Semiotics, 69 TEX. L. REV. 1779
Marijan Pavcnik (1997), Legal Decisionmaking as a Responsible Intellectual
    Activity: A Continental Point of View, 72 WASH. L. REV. 481
Chaim Perelman (1963), THE IDEA OF JUSTICE AND THE PROBLEM OF
    ARGUMENT (London: Routledge)
Chaim Perelman & Lucie Olbrechts-Tyteca (1963), The New Rhetoric, in CHAIM
    PERELMAN, THE IDEA OF JUSTICE AND THE PROBLEM OF
    ARGUMENT 134 (John Petrie, trans.) (London: Routledge)
Ingolf Pernice (1995), Carl Schmitt, Rudolf Smend und die europäische Integration,
    120 AöR 100
Michael J. Perry (1985), Authority of Text, Tradition, and Reason: A Theory of
    Constitutional Interpretation, 58 S. CAL. L. REV. 551
Christian von Pestalozza (1963), Kritische Bemerkungen zu Methoden und
    Prinzipien der Grundrechtsauslegung in der Bundesrepublik Deutschland,
    2 DER STAAT 425
Courtland H. Peterson (1982), Particularism in the Conflict of Laws, 10 HOFSTRA
    L. REV. 973

Michael J. Phillips (2001), THE LOCHNER COURT, MYTH AND REALITY
(Westport, CT: Praeger)

Richard H. Pildes (1994), Avoiding Balancing: The Role of Exclusionary Reasons in
Constitutional Law, 45 HASTINGS L.J. 711

Richard H. Pildes (2003), Conflicts between American and European Views of
Law: The Dark Side of Legalism, 44 VA. J. INT'L L. 145

J. G. A. Pocock (1962), The History of Political Thought: A Methodological
Inquiry, in J.G.A. POCOCK, POLITICAL THOUGHT AND HISTORY:
ESSAYS ON THEORY AND METHOD 3 (Cambridge University Press,
2009)

J.G.A. Pocock (1981), The Reconstruction of Discourse: Towards the Historiography
of Political Thought, 96 MODERN LANGUAGE NOTES 959

Douglas A. Poe (1968), The Legal Philosophy of John Marshall Harlan: Freedom
of Expression, Due Process, and Judicial Self Restraint, 21 VAND. L.
REV. 659

Iddo Porat (2006), The Dual Model of Balancing: A Model for the Proper Scope of
Balancing in Constitutional Law, 27 CARDOZO L. REV. 1393

Richard A. Posner (1990), What Has Pragmatism to Offer Law?, 63 S. CAL. L.
REV. 1563

Richard A. Posner (2002), Pragmatism Versus Purposivism in First Amendment
Analysis, 54 STAN. L. REV. 737

Richard A. Posner (2003), LAW, PRAGMATISM AND DEMOCRACY (Cambridge,
MA: Harvard University Press)

Roscoe Pound (1905a), Decadence of Equity, 5 COLUM. L. REV. 20

Roscoe Pound (1905b), Do We Need a Philosophy of Law?, 5 COLUM. L.
REV. 339

Roscoe Pound (1908), Mechanical Jurisprudence, 8 COLUM. L. REV. 605

Roscoe Pound (1909), Liberty of Contract, 18 YALE L.J. 454

Roscoe Pound (1910), Law in Books and Law in Action, 44 AMERICAN L.
REV. 12

Roscoe Pound (1911a), The Scope and Purpose of Sociological Jurisprudence, 24
HARV. L. REV 591

Roscoe Pound (1911b), The Scope and Purpose of Sociological Jurisprudence II, 25
HARV. L. REV. 140

Roscoe Pound (1912a), The Scope and Purpose of Sociological Jurisprudence III,
25 HARV. L. REV. 489

Roscoe Pound (1912b), Theories of Law, 22 YALE L.J. 114

Roscoe Pound (1912c), Social Justice and Legal Justice, 75 CENT. L.J. 455

Roscoe Pound (1913), Justice According to Law, 13 COLUM. L. REV. 696

Roscoe Pound (1914), The New Philosophies of Law, 27 HARV. L. REV. 718

Roscoe Pound (1921), Judge Holmes's Contributions to the Science of Law, 34
HARV. L. REV. 449

Roscoe Pound (1923), The Theory of Judicial Decision, 36 HARV. L. REV. 940

Roscoe Pound (1927), The Progress of the Law: Analytical Jurisprudence: 1914–1927, 41 HARV. L. REV. 174

Roscoe Pound (1943), A Survey of Social Interests, 57 HARV. L. REV. 1

Roscoe Pound (1959), *Jurisprudence* (5 Vols.) (St. Paul, MN: West Publishing)

L.A. Powe, Jr. (1989), Justice Douglas After Fifty Years: McCarthyism and Rights, 6 CONST. COMMENT. 267

L. V. Prott (1978), Updating the Judicial 'Hunch': Esser's Concept of Judicial Predisposition, 27 AM. J. COMP. L. 461

Peter E. Quint (1989), Free Speech and Private Law in German Constitutional Theory, 48 MD. L. REV. 247

Peter E. Quint (2011), A Return to Lüth, 16 ROGER WILLIAMS U. L. REV. 73

David M. Rabban (1981), Free Speech in its Forgotten Years, 90 YALE L.J. 514

David M. Rabban (1983), The Emergence of Modern First Amendment Doctrine, 50 U. CHI. L. REV. 1205

Gustav Radbruch (1957), DER MENSCH IM RECHT (Göttingen: Vandenbroeck & Ruprecht)

Margaret Jane Radin (1990), The Pragmatist and the Feminist, 63 S. CAL. L REV. 1699

Martin H. Redish (1971), The First Amendment in the Marketplace: Commercial Speech and the Values of Free Expression, 39 GEO. WASH. L. REV. 429

Martin H. Redish (1983) The Warren Court, the Burger Court and the First Amendment Overbreadth Doctrine, 78 NW. U. L. REV. 1031

Martin H. Redish (1984), FREEDOM OF EXPRESSION: A CRITICAL ANALYSIS (Charlottesvill, VA: Michie & Co.)

Charles A. Reich (1963), Mr. Justice Black and the Living Constitution, 76 HARV. L. REV. 673

Mathias Reimann (1990), Nineteenth Century German Legal Science, 31 BOSTON C. L. REV. 837

Thilo Rensmann (2007), WERTORDNUNG UND VERFASSUNG (Tübingen: Mohr Siebeck)

Charles E. Rice (1967), Justice Black, the Demonstrators, and a Constitutional Rule of Law, 14 UCLA L. REV. 454

Elliot L. Richardson (1951), Freedom of Expression and the Function of Courts, 65 HARV. L. REV. 1

Helmut K. J. Ridder (1954), Meinungsfreiheit, in GRUNDRECHTE II (F. Neumann, H.C. Nipperdey & U. Scheunea, eds.) (Berlin: Duncker & Humblot)

Annelise Riles (1999), Wigmore's Treasure Box: Comparative Law in the Era of Information, 40 HARV. INT'L L.J. 221

Annelise Riles (2000), The Transnational Appeal of Formalism: The case of Japan's Netting Law, Stanford/Yale Junior Faculty Forum Research Paper 2000, Nr. 3, 5, available at: http://papers.ssrn.com/sol3/papers.cfm?abstract_id=162588

Annelise Riles (2005), A New Agenda for the Cultural Study of Law: Taking On the Technicalities, 53 BUFF. L. REV. 973

Gerd Roellecke (1976), Prinzipien der Verfassungsinterpretation in der Rechtsprechung des Bundesverfassungsgerichts, in BUNDESVERFASSUNGSGERICHT UND GRUNDGESETZ II 23 (Christian Starck, ed.) (Tübingen: Mohr)

Patrick J. Rohan (1963), The Common Law Tradition: Situation Sense, Subjectivism, or Just-Result Jurisprudence, 32 FORDHAM L. REV. 51

Karl Rothenbücher (1928), Das Recht der freien Meinungsäußerung, 4 VVDSTRL 1

Gary D. Rowe (1999), Lochner Revisionism Revisited, 24 LAW & SOC. INQUIRY 221

Edward Rubin (2011), The Real Formalists, the Real Realists, and what they tell us about Judicial Decision Making and Legal Education, 109 MICH. L. REV. 863 (Book Review)

Max Rümelin (1930), Developments in Legal Theory and Teaching During my Lifetime, in THE JURISPRUDENCE OF INTERESTS 14 (Magdalena Schoch, trans. & ed.) (Cambridge, MA: Harvard University Press)

Benjamin Rusteberg (2009), DER GRUNDRECHTLICHE GEWÄHRLEISTUNGSGEHALT (Tübingen: Mohr Siebeck)

Bernd Rüthers (1968), DIE UNBEGRENZTE AUSLEGUNG: ZUM WANDEL DER PRIVATRECHTSORDNUNG IM NATIONALSOZIALISMUS (Tübingen: Mohr)

Wojciech Sadurski (2005), RIGHTS BEFORE COURTS: A STUDY OF CONSTITUTIONAL COURTS IN POSTCOMMUNIST STATES OF CENTRAL AND EASTERN EUROPE (Dordrecht: Springer)

Lawrence G. Sager (1978), Fair Measure: The Legal Status of Underenforced Constitutional Norms, 91 HARV. L. REV. 1212

Chaim Saiman (2008), Restitution in America: Why the US Refuses to Join the Global Restitution Party, 28 OXFORD J. LEGAL STUD. 99

Francis Bowes Sayre (1930), Labor and the Courts, 39 YALE L.J. 682

Antonin Scalia (1989), The Rule of Law as a Law of Rules, 56 U. CHI. L. REV. 1175

Antonin Scalia (1992), Open Justice in a Closed System, 13 CARDOZO L. REV. 1713

Antonin Scalia (1998), A MATTER OF INTERPRETATION: FEDERAL COURTS AND THE LAW (Princeton University Press)

Thomas Scanlon (1972), A Theory of Freedom of Expression, 1 PHIL. & PUB. AFF. 204

Frederick Schauer (1981), Categories and the First Amendment: A Play in Three Acts, 34 VAND. L. REV. 265

Frederick Schauer (1982), Codifying the First Amendment: New York v. Ferber, 1982 SUP. CT. REV. 285

Frederick Schauer (1984), Must Speech Be Special?, 78 Nw. U. L. Rev. 1284

Frederick Schauer (1985), Slippery Slopes, 99 Harv. L. Rev. 361

Frederick Schauer (1987), The Jurisprudence of Reasons, 85 Mich. L. Rev. 847

Frederick Schauer (1988), Formalism, 97 Yale L.J. 509

Frederick Schauer (1989), The Second-Best First Amendment, 31 Wm. & Mary L. Rev. 1

Frederick Schauer (1998), Principles, Institutions, and the First Amendment, 112 Harv. L. Rev. 84

Frederick Schauer (2004), The Boundaries of the First Amendment: A Preliminary Exploration of Constitutional Salience, 117 Harv. L. Rev. 1765

Frederick Schauer (2005), Freedom of Expression Adjudication in Europe and America: A Case study in Comparative Constitutional Architecture, in European and US Constitutionalism 49 (Georg Nolte, ed.) (Cambridge University Press)

Frederick Schauer (2010), Balancing, Subsumption, and the Constraining Role of Legal Text, 4(1) Law & Ethics of Human Rights 34

Ulrich Scheuner (1965), Pressefreiheit, 22 VVDStRL 1

Axel Schildt & Arnold Sywottek (1997), 'Reconstruction' and Modernization': West German Social History during the 1950s, in West Germany under Construction: Politics, Society, and Culture in the Adenauer Era 413 (Robert G. Möller, ed.) (Ann Arbor, MI: University of Michigan Press)

Pierre Schlag (1983), An Attack on Categorical Approaches to Freedom of Speech, 30 UCLA L. Rev. 761

Pierre Schlag (2002), The Aesthetics of American Law, 115 Harv. L. Rev. 1047

John Henry Schlegel (1995), American Legal Realism and Empirical Legal Science (Chapel Hill, NC: University of North Carolina Press)

Bernhard Schlink (1976), Abwägung im Verfassungsrecht (Berlin: Duncker & Humblot)

Bernard Schlink (2012), Proportionality in Constitutional Law: Why Everywhere but Here?, 22 Duke J. Int'l & Comp. L. 291

Christoph U. Schmid (2010), From *Effet Utile* to *Effet Neolibéral*: A Critique of the New Methodological Expansionism of the European Court of Justice, in Conflict of Laws and Laws of Conflict in Europe and Beyond: Patterns of Supranational and Transnational Juridification 295 (Rainer Nickel, ed.) (Antwerp: Intersentia)

Richard Schmid (1958), Ein Neues Kommunisten-Urteil des Supreme Court, JZ 501

Carl Schmitt (1928), Verfassungslehre (München, Leipzig: Duncker & Humblot)

Harald Schneider (1979), DIE GÜTERABWÄGUNG DES BUNDESVERFASSUNGSGERICHTS BEI GRUNDRECHTSKONFLIKTEN (Baden-Baden: Nomos)

Peter Schneider (1960), *In Dubio Pro Libertate*, in Hundert Jahre deutsches Rechtsleben II 263 (Ernst von Caemmerer, Ernst Friesenhand, Richard Lange, eds.) (Karlsruhe: C.F. Müller)

Peter Schneider (1963), Prinzipien der Verfassungsinterpretation, 20 VVDStRL 1

Roman Schnur (1965), Pressefreiheit, 22 VVDStRL 101

Miguel Schor (2009), The Strange Cases of *Marbury* and *Lochner* in the Constitutional Imagination, 87 TEX. L. REV. 1463

Glendon Schubert (1965), THE POLITICAL ROLE OF THE COURTS: JUDICIAL POLICY-MAKING (Chicago, IL: Scott, Foresman)

Bernard Schwartz (1994), Holmes versus Hand: Clear and Present Danger or Advocacy of Unlawful Action, 1994 SUP. CT. REV. 209

Louis M. Seidman (1987), Public Principle and Private Choice: The Uneasy Case for a Boundary Maintenance Theory of Constitutional Law, 96 YALE L.J. 1006

Martin Shapiro (1962), Judicial Modesty, Political Reality and Preferred Position, 47 CORNELL L. Q. 175

Martin Shapiro (1963a), The Supreme Court and Constitutional Adjudication: Of Politics and Neutral Principles, 31 GEO. WASH. L. REV. 587

Martin Shapiro (1963b), Political Jurisprudence, 52 KY. L. REV. 294

Steven Shiffrin (1984), The First Amendment and Economic Regulation: Away from a General Theory of the First Amendment, 78 NW. U. L. REV. 1212

Steven Shiffrin (1990), THE FIRST AMENDMENT, DEMOCRACY AND ROMANCE (Cambridge, MA: Harvard University Press)

Judith N. Shklar (1964), LEGALISM: LAW, MORALS, AND POLITICAL TRIALS (Cambridge, MA: Harvard University Press)

Stephen A. Siegel (1991), *Lochner* Era Jurisprudence and the American Constitutional Tradition, 70 N.C. L. REV. 1

Isidore Silver (1976), The Warren Court Critics: Where Are They Now That We Need Them?, 3 HASTINGS CONST. L.Q. 373

Joseph W. Singer (1988), Legal Realism Now, 76 CAL. L. REV. 517

Joseph W. Singer & Jack M. Beerman (1989), Baseline Questions in Legal Reasoning: The Example of Property in Jobs, 23 GA. L. REV. 911

Rudolf Smend (1928a), Das Recht der freien Meinungsäußerung, 4 VVDStRL, reprinted in STAATSRECHTLICHE ABHANDLUNGEN 89 (Berlin: Duncker & Humblot)

Rudolf Smend (1928b), Verfassung und Verfassungsrecht, Reprinted in STAATSRECHTLICHE ABHANDLUNGEN 119 (Berlin: Duncker & Humblot)

Francis G. Snyder (2000), THE EUROPEANISATION OF LAW: THE LEGAL EFFECTS OF EUROPEAN INTEGRATION (Oxford: Hart Publishing)

Peter Speiger (1984), INTERESSENJURISPRUDENZ IN DER DEUTSCHEN RECHTSPRECHUNG (Unpublished Doctoral Thesis, Freiburg) (on file)

Ernst Stampe (1905), RECHTSFINDUNG DURCH INTERESSENWÄGUNG, 1905 DJZ 713; Reprinted in INTERESSENJURISPRUDENZ 24 (Günter Ellscheid & Winfried Hassemer, eds.) (Darmstadt: Wissenschaftliche Buchgesellschaft)

Paul B. Stephan III (1982), The First Amendment and Content Discrimination, 68 VA. L. REV. 203

Klaus Stern (1993), General Assessment of the Basic Law – A German View, in GERMANY AND ITS BASIC LAW 17 (Paul Kirchhof & Donald P. Kommers, eds.) (Baden-Baden: Nomos)

Michael Stolleis (1992), GESCHICHTE DES ÖFFENTLICHEN RECHTS IN DEUTSCHLAND 2: STAATSRECHTSLEHRE UND VERWALTGS-SWISSENSCHAFT 1800–1914 (München: Beck)

Michael Stolleis (1999), GESCHICHTE DES ÖFFENTLICHEN RECHTS IN DEUTSCHLAND 3: STAATS- UND VERWALTUNGSRECH-TSWISSENSCHAFT IN REPUBLIK UND DIKTATUR 1914–1945 (München: Beck)

Michael Stolleis (2001), PUBLIC LAW IN GERMANY, 1800–1914 (Pamela Biel, trans.) (New York, NY: Berghahn Books)

Michael Stolleis (2004), A HISTORY OF PUBLIC LAW IN GERMANY 1914–1945 (Thomas Dunlap, trans.) (Oxford University Press)

Geoffrey R. Stone (1983), Content Regulation and the First Amendment, 25 WM. & MARY L. REV. 189

Geoffrey R. Stone (2004), PERILOUS TIMES (New York, NY: Norton)

Katherine van Wezel Stone (1981), The Post-War Paradigm in American Labor Law, 90 YALE L.J. 1509

Alec Stone Sweet (2003), Why Europe Rejected American Judicial Review – And Why It May Not Matter, 101 MICH. L. REV. 2744

Alec Stone Sweet (2004), THE JUDICIAL CONSTRUCTION OF EUROPE (Oxford University Press)

Alec Stone Sweet & Jud Mathews (2008), Proportionality Balancing and Global Constitutionalism, 47 COLUM. J. TRANSNAT'L L. 72

Frank R. Strong (1969), Fifty Years of Clear and Present Danger: From Schenck to Brandenburg – and Beyond, 1969 SUP. CT. REV. 41

Kathleen M. Sullivan (1992a), Foreword: The Justices of Rules and Standards, 106 HARV. L. REV. 22

Kathleen M. Sullivan (1992b), Post-Liberal Judging: The Roles of Categorization and Balancing, 63 U. COLO. L. REV. 293

Robert S. Summers (1978), Two Types of Substantive Reasons: The Core of a Theory of Common Law Justification, 63 CORNELL L. REV. 707

Robert S. Summers (1981), Pragmatic Instrumentalism in Twentieth Century American Legal Thought: a Synthesis and Critique of our Dominant General Theory about Law and its Use, 66 CORNELL L. REV. 861

Robert S. Summers (1982), INSTRUMENTALISM AND AMERICAN LEGAL THEORY (Ithaca, NY: Cornell University Press)

Robert S. Summers & Patrick S. Atiyah (1987), FORM AND SUBSTANCE IN ANGLO-AMERICAN LAW (Oxford: Clarendon Press)

Robert S. Summers (1992), The Formal Character of Law, 51 CAM. L.J. 1302

Robert S. Summers (1997), How Law is Formal and Why it Matters, 82 CORNELL L. REV. 1165

Cass R. Sunstein (1986), Pornography and the First Amendment, 4 DUKE L.J. 589

Cass R. Sunstein (1987), Lochner's Legacy, 87 COLUM. L. REV. 873

Cass R. Sunstein (1990), AFTER THE RIGHTS REVOLUTION (Cambridge, MA: Harvard University Press)

Cass R. Sunstein (1992), Neutrality in Constitutional Law (with Special Reference to Pornography, Abortion, and Surrogacy), 92 COLUM. L. REV. 1

Cass R. Sunstein (1993), On Analogical Reasoning, 106 HARV. L. REV. 741

Cass R. Sunstein (1995), Incompletely Theorized Agreements, 108 HARV. L. REV. 1733

Cass R. Sunstein (1996), Foreword: Leaving Things Undecided, 110 HARV. L. REV. 4

Cass R. Sunstein (1999), Must Formalism be Defended Empirically?, 66 U. CHI. L. REV. 636

Cass R. Sunstein (2005), RADICALS IN ROBES: WHY EXTREME RIGHT-WING COURTS ARE BAD FOR AMERICA (New York, NY: Basic Books)

Cass R. Sunstein (2007), Second-Order Perfectionism, 75 FORDHAM L. REV. 2867

Cass R. Sunstein (2008), Beyond Judicial Minimalism, 43 TULSA L. REV. 825

Brian Z. Tamanaha (1999), The View of Habermas from below: Doubts about the Centrality of Law and the Legitimation Enterprise, 76 DENVER U. L. REV. 989

Brian Z. Tamanaha (2006), LAW AS MEANS TO AN END: THREAT TO THE RULE OF LAW (Cambridge University Press)

Brian Z. Tamanaha (2009), BEYOND THE FORMALIST-REALIST DIVIDE: THE ROLE OF POLITICS IN JUDGING (Princeton University Press)

Gunther Teubner (1983), Substantive and Reflexive Elements in Modern Law, 17 LAW & SOC'Y REV. 239

Gunther Teubner (1998), Legal Irritants: Good Faith in British Law, or How Unifiying Law Ends up in New Divergences, 61 MOD. L. REV. 11

John E. Toews (1987), Intellectual History after the Linguistic Turn: The Autonomy of Meaning and the Irreducibility of Experience, 92 AM. HIST. REV. 879

Lawrence H. Tribe (1980), The Puzzling Persistence of Process-Based Constitutional Theories, 89 YALE L.J. 1063

David M. Trubek (1985), Reconstructing Max Weber's Sociology of Law, 37 STAN. L. REV. 919

Mark V. Tushnet (1985), Anti-Formalism in Recent Constitutional Theory, 83 MICH. L. REV. 1502

Mark V. Tushnet (1988), RED, WHITE AND BLUE: A CRITICAL ANALYSIS OF CONSTITUTIONAL LAW (Cambridge, MA: Harvard University Press)

Mark V. Tushnet (1999), TAKING THE CONSTITUTION AWAY FROM THE COURTS (Princeton University Press)

Mark Tushnet (2005), 'Our Perfect Constitution' Revisited, in TERRORISM, LAWS OF WAR, AND THE CONSTITUTION 131 (Peter Berkowitz, ed.) (Stanford, CA: Hoover Institution Press)

Mark Tushnet (2008), WEAK COURTS, STRONG RIGHTS: JUDICIAL REVIEW AND SOCIAL WELFARE RIGHTS IN COMPARATIVE CONSTITUTIONAL LAW (Princeton University Press)

Mark Tushnet (2009), The Inevitable Globalization of Constitutional Law, 49 VIRGINIA J. INT'L. L. 985

Roberto M. Unger (1986), THE CRITICAL LEGAL STUDIES MOVEMENT (Cambridge, MA: Harvard University Press)

Peter Unruh (2002), DER VERFASSUNGSBEGRIFF DES GRUNDGESETZES: EINE VERFASSUNGSTHEORETISCHE REKONSTRUKTION (Tübingen: Mohr Siebeck)

Catherine Valcke (2006), Comparative History and the Internal View of French, German, and English Private Law, 19 CAN. J. L. & JURISPRUDENCE. 133

Catherine Valcke (2012), Reflections on Comparative Methodology – Getting Inside Contract Law, in PRACTICE AND THEORY IN COMPARATIVE LAW 22 (Maurice Adams & Jacco Bomhoff, eds.) (Cambridge University Press)

Antoine Vauchez (2013), L'UNION PAR LE DROIT: L'INVENTION D'UN PROGRAMME (Paris: Les Presses de Sciences Po.)

Adrian Vermeule (2007), Instrumentalisms (Book Review), 120 HARV. L. REV. 2113

Jan Vetter (1983), Postwar Legal Scholarship on Judicial Decision Making, 33 J. LEGAL EDUC. 412

Theodor Viehweg, (1953) TOPIK UND JURISPRUDENZ: EIN BEITRAG ZUR RECHTSWISSENSCHAFTLICHEN GRUNDLAGENFORSCHUNG (München: Beck)

Richard Wasserstrom (1961), THE JUDICIAL DECISION: TOWARD A THEORY OF LEGAL JUSTIFICATION (Stanford University Press)

Grégoire C. N. Webber (2010), Proportionality, Balancing, and the Cult of Constitutional Rights Scholarship, 23 CAN. J. L. & JUR. 179

Max Weber (1907), CRITIQUE OF STAMMLER (New York, NY: Free Press, 1977)

Max Weber (1919), Science as a Vocation, reprinted in FROM MAX WEBER: ESSAYS IN SOCIOLOGY 155 (H.H. Gerth & C. Wright Mills, eds.) (New York, NY: Oxford University Press)

Max Weber (1925), MAX WEBER ON LAW IN ECONOMY AND SOCIETY 309 (Max Rheinstein ed., Max Rheinstein & Edward Shils, trans.) (New York, NY: Simon & Schuster, 1954) (German original from 1925)

Herbert Wechsler (1959), Toward Neutral Principles of Constitutional Law, 73 HARV. L. REV. 1

Herbert Wechsler & Harry Shulman (1941), Symposium on Civil Liberties, 9 AM. L. SCH. REV. 881

Ernest J. Weinrib (1988), Legal Formalism: On the Immanent Rationality of Law, 97 YALE L.J. 949

Lorraine E. Weinrib (1986), The Supreme Court and Section One, 10 SUP. CT. REV. 469

Lorraine E. Weinrib (2006), The Postwar Paradigm and American Exceptionalism, in THE MIGRATION OF CONSTITUTIONAL IDEAS 84 (Sujit Choudhry, ed.) (Cambridge University Press)

G. Edward White (1972), From Sociological Jurisprudence to Legal Realism: Jurisprudence and Social Change in Early Twentieth-Century America, 58 VA. L. REV. 999

G. Edward White (1973), The Evolution of Reasoned Elaboration: Jurisprudential Criticism and Social Change, 59 VA. L. REV. 279

G. Edward White (1996), The First Amendment Comes of Age: The Emergence of Free Speech in Twentieth Century America, 95 MICH. L. REV. 299

G. Edward White (2000), THE CONSTITUTION AND THE NEW DEAL (Cambridge, MA: Harvard University Press)

Morton White (1949), SOCIAL THOUGHT IN AMERICA: THE REVOLT AGAINST FORMALISM (New York, NY: Viking Press)

James Q. Whitman (1990), THE LEGACY OF ROMAN LAW IN THE GERMAN ROMANTIC ERA: HISTORICAL VISION AND LEGAL CHANGE (Princeton University Press)

Franz Wieacker (1990), Foundations of European Legal Culture, 38 AM. J. COMP. L. 1

Franz Wieacker (1995), A HISTORY OF PRIVATE LAW IN EUROPE (Tony
    Weir, trans.) (Oxford University Press)
Rudolf Wiethölter (1986), Materialization and Proceduralization in Modern
    Law, in DILEMMAS OF LAW IN THE WELFARE STATE 221 (Gunther
    Teubner, ed.) (New York, NY: de Gruyter), (reprinted in 12 GERMAN L.J.
    465, 2011)
Raymond L. Wise (1969), The Right to Dissent: A Judicial Commentary, 4
    SUFFOLK U. L. REV. 70
J. Skelly Wright (1971), Professor Bickel, the Scholarly Tradition, and the Supreme
    Court, 84 HARV. L. REV. 769
Hessel E. Yntema (1956), Comparative Legal Research: Some Remarks on 'Looking
    out of the Cave', 54 MICH. L. REV. 899
Reinhard Zimmermann (1996), Savigny's Legacy: Legal History, Comparative
    Law, and the Emergence of a European Legal Science, 112 LQR 576
Reinhold Zippelius (1962), WERTUNGSPROBLEME IM SYSTEM DER
    GRUNDRECHTE (München: Beck)
Peer Zumbansen (2007), The Law of Society: Governance through Contract, 14
    IND. J. GLOB. L. STUD. 191
Konrad Zweigert & Hein Kötz (1998), AN INTRODUCTION TO COMPARATIVE
    LAW, 3RD EDN. (Tony Weir, trans.) (Oxford University Press)

# INDEX

Alexy, Robert, 195, 219, 237

balancing
  anti-rules, as, 234
  characteristic, as, 12
  deference, and, 136
  definition, 17, 18
  formal and the substantive, 24–28
  formal vs substantive discourse, 7
  global age of, 10
  global pervasiveness, 9, 28, 243
  history, 33
  how formal and substantive, 26–28
  intuitive reasoning, 7
  judicial references, 11
  law's *proprium*, 24–26
  legalism, and, 2–6
  legitimacy, 21–24
  lens and an object, a, 16–18
  local meanings, 1, 6, 21–24
  nineteenth-century legal thought,
    and, 71
  optimization, 195
  problematic, 242
  process and discourse, as, 16–21
  relativity, 21–24
  rethinking, 6–9
  rise of, 4, 235
  role, 4
  scepticism vs faith dichotomy, 232
  scepticism, and, 5
  triumph of test, 56
  universality, 13
  value and interest, 4
Black, Hugo, 126, 132, 134, 137–39, 140,
  141, 142, 145, 146, 147–50, 151,
152, 153, 155, 156, 169, 170, 183,
184–86, 196, 250, 255, 262

Chafee, Zechariah, 157–60, 177,
  178, 196
civil rights
  balancing, and, 122
classes of expression, 186
classical orthodoxy, 31, 33–56
  autonomy and neutrality, 62–64
  autonomy, and, 36
  balancer's account, 34
  balancing and interests, 69–70
  balancing of interests, 61
  categorization and
    subsumption, 47–50
  conceptual reasoning, 47
  conceptual vocabulary, 34
  conceptualism, 46
  critique, 43, 46–56
  definition, 48
  degrees and
    interconnectedness, 64–66
  European vs United States, 48
  France, 57–60
  freedom of contract, 53
  gap-filling, 57
  gap-filling through sensible
    weighing, 61–62
  Gény, François, 57–60
  Germany, 60–64
  gradualism, 49
  Heck, Philipp, 60–64
  Langdellian legal science and legal
    education, 41–43
  legal formality, and, 48